ALSO AVAILABLE
30 Great Myths About Shakespeare
by Laurie Maguire and Emma Smith

OTHER BOOKS BY DUNCAN WU
Wordsworth's Reading 1770–1799
Wordsworth's Reading 1800–1815
Making Plays: Interviews with Contemporary British Dramatists and Directors
Wordsworth: An Inner Life
Wordsworth's Poets
Six Contemporary Dramatists: Bennett, Potter, Gray, Brenton, Hare, Ayckbourn
William Hazlitt: The First Modern Man

William Wordsworth: Selected Poems (co-edited with Stephen Gill)
Romanticism: A Critical Reader (editor)
William Wordsworth: The Five-Book Prelude (editor)
Women Romantic Poets: An Anthology (editor)
A Companion to Romanticism (editor)
William Hazlitt, The Plain Speaker: Key Essays (editor)
The Selected Writings of William Hazlitt, nine volumes (editor)
British Romanticism and the Edinburgh Review (co-edited with Massimiliano Demata)
William Wordsworth: The Earliest Poems 1785–1790 (editor)
Metaphysical Hazlitt (co-edited with Uttara Natarajan and Tom Paulin)
New Writings of William Hazlitt (editor)
Immortal Bird: Romantic Poems about Nightingales (editor)
The Happy Fireside: Romantic Poems about Cats and Dogs (editor)
Romanticism: An Anthology, Fourth Edition (editor)
Poetry of Witness: The Tradition in English, 1500–2001 (co-edited with Carolyn Forché)
'All that is worth remembering': Selected Essays of William Hazlitt (editor)

An early nineteenth-century cut-and-paste job. In 1825, after Byron's death, Pierre Louis Bouvier hijacked Thomas Phillips's 1813 portrait of Byron and superimposed on it an image of the plumed cavalry helmet the poet had designed himself, perpetuating the image of the archetypal Romantic who died on the battlefield in the cause of freedom (see Myth 19).
Source: Paul F. Betz Collection.

30 GREAT MYTHS ABOUT THE ROMANTICS

Duncan Wu

WILEY Blackwell

This edition first published 2015
© 2015 John Wiley & Sons Ltd

Registered Office
John Wiley & Sons Ltd, The Atrium, Southern Gate, Chichester, West Sussex, PO19 8SQ, UK

Editorial Offices
350 Main Street, Malden, MA 02148-5020, USA
9600 Garsington Road, Oxford, OX4 2DQ, UK
The Atrium, Southern Gate, Chichester, West Sussex, PO19 8SQ, UK

For details of our global editorial offices, for customer services, and for information about how to
apply for permission to reuse the copyright material in this book please see our website at
www.wiley.com/wiley-blackwell.

The right of Duncan Wu to be identified as the author of this work has been asserted in accordance
with the UK Copyright, Designs and Patents Act 1988.

Library of Congress Cataloging-in-Publication Data

Wu, Duncan.
  30 great myths about the Romantics / Duncan Wu.
    pages cm
  Includes bibliographical references and index.
  ISBN 978-1-118-84326-0 (cloth) – ISBN 978-1-118-84319-2 (pbk.) 1. English literature–19th
century–History and criticism. 2. English literature–18th century–History and criticism.
3. Romanticism–Great Britain. 4. Literature and society–Great Britain–History. I. Title. II. Title:
Thirty great myths about the Romantics.
  PR457.W84 2015
  820.9′145–dc23

                                                                        2014046950

A catalogue record for this book is available from the British Library.

Cover image: Illustration of Lord Byron, Private Collection / © Look and Learn / The Bridgeman
Art Library.

Set in 10/12pt Sabon by Laserwords Private Limited, Chennai, India
Printed and bound in Malaysia by Vivar Printing Sdn Bhd

1   2015

This book is dedicated to Catherine Payling and her companion, Poppy, the smooth fox terrier (1999–2013)

CONTENTS

ACKNOWLEDGEMENTS

I pay tribute to those whose writings I consulted during work on this book, from those who played their part in the editing of scholarly texts to the many who have written short notes correcting errors of fact in such indispensable publications as *Notes and Queries*. I pay tribute also to those whose arguments and debates played their part in shaping my thoughts. I have not agreed with everyone – that would be impossible – but have striven to summarize them accurately and with respect for their views.

The reports of the seven anonymous readers who analyzed my initial proposal have been constantly to hand; I thank them for their comments. I have not hesitated to turn to friends and colleagues for points of information or opinions on parts of this book, usually in return for nothing other than a sincere thank you, or the cut and thrust of continuing debate: G. E. Bentley, Jr., John Gardner, Sarah Wootton, Glenn Skaggs, Richard Gravil, Peter Cochran, Mary O'Connell, Jane Stabler, Paul Miner, Robert Morrison, Cian Duffy, Seamus Perry, John B. Pierce, Shelley King, Michael O'Neill, Susan J. Wolfson, and Nicholas Roe. Harry Mattison deserves particular thanks for surveying this book from a reader's perspective, and providing a list of adjustments. Charles E. Robinson has been a friend to this volume from its inception; he read several drafts and offered numerous corrigenda. I am grateful to the three anonymous readers who examined the final typescript and proposed emendations of tone and emphasis. Ben Thatcher, Project Editor at Wiley, has been helpful on production matters, Janet Moth has been a scrupulous and eagle-eyed copy-editor, while Deirdre Ilkson and Emma Bennett have been wise and responsive editors; I am grateful for their guidance, and that of my agent, Charlie Viney.

Giuseppe Albano, Curator of the Keats-Shelley Memorial House in Rome, and his colleague Luca Caddia, gave me access to Trelawny's earliest manuscript account of Shelley's seaside cremation, and provided the coveted photograph of his jawbone, published here for the first time (by kind permission of David Leigh Hunt on behalf of the Leigh Hunt family). As a member of the English Department at Georgetown I have been fortunate in having among my colleagues Paul F. Betz and Carolyn Forché, both of whom have advised me at various points along the way. Professor Betz provided some illustrations for these myths from his personal collection. The Master and Fellows of Campion Hall gave this book a home in Oxford in the summer of 2013, while Chester L. Gillis and Robert M. Groves, the Dean and Provost of Georgetown University, granted me time in which to finish it in the spring and summer of 2014.

This book has sent me back to basics in a way that leads me to reflect on the privilege of having enjoyed, at various times during my early career, the supervision of Jonathan Wordsworth and D. F. McKenzie – both of whom, directly and indirectly, shaped my approach to these essays. In turn I have learned, and continue to learn, from my students at Georgetown University, without whose insights this book would be the poorer. All errors, flights of fancy, and missed tricks are attributable exclusively to me.

My greatest debt is to Catherine Payling, who has assisted my work in countless respects. The dedication of this book to her and her companion Poppy the smooth fox terrier, for many years occupants of Keats House in Rome, is a small acknowledgement of all their endeavours on my behalf.

Duncan Wu
Georgetown University
July 2014

INTRODUCTION

Eternal Spirit! God of truth! to whom
All things seem as they are ...

Robert Pollok, *The Course of Time*, Book I

This book aims to reassert the humanity of Romantic writers. That is to say, its objective is to replace misconception and speculation with truth – or, where it is unknown, the admonition to be 'capable of being in uncertainties, Mysteries, doubts, without any irritable reaching after fact & reason'.[1] For some reason, the lethal combination of being both dead and 'Romantic' has abstracted writers of the late Georgian period to the point at which they have been divorced from the reality of their own lives and translated into the mini-mart of fantasy: Blake the presumptive inmate of Bedlam in a cell adjacent to that occupied by the artist John Martin, Wordsworth the ravisher of his own sister, Byron the poet slaughtered on the battlefield, Shelley keeping his sails raised in bad weather so as to precipitate his own demise, and Keats born, Christ-like, in a stable. They were (we are told) hostile to the Enlightenment, the Augustans, and the world of science while being atheists, drug users, wife-swappers and rock stars. It is as if the truth were judged harmful to the literature and displaced by a dog's breakfast of conjecture and surmise.

Even the label by which they are invoked inflicts upon them a species of violence: Romanticism is a flashy but brazenly opaque term.[2] None of the writers in this book would have used it to describe either themselves or the times in which they lived. From the vantage-point of an adult alive in 1805, when Wordsworth completed *The Thirteen-Book Prelude*, there

30 Great Myths About the Romantics, First Edition. Duncan Wu.
© 2015 John Wiley & Sons, Ltd. Published 2015 by John Wiley & Sons, Ltd.

was little romance to be found in recent history. The uprising of the United Irishmen was brutally suppressed in 1798 and again in 1803.[3] Since 1793, Britain had been suffering the privations of war – and I refer not to minor skirmishes but to arduous and drawn-out battles, fought on sea and land. For more than two decades much of the world became a potential battleground, the main protagonists (Britain and France) being international trading nations: the first few years of the French Revolutionary War were marked by clashes in Pondicherry, Guadeloupe, St Lucia, the Windward and Leeward Islands, and Trinidad.[4] No one grew up or came to maturity without being affected by it.[5]

What we call Romantic might more accurately be called Regency Wartime Literature were we to backdate the Regency, as some historians do, to 1788.[6] Just as the optimism associated with revolution shaped the sensibilities of those who witnessed it, so the impoverishment of war chilled the national psyche. The defeat of Napoleon brought temporary jubilation but pitched the country into internal conflict, deepened by the Corn Laws of 1815 (which kept food prices artificially high), economic recession, widespread unemployment, and indirect taxation (weighing disproportionately on the poor), to the point at which the country approached something not far from insurrection. None of this would have struck anyone as Romantic, and it might be argued such a hopeful word could be attached to these years only as a misnomer.

Small wonder that a blowzy concept imposed retrospectively on the past has been a vector for misconception. But then, given the flamboyance of those involved, that might have happened anyway. The Romantics must be among the most mythologized figures in the canon, their lives recounted in print and on stage, television, and celluloid. Perhaps the explanation has less to do with the immediacy of their writings than with the eventfulness of their lives. I wonder whether that has been their undoing. To take one example, who could be blamed for assuming Keats and Shelley were among the most widely read poets of their day? But if sales are anything to go by, there were few people awaiting their next book at the time: less than half the print-run (1,000 copies) of Keats's *Lamia, Isabella, The Eve of St Agnes, and Other Poems* (1820) had sold by the time he died in 1821, while Shelley's *Epipsychidion*, of which 250 copies were published in 1821, had sold roughly 90 copies by 1823.[7] The point is that the contemporary perspective was different from our own. Today Jane Austen is one of the most popular novelists of all time but in 1814 no one thought she would occupy that status, nor did they suspect an obscure

Figure 1 Samuel Rogers (1763–1855) was old enough to have been a friend of
Richard Brinsley Sheridan and the actress Sarah Siddons. His *The Pleasures
of Memory* (1792), in heroic couplets, became one of the most popular poems of
the day; by 1806 it had gone through fifteen editions.
Source: Paul F. Betz Collection.

engraver named Blake would 150 years later be hailed as a literary and
artistic genius.

Who *was* popular? Samuel Rogers was one of the period's best-known
poets, author of *The Pleasures of Memory* and *Italy*, and lived long
enough to be offered the laureateship upon Wordsworth's death in
1850.[8] His poems are now as seldom noticed as Thomas Campbell's *The*

Pleasures of Hope and Robert Pollok's ten-book epic, *The Course of Time*, best-sellers of their moment.[9] Byron, Scott, and Moore were the 'three great stars' of British poetry on the Continent.[10] Among serious poets, Robert Southey was highly regarded; Wordsworth once said his work would be 'cherished by posterity when the reputation of those, who now so insolently decry him, will be rotted away and dispersed upon the winds'.[11] But it is not easy to imagine a time when *Roderick, The Last of the Goths* will reclaim the readers it had during Southey's lifetime.[12]

In the theatre, nothing felt more enduring than the popularity of such melodramas as Lewis's *The Castle Spectre*, Kotzebue's *The Stranger*,[13] and Reynolds's *The Caravan* (featuring Carlo the dog, dubbed by Sheridan 'the author and preserver of Drury Lane Theatre'[14]); verse dramas including Milman's *The Fall of Jerusalem*;[15] and tragedies like Maturin's *Bertram*.[16] Few bother with them today; instead we read as classics works hardly known to contemporaries (*The Book of Urizen, The Prelude, Epipsychidion*, and *Lamia*) and dramas considered unactable – *Prometheus Unbound, Manfred, The Borderers, Osorio*, and *Otho the Great*.[17] Scott's novels continue to be read in our time, but other fictions of the day are now the haunt principally of students, such as Burney's *Camilla*, which sold 4,000 copies on its first outing (3,000 more than *Waverley*), and Amelia Opie's *Father and Daughter*, which sold 7,000 copies.[18] The current popularity of Mary Shelley's *Frankenstein* and Hogg's *Confessions of a Justified Sinner* would have been unimaginable to the scattered few who heard of them when they first appeared.[19]

What does that tell us? No one can know what will be read a century from now, and the impression given by anthologies and introductions – that Blake, Wordsworth, Coleridge, Keats, Byron, and Shelley were exemplary figures of their day, renowned and acknowledged as such – is misleading. The task of this book is to confront such notions with the contemporary perspective, assuming it can be reconstructed.

Some might ask: why bother with false trails and fake facts? Does it matter if we imagine Keats killed by a review or the Romantics' creativity drug-induced? It matters if the myth obscures the literature and those who created it. To take an example: Victorian readers wanted to believe Byron the author of manly poetry for a male readership. Writing in 1853, Charles Kingsley deplored the limp-wristed Shelley, hailing instead that 'sturdy peer, proud of his bull-neck and his boxing, who kept bears and bull-dogs, drilled Greek ruffians at Missolonghi, and "had no objection to a pot of beer,"[20] and who might, if he had reformed, have made a gallant English gentleman'.[21] This has enjoyed a protracted life in variant forms, including the beliefs Byron was a democrat (Myth 18), a liberator of the

Figure 2 Engraving of William Edward West's portrait of Byron. West thought his subject 'fat and rather effeminate'.
Source: Paul F. Betz Collection.

Greeks (Myth 19), and an impassioned heterosexual (Myth 17). It was as erroneous when first expounded as it is now; had Kingsley any notion of Byron's true predilections, he would probably have disdained to touch a copy of *Don Juan* with a pair of forceps.

Kingsley's blind eye was directed at the most incriminating evidence of all: what it was like to meet the man. Isaac D'Israeli encountered Byron before his grand tour of 1809, and never forgot him: 'Such a fantastic and effeminate thing I never saw. It was all rings and curls and lace. I was ashamed to speak to him; he looked more like a girl than a boy.'[22] D'Israeli was right. Byron was a dandy, though to say so hardly does him justice. His extensive jewellery collection ran to diamond brooches, necklaces, bracelets, and earrings.[23] Towards the end of his life, William Edward West described him as 'fat and rather effeminate'[24] – and the portrait he painted suggests a middle-aged Scottish midwife rather than a red-blooded aristocratic Lord. Kingsley did not have those testimonies to hand, but could have consulted those of Thomas Moore, who noted that in 'his caprices, fits of weeping, sudden affections and dislikes, – may be observed striking traces of a feminine cast of character';[25] of Marguerite, Countess of Blessington, who met Byron in Genoa, her first impression being that 'His voice and accent are peculiarly agreeable, but effeminate';[26] and of James Hamilton Browne, who sailed with Byron from Leghorn to Cephalonia:

> His delicately formed features were cast rather in an effeminate mould.... His eyes were rather prominent and full, of a dark blue, having that melting character which I have frequently observed in females, said to be a proof of extreme sensibility.

Byron's pout, Browne added, was that 'practised sometimes by a pretty coquette'.[27] On one occasion Scrope Davies surprised his friend 'with his hair *en papillote*' (the equivalent of curlers). 'Ha ha! Byron, I have at last caught you acting the part of the Sleeping Beauty', cried Davies. 'Do not, my dear Scrope, let the cat out of the bag', Byron pleaded, 'for I am as vain of my curls as a girl of sixteen.'[28] This was not a bull-necked boxer but a narcissist whose principal interest was boys – a taste that began at Cambridge where he fell in love with John Edleston, and which continued to the end of his life. Only such a man would describe Ali Pasha's grandsons as 'totally unlike our lads ... [they] have painted complexions like rouged dowagers, large black eyes & features perfectly regular. They are the prettiest little animals I ever saw'.[29] Kingsley may have been unaware of the proclivities of Byron's friends – Charles Matthews (who kept him abreast of sodomite news[30]), William Bankes MP (caught *in flagrante* with a guardsman[31]), and John Cam Hobhouse – whom Peter Cochran describes as 'a self-disgusted, cottaging heterosexual with ... a taste for spanking'.[32]

It is not just that Byron was never what Kingsley claimed him to have been but that, for as long as his view prevailed, it was impossible to read Byron's poetry and see its author plainly. Not until the 1950s, when G. Wilson Knight wrote explicitly about Byron's effeminacy, did critics begin fully to appreciate sexual ambiguity in his work.[33] In *Don Juan* Canto I, Byron has Donna Julia say, 'My brain is feminine',[34] a line now read as Byron's self-analysis.[35] But that would be in spite of Kingsley's platitudes, not because of them. The truth is always more revealing than myth, with the power to open pathways otherwise forbidden to us.

The limpet-like persistence of some myths may be related to the illusion they draw the Romantics closer to us. That tends to be the assumption of introductions to the subject, which foster the inclination to see them as poor relations whose insights and situation are 'the same' as our own. It is thus widely supposed they possessed the values and ideals of those who

Figure 3 Samuel Whitbread, MP (1764–1815), whose 'heart was in his broad, honest, English face'.
Source: Paul F. Betz Collection.

aspired to a modern liberal democracy when at the time barely 1.7 per cent of the population had the vote and most people thought the constitution a cause of pride.[36] To say women were permitted to write political pamphlets, canvass in elections, or be patrons of a borough (like Miss Elizabeth Lawrence, patron of Ripon in the first half of the nineteenth century), is to suggest they wielded political power, yet this was a society in which they were ineligible to vote or be elected as MPs – and no one recognized the anomaly.[37] It is claimed the Reform Bill of 1832 initiated an era of political freedom unknown to previous generations; throughout the Romantic period, however, 'democracy' remained a dirty word, tainted by implications of mob rule. Those pushing through the Reform Bill agreed with Thomas Macaulay, who described universal suffrage as 'fatal to the purposes for which government exists',[38] while in 1809 Samuel Whitbread condemned democracy as 'a form of government which I abhor;

violent, uncomfortable, ungrateful, cruel, unjust, only to be surpassed in wickedness by a savage, rooted, and confirmed despotism'.[39] Consider that for a moment: Whitbread was someone whose 'heart was in his broad, honest, English face';[40] as early as 1807 he introduced a Bill to give children at least two years of state-funded education regardless of parents' income,[41] and he was one of only three Whig politicians credited by E. P. Thompson for standing up 'again and again in the House to defend political liberties or social rights'.[42] *Even to him*, democracy was anathema. And even John Thelwall, today invoked as 'an avatar of Romantic radicalism',[43] was not, according to his friend Henry Crabb Robinson, 'an admirer of vulgar democracy'.[44] None of this was theoretical. Those who did advocate democracy could expect to be legislated against, pursued as criminals, or hounded into exile.

That should be enough to underline the importance of not assuming the Romantics were 'like us'. The glibness with which such ideas take root is one of the targets of this book, as indicated by the frequency with which I invoke that dangerous figure, anachronism. Readers have no business imposing their own socio-political assumptions on the past, then chiding it for not meeting standards of which it was innocent. The past is a foreign country; they do things differently there. And it is for us to learn its customs. We should endeavour imaginatively to reconstruct the beliefs that predisposed most people at the time to condemn democracy, the dominant political concept on which western societies are now based. To do so is to align ourselves with those who wrote the literature discussed in this volume rather than coerce them into agreement with perspectives to which they would never have consented.

The urge to define Romanticism is born of the desire to abstract, in the process of which blunt-force trauma is sometimes inflicted on the reality: 'The Romantics were misunderstood, solitary geniuses', 'English Romanticism was a reaction against the Enlightenment', 'The Romantics repudiated the Augustans'. The tendency of definitions to crack under pressure makes me wonder whether the thing itself remains incorrigibly elusive – though I have directed readers to a means of considering the concept (see page 4 below). Definers like straight lines – the kind of retrospective order critics imagine in the form of acts, intentions, designs, and psychological certainties that never were and never will be, which sometimes turn up in disquisitions on the subject. If this volume has any ambition it is to promote the claims of what one scholar calls the 'shapelessness of lives, the anarchy of thought, and the unpredictability of the future, as they are actually experienced'.[45] Though they make no contribution to an intellectually pleasing definition of Romanticism, they did exist: Keats cannot have known he would one day be a great poet. He died thinking his name writ in water even if, in more optimistic moods, he believed he would one day be counted among the greats. That, as we should recognize, is the nature of living in the moment; there are no certainties where literary reputation is concerned, any more than in other aspects of life. Were we to doubt that, we might do worse than bear in mind the Romantic period was one in which hardly anyone knew of *The Prelude*, while *The Course of Time* was 'distinguished ... by an originality of thought and style, a pure and sustained sublimity, that are deserving of the highest admiration'.[46]

*

This volume follows Wiley Blackwell's *30 Great Myths about Shakespeare* by Laurie Maguire and Emma Smith in its analysis of what might euphemistically be called factual slippage – exaggeration, speculation masquerading as fact, simplification, or outright error.[47] The profusion of Romantic myth is such that the learned reader may be alert to absentees; I have had no option but to be selective and exercise restraint towards certain writers and themes. It would have been easy to devote more space to their sex lives, and easier still to devote more than four chapters to Byron.[48] (I have no regrets about not finding space to discuss the spurious portraits of famous writers discovered in recent years, worthy of inclusion though they may be.)

It would be dishonest to pretend I have played no part in the perpetuation of the myths that follow; in fact, it was important that the book target those which, like the false idols of biblical times, still command respect, even (on occasion) from myself. I have sometimes supposed the throng of '-isms' by which Romanticism has for decades been beleaguered might have played their part in fostering them; I now doubt any such connection and believe that to suggest otherwise is to succumb to the temptation of overrating those '-isms' in the manner prescribed by their advocates. New Historicists are neither more nor less prone to misconception than anyone else, given though some might be to pointless obscurity; by the same token, no one has a monopoly on right-mindedness, and if this book has an agenda it is to remind readers that anyone who writes on the Romantics has a duty to earn our trust by respecting the truth.

I follow Maguire and Smith in favouring the 2,000- to 2,500-word essay as the device by which each myth is explored. The obvious drawback is that of being compelled to touch on, rather than explore at leisure, aspects of the topic at hand – though that adversity is not without blessing. I use annotation as the means by which to direct readers to sources that supplement my commentary. Brevity compels me, on occasion, to summarize other writers as cogently and accurately as space will allow. I have endeavoured to do so with respect for their good faith, even when I differ with them.

Invited to write introductions to Romanticism in the past, I have declined. It was with a shock of mild surprise, halfway through work on this book, that I recognized the challenge had caught up with me. *30 Great Myths about the Romantics* should serve as a guide to those new to the subject, for I have striven to write simply and directly, even when faced with complexity. I hope it sidesteps the usual pitfalls – of riding auctorial hobbyhorses too energetically and of failing to temper intellectual rigour with love of the subject. My objectives are comparatively modest. Foremost among them, I have tried to describe the Romantics truthfully and accurately, their follies, foibles, and eccentricities intact.

Notes

1 John Keats to George and Tom Keats, 21 December 1817, in *The Letters of John Keats 1814–1821*, ed. Hyder Edward Rollins (2 vols., Cambridge, MA: Harvard University Press, 1958), i. 193.

2 When introducing *The Portable Romantic Reader* in 1960, Howard E. Hugo put it slightly differently: '"Romantic" and "Romanticism" are troublesome words. It is small consolation for the common reader – all of us – that they were perplexing when they first appeared' (*The Portable Romantic Reader*, ed. Howard E. Hugo (New York: Viking, 1960), p. 1).

3 One of those who has most vividly remapped the Romantic period in the light of these events is Ian Haywood, *Bloody Romanticism: Spectacular Violence and the Politics of Representation, 1776–1832* (Houndmills, Basingstoke: Palgrave Macmillan, 2006).

4 See, *inter alia*, the useful account given by Robert Gardiner in his introduction to the 'War on Trade' section of *Fleet Battle and Blockade: The French Revolutionary War, 1793–1797* (London: Chatham Publishing, 1996), p. 61.

5 Mary A. Favret discusses the ways in which war shaped literature of the period in 'Writing, Reading and the Scenes of War', in *The Cambridge History of English Romantic Literature*, ed. James Chandler (Cambridge: Cambridge University Press, 2009), pp. 314–34.

6 They would include Venetia Murray, who explains her rationale in *An Elegant Madness: High Society in Regency England* (New York: Penguin Books, 1999), p. xiv. George III became patient to a mad-doctor, Francis Willis, in the summer of 1788. A Regency Bill was drawn up, and was a mere three days from coming into effect when on 17 February 1789 it was announced the king had recovered. (This story is recounted in dramatic form in Alan Bennett's play, *The Madness of George III*.)

7 William St Clair, *The Reading Nation in the Romantic Period* (Cambridge: Cambridge University Press, 2004), pp. 611–12, 650.

8 He had the good sense to decline; see R. Ellis Roberts, *Samuel Rogers and His Circle* (New York: Dutton, 1910), p. 63. I am reminded that Coleridge thought Rogers a 'drivelling booby'; see his letter to Thomas Poole, 13 February 1801, in *Collected Letters of Samuel Taylor Coleridge*, ed. Earl Leslie Griggs (6 vols., Oxford: Clarendon Press, 1956–71), ii. 676.

9 Campbell's poem went through nine editions within its first seven years of publication, and would go through many more. Pollok's poem had sold 78,000 copies by 1869, and as late as 1909 could be described as 'familiar to all lovers of literature'; see Mae Douglas Durrell Frazar, *Practical Guide to Great Britain and Ireland* (2 vols., Boston: Small, Maynard, 1909), ii. 197.

10 St Clair, *The Reading Nation in the Romantic Period*, p. 303. Rogers described Scott and Byron as 'the two *lions* of London' (*Reminiscences and Table-Talk of Samuel Rogers*, ed. G. H. Powell (London: R. Brimley Johnson, 1903), p. 153).

11 William Wordsworth to Charles Lamb, 21 November 1816, in *The Letters of William and Dorothy Wordsworth*, viii, *A Supplement of New Letters*, ed. Alan G. Hill (Oxford: Clarendon Press, 1993), p. 163.

12 *Roderick* was Southey's most financially successful poem.

13 *The Stranger* was a hit on both sides of the Atlantic, and remained in the repertory until the latter part of the nineteenth century.

14 Quoted in Laura Brown, *Homeless Dogs and Melancholy Apes: Humans and Other Animals in the Modern Literary Imagination* (Ithaca, NY: Cornell University Press, 2010), p. 132. Apparently there was a large pool onstage, and Carlo had to jump into it from a high rock in order to save the life of a small child. See Frederick Reynolds, *The Life and Times of Frederick Reynolds* (2 vols., London: Henry Colburn, 1826), ii. 349–52. For further information on Romantic melodrama and these plays in particular, see Felicia Hardison Londré, *The History of World Theater: From the English Restoration to the Present* (New York: Continuum, 1999), pp. 201–6.

15 Milman's play sold 7,250 copies in five separate editions.

16 *Bertram* went through nine editions in 1816.

17 David V. Erdman is illuminating on the subject of Byron's proclaimed intention to write 'for the closet'; see 'Byron's Stage Fright: The History of his Ambition and Fear of Writing for the Stage', *English Literary History* 6 (1939), 219–43.

18 Print runs from St Clair, *The Reading Nation in the Romantic Period*, pp. 584, 622. Burney's novel remains sufficiently prized that, at auction in New York on 5 December 2013, a copy of the first edition fetched $2,500 (£1,525), including the buyer's premium.

19 Throughout the first fourteen years of its life, *Frankenstein* existed in about 1,000 copies, fewer than most of the works of Scott and Byron sold on publication day. Blackwood printed 1,000 copies of Hogg's *Confessions* in 1824, but it was remaindered and reissued four years later as *The Suicide's Grave*; see St Clair, *The Reading Nation in the Romantic Period*, pp. 365, 610, 644.

20 Kingsley would have us suppose this a quotation from Byron but I have failed to trace it.

21 *Lord Byron: The Critical Heritage*, ed. Andrew Rutherford (London: Routledge & Kegan Paul, 1970), p. 355. Susan J. Wolfson has illustrated the alacrity

with which readers of *Sardanapalus* backed away from its protagonist's effeminacy, as if terrified of attributing that characteristic to its author. See Susan J. Wolfson, *Borderlines: The Shiftings of Gender in British Romanticism* (Stanford, CA: Stanford University Press, 2006), pp. 161–3. See also Alan Sinfield, *Cultural Politics – Queer Reading* (London: Routledge, 2005), p. 33.

22 C. L. Cline, 'Unpublished Notes on the Romantic Poets by Isaac D'Israeli', *Studies in English* 21 (1941), 138–46, p. 142.

23 Peter Cochran directs me to the lengthy inventory of Byron's jewellery collection at British Library, Egerton 2611 ff. 255–6.

24 Estill Curtis Pennington, 'Painting Lord Byron: An Account by William Edward West', *Archives of American Art Journal* 24 (1984), 16–21, p. 19. For a description of the painting and its various copies, see Annette Peach, 'Portraits of Byron', *The Volume of the Walpole Society* 62 (2000), 1–144, pp. 106–12.

25 Thomas Moore, *Letters and Journals of Lord Byron* (2 vols., London: John Murray, 1830), ii. 685.

26 Marguerite, Countess of Blessington, *Conversations of Lord Byron with the Countess of Blessington* (London: Henry Colburn, 1834), p. 3.

27 James Hamilton Browne, 'Voyage from Leghorn to Cephalonia with Lord Byron', *Blackwood's Edinburgh Magazine* 35 (January 1834), 56–67, pp. 56–7.

28 Rees Howell Gronow, *Reminiscences of Captain Gronow: being anecdotes of the camp, the court, and the clubs, at the close of the last war with France* (2nd ed., London: Smith, Elder, 1842), p. 210. The anecdote has been questioned, but Peter Cochran tells me it is plausible.

29 Byron to Mrs Catherine Gordon Byron, 12 November 1809, in *Byron's Letters and Journals*, ed. Leslie A. Marchand (13 vols., London: John Murray, 1973–94), i. 231.

30 See Matthews's letter to Byron of 13 January 1811, quoted in Louis Crompton, *Byron and Greek Love: Homophobia in 19th-Century England* (Berkeley: University of California Press, 1985), pp. 161–2. Cochran describes Matthews as 'an atheist and radical, as well as … an aspirational gay'; see 'Byron's Boyfriends', in *Byron and Women [and Men]*, ed. Peter Cochran (Newcastle upon Tyne: Cambridge Scholars, 2010), p. 36. See also D. S. Neff, 'Bitches, Mollies, and Tommies: Byron, Masculinity, and the History of Sexualities', *Journal of the History of Sexuality* 11 (2002), 395–438, pp. 407–8.

31 The fullest account of Bankes of which I am aware may be found in Cochran, 'Byron's Boyfriends', pp. 27–31.

32 Ibid., p. 37.

33 G. Wilson Knight, *Lord Byron: Christian Virtues* (London: Routledge & Kegan Paul, 1952), p. 81. There are numerous readings of effeminacy in Byron; foremost among them are those in Wolfson, *Borderlines*, chs. 5 and 6.

34 Byron, *Don Juan* I, stanza 195, l. 1557.

35 See, for instance, Jerome J. McGann, *Byron and Romanticism*, ed. James Soderholm (Cambridge: Cambridge University Press, 2002), p. 67.

36 For the range of radical opinion in the Romantic period, see Robert Sayre and Michael Löwy, 'Figures of Romantic Anticapitalism', in *Spirits of Fire: English Romantic Writers and Contemporary Historical Methods*, ed. G. A. Rosso and Daniel P. Watkins (London: Associated University Presses, 1990), pp. 23–68.

37 This is explored in detail by Judith Schneid Lewis, *Sacred to Female Patriotism: Gender, Class, and Politics in Late Georgian Britain* (London: Routledge, 2003), ch. 6.

38 See Robert J. Goldstein, *Political Repression in 19th-Century Europe* (London: Routledge, 1983), p. 3, and Eric J. Evans, *The Great Reform Act of 1832* (2nd ed., London: Routledge, 1994), p. 3.

39 This quotation is taken from the useful discussion by Joanna Innes, Mark Philp, and Robert Saunders, 'The Rise of Democratic Discourse in the Reform Era: Britain in the 1830s and 1840s', in *Re-imagining Democracy in the Age of Revolutions: America, France, Britain, Ireland 1750–1850*, ed. Joanna Innes and Mark Philp (Oxford: Oxford University Press, 2013), ch. 8.

40 *The Works of William Hazlitt*, ed. P. P. Howe (21 vols., London: Dent, 1930–4), xvii. 9.

41 Neil J. Smelser, *Social Paralysis and Social Change: British Working-Class Education in the Nineteenth Century* (Berkeley: University of California Press, 1991), p. 67.

42 E. P. Thompson, *The Making of the English Working Class* (New York: Pantheon Books, 1964), p. 451.

43 The phrase is used by Judith Thompson, *John Thelwall in the Wordsworth Circle: The Silenced Partner* (New York: Palgrave Macmillan, 2012).

44 Henry Crabb Robinson, MS Diary 4 (18 June 1814 to 31 December 1815), entry for 12 February 1815, 72^v (MS held at Dr Williams' Library, London). On a subsequent visit, Robinson found Thelwall 'not outrageously hostile to the Bourbons & not very friendly to Buon[aparte]: except that he prefers even him to a Bourb: Sovereign' (entry for Monday 15 May 1815, Diary 4, 110^v).

45 William St Clair, 'The Biographer as Archaeologist', in *Mapping Lives: The Uses of Biography* (Oxford: British Academy, 2002), pp. 217–34, 222.

46 *The Christian Review and Clerical Magazine* 1 (1827), 345.

47 I refer the reader to their percipient introduction, *30 Great Myths about Shakespeare* (Oxford: Wiley-Blackwell, 2013), pp. 1–2.

48 While working on this book, I have reflected that slippages of fact are prone to recur among those whose lives are most recounted.

A NOTE ON MONETARY VALUES

During the Romantic period, Britain used a pre-decimal currency of pounds, shillings, and pence. There were 12 pennies in a shilling and 20 shillings in a pound. Pennies were subdivided into quarters (or farthings). A sense of value is provided by William St Clair: 'For a price of 1.5 shillings (1s. 6d.) a week a bookseller's apprentice in Edinburgh could have a shared bedroom, a landlady to do the cooking, and the right to sit by the fire. His food could cost as little as 0.25 shillings (threepence) a day.'[1]

St Clair estimates a reasonable but not extravagant income for members of the upper or upper-middle classes to have been around £5 (100 shillings) a week;[2] clergymen, officers, doctors, merchants, widows, journalists, and university students might have lived on between 100 and 50 shillings (£5 and £2. 10s.); the highest-paid skilled workers in the country, printers, earned about 36 shillings (£1. 16s.); carpenters and weavers were paid about 25 shillings (£1. 5s.), while farm labourers and domestic servants made around 10 shillings a week.[3]

Books were an expensive luxury. Some volumes of poetry were comparatively cheap: in 1793 Blake priced *Songs of Innocence* at 5 shillings; *Lyrical Ballads* (1798) and Keats's earliest volume of *Poems* (1817) retailed at 6 shillings; Shelley's *Alastor* (1816) at 5 shillings; Hemans's *Records of Woman* (1828) was 8s. 6d. At the upper end, poetry could be as expensive as any other form of publication: Wordsworth's *The Excursion* (1814), Southey's *Madoc* (1805), and Scott's *Lady of the Lake* (1810)

30 Great Myths About the Romantics, First Edition. Duncan Wu.
© 2015 John Wiley & Sons, Ltd. Published 2015 by John Wiley & Sons, Ltd.

each cost 42 shillings (£2.2s.) – for which, as St Clair notes, a reader in Salisbury might have purchased 100 fat pigs.[4] Novels, which usually appeared in three volumes rather than one, were also costly: Scott's *Rob Roy* (1818) and Lady Caroline Lamb's *Glenarvon* (1816) sold for 24 shillings; Austen's *Pride and Prejudice* (1813) and *Mansfield Park* (1814) for 18 shillings; and Mary Shelley's *Frankenstein* (1818) for 16s. 6d.

Pricing was the key to reaching a wider audience. When in 1792 Thomas Paine dropped the price of *The Rights of Man* from 3s. 6d. to a mere sixpence, it became available to large numbers of people who normally had no access to such things. It is not known exactly how many copies went into circulation, but St Clair suggests 20,000, many of which were read aloud to enthusiastic listeners. Paine's success prompted his indictment for seditious libel by a government terrified of republicanism and revolution.[5] Twopence was the price charged by William Hone for his politically subversive pamphlets, *The Late John Wilkes's Catechism of a Ministerial Member*, *The Political Litany*, and *The Sinecurist's Creed, or Belief*, which precipitated his prosecution in 1817. As in the case of Paine, their low price made them widely available and thus a focus of government concern. When in 1823 Byron moved away from John Murray and began instead to publish with John Hunt, he agreed to a new form of publication. *Don Juan* was issued both in the octavo format favoured by middle-class readers, as well as in cheap editions costing a shilling, while excerpts appeared in twopenny magazines. By 1826 second-hand copies were changing hands for a halfpenny.[6] This lesson was quickly absorbed by newspaper proprietors. When in 1816 William Cobbett launched the mass-circulation broadsheet edition of his *Political Register*, he dropped its price from one shilling and a halfpenny to twopence – which caused its circulation to jump to between 40,000 and 70,000 copies a week.[7] It was not for nothing Hazlitt wrote of him: 'He is a kind of *fourth estate* in the politics of the country.'[8]

These data are applicable to the four decades or so covered by this book, but readers should be mindful that (for instance) food prices rose steeply between the early 1790s and 1815: in 1795 alone, the price of bread rose by 75 per cent.[9] That affected everyone in various degrees, not solely the poor – and had an effect on attitudes to book-purchasing, which remained principally an upper- and middle-class activity.

Notes

1 William St Clair, *The Reading Nation in the Romantic Period* (Cambridge: Cambridge University Press, 2004), p. 195.

2 Ibid., p. 194.
3 Ibid., p. 195.
4 Ibid., p. 202.
5 Ibid., pp. 624, 256.
6 Ibid., p. 327.
7 These are the figures given by Leonora Nattrass, *William Cobbett: The Politics of Style* (Cambridge: Cambridge University Press, 1995), p. 3.
8 'Character of Cobbett' in *Table Talk*; see *The Selected Writings of William Hazlitt*, ed. Duncan Wu (9 vols., London: Pickering & Chatto, 1998), vi. 43.
9 See, *inter alia*, Mark Harrison, *Crowds and History: Mass Phenomena in English Towns, 1790–1835* (Cambridge: Cambridge University Press, 1988), pp. 240–1; John E. Archer, *Social Unrest and Popular Protest in England, 1780–1840* (Cambridge: Cambridge University Press, 2000), ch. 3; John Bohstedt, 'Gender, Household and Community Politics: Women in English Riots 1790–1810', *Past and Present* 120 (1988), 88–122; Walter M. Stern, 'The Bread Crisis in Britain, 1795–96', *Economica* NS 31 (1964), 168–87.

Myth 1

ROMANTICISM BEGAN IN 1798

Once upon a time, as Karl Kroeber has observed, 'Romanticism was five poets, a Scottish novelist nobody read, and the years 1798–1832'.[1]

Even today, there are numerous authorities that proudly declare, with the *Routledge History of Literature in English* (2nd ed., 2001), that 'the period begins in 1798';[2] with the more recent *Britannica Guide to World Literature* (2011), that '*Lyrical Ballads* (1798) [began] the Romantic movement';[3] or with the *Cambridge History of Literary Criticism*, that 'British Romanticism … [has a] commonly accepted founding date of 1798 (the publication of *Lyrical ballads*)'.[4]

This is not unreasonable. Even to those alive at the time, the year was an important one – though not because it had anything to do with the 'R' word. The numbers that composed it, Hazlitt wrote in 1823, 'are to me like the "dreaded name of Demogorgon"'.[5] He may have been thinking of the uprising of the United Irishmen[6] or his first meetings with Wordsworth and Coleridge;[7] it is less likely he had in mind the year in which the Schlegel brothers began to publish in *The Athenaeum* writings that would activate the term 'Romantic'.[8]

The obvious objection is that 1798 consigns to the limbo of what used to be called 'pre-romanticism' most of Blake, Burns, Cowper, Mary Robinson, Anna Laetitia Barbauld, Charlotte Smith, Helen Maria Williams, and Ann Yearsley, not to mention early works of Wordsworth, Coleridge, Samuel Rogers, Crabbe, William Lisle Bowles, Ann Radcliffe, Hannah More, Elizabeth Inchbald, and the entire Revolution debate (Burke, Paine, Price, Wollstonecraft, Godwin, and Mackintosh, among others). One response is to backdate it to 1785, in line with the position taken by the *Norton Anthology of English Literature* from its sixth edition (1993) onwards. The *Norton*'s editors leave us to deduce for ourselves whether Romanticism began on 1 January 1785 – as opposed

30 Great Myths About the Romantics, First Edition. Duncan Wu.
© 2015 John Wiley & Sons, Ltd. Published 2015 by John Wiley & Sons, Ltd.

to 7 January, when a Frenchman and an American made the first crossing of the English Channel by hot-air balloon; 1 June, when John Adams, the American ambassador to Great Britain, had his first meeting with George III; or 6 July, when America adopted the dollar as its currency. Whatever their view, they include a number of works published prior to 1785: Barbauld's 'The Mouse's Petition' (1773), Charlotte Smith's 'Written at the Close of Spring' (1784), and John Newton's 'Amazing Grace!' (1779).

The *Norton* is guilty of inconsistency rather than confusion, and not without cause: theories about Romanticism have a tendency to fracture when crystallized as rules that have to be policed. That is because the concept has no exact correlative in historical time, unlike the Elizabethan age and the Restoration period (Sunday, 15 January 1559 being the date of Elizabeth's coronation, 29 May 1660 that of Charles II's triumphant entry to London). Instead, it is dependent on a post-mortem rationalization of the people and events with which it is associated, such rationalizations being seldom other than circular. That is to say, having determined Blake was not Romantic, we construct a definition excluding him; if we decide Hannah More and the Bluestockings *were*, we conceive it accordingly. And so on.

Which raises the matter of who we consider the Romantics to have been. No one today would question the eligibility of Keats, Shelley, and Blake, but in their own time they were either obscure or subject to ridicule. Then as now, successful writers were those whose books sold – such as James Montgomery (whose net sales amounted to 38,000 copies), Robert Bloomfield (100,000), George Crabbe (35,000), Henry Kirke White (21,000), and Robert Pollok, whose *The Course of Time* (1827) sold 17,750 copies in less than three years.[9] The most frequently read and discussed were Byron, Thomas Campbell, Coleridge, Thomas Moore, Samuel Rogers, Walter Scott, Southey, and Wordsworth.[10] If taxonomized at all, they were 'The Living Poets', a term Hazlitt used in his *Lectures on the English Poets* (1818), with the caveat, 'I cannot be absolutely certain that any body, twenty years hence, will think any thing about any of them'.[11] It was well advised: who, at the time of reading this essay, would confidently declare which poets of the present will be read decades from now? All the same, 'The Living Poets' stuck, perhaps because it was a label with no pretension other than to classify a diverse group by the one thing they had in common, and it persisted until around 1830, by which time one of them was dead.

During the Romantic period, 'romance' was meaningful only as a term by which certain kinds of novels or poems were taxonomized. In 1785, Clara Reeve used it to describe a 'wild, extravagant, fabulous Story' associated with epic and a likeable hero,[12] and contemporaries applied it similarly: Byron called *Childe Harold's Pilgrimage* a 'Romaunt'; Southey called *Thalaba* a 'rhythmical romance'; Scott's *Marmion* was 'a romance in six cantos', while Moore's *Lalla Rookh* was 'an oriental romance'. None of which would have caused anyone to brand them Romantic.[13] 'We are troubled with no controversies on Romanticism and Classicism', declared Carlyle as late as 1831, a little smugly.[14] The debate did not begin until long after the Romantics were capable of saying what they thought about it, and only in 1875 were Wordsworth, Southey, and Coleridge identified as comprising a Romantic school.[15] Even then, the term was slow to catch on. Mrs Oliphant's *Literary History of England* (1886) does not use it, referring instead to 'The New Brotherhood', while subsequent commentators mention 'The New Poetry'.

One wonders why anyone would posit a starting-point of 4 October 1798, even if that was the publication date of *Lyrical Ballads*. A precise date argues for specificity where the more politic option is that of vagueness, while placing emphasis on what, to most contemporaries, was a non-event. In March 1799, according to Sara Coleridge, 'The Lyrical Ballads are laughed at and disliked by all with very few excepted.'[16] Reviews were 'on the whole favorable, some of them laudatory', despite charges of 'babyism and social withdrawal'.[17] No one called it Romantic. And no one suggested, against the evidence, that Scott, Byron, Southey, Coleridge, and Wordsworth had anything in common until April 1820, when John Wilson wrote,

> This age has unquestionably produced a noble band of British Poets – each separated from all the rest by abundant peculiarities of style and manner – some far above others in skill to embrace and improve the appliances of popularity – but all of them successful in the best and noblest sense of that term, because all of them bound together, (however little some of themselves may suspect it) by rich participation in the stirring and exalting spirit of the same eventful age – an age distinguished above almost all its predecessors by the splendour of external things, but still more distinguished by the power and energy which these have reflected upon the intellect and imagination of its children.[18]

Wilson's commentary deals in generalities ('rich participation', 'the splendor of external things', and so on), the precise meaning of which may have been unclear even to him. Indeed, what might have struck contemporaries most forcibly were its implausibilities, especially given the animosities between some of those concerned.

Nonetheless, what he says is worth notice. He is reticent about assigning a *terminus a quo* to 'the stirring and exalting spirit of the same eventful age', despite having been one of its witnesses. And that was wise, for attempts at precise dating are probably doomed. Understandably, the trend among recent scholars has been to back away from 1798 (and *Lyrical Ballads*) and suggest, instead, 1789 (for example). Again, the argument is circular: by this means, Romanticism is defined in relation to events in France. Which is fine so long as that is deemed adequate to encompass the literature classed as Romantic.

Ernest Bernbaum dated the inception of Romanticism to 'c. 1783' for his *Anthology of Romanticism* (3rd edition 1948), which allowed him to begin with Blake's *Poetical Sketches*.[19] Such a move seems uncontroversial, as it is dependent not on a historical event but on a creative one. The problem lies with Romanticism as a concept, which has never been stable.[20] Blake was not essential to it until 1896, apparently. If you agreed with F. R. Leavis in 1932, Blake was out; if with Northrop Frye in 1947, he was in.[21] Southey took his place in the Romantic canon until Bernbaum's *Anthology*,[22] but failed to make the cut either in Auden and Pearson's *Portable Romantic Poets* (1950) or in Bloom and Trilling's *Romantic Poetry and Prose* (1973). He is absent from the ninth edition of the *Norton* (2012) which does, however, contain Letitia Landon, Horace Walpole, and Maria Edgeworth. As if that were not enough, there is the added complication of how the Romantics perceived themselves. Was Byron a Romantic? He didn't think so. In fact, he thought most poets after Pope, with the possible exceptions of George Crabbe and Samuel Rogers, a deviation from the true path – of Augustanism (see p. 34). That sort of opinion is put down to lordly eccentricity, but that this is Byron rather than Thomas Warton the younger should give us pause. To reiterate: the poet now reckoned the most Romantic of Romantics cast himself as Augustan, because to him Augustanism was the correct thing, rather than the incorrect thing of which all but two contemporaries were guilty – which was what? Anything but Romanticism, which did not yet exist.

This volume follows many others in the field in using the 'R' word unabashedly, which implies the obligation to offer readers some way of approaching it. I follow Roger Scruton in viewing Romanticism as the consequence of cultural developments that occurred during the Enlightenment.

> The course of Romantic art is one of ever deeper mourning for the life of 'natural piety' which Enlightenment destroyed. And from this mourning springs the Romantic hope – the hope of recreating in imagination the community that will never again exist in fact. Hence the importance of folk poetry, folk traditions, and 'ancestral voices'. Beneath the rational culture of Enlightenment, the Romantics searched for another and deeper culture – the culture of the people, rooted in mystery, and surviving in the inner sanctuary of the poet's self.[23]

By turning to 'the inner sanctuary of the poet's self', Scruton echoes Auden, who said that in Romantic literature 'the divine element in man is now held to be neither power nor free will nor reason, but self-consciousness .... the hero whom the poet must celebrate is himself, for the only consciousness accessible to him is his own'.[24] These thoughts may not amount to a definition, but do indicate a means by which Romanticism can be distinguished from what came before and after it.[25]

It is impossible to stick a precise date on when anyone (either individually or separately) started to think and act Romantically, but those who did were unlike their forebears. That is not to say they were opposed to them; after all, they were products of the Enlightenment. But if we regard them as preoccupied with the inner resources of the self, we apprehend something of what made them new. With that in mind, a quintessential Romantic moment might be found in a blank verse fragment of 1798 in which Wordsworth described a mystic experience when 'beauteous pictures'

> Rose in harmonious imagery – they rose
> As from some distant region of my soul
> And came along like dreams ....[26]

Composition of these lines in early 1798 might be taken to indicate that Romanticism had by then been conceived, but precise datings are probably best avoided if only because of the variation in what was being written at any one time. If Blake as Romantic composed *Urizen* in 1794, the same need not be argued of Henry James Pye as he wrote *The Siege of Meaux* the same year. We are enjoined neither to argue for consistency across the work of separate authors nor to demand it from a single writer across decades: Wordsworth in 1842 was not the same writer as in 1798 (Myth 12). Furthermore, the quality of whatever that thing was, as expressed through those on whom it alights, should be allowed to change. If we find it in 'Tintern Abbey', it need not be identical to what we find in *Childe Harold's Pilgrimage* Canto III or in 'Mont Blanc'.

Inexact that may be, but it exonerates us from nominating an entire country 'Romantic' for an arbitrary span determined in the ivory tower. If instead we think of Romanticism as mobile, localized, impermanent, and filtered through the prism of the individual, it becomes easier to see why attempts to restrict it to a definable moment remain perpetually open to debate. It is not stable in the same sense as historical events, being a retrospective judgement on a long-dead past. Far from invalidating it, acceptance of those inherent qualities – its variousness and selectivity – helps us consider it on its own terms, as it arises from the inner world of the individual writer, from his or her place within the culture, and as the agent of creative renewal, rather than as something monolithic, all-encompassing, and consistent, an edict imposed on an earlier time innocent of how it would be judged by a more knowing future.

Notes

1 Quoted by Harriet Kramer Linkin, 'The Current Canon in British Romantics Studies', *College English* 53 (1991), 548–70, p. 548.
2 Ronald Carter and John McRae, *The Routledge History of Literature in English: Britain and Ireland* (2nd ed., London: Routledge, 2001), p. 177.
3 *The Britannica Guide to World Literature: English Literature from the Restoration Through the Romantic Period*, ed. J. E. Luebering (New York: Britannica Educational Publishing, 2011), p. 155.
4 David Simpson, 'The French Revolution', in *The Cambridge History of Literary Criticism*, vol. v, *Romanticism*, ed. George Alexander Kennedy and Marshall Brown (Cambridge: Cambridge University Press, 2000), pp. 49–70, 52.
5 'My First Acquaintance with Poets', in *The Selected Writings of William Hazlitt*, ed. Duncan Wu (9 vols., London: Pickering & Chatto, 1998), ix. 95.
6 The suggestion is Tom Paulin's; see, *inter alia*, his 'Diary' article, *London Review of Books* 17 (24 August 1995), 24–5.
7 As David Higgins suggests; see *Romantic Genius and the Literary Magazine: Biography, Celebrity, Politics* (Abingdon, Oxon.: Routledge, 2005), p. 118.
8 Jonathan Arac, 'The Impact of Shakespeare', in *The Cambridge History of Literary Criticism*, vol. v, pp. 272–95, 273.
9 William St Clair, *The Reading Nation in the Romantic Period* (Cambridge: Cambridge University Press, 2004), pp. 217, 630.
10 Ibid., p. 210.
11 'On the Living Poets', in *Selected Writings of William Hazlitt*, ed. Wu, ii. 300. The very issue of posterity is one means by which modern critics have attempted to define Romanticism; see, in particular, Andrew Bennett, *Romantic Poets and the Culture of Posterity* (Cambridge: Cambridge University Press, 1999).
12 Richard Maxwell, 'The Historiography of Fiction in the Romantic Period', in *The Cambridge Companion to Fiction in the Romantic Period*, ed. Richard Maxwell and Katie Trumpener (Cambridge: Cambridge University Press, 2008), pp. 7–21, 8.
13 This is not to say that romance did not shape Romanticism; see, *inter alia*, David Duff, *Romance and Revolution: Shelley and the Politics of a Genre* (Cambridge: Cambridge University Press, 1994).
14 As quoted by Jane Moore and John Strachan, *Key Concepts in Romantic Literature* (Houndmills, Basingstoke: Palgrave Macmillan, 2010), p. 7.
15 St Clair, *The Reading Nation in the Romantic Period*, p. 212n10.

16 Sara Coleridge to Thomas *Poole*, March 1799, in *Minnow among Tritons: Mrs S. T. Coleridge's Letters to Thomas Poole, 1799–1834*, ed. Stephen Potter (London: Nonesuch Press, 1934), p. 4.

17 John O. Hayden, *The Romantic Reviewers 1802–1824* (London: Routledge & Kegan Paul, 1969), p. 78.

18 [John Wilson], 'Wordsworth's River Duddon', *Blackwood's Edinburgh Magazine* 7 (April 1820), 406. The quotation is cited by St Clair, *The Reading Nation in the Romantic Period*, p. 211n4.

19 *Anthology of Romanticism*, ed. Ernest Bernbaum (3rd ed., New York: Ronald Press, 1948), p. iii. This was also the dating adopted by Lionel Trilling and Harold Bloom for their *Romantic Poetry and Prose* (Oxford: Oxford University Press, 1973), the volume with which I was introduced to the period in the early 1980s.

20 See the quotations reproduced by Moore and Strachan, *Key Concepts in Romantic Literature*, pp. 9–14. John Beer provides a good potted history of its early evolution in his entry on Romanticism in *The Blackwell Companion to the Enlightenment*, ed. John W. Yolton, Roy Porter, Pat Rogers, and Barbara Maria Stafford (Oxford: Blackwell, 1991).

21 See Seamus Perry, 'Romanticism: The Brief History of a Concept', in *A Companion to Romanticism*, ed. Duncan Wu (Oxford: Blackwell, 1998), pp. 3–11, 8.

22 Bernbaum includes that old warhorse 'The Battle of Blenheim', along with 'The Holly Tree', 'On the Speech of Robert Emmet', 'My Days among the Dead are Passed', 'The Death of John Wesley', and extracts from Southey's *History of the Peninsular War*, *Life of Nelson*, and *The Doctor*.

23 Roger Scruton, *An Intelligent Person's Guide to Modern Culture* (South Bend, IN: St Augustine's Press, 2000), p. 49.

24 'Introduction', in *The Portable Romantic Poets*, ed. W. H. Auden and Norman Holmes Pearson (1950; New York: Penguin Books, 1977), pp. xii–xiv.

25 Those in search of a definition could do worse than to consult 'In Search of a Definition', the first chapter of Isaiah Berlin, *The Roots of Romanticism* (Princeton, NJ: Princeton University Press, 1999).

26 William Wordsworth, 'The Discharged Soldier', ll. 28–31. The fragment eventually found its way into *The Thirteen-Book Prelude*. See *Lyrical Ballads and Other Poems, 1797–1800*, ed. James A. Butler and Karen Green (Ithaca, NY: Cornell University Press, 1992), p. 278.

Myth

2

ENGLISH ROMANTICISM WAS A REACTION AGAINST THE ENLIGHTENMENT

The terms are as slippery as eels. I have already noticed the difficulty of defining Romanticism; the Enlightenment is, if anything, even more resistant to being pinned down, partly because it was never a single thing. We might venture, with Roger Scruton, that 'Enlightened people cease to define themselves in terms of place, history, tribe or dynasty, and lay claim instead to a universal human nature, whose laws are valid for all mankind.'[1] That claim precipitated loss: it stripped religion of authority, and suggested political power derived not from the Deity but from a 'social contract' between ruler and ruled.[2] The response of some Enlightenment thinkers was to find sacredness not in church and state but in nature; adventurers like Captain Cook and Sir Joseph Banks were thought to have found Eden in Tahiti, with its endless supply of breadfruit, coconuts, and Polynesian houris.[3]

The project of aestheticizing the primitive was a lengthy one, but it took Jean-Jacques Rousseau to give it the political dimension that would compel generations to come. For him, civilization was a disaster that had destroyed human freedom. Primitive people, he argued, 'lived as free, healthy, good and happy men so far as they could be',

> but from the instant one man needed the help of another, and it was found to be useful for one man to have provisions enough for two, equality disappeared, property was introduced, work became necessary, and vast forests were transformed into pleasant fields which had to be watered with the sweat of men, and where slavery and misery were soon seen to germinate and flourish with the crops.[4]

30 Great Myths About the Romantics, First Edition. Duncan Wu.
© 2015 John Wiley & Sons, Ltd. Published 2015 by John Wiley & Sons, Ltd.

That would prove a potent idea not least for its implied belief in a golden age when people were bound together by communal ties and religious faith, long before divisions of labour, property, and class prised them apart. It remains the ideal for which utopians and revolutionaries pine. Not for nothing were passages from Rousseau's inflammatory work, *The Social Contract*, read aloud to the Paris mob during the revolution.[5] To many it would seem he had, almost single-handedly, engineered the collapse of the *ancien régime*. But that was as spurious as to argue the Romantics precipitated the end of the Enlightenment. It would make more sense to ask whether the Enlightenment ever really ended. Probably not, as its influence extends into the present, through 'liberal democracy' and 'liberal nationalism'.[6]

All the same, the French Revolution did spell the end of something other than the royal family and their hangers-on. As Dorinda Outram notes, it was the first such event to have 'created something completely new, a break in the passage of history, and a "new order". This was the sense of "revolution" which was to be picked up by the French in 1789, and by all subsequent movements for change.'[7] She stops short of saying it marked the end of the Enlightenment, though a contemporary might have found significance in the fact that it coincided (roughly) with the death of Richard Price and emigration of Joseph Priestley, both of whom were identified with the Enlightenment in England.[8] For Coleridge, Blake, and (to some extent) Wordsworth, revolution in America and France, and the war that ensued in 1793, declared nothing less than the incipient millennium (Christ's thousand-year rule on earth as predicted in the Revelation of St John the Divine). 'Empire is no more!', wrote Blake in prophetic garb at the tumultuous conclusion of *The Marriage of Heaven and Hell* (1790) – 'and now the lion & wolf shall cease'[9] (echoing Isaiah's prophecy of a new heaven and earth in which 'the wolf and the lamb shall feed together', Isaiah 65:25). In 'Religious Musings' (1794–6), Coleridge would suggest the French Revolution represented the opening of the fifth of the seven seals, and that divine justice was at hand – a view consistent with those of Price and Priestley.[10] Coleridge's poem was a precursor of Wordsworth's millenarian epic, 'The Recluse', which would establish a necessitarian system of philosophy whereby love of nature would lead irresistibly to love of mankind.

> No naked hearts,
> No naked minds, shall then be left to mourn
> The burden of existence.
>
> ('Not useless do I deem', ll. 41–3[11])

Some scholars suggest the emergence of a 'simpler, more strident, democratic republicanism'[12] under Thomas Paine, and the evolution of a rationalistic, anarchistic philosophy under Godwin, signalled the end of the Enlightenment. Perhaps – but such judgements are the privilege of hindsight. For a contemporary to have thought Paine or Godwin signalled anything it was necessary first to understand the larger implications of their labours, and that was unclear from the vantage-point of 1793 (when Godwin published *Political Justice*). To the young men drawn to Utilitarianism in the early decades of the nineteenth century, the idea the Enlightenment was dead would have seemed questionable; they were, after all, disciples of a philosophy that gave renewed authority to Hume and Locke, the most eminent Enlightenment *savants* of all – and Benthamite theory would resonate for decades after its originator's death in 1832.[13] Which only goes to show the Romantics were products of what preceded them. Born in 1757, Blake was 2 years old when Johnson published *Rasselas* and Voltaire published *Candide*. When Blake was 10, Rousseau visited England and Sterne completed *Tristram Shandy*. Coleridge thought natural philosophers would transform the world in which he grew up, looking to statesmen-scientists such as Benjamin Franklin, Lavoisier in France, and Priestley in England.[14] He was also influenced by the philosophies of David Hartley and Bishop Berkeley, whose notions he conveyed enthusiastically to Wordsworth, and by German Enlightenment figures such as Herder and Lessing.[15] At Hawkshead Grammar School Wordsworth was a gifted student of Euclidean geometry, and as a Cambridge undergraduate he read Locke[16] within sight of Newton's statue at Trinity, 'with his Prism and silent Face'.[17] (For the Romantic attitude to science, and Newton in particular, see Myth 3.) The Romantics never assembled in opposition to the era that had preceded them; they emerged from it, carrying into the future its energies, aspirations, and customs.

Three examples might be invoked to bear this out, the first of which relates to the sociology of Romantic discourse.

2.1 New Forms of Sociability

As Outram points out, Enlightenment thinkers enjoyed 'new forms of sociability centring on ideas'[18] which originated in the London coffee-houses where, in the second half of the eighteenth century, Franklin read colonial newspapers and associated with his countrymen and their allies.[19] Those gatherings, less to do with social rank than with religious, political, and intellectual sympathies, are echoed by the networks through which the Romantics conceived and articulated their ideas. There are numerous instances, beginning with the Bluestockings (who included Burke and Reynolds), continuing with the philanthropic association

Figure 4 Marguerite Gardiner, Countess of Blessington (1789–1849), hostess of a glittering salon in her Park Lane house from 1830 onwards.
Source: Paul F. Betz Collection.

proposed by Shelley, the club which gathered round James Rice, the Zetosophian Society, the Breidden Society, Charles and Mary Lamb's 'at homes', through to the literary salon conducted by Marguerite, Countess of Blessington, at Gore House in the 1830s and 1840s.[20] One is reminded of less formal gatherings, including Coleridge's friendships with Robert Southey, Robert Lovell, John Thelwall, Humphry Davy, and William Wordsworth; Shelley's association with Thomas Jefferson Hogg, Byron, and Leigh Hunt; and Keats's with Charles Cowden Clarke, Benjamin Robert Haydon, Leigh Hunt (again), and John Hamilton Reynolds.

2.2 The Language of Passion

Rousseau's philosophy was echoed in a Romantic fascination with literary forms that were thought to pre-date the manner of which Pope and Dryden were exponents. 'In its ancient original condition', wrote the rhetorician Hugh Blair (thinking of ballad, folk song, and the oral tradition), poetry 'spoke the language of passion, and no other; for to passion it owed its birth.'[21] That was close to Wordsworth's claim that 'poetry is passion: it is the history or science of feelings',[22] and the politically loaded argument that it was preferable to write about 'low and rustic life … because in that condition the essential passions of the heart find a better soil in which they can attain their maturity, are less under restraint, and speak a plainer and more emphatic language'.[23] (For more on Wordsworth's indebtedness to eighteenth-century thinkers, see Myth 10, especially p. 85.) Romanticism has been so thoroughly digested by our own culture as to make such arguments uncontroversial: modern poets mine their emotions to the point of exhaustion and risk nothing by writing about 'low and rustic life'. Which makes it hard to appreciate how self-regardingly individual Wordsworth's arguments seemed in their day – though we should recall that Blair's theories, on which he drew, were in print by 1763.

2.3   The Poet as Prophet

Poets have compared themselves with prophets since classical times; the idea was revived in the eighteenth century and exploited with such conviction by the Romantics that entire books continue to be written on the subject.[24] At the end of *The Thirteen-Book Prelude* Wordsworth called himself and Coleridge 'Prophets of Nature' who would speak to readers 'Of their redemption, surely yet to come';[25] in his 'Defence of Poetry' Shelley described poets as 'hierophants of an unapprehended inspiration' (a hierophant being an explicator of sacred mysteries, like a priest or prophet);[26] Coleridge collected his poetry as sibylline leaves (the prophecies of the Erythraean Sibyl having been so inscribed);[27] Felicia Hemans impersonated a prophet in 'Second Sight' ('I see the blood-red future stain / On the warrior's gorgeous crest');[28] Keats, as he addressed Moneta in *The Fall of Hyperion* Canto I, mediates the poet's prophetic role; while Anna Laetitia Barbauld is said to have been 'ready to take the prophetic mantle for herself' from the late 1780s onwards, her late poem *Eighteen Hundred and Eleven* being 'prophetic in content but not really in style'.[29] Blake was a self-styled prophet. He described two of his early works as 'prophecies' and wrote of 'the Poetic Genius which is every where call'd the Spirit of Prophecy'.[30] When Coleridge hailed the poem we now know as *The Thirteen-Book Prelude* as 'An Orphic tale indeed',[31] he may have remembered how, when beginning 'The Recluse' in 1799, Wordsworth invoked the 'Soul of Man' for its vatic powers:

> Come, thou prophetic Spirit, Soul of Man,
> Thou human Soul of the wide earth that hast
> Thy metropolitan Temple in the hearts
> Of mighty Poets ... [32]

It is hard to imagine anyone other than the scattered mystics on the fringes of the culture at almost any historical moment saying anything like that before 1780. Pope was typical of his day in regarding even the concept of inspiration with caution: 'No Poet is always, and in every Word, an inspir'd person. 'Tis only when he Sings, and not when he Says, that this is his prerogative.'[33] The sacralizing of the poet-figure, and his assumption of prophetic garb, is attributable to the retreat of organized religion during the Enlightenment; only that, as Isaiah Berlin observes, explains why 'so many irrational persons wandered over [Europe] claiming adherence',[34] whether to Rosicrucianism or Freemasonry: 'This is the favoured age of all kinds of necromancers and chiromancers and hydromancers, whose various nostrums engage the attention and indeed capture the faith of a great many otherwise apparently sane and rational persons.'[35] The spiritual longing no longer satisfied by organized religion (the Church of England, in the case of most writers covered by this volume) had the result of prompting readers to think of poets not as craftsmen but as seers, visionaries, even prophets. Thomas Carlyle acknowledged that tendency in 1841 when he wrote: '*Vates* means both Prophet and Poet ... indeed they are still the same; in this most important respect especially, that they have penetrated both of them into the sacred mystery of the Universe, what Goethe calls "the open secret!"'[36]

*

Against the tendency to speak of Romanticism and the Enlightenment as if they inhabited different worlds, it might be truer to think of continuities, as Lilian R. Furst has suggested: 'English Romanticism is the freshest and freest [of European Romanticisms], the least self-conscious and codified because it evolved not against, but organically out of, the native tradition.'[37] Peter Gay rejects the idea that the Romantics reacted against the Enlightenment because it 'neglects both the intimate ties that bound many Romantics to the Age of Reason – I recall Byron's admiration of Voltaire – and the immense range of political ideas in what Lovejoy has properly called "Romanticisms", from the reactionary ideas of Novalis to the radicalism of Shelley'.[38] More recently still, Marshall Brown offers a view of Romanticism as revolutionary, 'yet it was not fundamentally a rebellion against its predecessors. Rather, it was revolutionary in that older and more encompassing sense in which a revolution gathers up and recollects, as it sweeps all with it toward the future.'[39] This has the advantage not only of providing a way of thinking about cultural developments of the 1790s and early 1800s, but of enjoining us to imagine how it felt to inhabit a world in which Romanticism and Enlightenment might have coexisted, and in which an understanding of the culture was focused on creative activity at specific moments. Brown reminds us that the emergence of one force out of another need not entail antipathy; it may be more accurately understood as cultural renewal, something that can arise from admiration, esteem, even affection.

Notes

1 Roger Scruton, *An Intelligent Person's Guide to Modern Culture* (South Bend, IN: St Augustine's Press, 2000), pp. 22–3. Isaiah Berlin provides a lengthier, more detailed definition of Enlightenment thought at the beginning of chapter 2 of *The Roots of Romanticism* (Princeton, NJ: Princeton University Press, 1999).

2 This was particularly true of Britain, where the divinity of the king had been vitiated by the Glorious Revolution of 1689; see Anthony Pagden, *The Enlightenment and Why It Still Matters* (New York: Random House, 2013), pp. 300–1.

3 Ibid., p. 220.

4 Jean-Jacques Rousseau, *A Discourse on Inequality*, tr. Maurice Cranston (Harmondsworth: Penguin Books, 1984), p. 116.

5 Pagden, *The Enlightenment*, p. 376.

6 Ibid., p. 389.

7 Dorinda Outram, *The Enlightenment* (3rd ed., Cambridge: Cambridge University Press, 2013), p. 141.

8 To some extent, I am indebted to Martin Fitzpatrick's helpful article on 'The Enlightenment' in *An Oxford Companion to the Romantic Age: British Culture 1776–1832*, ed. Iain McCalman (Oxford: Oxford University Press, 1999), esp. pp. 299–311.

9 *The Marriage of Heaven and Hell*, plate 27, in William Blake, *The Early Illuminated Books*, ed. Morris Eaves, Robert N. Essick, and Joseph Viscomi (London: William Blake Trust/Tate Gallery, 1993), pp. 192–3.

10 Jon Mee, *Dangerous Enthusiasm: William Blake and the Culture of Radicalism in the 1790s* (Oxford: Clarendon Press, 1992), pp. 38–40. See also Morton D. Paley, *Apocalypse and Millennium in English Romantic Poetry* (Oxford: Clarendon Press, 1999), ch. 2.

11 Wordsworth's fragmentary draft, given the provisional editorial title 'Not Useless do I deem', spells out the defining elements of 'The Recluse' as its author

understood them in spring 1798; see *Romanticism: An Anthology*, ed. Duncan Wu (4th ed., Oxford: Wiley-Blackwell, 2012), pp. 453–7.

12 Fitzpatrick, 'The Enlightenment', p. 308.

13 Frances Ferguson points out literary affinities of Benthamite Utilitarianism in 'Representation Restructured', in *The Cambridge History of English Romantic Literature*, ed. James Chandler (Cambridge: Cambridge University Press, 2009), pp. 598–600.

14 For Coleridge's views on Franklin, Lavoisier, and Priestley, see Ian Wylie, *Young Coleridge and the Philosophers of Nature* (Oxford: Clarendon Press, 1989). Jane Stabler helpfully compares Coleridge's understanding of Priestley with that of Barbauld in 'Space for Speculation: Coleridge, Barbauld, and the Poetics of Priestley', in *Samuel Taylor Coleridge and the Sciences of Life*, ed. Nicholas Roe (Oxford: Clarendon Press, 2001), pp. 174–204. Hazlitt's response to Priestley's lectures at Hackney is touched on by Duncan Wu, *William Hazlitt: The First Modern Man* (Oxford: Oxford University Press, 2008), pp. 53–4.

15 For a discussion of the influence on Coleridge of Herder and Lessing, see, *inter alia*, Anthony John Harding, *Coleridge and the Inspired Word* (Kingston and Montreal: McGill-Queen's University Press, 1985), ch. 1.

16 Wordsworth was examined on Locke in June 1789; see Duncan Wu, *Wordsworth's Reading 1770–1799* (Cambridge: Cambridge University Press, 1993), p. 167.

17 William Wordsworth, *The Thirteen-Book Prelude*, iii. 59.

18 Outram, *The Enlightenment*, p. 146.

19 J. A. Leo Lemay, *The Life of Benjamin Franklin* (2 vols., Philadelphia: University of Pennsylvania Press, 2006), i. 290.

20 See, on this subject, Jeffrey N. Cox, *Poetry and Politics in the Cockney School: Keats, Shelley, Hunt and Their Circle* (Cambridge: Cambridge University Press, 1998), pp. 3–6; Sylvia Harcstark Myers, *The Bluestocking Circle: Women, Friendship, and the Life of the Mind in Eighteenth-Century England* (Oxford: Clarendon Press, 1990) and *Bluestockings Displayed: Portraiture, Performance, and Patronage, 1730–1830*, ed. Elizabeth Eger (Cambridge: Cambridge University Press, 2013). Dickens encountered Landor at Gore House; see Michael Slater, *Charles Dickens: A Life Defined by Writing* (New Haven: Yale University Press, 2009), pp. 142–3.

21 This passage is helpfully discussed by M. H. Abrams, *The Mirror and the Lamp: Romantic Theory and the Critical Tradition* (New York: Oxford University Press, 1953), p. 96, and more recently by Fiona Stafford, 'Hugh Blair's Ossian, Romanticism and the Teaching of Literature', in *The Scottish Invention of English Literature*, ed. Robert Crawford (Cambridge: Cambridge University Press, 1998), p. 77.

22 William Wordsworth, 'Note to "The Thorn"', in *Romanticism: An Anthology*, ed. Wu, p. 519.

23 *Romanticism: An Anthology*, ed. Wu, p. 507. When Felicia Hemans described Wordsworth, her language suggests he was a kind of primitive: 'his manners are distinguished by that frank simplicity which I believe to be ever the characteristic of real genius'; see *Felicia Hemans: Selected Poems, Letters, Reception*

Materials, ed. Susan J. Wolfson (Princeton, NJ: Princeton University Press, 2000), p. 504.

24 See, *inter alia*, Shaun Irlam, *Elations: The Poetics of Enthusiasm in Eighteenth-Century Britain* (Stanford, CA: Stanford University Press, 1999), and Ian Balfour, *The Rhetoric of Romantic Prophecy* (Stanford, CA: Stanford University Press, 2002).

25 William Wordsworth, *The Thirteen-Book Prelude*, xiii. 441–2. The lines survive in *The Fourteen-Book Prelude*, xiv. 445–6.

26 *Romanticism: An Anthology*, ed. Wu, p. 1247.

27 Anthony Harding discusses the prophetic aspiration in *Coleridge and the Inspired Word*, p. 18.

28 *Romanticism: An Anthology*, ed. Wu, p. 1369.

29 Jon Mee, *Romanticism, Enthusiasm, and Regulation: Poetics and the Policing of Culture in the Romantic Period* (Oxford: Oxford University Press, 2003), pp. 177–8.

30 'All Religions are One', plate 8, in Blake, *The Early Illuminated Books*, ed. Eaves, Essick, and Viscomi, p. 51.

31 S. T. Coleridge, 'To William Wordsworth', l. 38, in *Romanticism: An Anthology*, ed. Wu, p. 707.

32 'Home at Grasmere' MS B, ll. 1026–9, in William Wordsworth, *Home at Grasmere: Part First, Book First, of The Recluse*, ed. Beth Darlington (Ithaca, NY: Cornell University Press, 1977), pp. 104, 106.

33 As quoted in Emerson Marks, 'Pope on Poetry and the Poet', *Criticism* 12 (1970), 271–80, p. 277.

34 Berlin, *The Roots of Romanticism*, p. 47.

35 Ibid. Scruton's argument is more detailed. He argues the Romantics sought to rescue an ethical view of human life which had existed in earlier times but which, with the retreat of religion in the Enlightenment period, had come under threat. That rescue, he writes, 'was a work of the imagination, in which the aesthetic attitude took over from religious worship as the source of intrinsic values' (Scruton, *An Intelligent Person's Guide to Modern Culture*, p. 52). One instance of the kind of imposture noticed by Berlin would be mesmerism, the history of which has been narrated in succinct but scholarly detail by Jonathan Miller, *On Further Reflection: 60 Years of Writing* (Newbold on Stour: Skyscraper Books, 2014), pp. 37–65.

36 As quoted in Cynthia Sheinberg, 'Victorian Poetry and Religious Diversity', in *The Cambridge Companion to Victorian Poetry*, ed. Joseph Bristow (Cambridge: Cambridge University Press, 2000), p. 159.

37 Lilian R. Furst, 'Romanticism in Historical Perspective', *Comparative Literature Studies* 5 (1968), 115–43, pp. 136, 142.

38 Peter Gay, 'The Enlightenment in the History of Political Theory', *Political Science Quarterly* 69 (1954), 374–89, p. 387.

39 Marshall Brown, 'Romanticism and Enlightenment', in *The Cambridge Companion to British Romanticism*, ed. Stuart Curran (Cambridge: Cambridge University Press, 1993), pp. 25–47, 46–7.

Myth 3

THE ROMANTICS HATED THE SCIENCES

The myth is ensnarled in anachronism: the modern meaning of the word 'science' had limited currency in the Romantic period, when its usual point of reference was systems of knowledge not limited to disciplines concerning the physical universe and its laws (see *OED* definitions 5(a) and (b)). Yet the myth continues to acquire credibility, so wedded to mysticism, the irrational, and everything opposed to scientific enquiry do we suppose the Romantics to have been. A cursory inspection of the evidence suggests the yawning insufficiency of such assumptions.

Were it true, it would make no sense for scientists and artists to have been one and the same: in Germany, Goethe conducted experiments with optics, while Hegel classified forms of scientific endeavour; Friedrich Schelling postulated a *Naturphilosophie* that would inspire Hans Christian Oersted's work on electromagnetism and J. W. Ritter's discovery of ultra-violet light.[1] In Grasmere, when not discussing the second volume of *Lyrical Ballads*, Coleridge and Wordsworth purchased microscopes and copies of Withering's *Botanical Arrangements of British Plants* so they could study botany[2] – a subject Mary Wollstonecraft suggested be taught to children, along with mechanics and astronomy.[3] As a young man, Shelley was deeply influenced by Dr James Lind, who inspired his life-long fascination with science, which led him to conduct electrical experiments with batteries[4] and distribute revolutionary pamphlets by means of a 'fire balloon';[5] Keats trained as apothecary-surgeon and then physician under Astley Cooper, passing the Licentiate's examination in 1816, an experience that influenced his poetry;[6] Blake attended anatomy lectures given by William Hunter, and knew his brother, the

30 Great Myths About the Romantics, First Edition. Duncan Wu.
© 2015 John Wiley & Sons, Ltd. Published 2015 by John Wiley & Sons, Ltd.

physiologist John Hunter.[7] And which poet composed this apostrophe to Nature?

> Oh, most magnificent and noble Nature!
> Have I not worshipped thee with such a love
> As never mortal man before displayed?
> Adored thee in thy majesty of visible creation,
> And searched into thy hidden and mysterious ways
> As Poet, as Philosopher, as Sage?[8]

Though known to us as the inventor of the miner's safety lamp and discoverer of iodine, Humphry Davy was capable of intense encounters with the natural world which inspired blank verse effusions not unlike those penned by his assistant in experiments with nitrous oxide, Samuel Taylor Coleridge.[9] The two men swapped roles with an ease that to us may appear to court frivolousness because they were not yet conceived *as* roles. The terms that to a modern mind set Davy and Coleridge apart had yet to be coined, and from their perspective no reason existed *not* to explore the other's territory, despite differences in the terrain.[10] Another scientist who passed muster as a poet (though in the mannered, high-tea guise of an Augustan) was Erasmus Darwin, whose *The Temple of Nature* (1803) expounded a theory of evolution in heroic couplets, establishing its author as 'the founding father of modern evolutionism'.[11]

It was an age of invention and discovery: inoculation (Jenner discovered how to vaccinate against smallpox in 1796),[12] the steam-powered printing press (patented March 1810), gas-light (introduced in Pall Mall in London, 1807), the steam-powered locomotive (the 'Puffing Billy', built at Wylam in 1813), the steam-ship (which made its first transatlantic crossing in 1819), and the telegraph (used in the Peninsular War).[13] Contemporary explorers such as Mungo Park and William Bartram published accounts of their journeys which spoke as eloquently to poets as they did to naturalists:[14] not for nothing did Keats, Shelley, and Leigh Hunt compete to write, in fifteen minutes, sonnets on the Nile.[15] Women whose scientific interests are reflected in poetry include Charlotte Smith, whose *Beachy Head* offers a natural history of the Sussex coastline, and Felicia Hemans,[16] both of whom were interested in geology. Indeed, the proliferation of rocks in Romantic poetry was not attributable solely to the proximity of mountains; Wordsworth and Coleridge were interested in what minerals revealed about that primordial moment

> ere Form
> From the conflicting powers of flood & fire
> Escaped, and stood fixed in permanence serene ... [17]

Admittedly, some took exception to *aspects* of scientific thought, and the remainder of this essay divides its attention among the best-known: Keats, Wordsworth, and Blake.

> Do not all charms fly
> At the mere touch of cold philosophy?
> There was an awful rainbow once in heaven:
> We know her woof, her texture; she is given
> In the dull catalogue of common things.
> Philosophy will clip an Angel's wings,
> Conquer all mysteries by rule and line,
> Empty the haunted air, and gnomed mine –
> Unweave a rainbow, as it erewhile made
> The tender-person'd Lamia melt into a shade.[18]

These lines are held to be emblematic of the 'romantic resistance to science',[19] even to the Enlightenment itself.[20] But they are approachable as such only when divorced from context. In Keats's *Lamia*, they state an opposition by which the drama is driven, as John Barnard notes: 'The poem is therefore about mutually exclusive categories of perception, and Lamia's doomed attempt to cross their boundaries…. Lamia's longings and Apollonius' philosophy are irreconcilable.'[21] Keats's critique is directed against 'cold philosophy', a manner of thought dependent on 'rule and line'. (A 'rule' is a measuring device, 'a straight-edged rectangle, square, or (formerly) cylinder of metal … typically marked at regular intervals and used to draw straight lines or measure distances'; a 'line' is 'a cord used by builders and others for taking measurements, or for making things level and straight' (*OED*).) Those who construct their universe by such tools have power to 'clip an angel's wings' and 'Unweave a rainbow'; put another way, if the lamia is to enchant the beholder, she must be allowed to inhabit a realm transcendent of mathematics. Her beauty is consistent with 'mysteries'.[22]

Keats used that word when speaking of 'negative capability' in December 1817: 'that is when man is capable of being in uncertainties, Mysteries, doubts, without any irritable reaching after fact & reason'.[23] The 'Mysteries' here and in *Lamia* are ineffable and unknowable. As Keats saw it, the fully imaginative mind had to accept whatever cannot be broken down by rational process. This was not an argument against science; it is pitched against the empiricist notion that experiment, observation, and measurement trump the intuited.[24] Perhaps, as commentators suggest, Keats associates that assumption with Newton (in which case it may be true he recalled him inaccurately[25]), but such claims miss the point: Keats's target is a way of thinking that is detrimental to imaginative vision. This is not an attack on science, and to read it as such is to misrepresent it; far from waging war on the sciences, he reflects their influence.[26]

His views are consistent with those of Wordsworth in 1798:

> Sweet is the lore which nature brings;
> Our meddling intellect
> Misshapes the beauteous forms of things;
> – We murder to dissect.
>
> (Wordsworth, 'The Tables Turned', ll. 25–8)

Keats did not know *The Two-Part Prelude*, addressed to Coleridge, but would have endorsed it if he had:

> Thou, my Friend, art one
> More deeply read in thy own thoughts, no slave
> Of that false secondary power by which
> In weakness we create distinctions, then
> Believe our puny boundaries are things
> Which we perceive and not which we have made.
> To thee, unblinded by these outward shews,
> The unity of all has been revealed,
> And thou wilt doubt with me, less aptly skilled
> Than many are to class the cabinet
> Of their sensations and in voluble phrase
> Run through the history and birth of each
> As of a single independent thing.[27]

At a moment when the science of psychology was in its infancy, with no consensus as to the workings of imagination and memory, Wordsworth is wondering how to analyse his mind. He rejects the idea of 'classifying' sensations as if they were specimens in a cabinet, of speaking about them as if they were 'independent' of the self. That would be a kind of 'murder' – of scientific truth as much as of the higher truth of the imagination. Wordsworth rejects approaches that deny revelation and apprehensions of unity – but not the science of the mind. And it should be emphasized there was a tradition of psychological thought which conceded the mind might depend on something more than physiology – the implication being it possessed an immaterial basis. Wordsworth would have been receptive to that; Alan Richardson has classed such theories under the rubric, 'neural sublime'.[28] Richardson argues that Romantic poets' beliefs concerning mental process were consistent with – and, in many cases, indebted to – those of contemporary science.[29]

It has long been acknowledged Wordsworth viewed scientists as creative beings. In the Preface to *Lyrical Ballads* (1802) he argued they were bound to the same path as poets.

> The Man of science seeks truth as a remote and unknown benefactor; he cherishes and loves it in his solitude: the Poet, singing a song in which all human beings join with him, rejoices in the presence of truth as our visible friend and hourly companion. Poetry is the breath and finer spirit of all knowledge; it is the impassioned expression which is in the countenance of all Science.[30]

A search for truth provides the fraternal connection between poet and scientist, indicating they are engaged on a joint labour: '[the poet will be] ready to follow the steps of the Man of science...he will be at his side, carrying sensation into the midst of the objects of the science itself'.[31] Wordsworth was inspired to write this by Humphry Davy, who proof-read *Lyrical Ballads* (1800).[32] Davy's lectures on science, delivered at the Royal Institution in London in early 1802, spoke of how 'The study of nature must always be more or less connected with the love of the beautiful and sublime...it is eminently calculated to gratify and to keep alive the more powerful passions and ambitions of the soul.'[33] That underpins Wordsworth's vision of a future in which the poet and man of science would be united – as potent a rebuttal of the view that he hated science as his idealized description of Newton's statue in Trinity College, Cambridge, which he could see from his rooms in St John's:

> And from my pillow, looking forth by light
> Of noon or favoring stars, I could behold
> The Antechapel, where the Statue stood
> Of Newton, with his prism, and silent face,
> The marble index of a Mind for ever
> Voyaging through strange seas of Thought, alone.
> (*The Fourteen-Book Prelude*, iii. 58–63[34])

The argument that the Romantics hated science is typically made by reference to Blake.[35] 'Blake thought he hated Newton even more profoundly than the earlier poets had adored him', wrote Marjorie Hope Nicolson in 1946,[36] before pointing out that he regarded concepts such as 'reason' and 'experiment' as anathema, along with such thinkers as Bacon, Descartes,

Figure 5 Blake's depiction of Sir Isaac Newton shows him drawing a geometrical figure on a scroll using compasses. In Blake's work, the scroll often symbolizes inspiration.
Source: The Art Archive / Tate Gallery London / Eileen Tweedy.

Locke, and Newton.[37] This is to misrepresent him. In his address to the Christians in *Jerusalem*, Blake admonished those

> who shall pretend to despise Art & Science! I call upon you in the name of Jesus! What is the Life of Man but Art & Science? ... What are the Pains of Hell but Ignorance, Bodily Lust, Idleness & devastation of the things of the Spirit[?] Answer this to yourselves, & expel from among you those who pretend to despise the labours of Art & Science, which alone are the labours of the Gospel ... .[38]

Blake's mission had nothing to do with hatred of science; his energies were invested in the need to preserve its union with the arts so that, when combined, they could generate wisdom. As he says elsewhere in *Jerusalem*: 'The Primeval State of Man, was Wisdom, Art and Science.'[39] Divorced from art, science became the foster-parent of materialism; Blake criticized Enlightenment thinkers only when their findings became detached from everything else.[40] Those who say this proves he detested them are mistaken; he praised them alongside the greatest poets in the language:

> The innumerable Chariots of the Almighty appeard in Heaven
> And Bacon & Newton & Locke. & Milton & Shakspear & Chaucer[41]

Blake was capable of demonizing this unholy trinity: they become a nightmarish monster in *Jerusalem*, the 'Three Forms, named Bacon & Newton & Locke'[42] – but not because he rejected the Enlightenment or science. He was dismayed by the materialist philosophies and faiths licensed by Enlightenment ideas. When it came to Newton, Blake could always be moved to admiration, as when he hailed 'the stars of heaven created like a golden chain',

> Travelling in silent majesty along their orderd ways
> In right lined paths outmeasurd by proportions of number weight
> And measure. mathematic motion wondrous.[43]

'mathematic motion wondrous': not a statement of hostility. Blake valued Newton's vision of the cosmos, but fought against its misuse – the growing tendency, especially among Deists, to regard the material universe as all there was. That was no imagined threat: Robert M. Ryan has shown that Newtonian science was employed by theologians to create 'a model of social and political relations that was concordant with the needs and structures of a new economic order' – in effect, physics 'had the effect of sacralizing the political and economic status quo that had evolved under the laissez-faire providence of an absentee Creator'.[44] In Blake's terms this was Satanic, a justification of self-interested materialism which erected Newton as idol, a figure identified with the mythic Urizen ('your reason'), who

> Compell'd others to serve him in moral gratitude & submission
> Being call'd God; setting himself above all that is called God … [45]

Urizen (and Newton) imitated God by forging a materialist universe that lay at the heart of the Blakean nightmare of infinite division into smaller and smaller constituent parts (the creation narrative recounted in *Urizen*). That was why, when Blake depicted Newton, it was as a figure holding a compass or dividers – tools by which the world would be carved up and broken down.

It is true *Frankenstein* admonishes the scientist who aspires to the status of deity,[46] while in *The Excursion* Wordsworth condemned the use of child labour in Lancashire's cotton mills.[47] If writers disliked aspects of scientific thought, they were not antagonistic to it. Confusion may stem from the notion there were those who, like Hamann, wrote in opposition to Enlightenment thought,[48] but English Romanticism did not emerge from opposition; it was 'an attitude concealed within' the Enlightenment.[49] And the Romantic interest in psychology hints at a wider fascination with other disciplines. When contemplating an epic poem in response to Milton, Coleridge contemplated a decade of preparatory study in which to 'warm my mind with universal science':

> I would be a tolerable Mathematician, I would thoroughly know Mechanics, Hydrostatics, Optics, and Astronomy, Botany, Metallurgy, Fossilism, Chemistry, Geology, Anatomy, Medicine – then the *mind of man* – then the *minds of men* – in all Travels, Voyages, and Histories.[50]

In recognizing a grasp of new discoveries as the writer's proper function, Coleridge was representative. His reaction indicates that, though capable of criticizing its unintended results, Romantic writers found science stimulating, challenging, and a cause for optimism.

Notes

1 All three of these German intellectuals are discussed in *Romanticism and the Sciences*, ed. Andrew Cunningham and Nicholas Jardine (Cambridge: Cambridge University Press, 1990), chs. 2, 14, and 16.

2 The microscopes and copies of Withering were purchased through Longman, the publisher; see Mark L. Reed, *Wordsworth: The Chronology of the*

Middle Years, 1800–1815 (Cambridge, MA: Harvard University Press, 1975), pp. 77–8.

3 Mary Wollstonecraft, *A Vindication of the Rights of Woman* (3rd ed., London: J. Johnson, 1796), p. 388.

4 *The Life of Percy Bysshe Shelley* (2 vols., London: Dent, 1933), i. 56; Richard Holmes, *Shelley: The Pursuit* (London: Quartet Books, 1974), p. 44.

5 Holmes, *Shelley: The Pursuit*, p. 149. See also Nora Crook and Derek Guiton, *Shelley's Venomed Melody* (Cambridge: Cambridge University Press, 1986), ch. 2.

6 See, for instance, R. S. White, *John Keats: A Literary Life* (Houndmills, Basingstoke: Palgrave Macmillan, 2010), ch. 2, and Alan Richardson, 'Keats and Romantic Science', in *The Cambridge Companion to Keats*, ed. Susan J. Wolfson (Cambridge: Cambridge University Press, 2001), pp. 230–45.

7 G. E. Bentley, Jr, *The Stranger from Paradise: A Biography of William Blake* (New Haven: Yale University Press, 2001), p. 50. A number of scholars have discussed Blake's knowledge of anatomy including F. B. Curtis, 'William Blake and Eighteenth-Century Medicine', *Blake Studies* 8.2 (1979), 187–99; Carmen S. Kreiter, 'Evolution and William Blake', *Studies in Romanticism* 4 (1965), 110–18; and Jon Mee, 'Bloody Blake: Nation and Circulation', in *Blake, Nation and Empire*, ed. Steve Clark and David Worrall (Basingstoke: Palgrave Macmillan, 2006), pp. 63–82.

8 *Fragmentary Remains, Literary and Scientific, of Sir Humphry, Davy, bart.*, ed. John Davy (London: John Churchill, 1858), p. 14.

9 For more on Davy, see Richard Holmes, *The Age of Wonder* (London: Harper-Press, 2008), ch. 6. Davy's friendship with Coleridge is analysed by David Knight, *Humphry Davy: Science and Power* (Oxford: Blackwell, 1992), pp. 29–33; June Z. Fullmer, *Sir Humphry Davy's Published Works* (Cambridge, MA: Harvard University Press, 1969), pp. 29–30, and Neil Vickers, *Coleridge and the Doctors* (Oxford: Clarendon Press, 2004), pp. 50–1.

10 One recent scholarly study puts it: 'If scientific thought was a kind of realization of poetry, poetry could be an exaltation of science'. See Tim Fulford, Debbie Lee, and Peter J. Kitson, *Literature, Science and Exploration in the Romantic Era: Bodies of Knowledge* (Cambridge: Cambridge University Press, 2004), p. 217.

11 *The Collected Letters of Erasmus Darwin*, ed. Desmond King-Hele (Cambridge: Cambridge University Press, 2007), p. x. For more on *The Temple of Nature*, see Desmond King-Hele, *Doctor of Revolution: The Life and Genius of Erasmus Darwin* (London: Faber & Faber, 1977), ch. 13.

12 For a cogent account of Jenner's work, see Fulford, Lee, and Kitson, *Literature, Science and Exploration*, ch. 9. See also Emily Lorraine de Montluzin, *Daily Life in Georgian England as Reported in* The Gentleman's Magazine (Lewiston, NY: Edwin Mellen Press, 2002), pp. 88–92.

13 Jan Golinski has discussed the literature of the new sciences in *The Cambridge History of English Romantic Literature*, ed. James Chandler (Cambridge: Cambridge University Press, 2009), pp. 527–52. Frederick Burwick provides a helpful survey of scientific developments of the period in 'Romantic Sciences',

in *A Concise Companion to the Romantic Age*, ed. Jon Klancher (Oxford: Wiley-Blackwell, 2009), ch. 8.

14 Fulford, Lee, and Kitson, *Literature, Science and Exploration*, p. 4.

15 Ibid., pp. 103–4.

16 See, for instance, Felicia Hemans's 'Epitaph on Mr Wilton, a Celebrated Mineralogist'.

17 These remarkable lines, from a draft towards *The Thirteen-Book Prelude*, were unpublished by Wordsworth; they indicate some knowledge of Thomas Burnet's *Sacred Theory of the Earth* (1681–9). See, *inter alia*, *The Thirteen-Book Prelude*, ed. Mark L. Reed (2 vols., Ithaca, NY: Cornell University Press, 1991), ii. 1008; Stephen Gill, *Wordsworth: The Prelude* (Cambridge: Cambridge University Press, 1991), p. 70; Noah Heringman, *Romantic Rocks, Aesthetic Geology* (Ithaca, NY: Cornell University Press, 2004); and John Wyatt, *Wordsworth and the Geologists* (Cambridge: Cambridge University Press, 1996).

18 John Keats, *Lamia*, ii. 229–38, in *The Poems of John Keats*, ed. Jack Stillinger (London: Heinemann, 1978), pp. 472–3.

19 Maurice S. Lee, *Uncertain Chances: Science, Skepticism, and Belief in Nineteenth-Century American Literature* (Oxford: Oxford University Press, 2012), p. 45.

20 Coleridge also expressed hostility to Newtonian physics in his extensive note to Book II of *Joan of Arc*; see *Joan of Arc* (Bristol, 1796), pp. 41–2.

21 John Barnard, *John Keats* (Cambridge: Cambridge University Press, 1987), p. 123. Nicholas Roe explains the context of Keats's lines in *John Keats and the Culture of Dissent* (Oxford: Clarendon Press, 1997), pp. 182–7; see also Richardson, 'Keats and Romantic Science'.

22 For a slightly different approach to Keats's view of Newton, see Julia L. Epstein and Mark L. Greenberg, 'Decomposing Newton's Rainbow', *Journal of the History of Ideas* 45 (1984), 115–40, pp. 136–7.

23 John Keats to George and Tom Keats, 21 December 1817, in *The Letters of John Keats 1814–1821*, ed. Hyder Edward Rollins (2 vols., Cambridge, MA: Harvard University Press, 1958), i. 193.

24 I am aware that there have been many interpretations of Keats's lines, and I believe mine to be consistent with most of them; compare, for instance, Tim Milnes, *The Truth about Romanticism: Pragmatism and Idealism in Keats, Shelley, Coleridge* (Cambridge: Cambridge University Press, 2010), pp. 94–6; Porscha Fermanis, *John Keats and the Ideas of the Enlightenment* (Edinburgh: Edinburgh University Press, 2009), pp. 116–18; Andrew Bennett, *Keats, Narrative and Audience: The Posthumous Life of Writing* (Cambridge: Cambridge University Press, 1994), pp. 176–8.

25 John Carey, for instance, observes that Keats exhibits 'a profound ignorance of Newton, who was, in fact, acutely aware of the mystery of the universe'; see *The Faber Book of Science*, ed. John Carey (London: Faber & Faber, 1995), p. 33.

26 See, for example, Alan Richardson, *British Romanticism and the Science of the Mind* (Cambridge: Cambridge University Press, 2001), ch. 5.

27 *The Two-Part Prelude*, ii. 249–61, in William Wordsworth, *The Prelude, 1798–1799*, ed. Stephen Parrish (Ithaca, NY: Cornell University Press, 1977), pp. 60–1.

28 Richardson, *British Romanticism and the Science of the Mind*, ch. 3.

29 See, in addition to the volume mentioned in the previous note, Alan Richardson, *The Neural Sublime: Cognitive Theories and Romantic Texts* (Baltimore, MD: Johns Hopkins University Press, 2010).

30 Preface to *Lyrical Ballads* (1850 text), in *The Prose Works of William Wordsworth*, ed. W. J. B. Owen and Jane Worthington Smyser (3 vols., Oxford: Clarendon Press, 1974), i. 141.

31 Ibid.

32 Roger Sharrock, 'The Chemist and the Poet: Sir Humphry Davy and the Preface to *Lyrical Ballads*', *Notes and Records of the Royal Society of London* 17 (1962), 57–76, p. 64. Catherine Ross observes that 'Davy's and Wordsworth's audiences read the same texts, attended the same lectures and social gatherings, knew both men directly and indirectly, and certainly would have recognized many of the similarities in their projects and discourse'; see 'Twin Labourers and Heirs of the Same Hopes: The Professional Rivalry of Humphry Davy and William Wordsworth', in *Romantic Science: The Literary Forms of Natural History*, ed. Noah Heringman (Albany, NY: State University of New York Press, 2003), pp. 23–52, 33.

33 Sharrock, 'The Chemist and the Poet', p. 66. Susan J. Wolfson reminds me that Davy's lectures were extremely well attended.

34 For more on Wordsworth's attitude towards Newton and physics, see W. K. Thomas and Warren U. Ober, *A Mind For Ever Voyaging: Wordsworth at Work Portraying Newton and Science* (Edmonton: University of Alberta Press, 1989).

35 One source for Blake's alleged hatred of science is his first biographer, Alexander Gilchrist: 'Scientific individuals would generally make him come out with something outrageous and unreasonable. For he had an indestructible animosity towards what, to his devout old-world imagination, seemed the keen polar atmosphere of modern science': *The Life of William Blake, 'Pictor Ignotus'* (2 vols., London: Macmillan, 1863), i. 328.

36 Marjorie Hope Nicolson, *Newton Demands the Muse: Newton's Opticks and the Eighteenth Century Poets* (Princeton, NJ: Princeton University Press, 1946), pp. 165–6.

37 Ibid., p. 169.

38 *Jerusalem*, plate 77 ('To the Christians'), in William Blake, *Jerusalem*, ed. Morton D. Paley (London: William Blake Trust/Tate Gallery, 1991), p. 258.

39 *Jerusalem*, plate 3, ibid., p. 133.

40 Entire books have been written about Blake and Newton, the most important of which remains Donald D. Ault, *Visionary Physics: Blake's Response to Newton* (Chicago: University of Chicago Press, 1974).

41 *Jerusalem*, plate 98, in *Jerusalem*, ed. Paley, p. 294.

42 *Jerusalem*, plate 70, ibid., p. 246.

43 *The Four Zoas*, p. 34, ll. 22–4, in *The Complete Poetry and Prose of William Blake*, ed. David V. Erdman (New York: Doubleday, 1988), p. 322.

44 Robert M. Ryan, *The Romantic Reformation: Religious Politics in English Literature, 1789–1824* (Cambridge: Cambridge University Press, 1997), pp. 65–6.

45 *Milton*, plate 9, ll. 11–12, in William Blake, *Milton a Poem*, ed. Robert N. Essick and Joseph Viscomi (London: William Blake Trust/Tate Gallery, 1993), p. 131.

46 See, for instance, Charles E. Robinson's invaluable introduction to Mary Wollstonecraft Shelley (with Percy Bysshe Shelley), *The Original Frankenstein*, ed. Charles E. Robinson (Oxford: Bodleian Library, 2008), pp. 31–5.

47 *The Excursion*, viii. 311–16.

48 For Hamann, see Isaiah Berlin's *Three Critics of the Enlightenment: Vico, Hamann, Herder*, ed. Henry Hardy (2nd ed., Princeton, NJ: Princeton University Press, 2013), 'The Magus of the North', pp. 301ff.

49 Roger Scruton, *An Intelligent Person's Guide to Modern Culture* (South Bend, IN: St Augustine's Press, 2000), p. 48.

50 S. T. Coleridge to Joseph Cottle, early April 1797, in *Collected Letters of Samuel Taylor Coleridge*, ed. Earl Leslie Griggs (6 vols., Oxford: Clarendon Press, 1956–71), i. 320–1.

Myth
4
THE ROMANTICS REPUDIATED THE AUGUSTANS, ESPECIALLY POPE AND DRYDEN

> The time which elapsed from the days of Dryden to those of Pope, is the dark age of English poetry.
>
> Robert Southey, *Specimens of the Later English Poets* (1807), I. xxix[1]

The myth constructs a scenario whereby Augustanism, the name by which critics refer to much of the literature produced between 1660 (especially the satirical poetry of Dryden and Pope) and Samuel Johnson's death in 1784, was rejected by the Romantics.[2] Though not wholly mistaken, it does scant justice to the truth; for instance, which well-known Augustan wrote the following?

> Ye kings, in wisdom, sense and power, supreme,
> These freaks are worse than any sick man's dream.
> To hated worth no Tyrant ere design'd
> Malice so subtle, vengeance so refin'd.[3]

These lines were written by Wordsworth for a satire he hoped to publish for £10 in 1795 – indicating a canny recognition that the popularity of Augustan verse continued to dictate its saleability. When amateurs such as Mary Leigh tried their hand at verse, it was often in heroic couplets.[4] That had been so for decades. Pope died in 1744 but, true to the adage that poets are never more in demand than when newly buried, the 1751–4 editions of his *Works* made a net profit of over £5,000, more than those of Shakespeare and Milton combined.[5]

30 Great Myths About the Romantics, First Edition. Duncan Wu.
© 2015 John Wiley & Sons, Ltd. Published 2015 by John Wiley & Sons, Ltd.

Success on that scale did not end quickly; Pope continued to be influential, though he was not without critics. In 1756 (the year before Blake's birth), Joseph Warton published his *Essay on the Genius and Writings of Pope*, which lamented Pope wrote 'from and to the head rather than the heart', neglecting the emotions.[6] Warton saw Pope as 'the great Poet of Reason', but at a cost: his imagination was 'withheld and stifled'.[7] More forthright still on the subject of Dryden, Warton thought *Absalom and Achitophel* 'does not partake of the essence of real poetry'.[8] But Warton was conflicted – on one hand, author of his own Pope-inspired verse, such as 'Fashion' (1742); on the other, eager to free himself from the constraints of his style.[9] He was not alone: William Cowper possessed a 'dislike of Pope [that] amounted to hatred … . He disliked Pope's manner as a poet, and his character as a man, and had formed the intention of attacking both.'[10] Yet Cowper's talents were as strongly shaped by Pope as Warton's had been; indeed, Pope has been described (with Milton) as one of 'Cowper's two most important models'.[11]

There was no such equivocation in Blake: 'I do not condemn Pope or Dryden because they did not understand Imagination but because they did not understand Verse.'[12] These were strong words and he meant them: he believed the Augustans distracted from the 'simpler' style of Milton and Bunyan, and that made him an enemy of Pope, Dryden, Sir Joshua Reynolds, Johnson, and William Hayley (among others).[13] One of the things that infuriated him was the saleability of work produced in the Augustan manner, and lack of interest in anything else: 'While the Works of Pope & Dryden are lookd upon as the Same Art with those of Milton & Shakespeare … there can be no Art in a Nation but such as is Subservient to the interest of the Monopolizing Trader.'[14]

Wordsworth's attitude is more complicated; as we have seen, he was capable of appealing to the fashion for satire in 1795, and had observed Augustan proprieties since producing his earliest surviving poem in 1785, 'a tame imitation of Pope's versification, and a little in his style'.[15] *An Evening Walk* and *Descriptive Sketches*, published January 1793, represent what one critic calls (rightly or wrongly) 'a final, indisputable mastery of the eighteenth-century poetic'.[16] Like Blake, Wordsworth memorized swathes of Augustan verse, as late as 1839 boasting he could recite 'several 1000 lines of Pope'.[17] Popean echoes are found in even his greatest work, including 'A Night-Piece', 'Tintern Abbey', 'The Winander Boy', and the skating episode in *The Two-Part Prelude*, to name a few.[18] To that extent, he was always a Popean.

Poetic maturity raised the challenge of finding new ways of writing. While they worked on *Lyrical Ballads*, Wordsworth and Coleridge defined themselves in opposition to Augustan style,[19] so that by 1797 Coleridge could condemn whatever 'the lovers of genuine poetry would call sensible and entertaining, such as the Ignoramuses & Pope-admirers would deem genuine Poetry'.[20] The Preface to *Lyrical Ballads*, ostensibly by Wordsworth (though the product of notes and discussions to which he and Coleridge were party – see Myth 10), cited a sonnet by Gray, the entirety of Pope's *Messiah*, a poem by Prior, and Johnson's 'The Ant' as comprising 'extravagant and absurd diction', 'a motley masquerade of tricks, quaintnesses, hieroglyphics, and enigmas'.[21] Johnson's poem was 'this hubbub of words'.[22] Wordsworth was consistent: the last of his 'Essays upon Epitaphs' expressed disappointment that eighteenth-century epitaphs were 'tainted by the artifices which have overrun our writings in metre since the days of Dryden and Pope',[23] and in the 'Essay, Supplementary to the Preface' (1815) he condemned Pope's belief that 'Nature was not to be trusted, at least in pastoral Poetry'.[24] As Robert J. Griffin observes, Wordsworth saw it as 'a question of nature versus artifice'.[25]

The evidence appears straightforward, but is complicated by Wordsworth's lifelong admiration of early Pope – the 'Ode on Solitude' ('Happy the man'), 'Eloisa to Abelard', *The Rape of the Lock*, and 'An Essay on Criticism'.[26] He consistently expressed dislike of the Homeric translations, compulsory schoolboy reading which 'decked out the bard in the raiment of a courtier to George I'.[27] In a letter to Walter Scott, Wordsworth said, 'It will require yet half a century completely to carry off the poison of Pope's Homer.'[28]

Coleridge's attitudes were equally complex. He too studied Pope's Homer at school, and it had a similar effect on him as on Wordsworth. In one of his lectures on literature in January 1812 he censured Pope's description of the moon in *The Iliad* for its 'absurdity of sense and diction'.[29] And in *Biographia Literaria* he objected to the manner in which, throughout Pope, 'a *point* was looked for at the end of each second line, and the whole was as it were a sorites, or if I may exchange a logical for a grammatical metaphor, a *conjunction disjunctive*, of epigrams'.[30] Like Wordsworth, he began as an Augustan, for among his schoolboy odes and sonnets there survives an accomplished attempt at the mock-heroic, clearly based on *The Rape of the Lock*.[31] Moreover, Coleridge was capable, in his 1813 lectures, of describing Pope as 'a delightful writer ... doubtless if everything that pleases be poetry, Pope's satires and epistles must be poetry'.[32] He was less equivocal in the case of Dryden, of whom 'I am & always have been a passionate admirer. I have always placed him among our greatest men.'[33]

His engagement with Johnson was just as equivocal: he was famous for calling him a 'fellow', sneering at the *Dictionary* as 'an entertaining *Quotation-book*', laughing at the 'bow-wow' manner of his conversation

Figure 6 Alexander Pope (1688–1744), who was never less influential than during the Romantic period, though much criticized. The staunchest of his admirers, Byron, deplored 'the unjustifiable attempts at depreciation begun by Warton – & carried on to & at this day by the new School of Critics & Scribblers who think themselves poets because they do *not* write like Pope'. Source: Paul F. Betz Collection.

(as recorded by Boswell), and ranking him with the overrated.[34] In his 1808 lectures he classed Pope and Johnson among those who 'did not comprehend' Shakespeare, and characterized Johnson as a 'Frog-Critic': 'How nimbly it leaps – how excellently it swims – only the fore-legs (it must be admitted) are too long & the hind ones too short.'[35] None of this prevented him using Johnson's works as a sourcebook.[36] 'Coleridge's famous formula about the psychology of reading – "that willing suspension of disbelief for the moment, that constitutes poetic faith" – refines and generalizes a concept already familiar through Johnson's Shakespearean criticism.'[37] H. J. Jackson has shown *Lives of the Poets* to have been the source for ideas in *Biographia Literaria*, including Coleridge's definition of a poem and criticism of Wordsworth.[38]

Keats was typical of his moment in elevating Milton and Spenser at the expense of the Augustans. As fellow-student Henry Stephens recalled,

'He was a great admirer of Spencer, his Fairy Queen was a great favorite with him. Byron was also in favor, Pope he maintained was no poet, only a versifier.'[39] He would have been encouraged in this by Leigh Hunt who, in his Preface to *Foliage* (1818), deplored in Pope 'and the other chief writers of the French school ... their narrow sphere of imagination, their knowledge of manners rather than natures, and their gross mistake about what they called classical, which was Horace and the Latin breeding, instead of the elementary inspiration of Greece'.[40] Keats felt sufficiently emboldened in 'Sleep and Poetry' to recall a time when beauty 'was awake', but the Augustans

> were dead
> To things ye knew not of, – were closely wed
> To musty laws lined out with wretched rule
> And compass vile: so that ye taught a school
> Of dolts to smooth, inlay, and clip, and fit,
> Till, like the certain wands of Jacob's wit,
> Their verses tallied. Easy was the task:
> A thousand handicraftsmen wore the mask
> Of Poesy.[41]

This was published before Keats heard Hazlitt's lectures on the English poets in 1818, which ridiculed 'those critics who are bigotted idolisers of [Pope]', the grammatical construction of whose poems 'is often lame or imperfect'.[42] That shocked and impressed Keats, who excitedly reported to his friend Benjamin Robert Haydon, 'Hazlitt has damned the bigotted ... how durst the Man?! he is your only good damner and if ever I am damn'd – I shouln't like him to damn me.'[43] As that suggests, he found Hazlitt's assessment bracing – perhaps because (like Keats himself) Hazlitt approached the matter from a Wordsworthian perspective. It must have intrigued Keats that Hazlitt did not reject Pope, preferring to value his satirical portraits, particularly those of Addison and Buckingham: 'shall we cut ourselves off from beauties like these with a theory?'[44] If Hazlitt was unembarrassed about opposing Wordsworth on poetic diction, he nonetheless aligned himself with his central thesis, stated at the beginning of his lecture: '[Pope] was, in a word, the poet, not of nature, but of art.'[45]

By May 1821, Shelley could observe Pope 'has been selected as the pivot of a dispute in taste, on which, until I understand it, I must profess myself neuter'.[46] He was addressing Byron, who was irritated by Keats's '*attack upon Pope*' in 'Sleep and Poetry'.[47] Under the circumstances, agnosticism was the politic recourse, for Shelley was aware that, to Byron, Pope represented the 'correct' literary path from which everything that followed had been a mistake. Byron's letter to his publisher, John Murray, in which his views on modern poetry are elucidated, takes us as close to an explanation as we are likely to get:

> With regard to poetry in general I am convinced the more I think of it – that he and *all* of us – Scott – Southey – Wordsworth – Moore – Campbell – I – are all in the wrong – one as much as another – that we are upon a wrong revolutionary poetical system – or systems – not worth a damn in itself – & from which none but Rogers and Crabbe are free – and that the present & next generations will finally be of this opinion. – I am the more confirmed in this – by having lately gone over some of our Classics – particularly *Pope* – whom I tried in this way – I took Moore's poems & my own & some others – & went over them side by side with Pope's – and I was really astonished (I ought not to have been so) and mortified – at the ineffable distance in point of sense – harmony – effect – and even *Imagination* Passion – & *Invention* – between the little Queen Anne's Man – & us of the lower Empire – depend upon it [it] is all Horace then, and Claudian now among us – and if I had to begin again – I would model myself accordingly ... .[48]

It seems extraordinary, from a modern perspective, that an intelligent man like Byron could rate the ornate but superficial verse of Rogers above that of Wordsworth, or that of Crabbe above his own.[49] But we should be mindful that he was in the majority, in his own day, in regarding 'the little Queen Anne's Man' as the dominant influence of the century.[50] Jane Austen's novels reflect Popean notions in 'her general ideas about self-love, reason, the passions, the predominant passions, instinct, happiness, the characters of men and women, the use of riches, and the various kinds of stupidity to be found in society'.[51] Like Byron, she admired Crabbe,[52] whose poetry rebuts any suggestion the Romantics were inherently antagonistic to the Augustans. Crabbe's poetry embodies many of the virtues of Augustan style while (in his later work) reflecting those of the poetry of the new century.[53]

After William Lisle Bowles censured Pope's moral and poetical character in a pamphlet of 1819, Byron poured his outrage into a pamphlet in Pope's defence.[54] Towering above 'the trashy Jingle of the crowd of "Schools" and upstarts', Pope was, Byron declared, 'the moral poet of all Civilization – and as such let us hope that he will one day be the National poet of Mankind'.[55] These bold, uncompromising words explain why, rather than become ensnared in argument, Shelley preferred to back away from the subject when writing to Byron in May 1821, though he added: 'I certainly do not think Pope, or *any* writer, a fit model for any succeeding writer'.[56] He was being politic, though modern critics now regard his poetry as Popean in style and content.[57]

The myth exposes the limitations of taxonomic approaches to literature: it is as untrue to say that everyone during the early eighteenth century was an imitator of Pope as to suggest that everyone during the early nineteenth was Romantic. Such distinctions are more clearly perceived by those who theorize in retrospect than by contemporaries; as Upali Amarasinghe was right to observe, 'taste and criticism during this period were extremely varied and complex, and reflected a wide variety of critical and creative preoccupations'.[58] The dominant trend of recent commentary has been to question the false opposition into which the Romantics and Augustans were once pitched, accepting the truth of Wordsworth's admission: 'I have a very high admiration of the talents both of Dryden and Pope, and ultimately, as from all good writers of whatever kind, their Country will be benefited greatly by their labours.'[59] Most contemporaries would have agreed; far from amounting to rejection, that counts as something very close to appreciation.

Notes

1 Rogers recalled: 'Southey told me that he had read Spenser through about *thirty* times, and that he could not read Pope through *once*' (*Reminiscences and Table-Talk of Samuel Rogers*, ed. G. H. Powell (London: R. Brimley Johnson, 1903), p. 159). There is not space here to explore Southey's view of the Augustans, and Pope in particular; but that job has been done by David Fairer, *Organizing Poetry: The Coleridge Circle, 1790–1798* (Oxford: Oxford University Press, 2009), ch. 5, esp. pp. 128–9. See also Upali Amarasinghe, *Dryden and Pope in the Early Nineteenth Century: A Study of Changing Literary Taste, 1800–1830* (Cambridge: Cambridge University Press, 1962), pp. 152–5.

2 Space does not permit me to deal with the extensive literature relating to theoretical discussions of what Augustan literature was; see, among many other articles, Donald Wesling, 'Justification and Breakup of a Period Style', *Texas Studies in Literature and Language* 22 (1980), 394–428.

3 William Wordsworth to the Revd Francis Wrangham, 20 November 1795, in *The Letters of William and Dorothy Wordsworth*, i, *The Early Years 1787–1805*, ed. Ernest de Selincourt, rev. Chester L. Shaver (2nd ed., Oxford: Clarendon Press, 1967), p. 157. 'Imitation of Juvenal, *Satire VIII*' is one of the poems most transformed by the new Cornell Wordsworth series; the text presented by Jared Curtis and Carol Landon runs to 278 lines. They date the various drafts of the poem to between summer 1795 and February 1797.

4 See David Selwyn, 'Poetry', in *Jane Austen in Context*, ed. Janet Todd (Cambridge: Cambridge University Press, 2005), p. 59.

5 William St Clair, *The Reading Nation in the Romantic Period* (Cambridge: Cambridge University Press, 2004), pp. 471–2.

6 Joseph Warton, *An Essay on the Writings and Genius of Pope* (3rd ed., London: Dodsley, 1772), p. 209. For a discussion of Warton's comments on the lack of sensibility in Pope, see John Mullan, 'Sensibility and Literary Criticism', in *The Cambridge History of Literary Criticism: The Eighteenth Century*, ed. Hugh Barr Nisbet, George Alexander Kennedy, and Claude Rawson (Cambridge: Cambridge University Press, 1997), pp. 425–7. See also Adam Rounce's introduction to *Alexander Pope and his Critics* (Abingdon, Oxon.: Routledge, 2004).

7 As quoted by Robert J. Griffin, *Wordsworth's Pope: A Study in Literary Historiography* (Cambridge: Cambridge University Press, 1995), p. 43.

8 As quoted in Amarasinghe, *Dryden and Pope in the Early Nineteenth Century*, p. 28.

9 Griffin has written well about Warton's conflict, and throughout this essay I am indebted to him: *Wordsworth's Pope*, pp. 39–42.

10 Ibid., p. 59.

11 Ibid., p. 60.

12 William Blake, 'Public Address', in *The Complete Poetry and Prose of William Blake*, ed. David V. Erdman (New York: Doubleday, 1988), p. 575.

13 Roger Murray, 'Blake and the Ideal of Simplicity', *Studies in Romanticism* 13 (1974), 89–104.

14 Blake, 'Public Address', p. 576.

15 'Autobiographical Memoranda', in *The Prose Works of William Wordsworth*, ed. W. J. B. Owen and Jane Worthington Smyser (3 vols., Oxford: Clarendon Press, 1974), iii. 372.

16 *The Earliest Wordsworth: Poems 1785–1790*, ed. Duncan Wu (Manchester: Carcanet, 2002), p. 132.

17 Griffin, *Wordsworth's Pope*, p. 91.

18 Ibid., pp. 97–110; Lawrence Lipking, 'Night Thoughts on Literary History', in *Literary History: Theory and Practice*, ed. Herbert L. Sussman (Boston: Northeastern University Press, 1984), p. 71.

19 Susan Manning examines the ballad tradition and its exponents in her essay, 'Antiquarianism, Balladry and the Rehabilitation of Romance', in *The Cambridge History of English Romantic Literature*, ed. James Chandler (Cambridge: Cambridge University Press, 2009), pp. 45–70.

20 S. T. Coleridge to Robert Southey, 10 November 1799, in *Collected Letters of Samuel Taylor Coleridge*, ed. Earl Leslie Griggs (6 vols., Oxford: Clarendon Press, 1956–71), i. 545.

21 'Appendix on Poetic Diction', in *The Prose Works of William Wordsworth*, ed. Owen and Smyser, i. 162.

22 Ibid., i. 163.

23 'Essays upon Epitaphs, III', ibid., iii. 84.

24 'Essay, Supplementary to the Preface', ibid., iii. 72. Griffin examines at greater length Wordsworth's treatment of Pope in the 'Essay, Supplementary': Griffin, *Wordsworth's Pope*, pp. 93–5.

25 Griffin, *Wordsworth's Pope*, p. 90.

26 See, *inter alia*, William Wordsworth to Alexander Dyce, 10 May 1830, and Wordsworth to Viscount Mahon, 11 April 1842, in *The Letters of William and Dorothy Wordsworth*, v, *The Later Years, Part 2: 1829–1834*, ed. Ernest de Selincourt, rev. Alan G. Hill (Oxford: Clarendon Press, 1979), p. 260; *The Letters of William and Dorothy Wordsworth*, v, *The Later Years, Part 4: 1840–1853*, ed. Ernest de Selincourt, rev. Alan G. Hill (Oxford: Clarendon Press, 1988), p. 324.

27 The description is that of William Logan, 'Keats's Chapman's Homer', *The Yale Review* 102 (April 2014), 1–25, p. 5.

28 William Wordsworth to Walter Scott, 18 January 1808, in *The Letters of William and Dorothy Wordsworth*, ii, *The Middle Years, Part 1: 1806–1811*, ed. Ernest de Selincourt, rev. Mary Moorman (2nd ed., Oxford: Clarendon Press, 1969), p. 191.

29 Samuel Taylor Coleridge, *Lectures 1808–1819: On Literature*, ed. R. A. Foakes (2 vols., Princeton, NJ: Princeton University Press, 1987), i. 406–7.

30 Samuel Taylor Coleridge, *Biographia Literaria*, ed. James Engell and Walter Jackson Bate (2 vols., Princeton, NJ: Princeton University Press, 1983), i. 18–19. A sorites is something 'heaped together'.

31 See, for instance, 'De medio fonte leporum surgit aliquid amari', dating from 1789; Samuel Taylor Coleridge, *Poetical Works*, ed. J. C. C. Mays (6 vols., Princeton, NJ: Princeton University Press, 2001), i. 11–12.

32 Coleridge, *Lectures 1808–1819: On Literature*, ed. Foakes, i. 515.

33 S. T. Coleridge to William Godwin, 8 July 1801, in *Collected Letters of Samuel Taylor Coleridge*, ed. Griggs, ii. 743.

34 H. J. Jackson, 'Johnson's Milton and Coleridge's Wordsworth', *Studies in Romanticism* 28 (1989), 29–47, pp. 30–1. Seamus Perry notes that Coleridge regarded the very transcribability of Johnson's conversation to mark the limits of his genius; see 'The Talker', in *The Cambridge Companion to Coleridge*, ed. Lucy Newlyn (Cambridge: Cambridge University Press, 2002), p. 119.

35 Coleridge, *Lectures 1808–1819: On Literature*, ed. Foakes, i. 117, 138. In a note, the editor points out that Coleridge 'saw Dr Johnson's defects as a critic of Shakespeare more clearly than his merits'. It is worth adding that Hugh Trevor-Roper traced the modern criticism of Gibbon that he was cold and unimaginative back to Coleridge; see *History and the Enlightenment* (New Haven: Yale University Press, 2010), p. 131.

36 This is confirmed by Coleridge's marginal notes in his copy of Johnson, which are often laudatory in tone; see Samuel Taylor Coleridge, *Marginalia*, ed. George Whalley and H. J. Jackson (6 vols., Princeton, NJ: Princeton University Press, 1983–2001), iii. 140–69.

37 Jackson, 'Johnson's Milton and Coleridge's Wordsworth', p. 32.

38 Ibid., pp. 36, 40–1.

39 Henry Stephens to G. F. Mathew, March 1847, in *The Keats Circle: Letters and Papers 1816–1878*, ed. Hyder Edward Rollins (2 vols., Cambridge, MA: Harvard University Press, 1948), ii. 209.

40 Leigh Hunt, *Foliage* (London: C. and J. Ollier, 1818), pp. 11–12.

41 John Keats, 'Sleep and Poetry', ll. 193–201, in *The Poems of John Keats*, ed. Jack Stillinger (London: Heinemann, 1978), pp. 73–4. See James Chandler's analysis of these lines, and the passage in which they appear, 'The Pope Controversy: Romantic Poetics and the English Canon', *Critical Inquiry* 10 (March 1984), 481–509, pp. 493–6. See also Donald Greene, 'An Anatomy of Pope-Bashing', in *The Enduring Legacy. Alexander Pope: Tercentenary Essays*, ed. G. S. Rousseau and Pat Rogers (Cambridge: Cambridge University Press, 1988), pp. 252–5.

42 *Lectures on the English Poets*, 'On Dryden and Pope', from *The Selected Writings of William Hazlitt*, ed. Duncan Wu (9 vols., London: Pickering & Chatto, 1998), ii. 234. Hazlitt was synchronous with Stendhal, who defined himself as 'un romantique', as opposed to Boileau and Racine, in 1818.

43 John Keats to Benjamin Robert Haydon, 21 March 1818, in *The Letters of John Keats 1814–1821*, ed. Hyder Edward Rollins (2 vols., Cambridge, MA: Harvard University Press, 1958), i. 252.

44 'On Dryden and Pope', from *Selected Writings of William Hazlitt*, ed. Wu, ii. 237.

45 Ibid., p. 229.

46 Percy Bysshe Shelley to Lord Byron, 4 May 1821, in *The Letters of Percy Bysshe Shelley*, ed. Frederick L. Jones (2 vols., Oxford: Clarendon Press, 1964), ii. 290.

47 Lord Byron to Percy Bysshe Shelley, 26 April 1821, in *Byron's Letters and Journals*, ed. Leslie A. Marchand (13 vols., London: John Murray, 1973–94), viii. 104. See also George Cheetham, 'Byron's Dislike of Keats's Poetry', *Keats-Shelley Journal* 32 (1983), 20–5.

48 Lord Byron to John Murray, 15 September 1817, in *Byron's Letters and Journals*, ed. Marchand, v. 265.

49 One of the most astute to address Byron's Augustan leanings is Jane Stabler, *Byron, Poetics and History* (Cambridge: Cambridge University Press, 2002), pp. 97–105.

50 This is verified by Upali Amarasinghe's survey of the periodicals and critics of the Romantic period; see *Dryden and Pope in the Early Nineteenth Century*, chs. 3–5.

51 Frank W. Bradbrook, *Jane Austen and Her Predecessors* (Cambridge: Cambridge University Press, 1966), p. 76.

52 Jane Stabler, 'Literary Influences', in *Jane Austen in Context*, ed. Todd, pp. 41–50, 44.

53 See, *inter alia*, Jerome J. McGann, 'The Anachronism of George Crabbe', *English Literary History* 48 (1981), 555–72, and Frank Whitehead, *George Crabbe, A Reappraisal* (London: Associated University Presses, 1995), pp. 151–5.

54 There is not space here to chart every blow in the Bowles/Pope controversy, but that is done with precision by Andrew Nicholson, *Lord Byron: The Complete Miscellaneous Prose* (Oxford: Clarendon Press, 1991), pp. 399–406.

55 Ibid., pp. 149, 150–1.

56 Percy Bysshe Shelley to Lord Byron, 4 May 1821, in *The Letters of Percy Bysshe Shelley*, ed. Jones, ii. 290.
57 Michael O'Neill and Paige Tovey, 'Shelley and the English Tradition', in *The Oxford Handbook of Percy Bysshe Shelley*, ed. Michael O'Neill and Anthony Howe, with the assistance of Madeleine Callaghan (Oxford: Oxford University Press, 2013), pp. 495–512, 504–12; Steven E. Jones, *Shelley's Satire: Violence, Exhortation, and Authority* (DeKalb: Northern Illinois University Press, 1994), pp. 49, 61–3.
58 *Dryden and Pope in the Early Nineteenth Century*, p. 209.
59 William Wordsworth to Walter Scott, 18 January 1808, in *The Letters of William and Dorothy Wordsworth*, ii, *The Middle Years, Part 1: 1806–1811*, ed. de Selincourt, rev. Moorman, p. 191.

Myth 5

THE ROMANTIC POETS WERE MISUNDERSTOOD, SOLITARY GENIUSES

The Romantic hero was a solitary genius who was ready to defy the world and sacrifice his life for a great cause.

Jackson Spielvogel, *Western Civilization*, ii. 742[1]

For the romantics, art is a production of the intuitive and solitary genius...

Nestór Garcia Canclini, in *The Visual Culture Reader*, p. 180[2]

It is little wonder the image of the lone Romantic continues to thrive: poets of the time portrayed themselves and their proxies as solitary – a hallmark of the sonnets of Charlotte Smith and William Lisle Bowles; Yearsley's *The Rural Lyre* (1796);[3] Helen Maria Williams's *A Farewell to England* (1791);[4] Ann Radcliffe's 'Song of a Spirit';[5] Ann Batten Cristall's 'Song on Leaving the Country' and 'Verses Written in the Spring';[6] Coleridge's conversation poems (most of which are addressed to other people); Amelia Opie's 'Ode to Borrowdale';[7] Byron's *Childe Harold* (often portrayed as solitary, though Byron was surrounded by hangers-on as he journeyed across Europe); Felicia Dorothea Hemans's *Records of Woman* (for instance, 'Indian Woman's Death Song' and 'Juana'), as well as poems about herself, including 'Second Sight' and 'Despondency and Aspiration';[8] Letitia Landon's poems about female poets and elegies to Hemans;[9] Keats's odes ('I cannot see what flowers are at my feet, / Nor

30 Great Myths About the Romantics, First Edition. Duncan Wu.
© 2015 John Wiley & Sons, Ltd. Published 2015 by John Wiley & Sons, Ltd.

what soft incense hangs upon the boughs'); Shelley's Christ-like posturing in 'Ode to the West Wind' ('I fall upon the thorns of life! I bleed!'), and his portrait of misunderstood artistry in *Adonais*, based more on himself than on Keats, of whom it is elegiac: 'A herd-abandoned deer struck by the hunter's dart' (l. 297).[10]

Those who portrayed themselves in this way followed Rousseau who, in his *Reveries of a Solitary Walker*, described retreat into exile:

> I scale rocks and mountains, or bury myself in valleys and woods, so as to hide as far as I can from the memory of men and the attacks of the wicked. Deep in the forest shades it seems to me that I can live free, forgotten and undisturbed as if I no longer had any enemies, or as if the foliage of the woods could protect me from their attacks as it obliterates them from my mind, and in my folly I imagine that if I do not think of them, they will not think of me.[11]

His solitary hours, wrote Rousseau, were 'the only ones when I can truly say that I am what nature meant me to be'.[12] The *Reveries* were influential; Hazlitt's 'On Going a Journey' recalls them, as does his recently discovered 'London Solitude',[13] while Shelley recalled Rousseau's *Reveries* as he composed *Alastor* and *The Triumph of Life*.[14] Rousseau's point is philosophical and not entirely true to his circumstances: at the time of writing was resident on a sixth-floor apartment in rue Plâtrière in Paris with his partner, Thérèse Levasseur.[15] Like him, the Romantics were social animals, their talents nurtured by teachers, their published writings socially produced.[16] Even those who wrote in secret were subject to the shaping influence of their society, and had eventually to show their work to someone, at which point any comment they received might have prompted revision. Friends such as John Hamilton Reynolds and Richard Woodhouse helped Keats edit and even compose.[17]

Writers are never truly alone. Their place within a social and cultural universe is proof of that, their work conveyed to readers through a range of socially constructed agencies. Jerome J. McGann has argued that the relations between those agencies 'do not sanction a theory of textual criticism based upon the concept of the autonomy of the author.'[18] That is to say, authors do not work in isolation and, when they deliver to a publisher, their writings become collaborative, laden with meanings determined not by one but by the many. The late, much-missed bibliographer D. F. McKenzie has described this way of thinking as follows: 'the text [is] always incomplete, and therefore open, unstable, subject to a perpetual re-making by its readers, performers, or audience'.[19] Or, to put it slightly differently, 'new readers of course make new texts, and … their new meanings are a function of their new forms'.[20]

This may be illustrated by the experiences of a range of female poets of the Romantic period. I turn to them because at first glance it might be assumed they worked in solitude, often surreptitiously, without hope they would be read by anyone else. Yet in truth their place within supportive networks of various kinds was a promise of literary success. Anna Laetitia Barbauld was part of Unitarian intellectual society in Warrington of which her father, a schoolmaster, was an important member. She was influenced by the philosopher Francis Hutcheson, and knew Joseph Priestley, to whom she addressed 'The Mouse's Petition'. She published her first book jointly with her brother John, a physician and accomplished writer.[21] Hannah More was a Bluestocking, a group of writers, artists, and intellectuals mutually encouraging of each other's labours. She knew Johnson, Reynolds, Walpole, Elizabeth Carter, Barbauld, and Elizabeth Montagu, the Queen of the Blues; in her turn, she was mentor to Ann Yearsley, whose pig received leftovers from her dining-table.[22] Yearsley's verse was admired by Georgiana Cavendish, Duchess of Devonshire, an accomplished poet (author of *The Passage of the Mountain of St Gothard* (1802)[23]) acquainted with Sheridan, Charles James Fox, and Mary Delany.[24] For a brief period in 1793 Cavendish looked after her niece, the 9-year-old Caroline Ponsonby (the future Lady Caroline Lamb), who would write compelling poetry as well as several novels including *Glenarvon* (1816), which fictionalized her liaison with Byron. Letitia Landon, one of the most successful poets of her day, was the protégée of William Jerdan, editor of the *Literary Gazette*, which carried her 'poetical sketches' and for which she was chief reviewer.[25]

The myth is fuelled by the Romantics' merciless crossfire, some of which tended to bolster the impression of solitary grandeur. On 27 October 1818, for instance, Keats sought to distance himself from 'the wordsworthian or egotistical sublime; which is a thing per se and stands alone'.[26] Ever since, Wordsworth has been branded a solipsist,[27] a charge that does scant justice to him and even less to Keats, who was arguing that Wordsworth 'was guilty of forcing himself upon both the material and the reader, and of allowing the self to obtrude upon the impersonality of great poetry'.[28] It is, in other words, a literary-critical judgement rather than a psychological one.

Keats may have recalled Hazlitt who, in his *Lectures on the English Poets*, hailed Wordsworth as a genius who 'sees nothing but himself and the universe.... His egotism is in some respects a madness; for he scorns even the admiration of himself, thinking it a presumption in any one to suppose that he has taste or sense enough to understand him.'[29] This might appear to go further than Keats, but its target is aesthetic: it concerns an attitude, a quality of the poetry, as much as Wordsworth's physical isolation.[30]

Despite the severity of his pride, Wordsworth was as much a social ani-
mal as the gregarious Hazlitt. In 1797, Coleridge urged him to continue
with 'The Ruined Cottage', advice which turned that poem into a tran-
sitional work in which Wordsworth discovered how to address 'the still,
sad music of humanity'.[31] In 1802 he revised 'The Leech-Gatherer' in
response to criticisms from Sara Hutchinson, prompting him to recast it
as 'Resolution and Independence'.[32] The views of Coleridge and Lamb
were instrumental in persuading him to withhold *The White Doe of Rylstone* from publication in 1808, precipitating revision before it appeared
in 1815.[33] In later years Wordsworth cultivated the rectitude and disposition of an Old Testament patriarch, so that wags like Leigh Hunt could
pretend to confuse him with the mountains about which he was thought
to write. In truth, he was acutely sensitive to his audience, and tailored
his work to their needs.

The myth of solitary genius has given rise to the idea the Romantics
were appreciated only long after their demise. But it would not be true to
suggest they were unappreciated, misunderstood, or that their work failed
to sell, with the possible exceptions of Blake, Shelley, and Keats. Shelley's
poetry was difficult: it presented readers with political and philosophical concepts to which not everyone would have been receptive had they
grasped them. It was mostly published in small editions, often at great distance from the author, issued by publishers who feared prosecution, and
reviewed (if at all) by hostile critics. It was largely ignored by the literary
world of his day and sales were poor: Scott and Byron sold more books
in an afternoon than Shelley did in his entire career.[34]

Yet the cliché of the solitary poet detached from reality and therefore
from an appreciative public does not hold. Among the reviewers there
were those such as John Wilson in *Blackwood's Edinburgh Magazine* who
thought Shelley 'a true poet' even though he detested his principles.[35]
And surviving correspondence proves Shelley understood the basis on
which booksellers retailed each other's publications on commission, as he
revealed when urging his publisher Charles Ollier to place as many copies
of his *Proposal for Putting Reform to the Vote* (1817) with other houses
as he could: 'get as many booksellers as you can to take copies on their
own account. Sherwood Neely & Co. *Hone* of Newgate St. Ridgeway, &
Stockdale are people likely to do so – Send 20 or 30 copies to Messrs.
Hookham & Co. Bond St. without explanation. I have arranged with
them.'[36] There then follows a list of prominent individuals and newspapers to whom he wanted Ollier to send copies as part of a marketing
campaign. Not long after this, Shelley instructed Ollier to advertise it 'in
all the morning papers of note'.[37] In subsequent years Shelley expanded
his repertoire of marketing devices including the use of bribes and hoax
reviews designed to draw readers' attention.[38] This was not the behaviour

of an ineffectual angel – isolated and otherworldly with no head for business. Shelley was fully engaged with the mechanics of the trade in which he was enmeshed, and displayed acumen when devising schemes to sell his work – which made it all the more frustrating when 'the literary world at large took little notice of him'.[39]

Despite predominantly good reviews, Keats was the victim of literary factionalism and branded a Cockney (a term denoting loose morals, poor literary taste, effeminacy, intellectual debility, and humble social status). The effect of these corrosive pronouncements is evident in sales figures for his three lifetime volumes: as late as 1824 (three years after his death), stocks of *Poems* (1817) were retailing at the original price of 6 shillings;[40] remainder copies of *Endymion* (1818) were sold by its publisher to Edward Stibbs, a cut-price bookseller, for one and a half pennies each, who remaindered them at 1s. 6d. a copy (its original price having been 9 shillings);[41] and the year after Keats's death, his publisher John Taylor reported feeble sales of his last (and greatest) collection, copies of which were in his warehouse when he went bankrupt in 1829.[42] Keats never received a penny from them. (Things had changed by 1840, when a cheap edition of his poems went to a print run of more than 3,000.[43]) Yet Keats was not solitary. His story is also, to some extent, that of his friends – the likes of Richard Woodhouse, who believed Keats would become the equal of Shakespeare and Milton; James Hessey, who loaned Keats £30 in 1819;[44] and John Taylor, who promised him £120 at a bank in Rome.[45]

Few suffered more by incomprehension than Blake: some (though by no means all) contemporaries thought him mad (Myth 7) and recognition on any scale came only in the mid-twentieth century. Neglect had to do with the content of his work and the means by which it was produced (in individual, bespoke, hand-coloured copies, of which barely 200 sold during his lifetime). He was not solitary, however. A number of people understood what he was attempting – acolytes like Frederick Tatham and patrons such as the government clerk Thomas Butts. Blake enjoyed the assistance of his wife, Catherine, which was not limited to psychological and spiritual support; she drew, engraved, and coloured his books. When he was commissioned to produce engravings, she sometimes saw them through the press.[46]

If the production of literary works was collaborative, interpretation too was a social event. The *Edinburgh Review* turned the intellectual cut-and-thrust of critical assessment into a public spectacle, just as bear-baiting had been in Elizabethan times, and its combination of self-righteous bossiness and splenetic asperity made it essential reading for the chattering classes: by 1818 it had a circulation of 13,500. It was followed by *Blackwood's Magazine*, the *London Magazine*, the *New Monthly*, and *Fraser's Magazine*, among others.[47] Influence gave the critics power. They brought Anna Laetitia Barbauld's publishing career to a premature end, her relatives being unwilling to allow her 'to expose again that honoured head to the scorns of the unmanly, the malignant, and the base',[48] and their ruderies were said to have 'killed' Keats (Myth 24). Even if their words lacked the power to kill, there can be no doubting the glee with which reviewers snarled and snapped at the poetry that came their way, especially those whose tastes were more than a century behind the times.[49] Their various weapons of choice included taxonomy: there was the Lake School, the Satanic School, and the Leg of Mutton School. They even mythologized themselves in fictional form, in 'Noctes Ambrosianae', in which John Wilson became 'Christopher North' alongside other members of the *Blackwood's* staff including their *éminence grise*, Mr Blackwood.

Few were more sensitive to reviews than Wordsworth, and he was preoccupied throughout his career by the relationship between artefact and audience. Having defended one of his poems against criticism, he told Lady Beaumont in 1807 'that every great and original writer, in proportion as he is great or original, must himself create the taste by which he is to be relished; he must teach the art by which he is to be seen ... and if this be possible, it must be a work *of time*'.[50] This is often invoked when critics write of Wordsworth's newness, and of the difficulty readers continue to have with a manner that can seem uncompromising and mumpish. It implies something else, however: he is acknowledging that the assessment of art and its absorption into the culture is a social act carried out by a community of readers over time. And that is how literary reputation works. It is socially constructed, like literature itself.

Notes

1 Jackson Spielvogel, *Western Civilization* (7th ed., 2 vols., Boston: Wadsworth, 2011).

2 Nestór Garcia Canclini, 'Remaking Passports: Visual Thought in the Debate on Multiculturalism', in *The Visual Culture Reader*, ed. Nicholas Mirzoeff (2nd ed., London: Routledge, 2002).

3 For instance, in her 'Extempore on hearing a Gentleman', in *Romantic Women Poets: An Anthology*, ed. Duncan Wu (Oxford: Blackwell, 1996), pp. 169–70.

4 Ibid., pp. 249–53.

5 Ibid., pp. 262–3.

6 Ibid., pp. 297–9.

7 Ibid., pp. 350–3.

8 *Romanticism: An Anthology*, ed. Duncan Wu (Oxford: Wiley-Blackwell, 2012), pp. 1336–8, 1344–5, 1369–74.

9 Ibid., pp. 1518–24. Susan J. Wolfson examines Landon's investigation of Byron; see *Romantic Interactions: Social Being and the Turns of Literary Action* (Baltimore, MD: Johns Hopkins University Press, 2010), pp. 270–8.

10 Timothy Clark has traced Shelley's self-portrayals as a solitary, misunderstood genius in *Embodying Revolution: The Figure of the Poet in Shelley* (Oxford: Clarendon Press, 1989).

11 Jean-Jacques Rousseau, *Reveries of the Solitary Walker*, tr. Peter France (Harmondsworth: Penguin, 1979), pp. 116–17.

12 Ibid., p. 35.

13 See *New Writings of William Hazlitt*, ed. Duncan Wu (2 vols., Oxford: Oxford University Press, 2007), ii. 353–5.

14 The complexities of the relationship are explored by Edward Duffy, *Rousseau in England* (Berkeley: University of California Press, 1979), pp. 93–5, 109–11, and Cian Duffy, *Shelley and the Revolutionary Sublime* (Cambridge: Cambridge University Press, 2005), pp. 196–201.

15 The apartment block is depicted in Leo Damrosch, *Jean-Jacques Rousseau: Restless Genius* (Boston: Houghton Mifflin, 2005), p. 466.

16 For a discussion of the social production of literature see, for instance, Jerome J. McGann, *A Critique of Modern Textual Criticism* (Chicago: University of Chicago Press, 1983), ch. 4. Zachary Leader has written persuasively about John Taylor's editing of Clare's poetry in *Revision and Romantic Authorship* (Oxford: Clarendon Press, 1996), ch. 5.

17 Jack Stillinger, *Multiple Authorship and the Myth of Solitary Genius* (New York: Oxford University Press, 1991), ch. 2. Greg Kucich has discussed 'Keats, Shelley, Byron, and the Hunt Circle', in *The Cambridge Companion to English Literature 1740–1830*, ed. Thomas Keymer and Jon Mee (Cambridge: Cambridge University Press, 2004), ch. 15.

18 McGann, *A Critique of Modern Textual Criticism*, p. 54.

19 D. F. McKenzie, *Bibliography and the Sociology of Texts: The Panizzi Lectures 1985* (London: British Library, 1986), p. 45.

20 Ibid., p. 20.

21 See, *inter alia*, *Anna Letitia Barbauld: Selected Poetry and Prose*, ed. William McCarthy and Elizabeth Kraft (Ontario: Broadview, 2002), introduction.

22 For More's coterie, see M. G. Jones, *Hannah More* (Cambridge: Cambridge University Press, 1952).

23 Cavendish's poem is most easily accessible in *Romantic Women Poets*, ed. Wu, pp. 170–7.

24 Of all these poets, Yearsley wrote poetry of a very public kind, often addressing public events and the state of society; see Moira Ferguson, *Eighteenth-Century Women Poets: Nation, Class, and Gender* (Albany: State University of New York Press, 1995), ch. 4.

25 These connections and many others are described in the headnotes to *Romantic Women Poets*, ed. Wu. Numerous scholars have written on these various writers; see, for example, Letitia Elizabeth Landon, *Selected Writings*,

ed. Jerome McGann and Daniel Riess (Peterborough, Ont.: Broadview, 1997), Glennis Stephenson, *Letitia Landon: The Woman Behind L.E.L.* (Manchester: Manchester University Press, 1995), and Paul Douglass, *Lady Caroline Lamb: A Biography* (New York: Palgrave Macmillan, 2004).

26 John Keats to Richard Woodhouse, 27 October 1818, in *The Letters of John Keats 1814–1821*, ed. Hyder Edward Rollins (2 vols., Cambridge, MA: Harvard University Press, 1958), i. 387.

27 For a discussion of this, see D. J. Moores, *Mystical Discourse in Wordsworth and Whitman: A Transatlantic Bridge* (Leuven: Peeters, 2006), pp. 58–9.

28 For this formulation I am grateful to John Barnard, who remains a trustworthy interpreter of Keats's poetry and correspondence; see *John Keats* (Cambridge: Cambridge University Press, 1987), p. 53.

29 *The Selected Writings of William Hazlitt*, ed. Duncan Wu (9 vols., London: Pickering & Chatto, 1998), ii. 316.

30 David Bromwich remains the finest explicator of Hazlitt's critique; see *Hazlitt: The Mind of a Critic* (New York: Oxford University Press, 1983), ch. 4.

31 Jonathan Wordsworth, *The Music of Humanity: A Critical Study of Wordsworth's Ruined Cottage* (London: Nelson, 1969), p. 195.

32 Jonathan Wordsworth, *William Wordsworth: The Borders of Vision* (Oxford: Clarendon Press, 1982), p. 159.

33 Duncan Wu, *Wordsworth: An Inner Life* (Oxford: Blackwell, 2002), ch. 11.

34 See William St Clair, *The Reading Nation in the Romantic Period* (Cambridge: Cambridge University Press, 2004), pp. 649–51.

35 *Shelley: The Critical Heritage*, ed. James E. Barcus (London: Routledge & Kegan Paul, 1975), p. 152.

36 Percy Bysshe Shelley to Charles Ollier, February 1817, in *The Letters of Percy Bysshe Shelley*, ed. Frederick L. Jones (2 vols., Oxford: Clarendon Press, 1964), i. 533.

37 Percy Bysshe Shelley to Charles Ollier, 22 February 1817, ibid., i. 534.

38 Behrendt points out that Shelley was the author of the only review of *Queen Mab*; see Stephen C. Behrendt, 'Shelley and His Publishers', in *The Oxford Handbook of Percy Bysshe Shelley*, ed. Michael O'Neill and Anthony Howe with the assistance of Madeleine Callaghan (Oxford: Oxford University Press, 2013), pp. 91–2.

39 *Shelley: The Critical Heritage*, ed. Barcus, p. 1.

40 St Clair, *The Reading Nation in the Romantic Period*, p. 611.

41 W. Carew Hazlitt, *Four Generations of a Literary Family: The Hazlitts in England, Ireland, and America, Their Friends and Their Fortunes 1725–1896* (2 vols., London: George Redway, 1897), i. 276; Tim Chilcott, *A Publisher and His Circle: The Life and Work of John Taylor, Keats's Publisher* (London: Routledge & Kegan Paul, 1972), p. 38.

42 St Clair, *The Reading Nation in the Romantic Period*, p. 612.

43 Ibid.

44 Nicholas Roe, *John Keats: A New Life* (New Haven: Yale University Press, 2012), p. 339.

45 Ibid., p. 378.

46 G. E. Bentley, Jr, *The Stranger from Paradise: A Biography of William Blake* (New Haven: Yale University Press, 2001), p. 71; G. E. Bentley, Jr., *Blake Records* (Oxford: Clarendon Press, 1969), p. 459.

47 One of the best accounts of the rise of the review journals is that given by Lee Erickson, *The Economy of Literary Form: English Literature and the Industrialization of Publishing, 1800–1850* (Baltimore, MD: Johns Hopkins University Press, 1996), ch. 3.

48 *Romantic Women Poets*, ed. Wu, p. 9.

49 The obvious example is John Wilson Croker (1780–1857), reviewer for the *Quarterly*, who assessed the poetry that came his way alongside that of Dryden and Pope, whom he regarded as having set the standard. As a result he admired Scott and Crabbe, and could be very critical of the Romantics.

50 William Wordsworth to Lady Beaumont, 21 May 1807, in *The Letters of William and Dorothy Wordsworth*, ii, *The Middle Years, Part 1: 1806–1811*, ed. Ernest de Selincourt, rev. Mary Moorman (2nd ed., Oxford: Clarendon Press, 1969), p. 150.

Myth

6

ROMANTIC POEMS WERE PRODUCED BY SPONTANEOUS INSPIRATION

'How is it, Bill, thee dost write such good verses? dost thee invoke Muses?'
Hawkshead schoolboy to young Wordsworth, c.1785[1]

Inspiration was the concept by which theologians explained how books of the Bible were written: their authors wrote while possessed of the Holy Spirit. The Romantic appropriation of the term secularized it, while preserving the idea that creativity was beyond the artist's conscious control. The most famous is Wordsworth's remark in the Preface to *Lyrical Ballads* that 'all good poetry is the spontaneous overflow of powerful feelings',[2] which converts it into psychological process. Letitia Landon may have had Wordsworth in mind when she insisted poetry was 'an art more connected with emotion than any of its sister sciences',[3] though in *The Improvisatrice* she constructed a model of poetic composition dependent on external influence.[4] Byron inclined towards a Wordsworthian notion of composition when he told Thomas Moore, 'I can never get people to understand that poetry is the expression of *excited passion*, and that there is no such thing as a life of passion any more than a continuous earthquake, or an eternal fever.'[5] His qualification is as important as the initial claim: he wanted Moore to understand creative 'passion' as temporary. Years before, he said he did not 'rank poetry or poets high in the scale of intellect', defining verse composition as 'the lava of the imagination whose eruption prevents an earth-quake'.[6] Throughout Hazlitt's critical writings on poetry he emphasized passion: poetry occurred, he declared, 'wherever a movement of imagination or passion is impressed on the mind, by which it seeks to prolong and repeat the emotion, to bring all other objects

30 Great Myths About the Romantics, First Edition. Duncan Wu.
© 2015 John Wiley & Sons, Ltd. Published 2015 by John Wiley & Sons, Ltd.

into accord with it, and to give the same movement of harmony ... to the sounds that express it'.[7]

In 'The Eolian Harp' Coleridge preferred an elaborate conceit by which a breeze sweeping across a stringed instrument was compared with imaginatively charged ideas as they passed through the receptive mind: 'And many idle flitting fantasies / Traverse my indolent and passive brain' (ll. 32–3). Shelley revised this in his 'Defence of Poetry', where he remarks:

> Man is an instrument over which a series of external and internal impressions are driven, like the alternations of an ever-changing wind over an Aeolian lyre, which move it, by their motion, to ever-changing melody. But there is a principle within the human being (and perhaps within all sentient beings) which acts otherwise than in the lyre, and produces not melody alone, but harmony, by an internal adjustment of the sounds or motions thus excited to the impressions which excite them.[8]

In 1818, Keats turned to nature to describe the process of composition when he wrote, 'if Poetry comes not as naturally as the Leaves to a tree it had better not come at all',[9] implying it was impulsive and unstoppable. As Jack Stillinger points out, Keats usually managed to get '*most* of the words right the first time. And for all the textual and biographical materials at our disposal, we really don't have the slightest idea how he managed to do this.'[10] Stillinger says Keats's drafts indicate 'a remarkable degree of *spontaneity* – composition on the spur of the moment'.[11]

This is a brief selection of testimony; there is more. The Romantics believed the urge to write was preceded by involuntary, unpremeditated processes:

> Visionary Power
> Attends upon the motions of the winds
> Embodied in the mystery of words.
> (Wordsworth, *The Thirteen-Book Prelude*, v. 619–21)

These assumptions followed such unforgivingly hard-nosed figures as Pope, who could describe Shakespeare's poetry as 'Inspiration indeed: he is not so much an Imitator, as an Instrument, of Nature'.[12] This essay seeks to balance the emphasis on unwilled creativity with an examination of these writers' practice.

What can we deduce about their work habits? On the surface, 'Tintern Abbey' might be thought to exemplify the part played by inspiration in the composition of Romantic poetry. It was written as Wordsworth toured the Wye with his sister in July 1798 and not, so far as we know, transcribed *currente calamo*; the likelihood is Wordsworth retained it in his memory, committing it to paper on return to Bristol, where it became the last thing added to *Lyrical Ballads*. But we tend to consider memory – the retention of hundreds of lines of poetry – as susceptible to the will. That in turn suggests poetic composition may be the work of the conscious mind, including the ability to organize. Moreover, it is likely that, as he composed his poem, Wordsworth knew it would be the culminating work of his new volume: that in turn suggests an element of calculation and the ability to fill a page-quota.

Wordsworth hints at this immediately after mentioning the spontaneous overflow of powerful feelings:

> But though this be true, poems to which any value can be attached were never produced on any variety of subjects but by a man who, being possessed of more than usual organic sensibility, had also thought long and deeply. For our continued influxes of feeling are modified and directed by our thoughts, which are indeed the representatives of all our past feelings.[13]

Wordsworth emphasizes the part played by 'long and deep' thought, hinting at the research, deliberation, and sheer hard work which might be said to accompany, and run concurrently with, composition. Keats's view is comparable; Woodhouse recorded he

> has repeatedly said ... that he never sits down to write unless he is full of ideas – and then thoughts come about him in troops, as tho' soliciting to be accepted & he selects – one of his Maxims is that if poetry does not come naturally, it had better not come at all. The moment he feels any dearth he discontinues writing & waits for a happier moment.[14]

Woodhouse's comments provide context for Keats's 'leaves to a tree' metaphor, making clear he is not referring to something beyond conscious control. He emphasizes the ability to select and discontinue, both of which are the product of editorial judgement. Stillinger concurs. He says Keats's manuscripts 'frequently show "correcting"', and points out that the kind of stylistic adjustments Keats made 'have very little to do with the creative process'.[15]

Of the Romantics, Byron was least amenable to the idea of writing as hard work – as anything besides play, leisure, gentlemanly distraction from *ennui*.[16] That ludic posture cannot be taken to imply he would have laid claim to inspiration; in fact, he despised poets who took themselves so seriously – such as Wordsworth, whose styling as a professional writer disgusted him: 'I thought that Poetry was an *art*, or an *attribute*, and not a *profession*'.[17] But even Byron was known to labour at it, as when he composed the opening cantos of *Don Juan*, among the most heavily revised of his writings: the Dedication and Canto I took four months to complete, Canto II took a month, Cantos III and IV three months. Admittedly, that was as nothing compared with Wordsworth's revisions of *The Prelude*, which extended across five decades and resulted in multiple versions of the same work, none published during the author's lifetime. But then, Wordsworth seems to have revised everything with the same irresistible compulsion, as the Cornell Wordsworth series reveals. To peruse facsimiles of Wordsworth's manuscripts, and compare multiple versions of *Benjamin the Waggoner*, *The White Doe of Rylstone*, and *The Ruined Cottage* (to name a few), is to recognize his determination to keep his writings in a form in which they were susceptible to further rewriting.

That is also the lesson of J. C. C. Mays's edition of Coleridge's poetry, which spans six volumes. Here are variants of his greatest, as well as least-known, poems, which testify to Coleridge's 'neurotic compulsion to tinker',[18] an activity some distance from unwilled inspiration. Coleridge dissimulated in order to claim possession of that ideal; as a result he 'would often hold over, and meticulously rework, several poems that would later be presented as "spontaneous" productions belonging to specific dates'. Such reworking, Richard Holmes tells us, 'becomes characteristic of almost all Coleridge's major poems'.[19] On occasion, the impulse led him to falsify the poem's source, so that he 'claimed as spontaneous work poems which were actually translations, paraphrases, or adaptations'.[20] (He was still a Cambridge undergraduate when he sent Mary Evans a poem called 'A Wish, Written in Jesus Wood, Feb. 10, 1792', which was in fact a translation of John Jortin's Latin 'Votum'.[21]) The entire text of 'Religious Musings' was, according to him, written on Christmas Eve 1794, but the actual dates of composition were '24 Dec 1794–28 Mar 1796; Jan–Jul 1797'.[22] In other words, the claim to have written a poem of 420 lines on a single evening belies a more plausible truth: it was written over fifteen months and revised after its first publication over the course of six months. It was, Coleridge wanted readers to understand, a gift from God. Another poem, 'The Eolian Harp', dramatizes its own composition, as if written in a single sitting, yet Mays dates it 'Aug–Oct 1795; also Feb? 1796',[23] indicating it was written over at least three months in the first instance, and revised some time later. Stillinger says it was revised sixteen times between 1796 and 1828.[24] He counts twelve versions of 'This Lime-Tree Bower my Prison' varying from fifty-five to seventy-seven lines in length,[25] ten of 'Frost at Midnight', and fifteen of 'Dejection: An Ode'.[26] Coleridge framed each as the product of a single inspirational bout, but all were overhauled across the decades. In Stillinger's view, 'Coleridge the famous advocate of unity may in fact have been one of the most scattered and *dis*unified poets in all of English literature.'[27]

Perhaps the most famous example is 'Kubla Khan' which, according to its Preface, came to its author in an opium dream 'without any sensation or consciousness of effort', after which 'he appeared to himself to have a distinct recollection of the whole, and taking his pen, ink, and paper, instantly and eagerly wrote down the lines that are here preserved'.[28] The will to suspend one's disbelief weakens here; Mays suggests a plausible date of composition might be 'Sept–Nov 1797?' before adding 'May 1798? Oct 1799?'[29] We know the poem underwent revision: Stillinger counts five distinct versions dating from between 1797 and 1834.[30] Experts on opium addiction doubt it could have been written at once, and even Coleridge's biographers are sceptical of his claims (see p. 245); as Fehrman remarks: 'In company with many contemporary scholars, we can doubt that the poem, in its highly structured form – and in spite of the gap or break – arose word for word as it now stands on paper.'[31]

Coleridge was not the only writer who claimed to have had such an experience: Mary Robinson said that, after consuming eighty drops of laudanum, she composed 'The Maniac', dictating it 'faster than it could be committed to paper'. The next morning she was 'unconscious of having been awake while she composed the poem'.[32] Scholars doubt this, saying she 'fabricated' her claim having been told by Coleridge of how he came to write 'Kubla Khan'.[33]

If revision was important to Byron, Wordsworth, and Coleridge, it was no less so to Shelley, as his manuscripts reveal. Indeed, the Bodleian Shelley manuscripts, which display him at work on such poems as 'Mont Blanc', indicate that composition for him was a painstaking process in which every line was drafted and redrafted. Robert Brinkley has traced the poem's evolution, showing its 'revisionary quality', while Donald H. Reiman's analysis of the notebooks reveals the intricate process by which Shelley 'could rapidly transfer raw feelings and thoughts into almost labyrinthine artifacts'.[34] Such care might not negate the possibility Shelley believed himself inspired, but it does oblige us to incorporate into our understanding of what poetic composition entailed such things as conscious deliberation, rational analysis, and editorial skill.

Blake would have none of that. Time and again, he insists on the primacy of inspiration. 'Inspiration & Vision', he says in his annotations to Reynolds's discourses, 'will always Remain my Element my Eternal Dwelling place'.[35] Yet in manuscripts we find him acting as editor, reviser, and self-critic – functions that to some extent vitiate the ideal of the artist inspired by outside forces. To take but one example, the 'mind-forged manacles' of 'London' appear in Blake's notebook as 'german forged

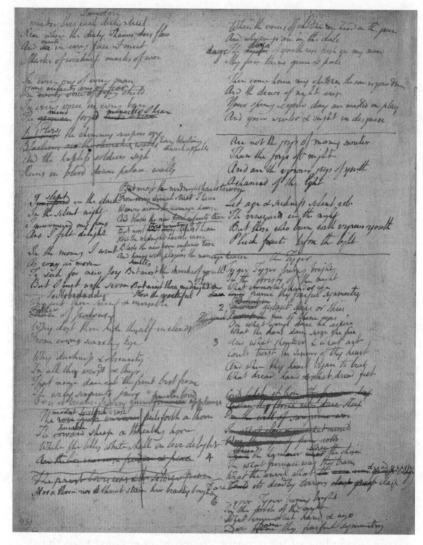

Figure 7 Blake's draft of 'London' from his notebook, showing revisions (at upper left).
Source: © The British Library Board, London, Add. 49460, f. 56.

links'.[36] Vincent Carretta suggests that revision shows Blake expanding his meaning 'inward' – moving from a political observation (a criticism of a political system dominated by a royal family imported from Germany) to a psychological one.[37] That would have entailed patient analysis, a willingness to submit to his inner editor, and act on his judgements. It was a journey as dependent on reason as on imagination.

The lesson of Blake's meticulous and detailed work on his illuminated books is more vivid still. Joseph Viscomi's examination of Blake's techniques, the most thorough so far attempted, reveals the craft and calculation of someone who composed directly onto copper plates. As Viscomi points out, that technique 'allowed each illuminated page and book to evolve organically, that is, to grow and take shapes not previously determined'.[38] Viscomi has done more than any scholar of recent years to understand the complex relationship between Blake's technique and thought:

> Creativity is, in this sense, an intense sensitivity to materials and methods and not just to one's feelings and mental images filtered through an aesthetic schemata. It is a sensitivity to the mind forming itself outside the body and inside the medium, a sensitivity predicated on the complete internalization of the medium. This union of invention and execution means that creative imagining and thinking occur simultaneously inside and outside the body.[39]

Though Viscomi is writing of Blake, I would hazard the thought that something similar could apply to most of the Romantics. If so, we should be wary of models of creativity that exalt the irrational, the illogical, and the mystic as the *sine qua non* of poetic composition, because the evidence lends them only limited credibility. It points instead to an equipoise of the kind described here: a process involving not just one's feelings but what Viscomi calls sensitivity, a union of invention and execution. And an important element of that process is painstaking, rational, analytical, self-critical reflection combined with the work of imagination.[40]

Notes

1 Edward Whately, *Personal and Family Glimpses of Remarkable People* (London: Hodder & Stoughton, 1889), p. 205.

2 *Romanticism: An Anthology*, ed. Duncan Wu (4th ed., Oxford: Wiley-Blackwell, 2012), p. 508.

3 *Critical Writings by Letitia Elizabeth Landon*, ed. F. J. Sypher (Delmar, NY: Scholars' Facsimiles, 1996), p. 66.

4 Anne DeLong, *Mesmerism, Medusa, and the Muse: The Romantic Discourse of Spontaneous Creativity* (Lanham, MD: Lexington Books, 2012), p. 37.

5 Lord Byron to Thomas Moore, 5 July 1821, in *Byron's Letters and Journals*, ed. Leslie A. Marchand (13 vols., London: John Murray, 1973–94), viii. 146.
6 Lord Byron to Annabella Milbanke, 29 November 1813, ibid., iii. 179.
7 'On Poetry in General', *Lectures on the English Poets*, in *The Selected Writings of William Hazlitt*, ed. Duncan Wu (9 vols., London: Pickering & Chatto, 1998), ii. 175.
8 *Romanticism: An Anthology*, ed. Wu, p. 1233.
9 John Keats to John Taylor, 27 February 1818, in *The Letters of John Keats 1814–1821*, ed. Hyder Edward Rollins (2 vols., Cambridge, MA: Harvard University Press, 1958), i. 238–9.
10 Jack Stillinger, 'Keats's Extempore Effusions and the Question of Intentionality', in *Romantic Revisions*, ed. Robert Brinkley and Keith Hanley (Cambridge: Cambridge University Press, 1992), pp. 307–20, 309.
11 Ibid.
12 *The Prose Works of Alexander Pope*, vol. i, ed. N. Ault (Oxford: Blackwell, 1936); vol. ii, ed. R. Cowler (Hamden, CT: Archon Books, 1986), p. 13.
13 *Romanticism: An Anthology*, ed. Wu, pp. 508–9.
14 *The Keats Circle: Letters and Papers 1816–1878*, ed. Hyder Edward Rollins (2 vols., Cambridge, MA: Harvard University Press, 1948), i. 128–9.
15 Jack Stillinger, *Coleridge and Textual Instability: The Multiple Versions of the Major Poems* (New York: Oxford University Press, 1994), pp. 103–4.
16 Byron was happy for Samuel Rogers to suppose that, after a hearty dinner, 'he would throw off sixty or eighty verses, which he would send to press next morning'. Rogers added that 'There is a great deal of incorrect and hasty writing in Byron's works; but it is overlooked in this age of hasty readers': *Reminiscences and Table-Talk of Samuel Rogers*, ed. G. H. Powell (London: R. Brimley Johnson, 1903), pp. 178, 187.
17 Lord Byron to Thomas Moore, 1 June 1818, in *Byron's Letters and Journals*, ed. Marchand, vi. 47.
18 Zachary Leader, *Revision and Romantic Authorship* (Oxford: Clarendon Press, 1996), p. 130.
19 Richard Holmes, *Coleridge: Early Visions* (London: Hodder & Stoughton, 1989), p. 113.
20 Ibid., p. 154.
21 Norman Fruman, 'Creative Process and Concealment in Coleridge's Poetry', in *Romantic Revisions*, ed. Brinkley and Hanley, pp. 154–68, 156.
22 Samuel Taylor Coleridge, *Poetical Works*, ed. J. C. C. Mays (6 vols., Princeton, NJ: Princeton University Press, 2001), i. 171.
23 Ibid., p. 231.
24 Jack Stillinger, 'The Multiple Versions of Coleridge's Poems: How Many "Mariners" Did Coleridge Write?', *Studies in Romanticism* 31 (Summer 1992), 127–46, p. 131. Stillinger examines each of the versions in *Coleridge and Textual Instability*, which profiles seven works which exist in different versions.
25 Stillinger, 'The Multiple Versions of Coleridge's Poems', p. 132.
26 Ibid., p. 133.

27 Ibid., p. 117.

28 Coleridge, *Poetical Works*, ed. Mays, i. 511–12.

29 Ibid., p. 509.

30 Stillinger, *Coleridge and Textual Instability*, pp. 73–9.

31 Carl Fehrman, *Poetic Creation: Inspiration or Craft* (Minneapolis: University of Minnesota Press, 1980), p. 70.

32 *Mary Robinson: Selected Poems*, ed. Judith Pascoe (Peterborough, Ont.: Broadview, 2000), pp. 122–3.

33 See, *inter alia*, Fehrman, *Poetic Creation*, p. 68. The dating would depend on Robinson having encountered Coleridge before retailing her story; to that end, Adam Sisman has challenged Paula Byrne's claim that Coleridge met Mary Robinson as early as 1796 ('The Mysterious "C"', *Times Literary Supplement*, 3 December 2004, p. 17). The suggestion they met on 15 January 1800 remains likely. See also Daniel Robinson, 'Coleridge, Mary Robinson, and the Prosody of Dreams', *Dreaming: Journal of the Association for the Study of Dreams* 7 (1997), 119–40, p. 123.

34 Robert Brinkley, 'Spaces Between Words: Writing *Mont Blanc*', in *Romantic Revisions*, ed. Brinkley and Hanley, pp. 243–67, 248; Donald H. Reiman, 'Shelley's Manuscripts and the Web of Circumstance', ibid., pp. 227–42, 237.

35 *The Complete Poetry and Prose of William Blake*, ed. David V. Erdman (New York: Doubleday, 1988), pp. 660–1.

36 *The Notebook of William Blake*, ed. David V. Erdman with the assistance of Donald K. Moore (Oxford: Clarendon Press, 1973), N109.

37 Vincent Carretta, *George III and the Satirists from Hogarth to Byron* (Athens: University of Georgia Press, 1990), pp. 158–9.

38 Joseph Viscomi, *Blake and the Idea of the Book* (Princeton, NJ: Princeton University Press, 1993), pp. 30–1.

39 Ibid., p. 43.

40 This is not far removed from Hölderlin's notion of 'calculated inspiration'; see Timothy Clark, *The Theory of Inspiration: Composition as a Crisis of Subjectivity in Romantic and Post-Romantic Writing* (Manchester: Manchester University Press, 1997), p. 116.

Figure 8 'Ghost of a Flea' encouraged doubts concerning Blake's sanity. It derives from two drawings of the head of a flea for Blake's series of Visionary Heads (c.1819–25); Blake seems always to have regarded it as a purely imaginative work.
Source: The Art Archive / Tate Gallery London / Eileen Tweedy.

Myth 7
BLAKE WAS MAD

Mad or Not Mad

> Alexander Gilchrist, *Life of William Blake* (1863), title of ch. 35

Madness, 2, 7, 19, 39n4, 42, 52–4, 57–8, 80, 105–6 and n2, 107–8, 138, 164–5, 171, 173–4, 180, 195, 208, 215–16 and n1, 217–20 and n2, 221 and nn2 and 4, 223, 226 and n2, 229 and n3, 232–3 and n1, 235–6, 244, 263, 268, 285, 299n1, 309, 321, 326, 352, 363, 367, 370, 372, 379–80, 387, 391 and n1, 396, 398–9, 401, 402 and n3, 424, 431n1, 432, 448–9, 455–6, 466n1, 477, 480 and n10, 489n1, 493–4, 499, 517, 519–20, 536–7, 539, 625–6

> Index entry, G. E. Bentley, Jr, *Blake Records* (1969)

Until the mid-twentieth century, Blake's madness was taken for granted. As far as most were concerned, he *was* mad, his work the outpouring of a disturbed psyche. For a long time, that provided the rationale for discounting his genius. The argument of this essay is not that he was free of mental disorder but that the epithet is too crude to do him justice. Such words should be used sparingly and with care: they say little, and have given rise to myths within myths – such as the mistaken notions that Blake was an inmate of Bedlam at the same time as John Martin and that he and his wife sat naked in their summer-house reciting *Paradise Lost*.[1]

Once upon a time, even Blake's champions felt they had no option but to concede the charge. 'There was nothing defective about Blake', G. K. Chesterton declared in 1910, before beating an undignified retreat: 'But if we ask whether there was not some madness about him, whether his naturally just mind was not subject to some kind of disturbing influence

---

30 Great Myths About the Romantics, First Edition. Duncan Wu.
© 2015 John Wiley & Sons, Ltd. Published 2015 by John Wiley & Sons, Ltd.

which was not essential to itself, then we ask a very different question .... there is a real sense in which Blake was mad.'[2] Even today, those who have worked for years on Blake admit he was 'perhaps insane'[3] and had 'glimpses of real madness'.[4] Such judgements are not crazy. W. J. T. Mitchell, one of Blake's sharpest commentators, takes a measured view: 'Another, less apocalyptic way of putting this is just to allow the possibility that Blake was a bit mad some of the time, in different ways on different occasions, and that he was equally sane (also in different ways) on others.'[5]

These judgements find corroboration among Blake's contemporaries – especially those who never met him. Wordsworth declared, 'There is no doubt this poor man was mad, but there is something in the madness of this man which interests me more than the Sanity of Lord Byron & Walter Scott.'[6] Robert Southey did encounter him (on 24 July 1811) and thought him so 'evidently insane, that the predominant feeling in conversing with him, or even looking at him, could only be sorrow & compassion'.[7] According to Henry Crabb Robinson, Blake had 'constant intercourse with the world of spirits – He receives visits from Shakespeare Milton Dante Voltaire &c &c &c And has given me repeatedly their very words in their conversations.'[8] He claimed also to have been visited by the Virgin Mary, the angel Gabriel, and the ghost of a flea. Even those who knew and liked him thought him deranged: Fuseli said 'Blake has something of madness about him', while Flaxman 'did not join in the ordinary derision of him as a madman' but referred to his irritability and remarked: 'I very much fear his abstracted habits are ... much at variance with the usual modes of human life'.[9]

Blake was aware of how he was regarded, as he reveals in his address to fellow engravers written to accompany his picture of the Canterbury pilgrims: 'It is very true what you have said for these thirty two Years I am Mad or Else you are so both of us cannot be in our right senses Posterity will judge by our Works.'[10] But it was not just a matter of facing down critics in his own profession; even during his lifetime, Blake suffered discrimination from those who presumed to judge his sanity by his art. When the Royal Academy declined to exhibit his work, he invited 'those Noblemen and Gentlemen, who are its Subscribers, to inspect what they have excluded: and those who have been told that my Works are but an unscientific and irregular Eccentricity, a Madman's Scrawls, I demand of them to do me the justice to examine before they decide'.[11]

Self-awareness of this order undercuts the accusation of insanity, as does Blake's recognition of the damage it wreaked upon his standing in the marketplace and in the profession. He alluded to it in annotations to Reynolds's *Discourses* when recounting how he 'spent the Vigour of my Youth & Genius under the Opression of Sr Joshua & his Gang of Cunning Hired Knaves Without Employment & as much as could possibly be Without Bread', before deploring the fact that, 'While Sr Joshua was rolling in Riches, Barry was Poor & Unemployd except by his own Energy, Mortimer was despised and mocked, calld a Madman & only Portrait Painting applauded & rewarded by the Rich & Great.'[12] These remarks testify to the conservatism of the academy and its propensity to label as mad whatever does not conform to its orthodoxies. Blake suffered by it, and saw the work of artists he admired – James Barry and John Hamilton Mortimer – 'despised and mocked'.

Blake's argument that the devaluing of serious art, and presumed madness of its creators, were products of a Reynoldsian aesthetic is a recurrent theme throughout his annotations, including the comment that 'Reynolds Wishd none but Fools to be in the Arts & in order to this, he calls all others Vague Enthusiasts or Madmen.'[13] In ancient Greece, enthusiasm entailed possession by a god; Blake suggests Reynolds equated it with mental illness as a way of denying serious consideration to others. The two men are divided partly by their attitude to 'reason' and 'rules'. Reynolds 'recommends long, laborious study and comparison of like objects'[14] and for that reason urged students to develop practical skills and not rely on what we would call talent: 'You must have no dependence on your own genius … mere enthusiasm will carry you but a little way.'[15] Such declarations infuriated Blake: 'Reynoldss Opinion was that Genius May be Taught & that all Pretence to Inspiration is a Lie & a Deceit to say the least of it – If the Inspiration is Great why Call it Madness.'[16] To Blake, Reynolds was the advocate of dullness, the 'idiot Reasoner [who] laughs at the Man of Imagination'.[17]

If 'enthusiasm' provides little basis for suspecting Blake of insanity, it is nonetheless true he suffered from depression. In a letter to his friend George Cumberland of July 1800, he wrote: 'I begin to Emerge from a Deep pit of Melancholy, Melancholy without any real reason for it, a Disease which God keep you from & all good men.'[18] This was sufficient to induce concern for his mental state, as on those occasions when he compared himself with Nebuchadnezzar, crawling on all fours in caves. Psychologists such as Hubert J. Norman suggest Blake's 'condition may, with little doubt, be classified as one of maniacal-depressive insanity'. Norman attributed Blake's mysticism to 'the disorderly functioning of unstable nerve-tissue, or to misunderstood organic reflexes'.[19] More recently, Kay Redfield Jamison has used the term 'manic-depressive illness' to describe Blake's ailment: 'This would account not only for Blake's visionary and psychotic states, but for his forays into and out of the rather more pro-saically rational world as well.'[20] She adds that

> the diagnosis of manic-depressive illness for Blake does not detract from the complexity of his life; it may, however, add a different kind of understand-ing to it. Likewise, it does not render his work any the less extraordinary, or make him any less a great visionary or prophet. Seeing Blake as some-one who suffered from an occasionally problematic illness – a constitutional predisposition shared in common with many other artists, writers, and com-posers – may not explain all or even most of who he was. But, surely, it does explain some.[21]

The 'mad' label caused Blake to be marginalized for more than a cen-tury after his death, a one-word description different in implication from the more specific diagnosis of manic-depressive illness – something from which Byron, Van Gogh, and Virginia Woolf also suffered, none of whose reputations were damaged as extensively, or for as long a time, as his.

Jamison's diagnosis has the endorsement of G. E. Bentley, Jr, who says Blake's writings are punctuated by 'Desperation', 'Desolation', and 'Death despair & everlasting brooding melancholy':

> His mood-swings, his unpredictability even to closest acquaintances, and his sudden anger at earnest friends working for his worldly welfare, all suggest an unstable personality and help to explain why friends like Hayley spoke of his 'dangerously acute' sensibility, of his 'Imagination utterly unfit to take due Care of himself', and of the need to 'Keep his too apprehensive Spirit for a Length of Time unruffled'.[22]

Blake described himself in terms suggesting more than a passing acquain-tance with what we would call depression: 'I have indeed fought thro a Hell of terrors & horrors', he wrote in 1804, and his friend Thomas Butts reminded him: 'you cannot but recollect the difficulties that have unceas-ingly arisen to prevent my discerning clearly whether your Angels are black white or grey'.[23] But it is possible to experience depression without actually going mad – a word that does scant justice to the symptoms Blake experienced. Paul Youngquist has written a book on the subject, *Madness and Blake's Myth* (1989), and agrees he 'was no stranger to despair, but he found a security against it in artistic activity, making mental distress his subject instead of passively becoming its victim'.[24] Youngquist suggests Blake's visions 'would today hold the interest of clinical investigators', and that his hallucinatory experience 'falls into a category we today con-sider at least potentially pathological'.[25] Blake dealt with this, he suggests,

by investigating psychological disturbance in his writings – a principal
example being *The Four Zoas*, the subject of which, Youngquist argues,
'is a form of madness that in many ways resembles what we today call
schizophrenia, whose fundamental symptoms Blake renders with uncanny
fidelity'.[26]

Only the sanest of artists could manage such a feat; the portrayal of
madness demands more objectivity than sufferers can manage. Judged in
that light, Blake ranks among the most level-headed artists who ever lived:
W. J. T. Mitchell discerns in his writings 'paranoia, depression, fixation,
obsession, compulsion, regression, rage, narcissism, melancholia, hysteria, mania, delusions of grandeur, fetishism'.[27] Even in Blake's mythical
anti-hero, Urizen, he finds the potential for mental imbalance:

> Urizen's rage for order, system, control, and law is consistently represented
> by Blake as producing the most pathological forms of madness, a 'petrific
> abominable chaos' in both the subjective mental life of the reasoner and the
> political sphere of rational social management – whether it is the authoritar-
> ian reason of traditional patriarchal societies or the mathematical, utopian
> rationality of modern revolutions.[28]

That Blake nurtured such ambitions rebuts the charge his myth-making
was an ongoing symptom of mental illness: only someone firmly rooted
in the world as we know it can find the resources to critique authoritar-
ianism and rationality. It has been said Blake attributed the human cost
of industrialization to 'the Newtonian worldview of materialism, mech-
anism, and rationalism'.[29] There is nothing irrational about that. And
when he denounced sexual repression and slavery, he said things that
would now be thought sane but which by the standards of his own day
appeared delusional.[30]

Those who say Blake was mad forget that, as G. E. Bentley, Jr, observes,
he became more serene after 1820. Having encountered him in 1825,
Henry Crabb Robinson revised his earlier opinion and said 'he had an
air of inspiration – But not such, as without a previous acquaintance
with him, or attending to *what* he said, would suggest the notion that
he was insane. There was nothing *wild* about his look.'[31] That is consistent with reports from the young artists who gathered round him in later
years: John Linnell believed there was no 'justice in calling him insane';
Edward Calvert testified 'I saw nothing but sanity ... saw nothing mad in
his conduct, actions, or character'; Francis Oliver Finch agreed: 'He was
not mad, but perverse and willful'; Cornelius Varley said 'There was nothing mad about him', and James Ward, who 'often met Blake in society and

talked with him, would never hear him called mad'.[32] In his final years, Samuel Palmer wrote feelingly of the injustice visited upon Blake by such allegations:

> I remember William Blake, in the quiet consistency of his daily life, as one of the sanest, if not the most thoroughly sane man I have ever known. The flights of his genius were scarcely more marvellous than the ceaseless industry and skilful management of affairs, which enabled him on a very small income to find time for very great works. And of this man the public are informed that he passed thirty years in a mad-house![33]

Notes

1 G. E. Bentley, Jr, *Blake Records* (Oxford: Clarendon Press, 1969), pp. 53–4, 299n1. There is no evidence Martin suffered significant mental health problems, other than a bout of depression in the 1830s; see *John Martin: Apocalypse*, ed. Martin Myrone (London: Tate Publishing, 2011), p. 132. I am guiltily aware of being among many who have repeated the story about Blake and his wife in their summer-house; the story appears to have originated with Thomas Butts. See Alexander Gilchrist, *The Life of William Blake, 'Pictor Ignotus'* (2 vols., London: Macmillan, 1863), i. 115.

2 G. K. Chesterton, *William Blake* (New York: Cosimo, 2005), pp. 71–2.

3 Morris Eaves, in *The Cambridge Companion to William Blake*, ed. Morris Eaves (Cambridge: Cambridge University Press, 2003), p. 10. Eaves has described *Milton* and *Jerusalem* as 'insane epics'; see 'On Blakes We Want and Blakes We Don't', *Huntington Library Quarterly* 58, no. 3/4, 'William Blake: Images and Texts' (1995), 413–39, p. 417.

4 Eric G. Wilson, *Blake's Infinite Writing: My Business is to Create* (Iowa City: University of Iowa Press, 2011), p. 77.

5 W. J. T. Mitchell, 'Chaosthetics: Blake's Sense of Form', *Huntington Library Quarterly* 58, no. 3/4, 'William Blake: Images and Texts' (1995), 441–58, p. 448.

6 *Blake: The Critical Heritage*, ed. G. E. Bentley, Jr (London: Routledge, 1975), p. 30.

7 Quoted by Mark Storey, *Robert Southey: A Life* (Oxford: Oxford University Press, 1997), p. 210. Henry Crabb Robinson reported that Southey 'held him for a decided madman …. he showed [him] a perfectly mad poem called Jerusalem – Oxford Street is in Jerusalem' (Bentley, *Blake Records*, p. 229).

8 Bentley, *Blake Records*, p. 324.

9 G. E. Bentley, Jr, *The Stranger from Paradise: A Biography of William Blake* (New Haven: Yale University Press, 2001), p. 380.

10 'Public Address', in *The Complete Poetry and Prose of William Blake*, ed. David V. Erdman (New York: Doubleday, 1988), p. 573.

11 'Advertisement of the 1809 Exhibition', ibid., pp. 527–8.

12 Ibid., p. 636. For an assessment of Blake's judgement of the Academy, see Aileen Ward, '"Sr Joshua and his Gang": William Blake and the Royal Academy', *Huntington Library Quarterly* 52 (1989), 75–95, pp. 85–6.

13 *The Complete Poetry and Prose of William Blake*, ed. Erdman, p. 647.

14 Hazard Adams, *Blake's Margins: An Interpretive Study of the Annotations* (Jefferson, NC: McFarland, 2009), p. 122.

15 *The Works of Sir Joshua Reynolds* (2nd ed., 3 vols., London: Cadell & Davies, 1798), i. 35, 43–4.

16 *The Complete Poetry and Prose of William Blake*, ed. Erdman, p. 642.

17 *Milton*, plate 32*(e), l. 7, in William Blake, *Milton a Poem*, ed. Robert N. Essick and Joseph Viscomi (London: William Blake Trust/Tate Gallery, 1993), p. 187.

18 William Blake to George Cumberland, 2 July 1800, in *The Complete Poetry and Prose of William Blake*, ed. Erdman, p. 706.

19 Hubert J. Norman, *William Blake* (London: Adlard, 1915), p. 240.

20 Kay Redfield Jamison, *Touched with Fire: Manic-Depressive Illness and the Artistic Temperament* (New York: Free Press, 1993), p. 94.

21 Ibid., pp. 94–5.

22 Bentley, *The Stranger from Paradise*, pp. 269–70.

23 Ibid., p. 271.

24 Paul Youngquist, *Madness and Blake's Myth* (University Park: Pennsylvania State University Press, 1989), p. 19.

25 Ibid., pp. 42–3.

26 Ibid., p. 101.

27 Mitchell, 'Chaosthetics: Blake's Sense of Form', p. 453.

28 Ibid.

29 Pamela Gossin, 'Literature and the Physical Sciences', in *The Cambridge History of Science*, vol. v, *The Modern Physical and Mathematical Sciences*, ed. Mary Jo Nye (Cambridge: Cambridge University Press, 2003), p. 97.

30 Other critics find portrayals of insanity in Blake's writings, including Mark L. Barr, 'Prophecy, the Law of Insanity, and "The First Book of Urizen"', *Studies in English Literature, 1500–1900* 46 (2006), 739–62. See also Josephine A. McQuail, 'Passion and Mysticism in William Blake', *Modern Language Studies* 30 (2000), 121–34. For examination of Blake's attitude to women and gender, see for instance Catherine L. McClenahan, 'No Face Like the Human Divine? Women and Gender in Blake's Pickering Manuscript', in *Spirits of Fire: English Romantic Writers and Contemporary Historical Methods*, ed. G. A. Rosso and Daniel P. Watkins (London: Associated University Presses, 1990), pp. 189–207.

31 Bentley, *The Stranger from Paradise*, p. 381.

32 Ibid.

33 *The Life and Letters of Samuel Palmer, Painter and Etcher*, ed. Alfred Herbert Palmer (London: Seeley, 1892), p. 23.

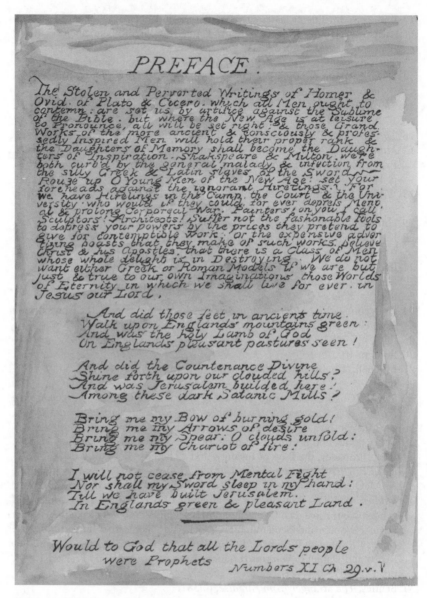

PREFACE.

The Stolen and Perverted Writings of Homer &
Ovid: of Plato & Cicero. which all Men ought to
contemn: are set us by artifice against the Sublime
of the Bible. but where the New Age is at leisure
to Pronounce, all will be set right: & those Grand
Works of the more ancient & consciously & professedly Inspired Men will hold their proper rank &
the Daughters of Memory shall become the Daughters of Inspiration. Shakspeare & Milton were
both curb'd by the general malady & infection from
the silly Greek & Latin slaves of the Sword,
Rouze up O Young Men of the New Age! set your
foreheads against the ignorant Hirelings! For
we have Hirelings in the Camp, the Court, & the University: who would if they could for ever depress Ment.
al & prolong Corporeal War. Painters! on you I call!
Sculptors! Architects! Suffer not the fashonable Fools
to depress your powers by the prices they pretend to
give for contemptible Work. or the expensive advor
tizing boasts that they make of such works: believe
Christ & his Apostles, that there is a Class of Men
whose whole delight is in Destroying. We do not
want either Greek or Roman Models if we are but
just & true to our own Imaginations, those Worlds
of Eternity in which we shall live for ever. in
Jesus our Lord.

And did those feet in ancient time.
Walk upon Englands mountains green:
And was the holy Lamb of God
On Englands pleasant pastures seen!

And did the Countenance Divine
Shine forth upon our clouded hills?
And was Jerusalem builded here.
Among these dark Satanic Mills?

Bring me my Bow of burning gold!
Bring me my Arrows of desire:
Bring me my Spear: O clouds unfold!
Bring me my Chariot of fire!

I will not cease from Mental Fight
Nor shall my Sword sleep in my hand:
Till we have built Jerusalem.
In Englands green & pleasant Land.

Would to God that all the Lords people
were Prophets
Numbers XI Ch 29.v.

Figure 9 The page from Blake's *Milton* containing the lyric now known as 'Jerusalem', of which he printed only two copies.
Source: © The British Library Board, London, Tab. 435.c.8, page 2.

Myth
8
BLAKE WROTE 'JERUSALEM' AS AN ANTHEM TO ENGLISHNESS

When did Blake write 'Jerusalem'? The question is anachronistic. No one in Blake's day, not even Blake, called it that. And it is something of a misnomer, because the lyric was originally part of the prose introduction to his prophetic poem *Milton*. The engraved plate on which it appears has been dated to c.1808.[1] Four copies of *Milton* were struck off in Blake's workshop, only two of which contained it.[2] At the time of its author's death it had no circulation and was completely unknown. And there it remained, becalmed in the horse-latitudes of obscurity, known (if at all) to scattered enthusiasts – bibliophiles such as William Michael Rossetti, Algernon Charles Swinburne, and William Butler Yeats, whose obsessive engagement with the Blakean mythos made its originator look like an amateur.

It was included by Alexander Gilchrist in his biography of Blake in 1863[3] but not reprinted in a form accessible to a large readership until 1916, when Robert Bridges (then Poet Laureate) included it in his wartime anthology, *The Spirit of Man*, as a recourse from 'the great scheme of tyranny' envisaged by 'the evil spirit' of the Germans.[4] In resurrected form it was always a political work, its first incarnation framed to embody the optimism demanded of those whose forlorn task it was to engage in the deadliest war anyone could remember. No one recognized its potential better than Bridges, and he commissioned Sir Hubert Parry to set it to music for 'Fight for Right', an organization whose mission was to reignite the waning bellicosity of a nation that had begun to realize the war would not be over by Christmas. Feeling understandable unease, Parry withdrew his setting before it could be sucked into the maw of the propaganda machine, preferring instead to donate it to the 'Votes for Women'

30 Great Myths About the Romantics, First Edition. Duncan Wu.
© 2015 John Wiley & Sons, Ltd. Published 2015 by John Wiley & Sons, Ltd.

campaign, allowing suffragettes to sing it at a concert at the Royal Albert Hall on 13 March 1916.

From that point onwards, its fate was sealed. Between 1920 and 1990, Blake's lines, now entitled 'Jerusalem', would appear in more than a dozen collections of popular hymns – not an outcome that would have given their author any pleasure, given his dislike of organized religion. (Anglicans have reciprocated: in 2001 the vicar of Cheadle parish church refused to allow it to be sung at a wedding because it declared the merits of a 'socialist-type utopia'.[5]) It would receive its biggest boost when in 1922 Elgar recast Parry's setting for symphony orchestra in the bombastic, barnstorming version, marinated in its own gravitas, performed at the Last Night of the Proms. As anyone who has ever watched the Olympics will know, anthems are usually the opportunity for the world to observe the extremes of witlessness known as state-sponsored art; Elgar and Parry's 'Jerusalem' is the exception, perhaps because it was neither official nor state-sponsored. Theirs is a fierce paean to Englishness, composed at the last moment such a thing was imaginable, sung by a mezzo-soprano wrapped in the banner of St George. For nearly a century it has saturated English culture with its own distinctive brand of defiant self-celebration – adopted by the Women's Institute in 1924; sung by the Jarrow marchers in 1936; recited by Clement Attlee at the Labour Party conference of 1945, in a speech declaring his vision of a welfare state. Since 1970 it has been recorded on more than a thousand occasions by such artists as the Grimethorpe Colliery Band, the England cricket team, and Emerson, Lake and Palmer.[6] It continues to be chanted at sporting events, particularly test matches and cup finals, and from 2000 onwards the British National Party, an extreme right-wing political organization, attempted to appropriate it as its unofficial anthem.[7]

It would be wrong to perceive strength in such transparent permeability. Any poem desperate to set up house with so many different bedfellows – some honourable, some frivolous, others patently certifiable – is in need of professional help. The point is not just that Blake would have disapproved but that in its present form the lyric is orphaned from whatever originally gave it meaning. This essay seeks to reconnect it to its sources.

In one sense, the re-gearing of 'Jerusalem' to First World War politics was not a wholesale betrayal of its origins; it was a war poem, of sorts. When Blake composed it Britain had been involved for fifteen long years in global conflict. (There had been a brief truce with France, from March 1802 to May 1803, but otherwise the war that began in 1793 would continue until Napoleon's defeat at Waterloo in 1815.) Those years devastated British society as thoroughly as the more intense conflagration that began in 1914. By 1808 an entire generation had been either killed or invalided out of the army with chronic illness or terrible injuries, and there was no prospect the suffering would end. At home, conditions were unspeakable. The French Revolutionary and Napoleonic wars took place against the background of rapid industrialization which depended on an army of underpaid woman and child labourers; not until 1802 did Parliament pass the first regulations to safeguard the health of apprentices, and only in 1819 would it prohibit children under the age of 9 from working in factories. War deepened a pre-existing poverty that horrified Blake as much when he moved to Sussex as when he lived in London, his sympathies being with the oppressed – those forced 'to live upon a Crust of bread', the farmer who 'plows for bread in vain'.[8]

'Jerusalem' occurs at a moment in the Preface to *Milton* when Blake condemns the materialist errors and evils of classical culture, as compared with 'the Sublime of the Bible', and envisages a time when 'professedly Inspired Men' (the Hebrew prophets, Jesus and his apostles, Milton, and Blake) will 'hold their proper rank'. He is angered by the neoclassical revival, the passion for Greek and Roman antiquity which had the effect of devaluing everything else. In response he demands a revolt in taste led by fellow artisans: 'Rouze up O Young Men of the New Age! set your foreheads against the ignorant Hirelings! For we have Hirelings in the Camp, the Court, & the University: who would if they could, for ever depress Mental & prolong Corporeal War. Painters! on you I call! Sculptors! Architects!'[9] Blake is not advocating physical conflict; his reference to 'Corporeal War' is intended to draw an implicit distinction between the battlefield and the inner struggle entailed by artistic creation. In his lyric, he will oppose the one and promote the other. There is nothing jingoistic about it. (The attack on 'Hirelings' is also directed against journeyman engravers like Blake himself, who had in the past shackled himself to such patrons as William Hayley, now regarded with contempt.)

The Preface continues:

> Suffer not the fash[i]onable Fools to depress your powers by the prices they pretend to give for contemptible works or the expensive advertizing boasts that they make of such works; believe Christ & his Apostles that there is a Class of Men whose whole delight is in Destroying. We do not want either Greek or Roman Models if we are but just & true to our own Imaginations, those Worlds of Eternity in which we shall live for ever; in Jesus our Lord.

Speaking from the soapbox placed before his fellow artists, Blake urges they recognize the corrupting influence of the market on taste. Again, he counsels abandonment of neoclassical trends and adoption of 'those Worlds of Eternity' accessible through 'our own Imaginations'. It is at this moment that Blake elaborates his argument in verse, declaring a readiness to fight *not on the battlefield* but in the studio, armed with artist's tools, which will give physical shape to the insights of the imagination. And he begins with an image no one, having read the Preface, could have predicted – that of Christ's feet striding the fields and mountains of his native land.[10]

> And did those feet in ancient time
> Walk upon England's mountains green:
> And was the holy Lamb of God
> On England's pleasant pastures seen![11]

Editors fuss needlessly about Blake's punctuation, like underemployed waiters, inserting question marks at the end of lines 2 and 4.[12] Blake omits them because he states with certainty that England was indeed hallowed by the 'Lamb of God' – a phrase that recalls the Gospel of St John: 'The next day John seeth Jesus coming unto him, and saith, Behold the Lamb of God, which taketh away the sin of the world' (John 1:29). The idea of seeing Christ on English fields may seem bizarre, but is the kind of experience Blake was capable of having. He describes it again in *Jerusalem*, parts of which were composed in the same period as *Milton*, when he locates Jerusalem in London: 'The fields from Islington to Marybone ... builded over with pillars of gold, / And there Jerusalems pillars stood', with 'The Lamb of God'.[13] For Blake, 'ancient time' does not denote a distant past; Christ's visit to England remains visible to us in the here and now, although it took place many centuries ago.[14]

There is another echo of the Bible, recalling Isaiah 52:7: 'How beautiful upon the mountains are the feet of him that bringeth good tidings, that publisheth peace; that bringeth good tidings of good, that publisheth salvation; that saith unto Zion, thy God reigneth!'[15] That messenger of good tidings is the Lamb of God, and his message is that Zion's (Jerusalem's) God reigns in England now, as elsewhere and throughout eternity.

> And did the Countenance Divine,
> Shine forth upon our clouded hills?
> And was Jerusalem builded here,
> Among these dark Satanic Mills?

This time the question marks *are* Blake's, and the doubt at which they hint comes from refusal to blind himself to the evidence of his senses – that he inhabits a fallen world. He is well aware that the fields north of London do not contain the new Jerusalem (and that, in reality, they swarmed with thieves and prostitutes[16]) just as the clouded hills look down on 'dark

Satanic Mills', prisons of rationality for mind and body. In that knowledge, he responds:

> Bring me my Bow of burning gold;
> Bring me my Arrows of desire:
> Bring me my Spear: O clouds unfold!
> Bring me my Chariot of fire!

Blake's exclamations recall his demand that 'Young Men of the New Age! set your foreheads against the ignorant Hirelings! ... Painters! on you I call! Sculptors! Architects!' War has been declared not on France or any other 'Corporeal' entity but on those who assert the claims of 'dark Satanic Mills' against the new Jerusalem. Blake declares his intention to join that fight, armed not with literal weapons but with visionary ones corresponding with his metal plates, etching tools, and engraving acids. The chariot confirms his knowledge that he is prosecuting the will of God, for it was used by Elijah at 2 Kings 2:11: 'And it came to pass, as they still went on, and talked, that, behold, there appeared a chariot of fire, and horses of fire, and parted them both asunder; and Elijah went up by a whirlwind into heaven.'

It bears repeating that, as Blake gathers together bow, arrows, spear, and chariot, he does so not in a literal sense. This is not an act of physical violence but a creative one by which he will become what he elsewhere calls a golden builder,[17] someone who will articulate in physical form the divinely inspired visions of the imagination. The dark Satanic mills have turned the fallen England into hell; Blake will regenerate it through art.

> I will not cease from Mental Fight,
> Nor shall my Sword sleep in my hand:
> Till we have built Jerusalem,
> In England's green and pleasant Land.

Jerusalem literally means 'foundation of peace'. Blake believes it is possible to turn the nation in which he lives, enslaved to war, into something different. 'Mental Fight' – that is, the striving of imaginative faculties – will enable the new Jerusalem to be built. That he will succeed is implicit in that phrase, 'green and pleasant Land', which reminds us England still remains, *in potentia*, the paradise Blake believes it to be, if only golden builders are permitted to do their work. Immediately after his lyric, Blake adds: 'Would to God that all the Lords people were Prophets. Numbers XI. Ch 29 v.' He is quoting the Bible, where Moses says: 'Would God that all the Lord's people were prophets, and that the Lord would put his spirit upon them!' Blake's task is to reveal to his readers a higher truth – that the new Jerusalem is within reach of all, not as idea but as reality.

It should by now be clear how thoroughly the appropriation of Blake's lyric as anthem for war or white English supremacy betrays its author's most deeply held convictions. Blake preached a form of pacifistic enlightenment by which England might be seen as a haven for those who love peace and beauty, its claims as a source of imaginative strength exalted above those of ancient Greece and Rome (which to him were a false lure). 'Jerusalem' champions not the mean, exclusionary, ruddy-faced nationalism of those who would have it serve their self-befouling cause, but the inclusivity of visionary power on home ground – accessible to 'all the Lord's people', English or not.

> And did those feet in ancient time,
> Walk upon England's mountains green:
> And was the holy Lamb of God
> On England's pleasant pastures seen!
>
> And did the Countenance Divine,
> Shine forth upon our clouded hills?
> And was Jerusalem builded here,
> Among these dark Satanic Mills?
>
> Bring me my Bow of burning gold;
> Bring me my Arrows of desire:
> Bring me my Spear: O clouds unfold!
> Bring me my Chariot of fire!
>
> I will not cease from Mental Fight,
> Nor shall my Sword sleep in my hand:
> Till we have built Jerusalem,
> In England's green and pleasant Land.

Notes

1 Joseph Viscomi, *Blake and the Idea of the Book* (Princeton, NJ: Princeton University Press, 1993), pp. 320–1.
2 For full details, see G. E. Bentley, Jr, *Blake Books* (Oxford: Clarendon Press, 1977), pp. 304–20. Essick and Viscomi speculate that Blake abandoned the Preface for copies C and D of *Milton* in part because he stopped believing he would reach the large audience anticipated in it; see William Blake, *Milton a Poem*, ed. Robert N. Essick and Joseph Viscomi (London: William Blake Trust/Tate Gallery, p. 40.
3 Gilchrist introduces it by saying *Milton* 'is very like the *Jerusalem* in style: it would seem, in fact, to be a sort of continuation; an idea that is borne out by the verses with which its singular Preface concludes': *The Life of William Blake, 'Pictor Ignotus'* (2 vols., London: Macmillan, 1863), i. 195.

4 Robert Bridges, *The Spirit of Man* (London: Longman, 1916), preface, p. 3.

5 See, *inter alia*, 'Why we believed that Jerusalem is not a nationalist hymn', *Times Higher Education*, 17 August 2001.

6 The cultural history of Blake's poem is explored at length by Roger Whitson and Jason Whitaker, *William Blake and the Digital Humanities: Collaboration, Participation, and Social Media* (Abingdon, Oxon.: Routledge, 2013), ch. 3.

7 See Jason Whitaker, 'Albion's Spectre: Building the New Jerusalem', in *Mysticism, Myth and Celtic Identity*, ed. Marion Gibson, Shelley Trower, and Garry Tregidga (Abingdon, Oxon.: Routledge, 2013), pp. 220–1.

8 Quoted from G. E. Bentley, Jr, *The Stranger from Paradise: A Biography of William Blake* (New Haven: Yale University Press, 2001), p. 215.

9 *The Complete Poetry and Prose of William Blake*, ed. David V. Erdman (New York: Doubleday, 1988), p. 95.

10 Blake was the first writer to imagine this. The folk legend of Christ's visit to the tin mines in the West Country in the company of his uncle, Joseph of Arimathea, dates from the 1890s and cannot have been known to him; see A. W. Smith, '"And Did Those Feet … ?": The "Legend" of Christ's Visit to Britain', *Folklore* 100 (1989), 63–83, and William John Lyons, *Joseph of Arimathea: A Study in Reception History* (Oxford: Oxford University Press, 2014), pp. 105–15. I follow Essick and Viscomi in identifying the feet as Christ's; *Milton a Poem*, ed. Essick and Viscomi, p. 214.

11 I have taken my text of Blake's poem from *Milton a Poem*, ed. Essick and Viscomi, p. 214. For ease of reading, I have preferred to expand ampersands to 'and', and insert apostrophes where necessary.

12 I say this in the full knowledge I am one of the worst culprits.

13 *Jerusalem*, plate 27, ll. 1–4; see William Blake, *Jerusalem*, ed. Morton Paley (London: William Blake Trust/Tate Gallery, 1991), p. 170. Paul Miner draws my attention to this passage; see 'Blake's London: Times & Spaces', *Studies in Romanticism* 41 (2002), 279–316, p. 310.

14 This point is made by Nancy Moore Goslee, '"In England's Green & Pleasant Land": The Building of Vision in Blake's Stanzas from "Milton"', *Studies in Romanticism* 13 (1974), 105–25, p. 110.

15 I am grateful to Paul Miner for bringing the biblical echo to my attention.

16 Again, see Miner, 'Blake's London', p. 311.

17 See *Jerusalem*, plate 27, l. 25, in *Jerusalem*, ed. Paley, p. 171.

Myth

9

LYRICAL BALLADS (1798) WAS DESIGNED TO ILLUSTRATE 'THE TWO CARDINAL POINTS OF POETRY', USING POEMS ABOUT EVERYDAY LIFE AND THE SUPERNATURAL

The myth is Coleridge's, a token of his autocracy when rewriting history. In *Biographia Literaria* chapter 14, he claimed that, during their year in Somerset, 1797–8, he and Wordsworth discussed 'the two cardinal points of poetry, the power of exciting the sympathy of the reader by a faithful adherence to the truth of nature, and the power of giving the interest of novelty by the modifying colours of imagination'. He then said either he or Wordsworth suggested they write poems of both kinds for a book:

> In the one, the incidents and agents were to be, in part at least, super-natural... For the second class, subjects were to be chosen from ordinary life; the characters and incidents were to be such, as will be found in every village and its vicinity, where there is a meditative and feeling mind to seek after them, or to notice them, when they present themselves.[1]

30 Great Myths About the Romantics, First Edition. Duncan Wu.
© 2015 John Wiley & Sons, Ltd. Published 2015 by John Wiley & Sons, Ltd.

This version of how *Lyrical Ballads* came into existence has been cited as fact by generations of editors, critics, biographers, and scholars, not to mention (despite one or two honourable exceptions) the petrified forest of Readers, Companions, student texts, anthologies, and other instruments of indoctrination.

How misleading is this version of events? Let me count the ways. The first thing that should give us pause is the claim that *Lyrical Ballads* was written during Wordsworth's stay at Alfoxden (June 1797 to July 1798), when it is known a number of its component poems were in existence before that: 'The Female Vagrant' (originally composed as part of 'Salisbury Plain' in late July and September 1793[2]), 'The Convict' (March to early October 1796), 'Lines written near Richmond, upon the Thames, at Evening' and 'Lines written when sailing in a Boat' (derived from a sonnet originally composed around late 1788 and 1791, reworked by 29 March 1797[3]). To these can be added 'The Foster Mother's Tale' and 'The Dungeon' (not inspired in the way Coleridge suggests because they were extracted from his play *Osorio*, written for the London stage, April to September 1797), as well as 'Lewti', which appears in some early copies of *Lyrical Ballads*.[4] We should also exclude 'The Rime of the Ancient Mariner' which, as Wordsworth recounted, was planned as a joint project 'to defray the expence'[5] of a walking tour to Lynton and the Valley of Stones in north Devon. Wordsworth handed it to Coleridge shortly after the principal incidents had been sketched out, and it was largely complete by November 1797,[6] when Coleridge reported to his publisher Joseph Cottle, 'I have written a ballad of about 300 lines'.[7] Lest we doubt it was written as a pot-boiler, Coleridge declared in early January 1798 he would 'sell my Ballad to Phillips who I doubt not will give me 5£ for it'[8] (Richard Phillips was proprietor of the *Monthly Magazine*). In any case, 'The Ancient Mariner' cannot have been written for *Lyrical Ballads* as the book had not then been thought of. Its exclusion from Coleridge's *Biographia* account is problematic because it must be the work he has in mind when referring to that in which 'the incidents and agents were to be, in part at least, supernatural'. Even were that not so, the other poems I have mentioned add up to a substantial proportion of those which comprised *Lyrical Ballads* (1798).

What of the remainder? Coleridge's story of how *Lyrical Ballads* (1798) was conceived places the following events in the following order: (1) conversation about 'two sorts' of poetry; (2) proposal that a book be written containing them; (3) its writing by Wordsworth and Coleridge. Everything we know about its evolution stands in contradiction to that orderly schema. The most important point is that the writing of many of them *preceded* conception of *Lyrical Ballads* as a volume.

Coleridge knew that as well as anyone. In 1797–8 he acted as literary agent for himself and Wordsworth. Having estimated they needed 30 guineas to relocate to Germany (renewal of the lease on Alfoxden House having been declined[9]), Coleridge wrote to his publisher Joseph Cottle, around 13 March 1798, with two publishing projects: (1) 'Our two tragedies – with small prefaces containing an analysis of our principal characters' (*The Borderers* and *Osorio*); (2) 'Wordsworth's Salisbury Plain & Tale of a Woman which two poems with a few others which he will add'[10] ('Tale of a Woman' was the poem now known as 'The Ruined Cottage'). There is no mention of *Lyrical Ballads* even though Wordsworth had composed 'Lines written at a small distance from my House' (on 6–9 March 1798) and 'Goody Blake and Harry Gill' (7–13 March). If Coleridge's claims in *Biographia* were correct, we would expect discussion about 'two sorts' of poetry to have preceded composition of them and for Coleridge to have mentioned the joint volume to Cottle as a matter of urgency, given the need for money. He didn't. Why? Because no such conversation had taken place and no such plan was yet agreed. Instead he proposed everything else he could think of.

Two weeks later, in early April, Coleridge wrote again to Cottle, withdrawing the dramas but instead proposing a 'volume of Wordsworth's poems' for which he was asked to pay 30 guineas at the end of July.[11] This would gradually mutate into *Lyrical Ballads*: it was inspired not by conversations about 'two sorts' of poem but by the fact Wordsworth was in the midst of frantic composition. In addition to those works already mentioned, he might by now have been working on any or all of 'Simon Lee', 'Anecdote for Fathers', 'We Are Seven', 'Lines written in Early Spring', 'The Thorn', 'The Last of the Flock', 'The Mad Mother', and 'The Idiot Boy'. Coleridge does not say the proposed volume would contain anything by himself. He does not even mention 'The Ancient Mariner' (which, for all we know, was still destined for a periodical): the only acceptable project is 'the volume of Wordsworth's Poems', later referred to as '*his* Poems'.[12] If as late as early April 1798 the sole project in negotiation with Cottle was a book of poetry by Wordsworth – that is to say, one that excluded anything by Coleridge – the account given in *Biographia* cannot be correct.

By mid-April Wordsworth had a clearer sense of what his forthcoming book might contain, for he told Cottle he had been 'very rapidly adding to my stock of poetry'.[13] Even so, its contents were still uncertain: at the end of April Dorothy Wordsworth told her brother Richard that William was preparing to publish *two* volumes of poetry: 'He is to have twenty guineas for one volume, and he expects more than twice as much for another which is nearly ready for publishing.'[14] There is no hint either would contain anything by Coleridge – and no mention of supernatural poems. Nor was there mention of its title – perhaps not surprisingly, given that in early May Wordsworth again wrote to Cottle suggesting the new book would contain 'Salisbury Plain'.[15] By the end of the month, however, the book had assumed a shape vaguely resembling that in which it would be published. Cottle visited Wordsworth and Coleridge, taking back to Bristol the manuscript of 'The Ancient Mariner' and probably copies of some of Wordsworth's poems – though there is no indication that at this point 'The Ancient Mariner' was considered part of Wordsworth's book.[16] As Dorothy told her brother Richard on the last day of May: 'William has now some poems in the Bristol press ... William has sold his poems very advantageously'.[17] She refers to publication solely by Wordsworth, with no suggestion of a co-author. Not until 4 June, when Coleridge wrote to Cottle, was collaboration mooted: Wordsworth 'would not object to the publishing of Peter Bell *or* the Salisbury Plain, singly; but to the publishing of *his poems* in two volumes he is decisively repugnant & oppugnant – He deems that they would want variety &c &c – if this apply in his case, it applies with tenfold force to mine.'[18] The solution? A volume containing poems by both men. Of the twenty-three works eventually included in the 1798 edition of *Lyrical Ballads*, all but one were in draft by the time it had been agreed the volume would contain two poets' work.[19] If the version of events given in *Biographia* has any validity, the only poem that can possibly have been affected by the alleged discussions about 'two sorts' of poems was that not written by 4 June: 'Tintern Abbey', which is neither supernatural nor concerned with everyday life.

The information by which Coleridge's account is contradicted would not have been available to readers of *Biographia Literaria* when first published but has been available to modern readers for decades. Yet for some reason Coleridge's version of events continues to be trotted out as if it commanded biblical authority. Critics should know better: it is inconsistent with everything we know about how creative works are conceived and written. Seldom, if ever, are they the result of debate, the drawing up of an agenda, and bespoke composition; Coleridge makes no allowance for the unpredictability and changeability of the human imagination, or the random accidents that make life other than orderly. Perhaps that explains the appeal his story has for those drawn to neatness, clarity, and straight lines – which rarely figure in the lives of poets or, indeed, anyone else.

Why invent it? Coleridge's ersatz history established him as one of the architects and principal creators of *Lyrical Ballads*, a much-needed corrective to the popular misconception of it as wholly Wordsworth's. But it came at a price – the truth. Its biggest distortion was to impose on the past a version of high-minded interest in 'two sorts' of poetry as the volume's inspiration, effacing the book's true *raison d'être* – the one too blowzy and disreputable to be allowed to speak its name: lucre. Coleridge and Wordsworth united under the *Lyrical Ballads* banner only when squeezed to generate the cash that would get them to Germany. They would not have done so otherwise.

This is seen most vividly when one takes into account Wordsworth's resistance to publication. He loathed it because the setting in print of verse was deadening; by keeping his poems to himself he maintained their vitality. Faced with the need to publish in spring 1798, he could have handed Cottle any number of works from his bottom drawer – 'The Borderers', 'Salisbury Plain', 'Adventures on Salisbury Plain', 'The Discharged Soldier', 'Peter Bell', 'A Night-Piece', 'The Old Cumberland Beggar', 'A Somersetshire Tragedy', 'The Ruined Cottage', 'The Pedlar', or the long Juvenalian satire he had co-authored with Francis Wrangham from Racedown. A few were proposed, but when asked to release more than one, he declared himself 'decisively repugnant & oppugnant'. Instead he produced a series of shorter poems, two derived from a sonnet he had written a decade before; he undertook major surgery on 'Salisbury Plain' to extract the female vagrant's tale as a free-standing narrative; and, when really desperate, scrambled his literary agent (who doubled as a poet), thus permitting inclusion of two poems amputated from *Osorio*, a lengthy supernatural ballad unlike anything else in the volume, and 'The Nightingale'. *Lyrical Ballads* was not written after the preparatory discussions Coleridge implies took place; its contents are drawn from disparate sources some of which were ransacked for the purpose of making up the required number of pages.[20]

The problem when writing the 'Advertisement' was to find an overarching rationale. Wordsworth's genius revealed itself when he came up with the sentence, 'The majority of the following poems are to be considered as experiments'[21] – as compelling a thesis as any. Our tendency is to think that was Wordsworth and Coleridge's objective all along, reading it backwards to the moment of the book's conception, as befits the status now conferred on it as 'a revolution in Romantic literature' (another myth). But that would not have been Wordsworth's view in July 1798. The book he was putting through the press had taken many months to assume its final shape, and only afterwards was he in a position to understand how best to explain its contents to readers. From that vantage-point, the collection really *was* experimental.

Wordsworth and Coleridge *did* talk about poems that dealt with the supernatural, and were sufficiently engaged to write 'The Ballad of the

Dark Ladiè', 'Christabel', 'The Three Graves', and 'The Ancient Mariner'. Wordsworth wrote Gothic poetry even as a schoolboy at Hawkshead, and several lyrical ballads (including 'Goody Blake and Harry Gill', 'The Thorn', and 'The Idiot Boy') interrogate the genre.[22] But that does not prove *Lyrical Ballads* was intended to showcase 'two sorts' of poetry. Coleridge's scheme fails not only to explain the diversity of the volume's contents but to account for the false starts, second thoughts, and haphazard route by which the volume assumed its eventual shape. Wordsworth would have perceived Coleridge's rewriting of history as soon as he set eyes on *Biographia* chapter 14 nearly twenty years later. When asked his opinion of it, he opted for a politic response, saying he had 'contented myself with skimming parts of it', before adding: 'I am heartily sick of even the best criticism'.[23]

Notes

1 Samuel Taylor Coleridge, *Biographia Literaria*, ed. James Engell and Walter Jackson Bate (2 vols., Princeton, NJ: Princeton University Press, 1983), ii. 5–6.

2 Wordsworth recounts the circumstances of its composition in his letter to John Kenyon of summer 1838, *The Letters of William and Dorothy Wordsworth*, vi, *The Later Years, Part 3: 1835–1839*, ed. Ernest de Selincourt, rev. Alan G. Hill (2nd ed., Oxford: Clarendon Press, 1982), p. 616. Throughout this essay I have observed the dates of composition stipulated by Mark L. Reed, *Wordsworth: The Chronology of the Early Years 1770–1799* (Cambridge, MA: Harvard University Press, 1967). Slightly more precise datings are to be found in Mary Jacobus, *Tradition and Experiment in Wordsworth's Lyrical Ballads 1798* (Oxford: Clarendon Press, 1976), pp. 273–6.

3 The relation of the two lyrical ballads to the early sonnet is discussed by Duncan Wu, *William Wordsworth: The Earliest Poems 1785–1790* (Manchester: Carcanet, 2002), pp. 126–8.

4 Coleridge derived 'Lewti' from 'Beauty and Moonlight: An Ode', a poem Wordsworth composed as a schoolboy at Hawkshead in 1786, with the specific intention of making money from the *Morning Post*, where it was first published on 13 April 1798. It is discussed by the editors of William Wordsworth, *Lyrical Ballads and Other Poems, 1797–1800*, ed. James Butler and Karen Green (Ithaca, NY: Cornell University Press, 1992), p. 766; Robert S. Woof, 'Wordsworth's Poetry and Stuart's Newspapers: 1797–1803', *Studies in Bibliography* 15 (1962), 149–89, p. 170; and Samuel Taylor Coleridge, *Poetical Works*, ed. J. C. C. Mays (6 vols., Princeton, NJ: Princeton University Press, 2001), i. 457–8.

5 The phrase is Wordsworth's; see *Lyrical Ballads and Other Poems*, ed. Butler and Green, p. 347.

6 As J. C. C. Mays observes, it was reworked and amplified up to 23 March 1798; see Coleridge, *Poetical Works*, ed. Mays, i. 365.

7 S. T. Coleridge to Joseph Cottle, c. 20 November 1797, in *Collected Letters of Samuel Taylor Coleridge*, ed. Earl Leslie Griggs (6 vols., Oxford: Clarendon Press, 1956–71), i. 357. Mary Moorman deals with Coleridge's debt to Wordsworth in *William Wordsworth: A Biography. The Early Years 1770–1803* (Oxford: Clarendon Press, 1957), pp. 347–9.

8 S. T. Coleridge to John Prior Estlin, [6 January 1798], in *Collected Letters of Samuel Taylor Coleridge*, ed. Griggs, i. 368.

9 Wordsworth reported this to his friend James Webbe Tobin on 6 March; *The Letters of William and Dorothy Wordsworth*, i, *The Early Years 1787–1805*, ed. Ernest de Selincourt, rev. Chester L. Shaver (2nd ed., Oxford: Clarendon Press, 1967), p. 211.

10 S. T. Coleridge to Joseph Cottle, c. 13 March 1798, in *Collected Letters of Samuel Taylor Coleridge*, ed. Griggs, i. 400.

11 S. T. Coleridge to Joseph Cottle, [early April 1798], ibid., i. 402.

12 Ibid., i. 402–3. As the editors of the Cornell edition of *Lyrical Ballads* suggest, the volume proposed to Cottle in March may then have been thought to include poems which would not appear in the finished volume, such as the complete text of 'Salisbury Plain', 'The Ruined Cottage', 'The Old Cumberland Beggar', and 'The Discharged Soldier'. See *Lyrical Ballads and Other Poems*, ed. Butler and Green, p. 9.

13 William Wordsworth to Joseph Cottle, 12 April 1798, in *The Letters of William and Dorothy Wordsworth*, i, *The Early Years*, ed. de Selincourt, p. 215.

14 Dorothy Wordsworth to Richard Wordsworth, 30 April 1798, ibid., p. 216.

15 William Wordsworth to Joseph Cottle, 9 May 1798, ibid., p. 218.

16 I follow the surmise of James Butler and Karen Green; see *Lyrical Ballads and Other Poems*, ed. Butler and Green, p. 12.

17 Dorothy Wordsworth to Richard Wordsworth, 31 May 1798, in *The Letters of William and Dorothy Wordsworth: The Early Years 1787–1805*, ed. de Selincourt, p. 219.

18 S. T. Coleridge to Joseph Cottle, 4 June 1798, in *Collected Letters of Samuel Taylor Coleridge*, ed. Griggs, i. 411–12. Griggs dates this letter to 28 May 1798, but Shaver argues persuasively for the later date, an argument accepted by Butler and Green.

19 This is corroborated by Butler and Green; see *Lyrical Ballads and Other Poems*, ed. Butler and Green, p. 12.

20 That is not to say the volume is disorganized or incoherent; its contents were drawn together with forethought and discrimination, as argued by, *inter alia*, Neil Fraistat, *The Poem and the Book: Interpreting Collections of Romantic Poetry* (Chapel Hill: University of North Carolina Press, 1985), ch. 3, and Stephen Maxfield Parrish, *The Art of the Lyrical Ballads* (Cambridge, MA: Harvard University Press, 1973).

21 'Advertisement to *Lyrical Ballads* (1798)', in *The Prose Works of William Wordsworth*, ed. W. J. B. Owen and Jane Worthington Smyser (3 vols., Oxford: Clarendon Press, 1974), i. 116.

22 For further discussion of Gothicism in Wordsworth's 1798 poetry, see Jacobus, *Tradition and Experiment in Wordsworth's Lyrical Ballads 1798*, esp. chs. 9 and 10. Wordsworth's schoolboy Gothicism is seen most obviously in 'The Vale of Esthwaite', for which see *William Wordsworth: The Earliest Poems 1785–1790*, ed. Wu, pp. 14–27.

23 William Wordsworth to R. P. Gillies, 19 September 1817, in *The Letters of William and Dorothy Wordsworth*, iii, *The Middle Years, Part 2: 1812–1820*, ed. Ernest de Selincourt, rev. Mary Moorman and Alan G. Hill (2nd ed., Oxford: Clarendon Press, 1970), p. 399.

Myth

10 WORDSWORTH'S PREFACE TO *LYRICAL BALLADS* WAS A MANIFESTO FOR THE ROMANTIC REVOLUTION

The myth would have us suppose Wordsworth, in 1800, leader in a revolutionary campaign against the eighteenth century – or at least the Augustans. It is one of the most repeated claims by writers on Romanticism and I have never seen it questioned.

The *OED* defines 'manifesto' as 'propounding a theory or argument', and in that limited sense it might describe the Preface to *Lyrical Ballads*. But such labels only expose the limitations of taxonomy; when applied to poets and their work, they are ungainly, blunt-force implements that violate inconsistency, unpredictability, and originality – whatever makes writers human, in other words. In this case the idea of the Preface as manifesto has the effect of superseding any other way of understanding it, turning it into something like *The Germ* (the Pre-Raphaelite journal) or *BLAST* (that of the Vorticists), when – unlike either of them – it was not the result of a group decision to articulate, in public, the shock of the new.

Wordsworth and Coleridge did not see themselves as founders of a movement or trend, nor as guerrillas fending off the exemplary monsters of previous centuries; they wanted to describe the style developed for *Lyrical Ballads* in contrast to that used by some other writers.[1] Which leads me to another point: though Wordsworth was author of the Preface, it was not exclusively his. 'The Preface contains our joint

30 Great Myths About the Romantics, First Edition. Duncan Wu.
© 2015 John Wiley & Sons, Ltd. Published 2015 by John Wiley & Sons, Ltd.

opinions on Poetry', Coleridge declared on 30 September 1800,[2] having seen the finished essay four days before.[3] The text we now read is rightly considered Wordsworth's 'most original essay in aesthetics',[4] but it began as Coleridge's, who meant to write it himself, as he told William Sotheby:

> It is most certain, that the P[reface arose from] the heads of our mutual Conversations &c – &c the f[irst pass]ages were indeed partly taken from notes of mine / for it was at first intended, that the Preface should be written by me – and it is likewise true, that I warmly accord with W. in his abhorrence of these poetic Licences, as they are called, which are indeed mere tricks of Convenience & Laziness.[5]

'It is most certain ... it is likewise true': Coleridge garnishes his recollection with certitudes. Given the proximity in time (composition of the Preface took place only fourteen or fifteen months before), we have no cause to question either his involvement or 'accord' with Wordsworth's critique of 'poetic Licences'. Nor should we regard him as less complicit in the Preface as it appeared in revised form in *Lyrical Ballads* (1802), when he told Southey:

> Wordsworth's Preface is half a child of my own Brain / & so arose out of Conversations, so frequent, that with few exceptions we could scarcely either of us perhaps positively say, which first started any particular Thought – I am speaking of the Preface as it stood in the second Volume [edition?] ...[6]

Scholars take the 'Friends' mentioned in the Preface to refer to Coleridge alone, looking over Wordsworth's shoulder as he composed,[7] and have found jottings in Coleridge's notebook that contributed, including one with the phrase, 'recalling of passion in tranquillity', similar to the Preface's 'emotion recollected in tranquillity'.[8]

For all that, Wordsworth was its sole writer (the bossy sententiae and serpentine cadences could only be his) though the inspiration and some of its ideas are attributable to Coleridge. At its inception, it was collaborative, and Wordsworth's involvement seems to have been – at least at the outset – hesitant. 'I never cared a straw about the theory', he protested, '& the Preface was written at the request of Mr Coleridge out of sheer good nature. I recollect the very spot, a deserted Quarry in the Vale of Grasmere where he pressed the thing upon me, & but for that it would never have been thought of.'[9] Coleridge wore philosophy like a pair of well-fitting brogues, and had he composed the Preface it might have been a disquisition to match Aristotle. But then, Coleridge was in the habit of projecting all manner of discursive works that failed to materialize.[10] Years later, Wordsworth would admit: 'I am not a Critic – and set little value upon the art. The preface which I wrote long ago to my own Poems I was put upon by the urgent entreaties of a friend, and heartily regret I ever had any thing to do with it.'[11] Wordsworth's gifts did not dispose him to that kind of writing, as Mark L. Reed points out: 'His imperfections as a handler of dialectical nuance now and later prevented his elaboration of a completely integrated and cohesive description of the poems.'[12] Wordsworth needed Coleridge's notes, just as he would need assistance with the other project Coleridge convinced him to pursue – the philosophical poem called 'The Recluse'.[13]

Yet he did accept the challenge, and critics find the Preface laden with inconsistencies that reflect his authorship. When taking the knife to it in *Biographia Literaria*, Coleridge was among the first to note its failure to conform with its author's practice; or, as he put it in a letter of July 1815: 'I have done my Duty to myself and to the Public, in (as I believe) compleatly subverting the Theory & in proving that the Poet himself has never acted on it except in particular Stanzas which are the Blots of his Compositions.'[14] Coleridge was disingenuous in pretending he had no part in the Preface, but his reservations about Wordsworth's thought are well grounded. W. J. B. Owen goes further: Wordsworth's comments on 'the best part of language' are 'at best, only partially true'; the Preface fails to 'make any positive statement on what the language of prose is'; Wordsworth's aspiration towards a poetry 'well adapted to interest mankind permanently' 'fails, not unnaturally, to prove an impossible thesis'; his theory of metre is 'incomplete', and his notion concerning the spontaneous overflow of powerful feelings 'is widely but not generally applicable'. In its 1800 and 1802 versions, the Preface 'is at odds with itself in its general theory of poetics'.[15]

But then, the Preface was never designed as a philosophical work, as recent critics point out,[16] and it is not unusual for prefaces to enshrine their authors' inconsistences and contradictions. None of which can be said of manifestoes – formal statements often written by committee, designed to set out a programme for future courses of action. The Preface is not that kind of statement, and I wonder whether Coleridge knew that as soon as he read the completed draft on 26 September 1800. That may be why, on 9 October, he told Humphry Davy he wanted to write 'an Essay on the Elements of Poetry' which 'would in reality be a *disguised* System of Morals & Politics'[17] – that is, a work as individual in its thought as Wordsworth's Preface, though of a more formal, academic kind. Eighteen months later, in the summer of 1802, Wordsworth and Coleridge were aware their opinions about poetry had diverged – something attributable as much to Coleridge's worsening health as to his disappointment with Wordsworth's failure to write 'The Recluse'. Having seen an extended version of the Preface to *Lyrical Ballads*, Coleridge told Southey, 'I am far from going all lengths with Wordsworth ... I rather suspect that some where or other there is a radical Difference in our theoretical opinions respecting Poetry –/ this I shall endeavor to go to the Bottom of.'[18] There is no evidence he differed with the Preface prior to this but, once convinced Wordsworth's views were not aligned with his own, his reservations deepened, a process accelerated by the rift in their relationship after 1810. When he came to write *Biographia Literaria* in the summer of 1815, Coleridge was inclined to portray Wordsworth's ideas as contentious from the outset: 'With many parts of this preface ... I never concurred; but on the contrary objected to them as erroneous in principle.'[19] He had conveniently forgotten what, at the time of its writing, he took for granted – that it 'contains our joint opinions on Poetry' – enabling him to paint Wordsworth a jabbering humbug. None of this supports the idea that the Preface was regarded by either Coleridge or Wordsworth as a manifesto. It was always a highly individual account of one man's poetics, with all the eccentricities arising from his authorship.

Those who insist it is a manifesto rely on the assumption of newness, yet it is hardly innovatory in its arguments.[20] The editors of Wordsworth's prose works say it is 'less original than has sometimes been thought ... in that many of its aesthetic, psychological, and sociological presuppositions are quite commonplace'.[21] Far from waging war on writers of earlier decades, Wordsworth drew on eighteenth-century authorities – Hugh Blair's *Lectures on Rhetoric and Belles Lettres* (1783);[22] Joanna Baillie's 'Introductory Discourse' to her *Series of Plays* (1798);[23] William Enfield's 'Is Verse Essential to Poetry?' in the *Monthly Magazine* (1796); John Dennis's theory of the passions;[24] and Erasmus Darwin's *The Loves of the Plants* (1789) – not to mention Quintilian and Aristotle.[25] To take two representative examples: Wordsworth's celebrated attack on 'what is usually called poetic diction'[26] depends in part on Enfield, who noted the impropriety of 'the artificial diction of modern poetry'.[27] And when Wordsworth recommended 'the essential passions of the heart' as the fittest subject for poetry,[28] he had in mind Blair's praise of 'language of passion'.[29]

If we are to believe the Preface was 'the great manifesto of the Romantic revolution in England', we must force-feed ourselves the idea Wordsworth spoke not just for himself but for everyone else we nominate revolutionary – writers such as Keats (who in 1800 was 5 years old),[30] Shelley (8), Byron (12), Felicia Dorothea Hemans (7), Letitia Landon (not born until 1802), and perhaps even Elizabeth Barrett (not born until 1806). Were that granted, we would have to assume first that they understood it, and then that they agreed with it – not the firmest of foundations on which to build. One need not look far for evidence undermining the view that Wordsworth spoke on others' behalf. Like its author, the Preface was full of moody singularity, disinclined to ingratiate itself with anyone, far less make friends. So it didn't.[31] Blake objected angrily to Wordsworth's 1815 Preface and is likely to have been equally unresponsive to that of 1800,[32] while Byron had the Preface in mind when expressing revulsion at Wordsworth being thought 'at the head of his own *profession*, in the *eyes* of *those* who followed it', because 'his principles [had] turned as perverted as his *soi-disant* poetry'. He was thinking of Wordsworth's critique of Augustan style; as he remarked elsewhere, 'This comes of Southey and Turdsworth and such renegado rascals with their systems.'[33] (The indignation comes not at the beginning, nor at the middle, but at the end of that sentence, with its final, hissed sibilants.)

Byron cast Wordsworth and Southey as partners in crime because he embraced the overwrought denunciations of Francis Jeffrey, originator of the myth of the Preface as manifesto. In October 1802 Jeffrey nominated Coleridge, Southey, and Wordsworth as 'the Lake School' and condemned the Preface as 'a kind of manifesto, that preceded one of their most flagrant acts of hostility'.[34] Like most acts of critical taxonomy, this was roughsawn, crudely utilitarian, and misleading.[35] Those concerned were quick to recognize the injustice; as Southey observed, 'it is odd enough that my fellow-conspirator, Wordsworth, should be almost a stranger to me, – a man with whom I have scarcely had any intercourse, not even of common acquaintanceship'.[36] Jeffrey's coinage might best be considered a metaphor by which Wordsworth was head of a gang of three whose half-baked views on diction were alleged to reveal a 'perverted taste for simplicity'.[37] The real bone of contention was politics. Jeffrey's reading of 'The Convict' and 'The Female Vagrant' alongside the Preface's championing of the language of rustics led him to consider Wordsworth a Jacobinical hothead: 'A splenetic and idle discontent with the existing institutions of society, seems to be at the bottom of all their serious and peculiar sentiments .... For all sorts of vice and profligacy in the lower orders of society, they have the same virtuous horror, and the same tender compassion.'[38] From the outset, the myth tarred and feathered Wordsworth as dangerously subversive so as to discourage imitators; its alarmist posture offers modern readers a sound reason for rejecting it.

When Jeffrey used the term 'manifesto' he invoked it hyperbolically – puffing up the Preface so as to maximize its deflation. But Wordsworth never meant to articulate the vision of a school, was not attempting to be 'revolutionary', and had no suspicion he was defining Romanticism (whatever that feathered, four-legged thing might be). He wanted to elucidate some of the ideas that informed *Lyrical Ballads*. Those who persist in labelling the Preface a manifesto attribute to its author and his silent collaborator, Coleridge, a foreknowledge and presumption of which they were innocent, and forsake a truthful rendering of the past for one that is false and crudely dramatized.

Notes

1 As W. J. B. Owen points out, 'The main object of the Preface of 1800 is to define and defend a particular rhetoric: to assert the poetic value of "a selection of the real language of men in a state of vivid sensation" and of "the language of prose"'; see *Wordsworth as Critic* (Toronto: University of Toronto Press, 1969), p. 3.

2 S. T. Coleridge to Daniel Stuart, 30 September 1800, in *Collected Letters of Samuel Taylor Coleridge*, ed. Earl Leslie Griggs (6 vols., Oxford: Clarendon Press, 1956–71), i. 627.

3 For Coleridge's presence in Grasmere on 26 September 1800 see Mark L. Reed, *Wordsworth: The Chronology of the Middle Years, 1800–1815* (Cambridge, MA: Harvard University Press, 1975), p. 87. According to Reed, the Preface was 'basically composed' by 27 September 1800 (p. 19).

4 Introduction to the Preface to *Lyrical Ballads*; *The Prose Works of William Wordsworth*, ed. W. J. B. Owen and Jane Worthington Smyser (3 vols., Oxford: Clarendon Press, 1974), i. 112.

5 S. T. Coleridge to William Sotheby, 13 July 1802, in *Collected Letters of Samuel Taylor Coleridge*, ed. Griggs, ii. 811.

6 S. T. Coleridge to Robert Southey, 29 July 1802, ibid., ii. 830. Max F. Schultz suggests what some of these ideas might have been in 'Coleridge, Wordsworth, and the 1800 Preface to Lyrical Ballads', *Studies in English Literature, 1500–1900* 5 (1965), 619–39, pp. 624–5.

7 See *The Prose Works of William Wordsworth*, ed. Owen and Smyser, i. 113, 167.

8 See *The Notebooks of Samuel Taylor Coleridge*, vol. i, ed. Kathleen Coburn (New York: Pantheon Books, 1957), entry 787 and note.

9 *Barron Field's Memoirs of Wordsworth*, ed. Geoffrey Little (Sydney: Sydney University Press, 1975), p. 62.

10 *The Notebooks of Samuel Taylor Coleridge*, ed. Coburn, entry 803. The entry is dated to early September 1800, at the time the Preface was being discussed.

11 William Wordsworth to John Abraham Heraud, 23 November 1830, in *The Letters of William and Dorothy Wordsworth*, v, *The Later Years, Part 2: 1829–1834*, ed. Ernest de Selincourt, rev. Alan G. Hill (2nd ed., Oxford: Clarendon Press, 1979), p. 352.

12 Mark L. Reed, 'Wordsworth, Coleridge, and the "Plan" of the *Lyrical Ballads*', *University of Toronto Quarterly* 34 (1965), 238–53, p. 250.

13 Jonathan Wordsworth provides a cogent scholarly analysis of 'The Recluse' in the epilogue to *William Wordsworth: The Borders of Vision* (Oxford:

Clarendon Press, 1982). Michael Gamer suggests Wordsworth's criticism of the Gothic was largely instigated by Coleridge; see *Romanticism and the Gothic: Genre, Reception, and Canon Formation* (Cambridge: Cambridge University Press, 2000), pp. 98–107.

14 S. T. Coleridge to R. H. Brabant, 29 July 1815, in *Collected Letters of Samuel Taylor Coleridge*, ed. Griggs, iv. 579.

15 Owen, *Wordsworth as Critic*, pp. 14, 15, 23, 25, 36, 56, 116.

16 See, for instance, John R. Nabholtz, 'My Reader, My Fellow-Labourer': A Study of English Romantic Prose (Columbia: University of Missouri Press, 1986), pp. 68–72, and Anuradha Dingwaney and Lawrence Needham, '(Un)Creating Taste: Wordsworth's Platonic Defense in the Preface to *Lyrical Ballads*', *Rhetoric Society Quarterly* 19 (1989), 333–47.

17 S. T. Coleridge to Humphry Davy, 9 October 1800, in *Collected Letters of Samuel Taylor Coleridge*, ed. Griggs, i. 632.

18 S. T. Coleridge to Robert Southey, 29 July 1802, ibid., ii. 830. Stephen Maxfield Parrish suggests some of these differences related to Wordsworth's comments on metre; see *The Art of the Lyrical Ballads* (Cambridge, MA: Harvard University Press, 1973), pp. 22–3.

19 Samuel Taylor Coleridge, *Biographia Literaria*, ed. James Engell and Walter Jackson Bate (2 vols., Princeton, NJ: Princeton University Press, 1983), ii. 9.

20 Judith Thompson suggests one possible influence is that of John Thelwall; see *John Thelwall in the Wordsworth Circle: The Silenced Partner* (Houndmills, Basingstoke: Palgrave Macmillan, 2012), pp. 174–6.

21 *The Prose Works of William Wordsworth*, ed. Owen and Smyser, i. 112.

22 Owen did not find any specific debt to Blair in the Preface, but the more general similarities are documented by M. H. Abrams, *The Mirror and the Lamp: Romantic Theory and the Critical Tradition* (New York: Oxford University Press, 1953), pp. 95–7.

23 See, *inter alia*, Mary F. Yudin, 'Joanna Baillie's Introductory Discourse as a Precursor to Wordsworth's Preface to *Lyrical Ballads*', *Compar(a)ison* 1 (1994), 101–11, and William D. Brewer, 'The Prefaces of Joanna Baillie and William Wordsworth', *The Friend: Comment on Romanticism* 1 (1991–2), 34–47.

24 See Owen, *Wordsworth as Critic*, p. 36.

25 See Duncan Wu, *Wordsworth's Reading 1770–1799* (Cambridge: Cambridge University Press, 1993), pp. 8–9, 44, 181–2; *Wordsworth's Reading 1800–1815* (Cambridge: Cambridge University Press, 1995), pp. 24, 70, 85. W. J. B. Owen discusses Enfield and Darwin in his introduction to his edition of the Preface; see *Wordsworth's Preface to Lyrical Ballads*, ed. W. J. B. Owen (Copenhagen: Rosenkilde & Bagger, 1957), pp. 23–5. William Keach has also proposed the influence of Herder and Sulzer, though I know of no evidence Wordsworth read either author; see 'Poetry, after 1740', in *The Cambridge History of Literary Criticism*, vol. iv, *The Eighteenth Century*, ed. H. B. Nisbet and Claude Rawson (Cambridge: Cambridge University Press, 1997), pp. 117–66.

26 'The Preface to *Lyrical Ballads* (1800)', in *The Prose Works of William Wordsworth*, ed. Owen and Smyser, i. 130.

27 Ibid., p. 173.

28 Ibid., p. 124.

29 Hugh Blair, *A Critical Dissertation on the Poems of Ossian* (London, 1763), p. 65. See Abrams, *The Mirror and the Lamp*, pp. 95–7.

30 At the same time it should be noted some critics have detected the influence of Wordsworth's Preface on Keatsian poetics; see Beth Lau, *Keats's Reading of the Romantic Poets* (Ann Arbor: University of Michigan Press, 1991), p. 36.

31 Having said which, it was cherished by Hazlitt, who cites it in his first book, his *Essay on the Principles of Human Action*; see *Selected Writings of William Hazlitt*, ed. Duncan Wu (9 vols., London: Pickering & Chatto, 1998), i. 41.

32 *The Complete Poetry and Prose of William Blake*, ed. David V. Erdman (New York: Doubleday, 1988), pp. 665–6.

33 Lord Byron to Thomas Moore, 1 June 1818, in *Byron's Letters and Journals*, ed. Leslie A. Marchand (13 vols., London: John Murray, 1973–94), vi. 47, and Byron to Francis Hodgson, 22 October 1820, ibid., vii. 253.

34 Francis Jeffrey, review of Southey's *Thalaba*, in *Edinburgh Review* 1 (October 1802), 63–83, p. 65.

35 Hazlitt never forgave Jeffrey for failing to recognize the genius of the *Lyrical Ballads*; see his essay in *The Spirit of the Age*, in *Selected Writings of William Hazlitt*, ed. Wu, vii. 194.

36 *A Memoir of the Life and Writings of William Taylor of Norwich*, ed. J. W. Robberds (2 vols., London: John Murray, 1843), i. 440.

37 Jeffrey, review of Southey's *Thalaba*, p. 68.

38 Ibid., p. 71.

Myth

11

WORDSWORTH HAD AN INCESTUOUS RELATIONSHIP WITH HIS SISTER

Behind this myth lies the suspicion incest might be a lifestyle choice, like smoking grass or riding a Harley, the pastimes of the leisured class we know poets to be. And it is not just Wordsworth; Austen and Byron seem to have followed (Myths 14 and 16). Once they have joined the party, hardly anyone seems untouched by it.

> Brother-sister incest is a major theme in English Romantic and Victorian literature and on into early modernism. Unlike parent-child incest, usually regarded with horror, brother-sister incest is tolerated, even covertly admired, by many of the great romantics and their successors, some of whom had relationships with their siblings that were at least on the subconscious level incestuous.[1]

'Who?', one wants to ask. Who are these 'many' Romantics who 'admired' sibling incest and even committed it, albeit in the privacy of their own subconscious? The question deliquesces into meaninglessness: how can someone have a sexual relationship with their sibling (or, indeed, anyone at all) *in their subconscious*? But that is the point. The subconscious contains no visitor books, logs, or calling cards: it is an untouchable realm beyond the reach of sense – doubly so, in the case of the deceased. And therein lies its value. Any critic who refers us to the subconscious arrogates to himself the powers of psychic and psychiatrist – which is as good as no argument at all, being resistant to confirmation

30 Great Myths About the Romantics, First Edition. Duncan Wu.
© 2015 John Wiley & Sons, Ltd. Published 2015 by John Wiley & Sons, Ltd.

even were the author resurrected from the dead and given the third degree, for who can claim to be privy to their subconscious? It is speculation about speculation.

In this case, speculator-in-chief was Oxford don F. W. Bateson, who in *Wordsworth: A Re-Interpretation* (1956) posited incestuous feeling between the poet and his sister for which he claimed marriage to Mary Hutchinson was a 'cure'. Bateson was careful to insist this was not consciously acknowledged by any of them:

> To say that the relationship between William and Dorothy changed in the course of this year from that of brother and sister to that of lovers is to invite misapprehension. There was no physical basis to this love-affair and for some time they were neither of them conscious of its quasi-sexual character, but it is no accident that 'Tintern Abbey' ends with the famous tribute to Dorothy Wordsworth.

'but it is no accident...': meaning what? That the conclusion of Wordsworth's poem proves he wanted to have sex with his sister, though he never did? Balancing one insinuation precariously on another, Bateson added a footnote in which he said that in 1938 L. A. Willoughby discussed 'the lover-like terms on which [Dorothy] stood with her brother', and that two 'crucial' pages torn from her Grasmere journals 'seem to me to clinch the matter'.[2] In other words, the sole piece of scholarly evidence Bateson brought to the argument (other than the conclusion of 'Tintern Abbey') is two manuscript pages the contents of which are unknown. One can only marvel at the rapidity with which this banquet of innuendo congealed as ersatz fact; in 1967 another critic, Geoffrey Yarlott, concluded Bateson said Wordsworth had 'a love-relationship with Dorothy'[3] when he had said no such thing; in fact he denied it.

In the course of a critical essay in 1978, Donald H. Reiman pursued an argument similar to Bateson's, saying Wordsworth had to remind himself '(probably subconsciously) that Dorothy was unacceptable as the object of a romantic or sexual attachment'. By what mental contortion, one wonders, is it possible for anyone to remind their subconscious self of anything? But then, why bother with logic when arguing something so far beyond proof? Such terms as 'probably' are defensive postures in the face of mounting improbability. The Lucy poems were inspired by a dream of Dorothy's death, wrote Reiman, their origins 'in William's subconscious struggle to avoid focusing his obviously strong sexual drive on the sister he lived with for seven years'.[4] He declined to reveal how he assessed the libido of a man who had died more than a century before.

The first responsibility of any biographer is to the truth, yet the dime-store psychology sketched by Bateson has been a constant lure, perhaps because incest makes for a colourful story. In *The Hidden Wordsworth: Poet, Lover, Rebel, Spy* (1998), Kenneth R. Johnston weighed the matter hesitantly: 'While it is hard to conceive of a physically incestuous relation between William and Dorothy Wordsworth, it is equally hard to believe that the possibility was not often on their minds, whether as a temptation or a threat, at critical times like the Goslar months.'[5] To which the obvious response is, 'Why?' Who says the possibility was 'often' on their minds? And had it been, how would Johnston know about it? But that hardly matters. He is constructing a drama in which the poet sensed a 'possibility' he sought later to prevent: 'the depths of Dorothy's passions were revealed in Germany, and they both realized the need for him to attach his sexual passions elsewhere'.[6] This is stated as fact, yet if you consult Mark L. Reed's *Chronology of the Early Years, 1770–1799* (1967) you will find nothing to corroborate it. At least Johnston does not claim the entire thing took place in anyone's subconscious.

Those who study the incarnations of this myth quickly come to realize how readily the literary scholar adopts the robe of clinical diagnostician. Molly Lefebure worked as a pathologist before she wrote about Wordsworth and his sister, and her tendency is to perceive them as ailments on legs. Her reading of the Grasmere journal leads her to say that 'the picture that emerges … is one of a woman deeply in love with a man who reciprocates her love to the full, but is forced to marry another. The struggle of the lovers to accept this harsh fate and the tensions arising from their struggle (tensions intensified by the fact that the frustrated pair live intimately together) result in constant physical distress, severe headaches, nausea and insomnia.'[7] Readers might be forgiven for not realizing how conjectural is Lefebure's connection between illness and the purported relationship. It sounds as if she is giving a considered medical opinion, but on what basis? Not an encounter with the 'patients' or their medical records, which do not exist.

Anyone touting a thesis so prone to inward collapse might be expected to show respect for alternative views, but Lefebure pooh-poohs incest-deniers before insisting: 'every fact we know about [the Wordsworths] indicates an incestuous relationship; indeed, there is more hard factual evidence to support the allegations of such a relationship than can possibly be brought forward to refute it'.[8] Her case is more dependent on bluster than on 'hard factual evidence'. 'Incestuous relationships are of far greater occurrence, in all walks of life, than is usually assumed',[9] she says. Even were that true,[10] there are no data to support the notion incest occurred 'in all walks of life' during the Romantic period. And if there were, and they bore out what she alleges, that would prove nothing in relation to the Wordsworths.

Kathleen Jones argues in favour of incest on grounds borrowed from Lefebure in *A Passionate Sisterhood* (2000), with the difference that she offers indecisiveness masquerading as trenchancy. She begins by saying it is 'indisputable' Dorothy loved her brother, then says 'Dorothy and William were *not* physical lovers' (my emphasis), adding it is unlikely they had intercourse because of the risk of pregnancy (a point missed by male critics and biographers), before concluding: 'all this does not preclude the possibility that there may have been physical lovemaking between them, stopping short of actual intercourse'.[11] In other words, the very thing she uses to argue *against* a sexual relationship is invoked to suggest one took place.

In *Thicker Than Water* (2011), Leonore Davidoff studies sibling relationships between 1780 and 1920, adopting the Wordsworths as a case study. She has at her fingertips the information necessary to make a judgement but prefers to retreat from that duty, instead citing Kathleen Jones's observation that 'the nature of their passion for each other is a nettle left ungrasped by most ... biographers'.[12] As arguments go, it is not one of Jones's more persuasive given the throng of those who have not only plucked the nettle but clutched it to their bosom as if their credibility depended on it (including several omitted here for lack of space). Such is the consensus, it has become unfashionable – even shameful – to dispute it.

Yet there are dissenters including G. Kim Blank,[13] Juliet Barker,[14] and Frances Wilson, who writes: 'The relationship between the Wordsworths was organized around a notion of perfect and exclusive brother-sister love which was imaginatively assimilated by them both to the point where it became the source of their creative energy, but its physical expression would have been of no interest to them.'[15] The sentence is so understated you might almost miss its plain-spoken common sense. Wilson explains the endearments in Dorothy's journals, placing them in a context that need not entail incest. John Worthen admits the relationship was 'physically intimate' though 'there was nothing sexual about it'.[16]

> In the first place, nearly all the evidence of the details of the relationship come from Dorothy's own journal, where – all unconsciously – she provided language and behavior which a post-Freudian age finds sexual ... If, however, she had been attempting to conceal the nature of her relationship (for incest, ma'am, is a crime), she would have been a good deal more careful. It is precisely because she was *not* trying to conceal it that the 'evidence' stands out.[17]

What do we know about incest today? For one thing, it is not confined to the subconscious. Psychologists who study women in such relationships find them prone to depression and poor self-esteem like other victims of physical abuse.[18] Rape is often an aggravating factor and, where an older brother is the aggressor, he usually follows the example of an abusive father.[19] Victims suffer long-term psychological effects including shame, high levels of anxiety, depression, sleep disturbance, and sexual problems.[20] Sibling incest 'can have devastating psychological effects on survivors, whether the perpetrator of the abuse was an adult or a sibling'.[21] In short, brother–sister incest is a form of family violence highly abusive in nature.

Incest advocates should reflect on whether this shambling, self-serving conceit is worth the steroids they pump into it. If it is, they should be prepared to profile Wordsworth as potential sexual predator and his sister as victim – something no one has so far contemplated. In fact, none of those who cry incest cite any of the clinical studies. But then, were they to read them, they would be dismayed to find that nothing any clinical researcher has to say about sibling incest in the real world squares with evidence concerning the Wordsworths.

Advocates argue Wordsworth's union with Mary Hutchinson was strategic – a way of preventing incest from occurring – which obliges them to denigrate the marriage. Bateson says Mary Hutchinson was 'a kindly, sensible, ordinary woman, with a "delicate feeling for propriety"' and a habit 'of unembarrassed, unembarrassing silence';[22] in short, an all-round embarrassment, dull and stupid, someone in whom Wordsworth had no genuine interest. 'There had been some sort of a flirtation with Mary in Wordsworth's undergraduate days', sneers Bateson,[23] as if to imply the poet had been distracted from the more appetizing alternative of Dorothy.

Bateson's commentary falsifies everything it touches. William and Mary had known each other since attending dame school at Penrith, where both families had roots;[24] both were orphaned at an early age and sent to live with relatives. Far from being what Bateson condescendingly describes, Mary possessed what one scholar calls 'a similar intellectual calibre [to Wordsworth in which] lay the real source of their congeniality'.[25] Henry Crabb Robinson acknowledged the superiority of her diary to his own: 'She saw so much more than I did, though we were side by side during a great part of the time.'[26] She is an influence throughout the poetry – author of two of the most memorable lines in the canon;[27] inspiration for 'She was a phantom of delight'; and probable subject of two love poems written when Wordsworth was 16 ('Anacreon Imitated' and 'Beauty and Moonlight'). Far from being a convenience, the marriage was happy and the couple well matched: a decade into it Wordsworth wrote to Mary from London,

> How I long ... to be with thee; every hour of absence now is a grievous loss, because we have been parted sufficiently to feel how profoundly in soul and body we love each other; and to be taught what a sublime treasure we possess in each others love. ... Oh my beloved – but I ought not to trust myself to this senseless and visible sheet of paper; speak for me to thyself, find the evidence of what is passing within me in *thy* heart, in thy mind, in thy steps as they touch the green grass, in thy limbs as they are stretched upon the soft earth; in thy own involuntary sighs and ejaculations, in the trembling of thy hands, in the tottering of thy knees, in the blessings which thy lips pronounce, find it in thy lips themselves, and such kisses as I often give to the empty air, and in the aching of thy bosom, and let a voice speak for me in every thing within thee and without thee.[28]

Incest advocates would read this as the utterance of someone whose deepest wish was to bed his own sister. Wordsworth's love letters to his wife have, in the words of their editor, 'revolutionized the commonly-held view of the poet's marriage and the dynamics of the Wordsworth family circle'.[29] Despite being available to most of those mentioned above (with the exception of Bateson and Reiman[30]), they are studiously disregarded because they lend the incest theory no support. Yet the evidence is clear: Dorothy's journal and correspondence suggest a comfortable relationship in which both siblings felt relaxed about saying whatever they wanted,[31] distinct in kind and degree from the impassioned devotion expressed by Wordsworth to his wife.

Dorothy and William's decision to live together in the mid-1790s was not incestuous. At a time when women were not permitted to pursue a career, brothers had little choice but to take care of sisters – there are many examples of adult siblings living under the same roof throughout the nineteenth century on both sides of the Atlantic. Charles Lamb lived all his life with his sister Mary, who was also his writing partner, yet no one suggests they had an affair. As Barker observes, 'before we were taught to see through Freud's distorting lens, such relationships were not only commonplace but also held up for admiration'.[32]

Notes

1 Frederick Turner, *Epic: Form, Content and History* (New Brunswick, NJ: Transaction, 2012), p. 140.
2 F. W. Bateson, *Wordsworth: A Re-Interpretation* (2nd ed., Harlow: Longman, 1956), p. 143.

3 Geoffrey Yarlott, *Coleridge and the Abyssinian Maid* (London: Methuen, 1967), p. 237.

4 Donald H. Reiman, 'The Poetry of Familiarity: Wordsworth, Dorothy, and Mary Hutchinson', in *The Evidence of the Imagination: Studies of Interactions between Life and Art in English Romantic Literature*, ed. Donald H. Reiman, Michael C. Jaye, and Betty T. Bennett (New York: New York University Press, 1978), pp. 142–77, 158.

5 Kenneth R. Johnston, *The Hidden Wordsworth: Poet, Lover, Rebel, Spy* (New York: W. W. Norton, 1998), p. 635.

6 Ibid., p. 716. Johnston clarifies his intended meanings in 'A Tale of Two Titles', in *Romantic Biography*, ed. Arthur Bradley and Alan Rawes (Aldershot, Hants.: Ashgate, 2003), pp. 48–57, esp. p. 52.

7 Molly Lefebure, *Samuel Taylor Coleridge: A Bondage of Opium* (London: Quartet, 1974), p. 352.

8 Ibid., p. 278.

9 Ibid.

10 *The Encyclopedia of Relationships Across the Lifespan* (1996) points out that 'sibling incest is … believed to be widespread, but it is rarely reported. The most prevalent sibling incest pattern appears to be the abuse of younger sisters and brothers by an older male sibling' (Jeffrey S. Turner, *Encyclopedia of Relationships Across the Lifespan* (Westport, CT: Greenwood Press, 1996), p. 92). However, this does not support Lefebure's point, which is that incest is more widespread 'in all walks of life' – that is to say, in all social classes – than is currently thought.

11 Kathleen Jones, *A Passionate Sisterhood: The Sisters, Wives and Daughters of the Lake Poets* (New York: St Martin's Press, 2000), p. 101.

12 Leonore Davidoff, *Thicker Than Water: Siblings and Their Relations, 1780–1920* (Oxford: Oxford University Press, 2011), pp. 214–15. Davidoff's quotation is from Jones, *A Passionate Sisterhood*, p. 101.

13 G. Kim Blank, *Wordsworth and Feeling: The Poetry of an Adult Child* (Rutherford, NJ: Farleigh Dickinson University Press, 1995), p. 71.

14 Juliet Barker, *Wordsworth: A Life* (London: Viking, 2000), pp. 231–2.

15 Frances Wilson, *The Ballad of Dorothy Wordsworth* (London: Faber & Faber, 2008), p. 146.

16 John Worthen, *The Gang: Coleridge, the Hutchinsons and the Wordsworths in 1802* (New Haven: Yale University Press, 2001), p. 50.

17 Ibid.

18 Richard Green, *Sexual Science and the Law* (Cambridge, MA: Harvard University Press, 1992), p. 131.

19 Sam Kirschner, Diana Adile Kirschner, and Richard L. Rappaport, *Working with Adult Incest Survivors: The Healing Journey* (New York: Brunner/Mazel, 1993), pp. 46–7.

20 See, for instance, Thomas Michael McGrath, 'The Long-Term Psychological Effects for Survivors of Sibling Incest and Their Capacities to Have Adult Relationships That Are Intimate and Autonomous' (Ph.D. thesis, Seton Hall University, 2008).

21 Vernon R. Wiehe, *Sibling Abuse: Hidden Physical, Emotional and Sexual Trauma* (2nd ed., Thousand Oaks, CA: Sage, 1997), p. 133.

22 Bateson, *Wordsworth: A Re-Interpretation*, p. 155.

23 Ibid.

24 For more details concerning Dame Birkett's school, see Mary Moorman, *William Wordsworth: A Biography. The Early Years 1770–1803* (Oxford: Clarendon Press, 1957), p. 15.

25 'Introduction', in *The Letters of Mary Wordsworth 1800–1855*, ed. Mary E. Burton (Oxford: Clarendon Press, 1958), p. xviii.

26 As quoted by Burton, ibid., p. xvii.

27 'They flash upon that inward eye / Which is the bliss of solitude' ('I wandered lonely as a cloud', ll. 21–2).

28 William Wordsworth to Mary Wordsworth, 3–4 June 1812, in *The Letters of William and Dorothy Wordsworth*, viii, *A Supplement of New Letters*, ed. Alan G. Hill (Oxford: Clarendon Press, 1993), pp. 109–10.

29 Preface, ibid., p. v.

30 They did not appear in the standard edition of Wordsworth's correspondence until 1993.

31 When critics and biographers argue Wordsworth and Dorothy had a 'subconscious' love affair, they usually refer to the journal entries in which Dorothy speaks of her brother as 'beloved' and avoid those more routine letters such as that in which Dorothy complains of 'a pain in my bowels' (Dorothy Wordsworth to William Wordsworth, 19 August 1810, in *The Letters of William and Dorothy Wordsworth*, viii, *A Supplement of New Letters*, ed. Hill, p. 39).

32 Barker, *Wordsworth: A Life*, p. 232.

Myth 12 TORY WORDSWORTH

The myth is anachronistic, Toryism having a different meaning today than it did in 1840. It does not mean Wordsworth would have opposed membership of the EU or despised the welfare state; it would be closer to the mark to note Hazlitt never forgave him for commemorating the end of the war with France with a Thanksgiving Ode that declared carnage the daughter of God[1] – lines I have no wish to defend. And who does not join with Keats in lamenting Wordsworth's support of the campaign of Tory placeman, Lord Lowther: 'Sad – sad – sad'?[2] The problem is that unglossed references to conservatism give the impression Wordsworth betrayed his earlier beliefs wholesale and adopted views we might identify with present-day Tories. This essay suggests such terms are too crude to describe Wordsworth's complex views. (I have nothing to say about the decades-old canard that Wordsworth was always a Tory, demolished years ago by others at greater length than is possible here.[3])

If Wordsworth was a regicide who turned 'Tory at / Last',[4] it would be as well to understand what was meant by the term, British Toryism then being as varied as now.[5] Which is to say, we should be able to distinguish his views from those of Southey, who thought pauperism the result of 'misconduct' and attributed the situation in Ireland to the 'almost irreclaimable barbarity of its population', most of whom deserved to be shipped to the colonies,[6] and those of De Quincey, who opposed missionary expeditions to China on the grounds that the natives were 'so unspiritual', and blamed the Indian Mutiny on 'infatuated savages' (the sepoys).[7]

Wordsworth's conservatism might be defined by his response to the Reform Act of 1832. He was not alone in opposing it: the young

30 Great Myths About the Romantics, First Edition. Duncan Wu.
© 2015 John Wiley & Sons, Ltd. Published 2015 by John Wiley & Sons, Ltd.

William Ewart Gladstone who, twenty years later, was responsible for the third Reform Act of the century, was also a dissenter, and for similar reasons. Both Wordsworth, who witnessed the French Revolution, and Gladstone, who only read about it, feared reform might precipitate social breakdown. This was not unreasonable, but it was conservative: both men recalled Burke's *Reflections on the Revolution in France* when putting their case.[8]

Wordsworth said he objected to 'all *hot* Reformations; i.e. to every sudden change in political institutions upon a large scale'.[9] The Reform Act made too great a concession to 'the most selfish, perhaps, and ignorant class of the community'[10] – that is to say, the 'ten pound Raters or Renters' (what we would call the lower middle class) who it made the largest category of voter.[11] Wordsworth feared it might precipitate universal suffrage, which he saw as a betrayal of the sacred, time-honoured system whereby a benevolent aristocracy controlled the body politic.

The existing system provided a legislature dominated by men of property, education, and pedigree, something in which Wordsworth believed:

> The Constitution of England which seems about to be destroyed, offers to my mind the sublimest contemplation which the History of Society and Govern[t] have ever presented to it; and for this cause especially, that its principles have the character of preconceived ideas, archetypes of the pure intellect, while they are in fact the results of a humble-minded experience.[12]

This 'humble-minded experience' was based on a conviction in the 'spiritual community binding together the living and the dead; the good, the brave, and the wise, of all ages',[13] recalling Burke, who insisted that 'Society is, indeed, a contract …. it becomes a partnership not only between those who are living, but between those who are living, those who are dead, and those who are to be born.'[14] This is a clear example of an opinion Wordsworth changed, for in his republican *Letter to the Bishop of Llandaff* (written 1793) he ridiculed it.[15]

Wordsworth's anxiety at the revival of revolutionary forces is glimpsed in his remarks to Lord John Russell when they met in London in 1831. Wordsworth told him 'the middle and lower classes were naturally envious haters of the Aristocracy' and that Russell was in danger of giving them the power to 'pull you down – that power, all at once, are you now giving them through your ten pound renters who to effect their purpose will soon call in the aid of others below them till you have the blessing of universal suffrage'.[16] He was not alone: even framers of the Bill spoke against universal suffrage, Lord Grey ruling out even manhood suffrage.[17]

Wordsworth's position, and his philosophy, may on that occasion have been conservative, but how conservative was he in arguing reform be implemented on a limited scale as an experiment?

> If it could have been shewn of such or such a Borough that it claimed the right to send Members to Parliament, upon usurpation, or that it had made a grossly corrupt use of a legal privilege – in both these cases I would dis-franchise – and also with the consent of the owners of burgage Tenure, but beyond this I would not have gone a step. As to transferring the right of voting to large Towns; my conviction is that they will be little the better for it – if at all – but een let them have their humour in certain cases and try the result.[18]

His response when the Bill passed traces his anxieties to their source: 'I have witnessed one revolution in a foreign Country, and I have not courage to think of facing another in my own.'[19] When Wordsworth's political apostasy comes under discussion, he is often portrayed as hav-ing changed completely in middle age, denying everything he witnessed in France. Such assumptions do scant justice to the truth. Wordsworth was not alone in fearing revolution in the early 1830s. The French Revolution of July 1830 had driven Charles X into exile, replacing him with Louis Philippe, who promptly doubled the number of voters, a measure which had the effect both of prompting reform in Britain and deepening con-servative opposition to it. Wordsworth was among those with first-hand experience of the earlier revolution and its impact on the poor, and to that extent he was innocent of inconsistency. It would be difficult to sus-tain the view he was arguing from prejudice: 'In my Youth I witnessed in France the calamities brought upon all classes, and especially the poor, by a Revolution, so that my heart aches at the thought of what we are now threatened with.'[20]

Wordsworth's opposition to the Catholic Relief Bill of 1829 also depended on a belief that tried and tested experience was superior to the unknown. 'Are not the same Arguments that induced our Forefathers to withdraw from the Roman faith 300 years ago still applicable?', he asked.[21] His principal anxiety was that if Catholics were allowed to vote, sit in Parliament, and hold civil office, they could precipitate disestablishment of the Church of England. It was a constitutional matter. Opposition to it sets Wordsworth to the right of such figures as the Home Secretary, Robert Peel, and his prime minister, the Duke of Wellington, both of whom look, from the perspective of the twenty-first century, conservative enough.[22]

A charge made of the later Wordsworth is that he betrayed principles held in youth, and the usual example of this is his stance during and after the French Revolution. But who among those that supported the revolution was unshaken by the rise of Robespierre? It was the first time anyone had seen revolution up close, with its potential for bloodshed and tyranny; in fact, Wordsworth was one of very few Englishmen who may have seen at first hand public executions in Paris, including that of Gorsas, the first Deputy to go to the scaffold.[23] It is not surprising that, having borne witness to the Terror, Wordsworth questioned the efficacy of revolution as a vehicle of change. None of which makes him conservative; in his own judgement he remained faithful to his ideals.

> If I were addressing those who have dealt so liberally with the words Renegado, Apostate etc, I should retort the charge upon them, and say, *you* have been deluded by Places and Persons, while I have stuck to Principles – I abandoned France, and her Rulers, when they abandoned the struggle for Liberty, gave themselves up to Tyranny, and endeavoured to enslave the world.[24]

His consistency is demonstrable on other counts. The best example is his response to the Poor Law Amendment Act of 1834, which saw vagrants as a 'moral plague' that should be locked in workhouses and chained to treadmills.[25] The Poor Law was met with widespread resistance,[26] and Wordsworth was in the vanguard of opposition. He rebutted the hatchet-faced utilitarianism by which it was underpinned as long before as 1797, in 'The Old Cumberland Beggar', and returned to the debate in 1835 with an essay arguing that '*all* persons who cannot find employment, or procure wages sufficient to support the body in health and strength, are entitled to a maintenance by law'.[27] That is to say, everyone has 'a right (not to be gainsaid by utilitarians and economists) to public support when, from any cause, they may be unable to support themselves'.[28] By this date, it is claimed, Wordsworth was a Tory, yet on this matter he fought alongside that wily old radical William Cobbett, who argued 'the poor had a universal legal right to relief'.[29] After the passing of the Poor Law, Cobbett called for armed insurrection; Wordsworth would never have gone along with that, but his stance exposed Whig conservatism for what it was.

There were two causes for which Wordsworth agitated vigorously during his final decade. The Copyright Act of 1814 limited copyright to a term of twenty-eight years or the remainder of the author's life if he or she outlived that term. As a result, there were many cases in which authors died while their books continued to sell, providing nothing for their bereaved families. In the interest not only of his own family but also those of others, Wordsworth campaigned for extension of copyright to sixty years.[30] He had argued for fairer compensation for authors since 1808 – so in this instance too his work was consistent with earlier beliefs; indeed, it proves he could remain true to his principles over decades. These struggles bore fruit: his contribution to the Copyright Act of 1842 has been described as 'enormous',[31] laying the foundation for laws which protect the rights of writers and musicians today.[32]

The second cause was the environment. When in 1844 it was proposed to build a railway from Oxenholme to Windermere, Wordsworth opposed it because it would change the countryside forever, not only by facilitating industrialization, but by attracting many thousands of tourists. It would be better, he argued, if 'artisans and labourers, and the humbler classes of shopkeepers' were to make 'little excursions with their wives and children among neighbouring fields'.[33] Although his tone towards working-class and lower-middle-class folk may carry a whiff of condescension, it is important to note, with Jonathan Bate, that 'it was to the *rash* assault that he objected'.[34] He wanted to protect the Lake District 'for the sake of every one, however humble his condition, who coming hither shall bring with him an eye to perceive, and a heart to feel and worthily enjoy'.[35] This was a conservationist stand; the septuagenarian Wordsworth was a pioneer ecologist.

An excellent way of inciting scholars to fisticuffs would be to ask them to date the inception of Wordsworth's conservatism; no two seem to agree. For instance, the *Encyclopedia of British Writers* says his poetic powers declined after 1807, at which point he 'became increasingly conservative',[36] while *The Romanticism Handbook* suggests he entered a period of 'introspective conservatism' after moving to Dove Cottage[37] – that is, from December 1799 onwards. If so, can someone please explain why Joseph Farington reported in his diary on 17 June 1806 that Wordsworth was 'strongly disposed towards Republicanism',[38] and three years later Sir George Beaumont noted the 'terrific democratic notions' that made him fearful of introducing Wordsworth into polite society?[39] That same year (1809) Wordsworth wrote a pamphlet deploring the Convention of Cintra, in support of Spanish and Portuguese freedom fighters and 'this new-born spirit of resistance, rising from the most sacred feelings of the human heart'.[40] As Deirdre Coleman observes, Wordsworth's hope was that, so long as 'the people held fast to their hard-won liberties, the "open field of a republic" remained a sublime possibility'.[41] None of which is self-evidently conservative.[42]

The myth of the youthful radical who turned in middle age has unstoppable momentum, perhaps because it allows us to drag the great writer down to our level, at least for a moment. It was the judgement of Browning, who met Wordsworth in 1835 –

> Just for a handful of silver he left us,
> Just for a riband to stick in his coat
>
> (Robert Browning, 'The Lost Leader', ll. 1–2)

– which takes its place among the countless opinions posing as fact. It may be that the taxonomizing of other people's politics is a job for the gambler rather than the brain surgeon. The assumption of inconsistency often follows in the wake of words like 'conservative' and 'Tory'. And everyone knows what conservatism meant in 1835, don't they? (Well, who was prime minister that year? Two correct answers: Sir Robert Peel up to 8 April, Lord Melbourne thereafter.)

Yes, Wordsworth backed Tory interests in 1818 – but, as Stephen Gill has shown, the Lowther campaign was not an act of political betrayal; it was contiguous with Wordsworth's long-standing desire 'to get the voters of Westmorland to see the "ancient frame of society" as a value to be transmitted, not something obsolete rudely to be swept away'.[43] It does not prove Wordsworth was anyone's stooge; in 1812 he told his wife, 'I have no confidence in any public man or set of men; I mean I have no confidence in their Knowledge and Talents',[44] and he was wont to pass similar comments throughout his life. If he really considered himself Tory, he had a strange way of showing it: at a period when commentators would have him a paid-up party member, he demurred at proposals curbing freedom of the press; resisted enclosure in Grasmere; protested 'the privations of the labouring poor'; and (as late as 1843) declared, 'as far as the people are capable of governing themselves I am a Democrat'.[45] There were numerous Whigs who regarded his views, on some issues, as extreme: he clashed with Lord John Russell over copyright and with Brougham over the Poor Law.[46] If 'Tory' is to be shorthand for Wordsworth's later thought, then let it be mitigated by definition – or better still, as Richard Gravil advises, it might be preferable 'to avoid such blanket terms as radical or conservative when discussing Romantic politics, and to focus on the content of belief'.[47]

Notes

1 See Wordsworth's *Ode. The Morning of the Day Appointed for a General Thanksgiving. January 18, 1816*, l. 282: 'Yea, Carnage is thy daughter!' See, *inter alia*, Uttara Natarajan, 'William Hazlitt', in *Great Shakespeareans: Lamb, Hazlitt, Keats* (London: Continuum, 2010), p. 87; and David Bromwich, *Hazlitt: The Mind of a Critic* (New York: Oxford University Press, 1983), p. 66.

2 John Keats to Tom Keats, 26 June 1818, in *The Letters of John Keats* ed. Hyder Edward Rollins (2 vols., Cambridge, MA: Harvard University Press, 1958), i. 299.

3 See, for example, Nicholas Roe, *The Politics of Nature: William Wordsworth and Some Contemporaries* (2nd ed., Houndmills, Basingstoke: Palgrave

Macmillan, 2002), introduction; and Thomas McFarland, *William Wordsworth: Intensity and Achievement* (Oxford: Clarendon Press, 1992), ch. 1, etc.

4 Byron, Dedication to *Don Juan*, ll. 3–4, which actually refers to Robert Southey.

5 Peter Viereck posited that Wordsworth wavered between 'ottantottist' and Burkean conservatism; see *Conservative Thinkers: From John Adams to Winston Churchill* (Brunswick, NJ: Transaction, 2006), pp. 33–4.

6 See W. A. Speck, *Robert Southey: Entire Man of Letters* (New Haven: Yale University Press, 2006), pp. 174, 129.

7 Robert Morrison, *The English Opium Eater: A Biography of Thomas De Quincey* (London: Weidenfeld & Nicolson, 2009), pp. 388–9.

8 For Gladstone's Burkean views, see Roland Quinault, 'Gladstone and Parliamentary Reform', in *Gladstone: Centenary Essays*, ed. David Bebbington and Roger Swift (Liverpool: Liverpool University Press, 2000), p. 78.

9 William Wordsworth to Benjamin Robert Haydon, 8 July 1831, in *The Letters of William and Dorothy Wordsworth*, v, *The Later Years, Part 2: 1829–1834*, ed. Ernest de Selincourt, rev. Alan G. Hill (2nd ed., Oxford: Clarendon Press, 1979), p. 408.

10 William Wordsworth to John Gardner, 27 December 1831, ibid., p. 470.

11 Wordsworth had known such a man: William Hazlitt, whose move to Westminster in the summer of 1813 may have been motivated by his desire to exercise the potwalloper's right to vote. See Duncan Wu, *William Hazlitt: The First Modern Man* (Oxford: Oxford University Press, 2008), p. 268.

12 William Wordsworth to W. R. Hamilton, 22 November 1831, in *The Letters of William and Dorothy Wordsworth*, v, *The Later Years, Part 2: 1829–1834*, ed. de Selincourt, p. 455.

13 *The Convention of Cintra*, in *The Prose Works of William Wordsworth*, ed. W. J. B. Owen and Jane Worthington Smyser (3 vols., Oxford: Clarendon Press, 1974), i. 339.

14 Edmund Burke, *Reflections on the Revolution in France*, ed. L. G. Mitchell (Oxford: Clarendon Press, 1993), p. 96.

15 See 'A Letter to the Bishop of Llandaff', in *The Prose Works of William Wordsworth*, ed. Owen and Smyser, i. 48. For further discussion, see James K. Chandler, *Wordsworth's Second Nature: A Study of the Poetry and Politics* (Chicago: University of Chicago Press, 1984), pp. 43–4.

16 William Wordsworth to Benjamin Robert Haydon, 8 July 1831, in *The Letters of William and Dorothy Wordsworth*, v, *The Later Years, Part 2: 1829–1834*, ed. de Selincourt, p. 408.

17 John Ashton Cannon, *Parliamentary Reform 1640–1832* (Cambridge: Cambridge University Press, 1972), p. 205

18 William Wordsworth to Benjamin Robert Haydon, 8 July 1831, in *The Letters of William and Dorothy Wordsworth*, v, *The Later Years, Part 2: 1829–1834*, ed. de Selincourt, p. 408.

19 William Wordsworth to Christopher Wordsworth, 1 April 1832, ibid., p. 517.

20 William Wordsworth to Eliza Hamilton, 10 January 1833, ibid., p. 581.

21 William Wordsworth to Sir Robert Inglis, 11 June 1825, in *The Letters of William and Dorothy Wordsworth*, iv, *The Later Years, Part 1: 1821–1828*, ed. Ernest de Selincourt, rev. Alan G. Hill (2nd ed., Oxford: Clarendon Press, 1978), p. 359.

22 There is some irony in the fact that Wordsworth was closely associated with the Oxford Movement, one of whose members published a pamphlet entitled *Contributions of William Wordsworth to the Revival of Catholic Truths* (1842). See, for further information, Stephen Gill, *Wordsworth and the Victorians* (Oxford: Clarendon Press, 1998), pp. 63ff.

23 Wordsworth's presence in France during the Terror continues to be the subject of debate, but is accepted as a possibility by Mary Moorman, *William Wordsworth: A Biography. The Early Years 1770–1803* (Oxford: Clarendon Press, 1957), p. 240; Stephen Gill, *William Wordsworth: A Life* (Oxford: Clarendon Press, 1989), p. 77; Roe, *The Politics of Nature*, pp. 146–58; and David Bromwich, *Disowned by Memory: Wordsworth's Poetry of the 1790s* (Chicago: University of Chicago Press, 1998), p. 13. It is questioned by Juliet Barker, *Wordsworth: A Life* (London: Viking, 2000), pp. 136–7.

24 William Wordsworth to James Losh, 4 December 1821, in *The Letters of William and Dorothy Wordsworth*, iv, *The Later Years, Part 1: 1821–1828*, ed. de Selincourt, p. 97.

25 David R. Green, *Pauper Capital: London and the Poor Law, 1790–1870* (Farnham, Surrey: Ashgate, 2010), p. 116; Felix Driver, *Power and Pauperism: The Workhouse System, 1834–1884* (Cambridge: Cambridge University Press, 1993), p. 18.

26 See Lynn Hollen Lees, *The Solidarities of Strangers: The English Poor Laws and the People, 1700–1948* (Cambridge: Cambridge University Press, 1998), pp. 164–5; Nicholas C. Edsall, *The Anti-Poor Law Movement* (Manchester: Manchester University Press, 1971); Driver, *Power and Pauperism*, ch. 7; Elaine Hadley, *Melodramatic Tactics: Theatricalized Dissent in the English Marketplace, 1800–1885* (Stanford, CA: Stanford University Press, 1995), ch. 3.

27 'Postscript, 1835', in *The Prose Works of William Wordsworth*, ed. Owen and Smyser, iii. 240. Fulford notes continuities in Wordsworth's thought; see Tim Fulford, *Landscape, Liberty and Authority: Poetry, Criticism and Politics from Thomson to Wordsworth* (Cambridge: Cambridge University Press, 1996), p. 160.

28 'Postscript, 1835', in *The Prose Works of William Wordsworth*, ed. Owen and Smyser, iii. 242.

29 James P. Huzel, *The Popularization of Malthus in Early Nineteenth-Century England: Martineau, Cobbett and the Pauper Press* (Aldershot, Hants.: Ashgate, 2006), p. 138.

30 The full story of this fight, and Wordsworth's part in it, has been told by Catherine Seville, *Literary Copyright Reform in Early Victorian England: The Framing of the 1842 Copyright Act* (Cambridge: Cambridge University Press, 1999).

31 Ibid., p. 175.

32 That case is made by Lee Marshall, *Bootlegging: Romanticism and Copyright in the Music Industry* (London: Sage, 2005).

33 'Kendal and Windermere Railway', in *The Prose Works of William Wordsworth*, ed. Owen and Smyser, iii. 344.

34 Jonathan Bate, *Romantic Ecology: Wordsworth and the Environmental Tradition* (London: Routledge, 1991), p. 50.

35 'Kendal and Windermere Railway', in *The Prose Works of William Wordsworth*, ed. Owen and Smyser, iii. 355.

36 *The Encyclopedia of British Writers: 19th and 20th Centuries*, ed. George Stade, Karen Karbiener, and Christine L. Krueger (New York: Book Builders, 2003), p. 364. The entry for Wordsworth describes *The Excursion* as 'primarily of interest today as autobiography'.

37 *The Romanticism Handbook*, ed. Sue Chaplin and Joel Faflak (London: Continuum, 2011), pp. 33, 37.

38 *The Diary of Joseph Farington*, ed. Kenneth Garlick, Angus Macintyre, and Kathryn Cave (17 vols., New Haven: Yale University Press, 1978–98), vii. 2785.

39 *The Autobiography of Benjamin Robert Haydon*, ed. Tom Taylor (Oxford: Oxford University Press, 1927), p. 126.

40 'The Convention of Cintra', in *The Prose Works of William Wordsworth*, ed. Owen and Smyser, i. 228. Richard Gravil offers a persuasive analysis of Wordsworth's politics in 1809 in *Wordsworth's Bardic Vocation, 1787–1842* (Houndmills, Basingstoke: Palgrave Macmillan, 2003), pp. 229–34. David Bromwich is among the distinguished critics to have conceded Wordsworth's continuing fidelity to democratic idealism a full decade after Napoleon's attack on the Swiss republic; see Bromwich, *Disowned by Memory*, p. 6.

41 Deirdre Coleman, 'Re-living Jacobinism: Wordsworth and the Convention of Cintra', *The Yearbook of English Studies* 19 ('The French Revolution in English Literature and Art' special number) (1989), 144–61, p. 161.

42 One of the more thoughtful such arguments is that by James K. Chandler, who proposes 1815 as a culminating year in Wordsworth's political development; see '"Wordsworth" after Waterloo', in *The Age of William Wordsworth: Critical Essays on the Romantic Tradition*, ed. Kenneth R. Johnston and Gene W. Ruoff (New Brunswick: Rutgers University Press, 1987), pp. 84–111.

43 No one has written more perceptively about this episode; see Stephen Gill, *Wordsworth's Revisitings* (Oxford: Oxford University Press, 2011), p. 114.

44 William Wordsworth to Mary Wordsworth, 23 May 1812, in *The Letters of William and Dorothy Wordsworth*, viii, *A Supplement of New Letters*, ed. Alan G. Hill (Oxford: Clarendon Press, 1993), p. 89.

45 See, *inter alia*, William Wordsworth to Viscount Lowther, mid-October 1819, and William Wordsworth to Lord Lonsdale, 6 December 1824, in *The Letters of William and Dorothy Wordsworth*, viii, *A Supplement of New Letters*, ed. Hill, pp. 171, 189; William Wordsworth to Henry Crabb Robinson, 8 December 1844, and William Wordsworth to Henry Reed, 10 November 1843, in *The Letters of William and Dorothy Wordsworth*, vii, *The Later*

Years, Part 4: 1840–1853, ed. Ernest de Selincourt, rev. Alan G. Hill (2nd ed., Oxford: Clarendon Press, 1988), pp. 633, 496.

46 See William Wordsworth to Edward Moxon, 29 July 1838, in *The Letters of William and Dorothy Wordsworth*, vi, *The Later Years, Part 3: 1835–1839*, ed. Ernest de Selincourt, rev. Alan G. Hill (2nd ed., Oxford: Clarendon Press, 1982), p. 623; and William Wordsworth to Robert Ferguson, 4 July 1842, in *The Letters of William and Dorothy Wordsworth*, vii, *The Later Years, Part 4: 1840–1853*, ed. de Selincourt, p. 350.

47 Richard Gravil, *Lyrical Ballads (1798) with Some Poems of 1800* (Penrith, Cumbria: Humanities-Ebooks, 2007).

Myth
13 THE PERSON FROM PORLOCK

The origin myth of 'Kubla Khan' is that of the young genius who retires to 'a lonely farmhouse between Porlock and Lynton' suffering 'a slight indisposition' (dysentery) for which he self-administers 'an anodyne' (that is, opium),

> from the effects of which he fell asleep in his chair at the moment that he was reading the following sentence, or words of the same substance, in Purchas's *Pilgrimage*: 'Here the Khan Kubla commanded a palace to be built, and a stately garden thereunto. And thus ten miles of fertile ground were inclosed with a wall.' The author continued for about three hours in a profound sleep, at least of the external senses, during which time he has the most vivid confidence, that he could not have composed less than from two to three hundred lines.... On awaking he appeared to himself to have a distinct recollection of the whole, and taking his pen, ink, and paper, instantly and eagerly wrote down the lines that are here preserved. At this moment he was unfortunately called out by a person on business from Porlock, and detained by him above an hour, and on his return to his room, found to his no small surprise and mortification, that though he still retained some vague and dim recollection of the general purpose of the vision, yet, with the exception of some eight or ten scattered lines and images, all the rest had passed away like the images on the surface of a stream into which a stone has been cast, but, alas! without the after restoration of the latter. ... [1]

Experience cautions that we stand back from Coleridge's claims about where his poems came from, so removed are they from the truth (see p. 52). Though he loved to claim himself the recipient of inspirational fits, it is widely believed that 'Kubla Khan', like most of his works, was written over a longer period than he was prepared to admit; the editor of the

30 Great Myths About the Romantics, First Edition. Duncan Wu.
© 2015 John Wiley & Sons, Ltd. Published 2015 by John Wiley & Sons, Ltd.

standard edition of his poetry opts for a composition date of September to November 1797, while Jack Stillinger finds that Coleridge wrote five distinct versions of the poem between 1797 and 1834.[2] Yet among such stories this enjoys a unique status, opening the portal to a new way of thinking about creativity. It is a fable of frustration about a perfect conception truncated by interruption. That conceit – a shaggy dog story so ensnarled in its own essential shagginess it transcends the genre – was designed not only to suggest 'Kubla Khan' was a mere 'psychological curiosity', but to relegate it to the dream that preceded it and suggest that (worse still) the poem offers us the palest reflection of the ideal dreamt by its author.[3]

Scholars respond with the urge to escape the myth's slipperiness and pin it to certainties: they debate the location of the farmhouse to which Coleridge 'retired';[4] map the restless topography of Culbone – and, most compulsively of all, question the identity of Coleridge's visitor. Was it Coleridge's wife? Was it Wordsworth? Their publisher and friend, Joseph Cottle? Each has their advocate. For Richard Holmes, the visitor's identity matters less than what he or she represented: the person from Porlock is symbolic of 'the humdrum world (the world of business, money, domestic affairs) breaking into the fine, solitary, detached world of artistic creation'.[5] Walter Jackson Bate sees him as a destructive figure, the enemy of promise: 'If there is any man in the history of literature who should be hanged, drawn and quartered, it is the man on business from Porlock.'[6]

But that would be to read Coleridge's account literally. The more pressing question is: did the person from Porlock really exist? That he makes no appearance in the earliest manuscript of the poem (the Crewe MS, retained at the British Library), which nonetheless contains a truncated prose account of the poem's origins, suggests he may have been the fancy stitching on the preposterously embroidered fiction Coleridge manufactured in the Preface to its 1816 publication. If so, the entire story is thrown into question – and critics have not been slow to poke holes in it. Why, Bate asked, 'should he be seeking out Coleridge, who had so few business dealings, and how, even so, would he have known that Coleridge, who had been seeking seclusion, was staying at this particular place?'[7] Norman Fruman expressed kindred doubts as to Coleridge's plausibility: 'Why any man on business would be meeting Coleridge in a lonely farm house twenty miles from his home is baffling. There would have had to be an appointment, and Coleridge could not have been in the habit of meeting men on business in such places.'[8] John Worthen says Coleridge's guest was 'certainly fictitious';[9] Rosemary Ashton that he was 'invented'.[10]

One of the most ingenious Coleridge-watchers, Hugh Haughton, says the myth elevates interruption to a fine art, presenting 'Kubla Khan' as

> an interrupted transcription of a dream triggered by an interrupted sentence he was reading in an old travel book. The dream is itself an interruption, he seems to suggest, an eruption of the poet's unconscious into the text he had been reading, the text of which we are reading when we read the poem. According to Coleridge's account, in other words, it was an interruption that inspired the poem as well as apparently terminated its transcription.[11]

The poem is interrupted; the dream that inspired it was an interruption; the reading that inspired the poem was interrupted by the dream. The obsessive patterning in Coleridge's tale declares its author's part in its devising and bespeaks an almost paranoid obsession with the motif. Played on a loop, ad infinitum, the repetition becomes nightmare.

But, then, the myth was invented to distract attention from the oneiric, subdural world of the poem. It prefaces 'Kubla Khan' with a story that seems to surrender its author to view while offering no more than reiterated, fleeting reflections in a hall of mirrors. The one character whose reality is never in doubt is the one Coleridge presumably fabricated – the person from Porlock, who becomes, as Haughton reminds us, 'the figure of and for the "third person." His much-maligned and much-lamented visit – scorned not least because he comes on "business" to intrude on the world of art – is the infinite interruption that marks, and does not cancel or block, the relation to the other.'[12] The person from Porlock enters the world of creativity from the Heraclitean flux of the quotidian, providing us with a proxy in the clockwork universe where sequential interruptions are doomed to recur. For David Perkins, that makes him angel rather than devil: the person from Porlock served 'to reestablish everyday, rational consciousness; to end the solitude of the poet and associate him again with ordinary human beings; to turn the poem into a fragment, and to stop a transgression'.[13] No figure is more ordinary than a businessman, yet none could be more extraordinary than that from Porlock.

What happens when a character escapes the treadmill of myth? The person from Porlock is such a beast. Nearly a century after his first appearance in print, he was incarnated as Fred Porlock, sidekick of the evil Moriarty, in Conan Doyle's *The Valley of Fear* (1915). He provides the inciting incident of the narrative by writing to Sherlock Holmes, who recognizes his correspondent's hand immediately: 'I can hardly doubt that it is Porlock's writing, though I have only seen it twice before. The Greek "e" with the peculiar top flourish is distinctive. But if it is Porlock, then it must be something of the very first importance.'[14] The story has only just begun, and Porlock's role in its unravelling will be crucial.

He became an extraterrestrial being in human form in Raymond F. Jones's classic story, 'The Person from Porlock', published in *Astounding* magazine in 1947 (and perhaps he was always such a creature). Jones's protagonist is working on a teleportation machine, but finds himself hampered by endless interruptions and screw-ups attributable to aliens whose sole purpose is to obstruct humans:

> They make mistakes in important work entrusted to them. They interfere with others who are doing intense and concentrated work so that trains of thought are broken and perhaps lost forever, as in the case of Coleridge. And as in my own case. I could tell of at least a hundred times when I have been deliberately interrupted at critical points of my calculations so that work had to be repeated and some points, only faintly conceived, were totally lost.[15]

It transpires Coleridge's 'Kubla Khan' was an attempt to describe these aliens; to prevent him from completing it, they sent an emissary to disrupt his labours.

Vladimir Nabokov was unable to shake off everyone's favourite traveller from inner space. As early as 1942, 'The Person from Porlock' was the working title for *Bend Sinister*,[16] while 'The Vane Sisters', a story from 1951, alludes to

> an eccentric librarian called Porlock who in the last years of his dusty life had been engaged in examining old books for miraculous misprints such as the substitution of 'l' for the second 'h' in the word 'hither.' Contrary to Cynthia, he cared nothing for the thrill of obscure predictions; all he sought was the freak itself, the chance that mimics choice, the flaw that looks like a flower; and Cynthia, a much more perverse amateur of misshapen or illicitly connected words, puns, logographs, and so on, had helped the poor crank to pursue a quest that in the light of the example she cited struck me as statistically insane.[17]

In Nabokov's most famous novel, *Lolita*, Humbert Humbert's suspicion that he and his under-age companion are trailed by an invisible observer as they proceed from one motel to the next is confirmed when he sees, in a register, the name, 'A. Person, Porlock, England'.[18] Despite its outward innocence, the association with Coleridge's unexpected visitor is sinister – a hint to Humbert he is under surveillance and his continuing freedom conditional.

By this time, the person from Porlock was acquiring supernatural associations. When he turned up in Louis MacNeice's final radio play, broadcast in August 1963, he was identified with the grim reaper. Meeting him at the end of the play, its protagonist, an artist called Hank, is told his paintings will now sell. Why? 'Because they will say you met a noble – well, a noble person from Porlock.'[19] Hank has yet to realize he has passed on.

The association with death flows into Stevie Smith's 'Thoughts on the Person from Porlock':

I long for the Person from Porlock
To bring my thoughts to an end,
I am becoming impatient to see him
I think of him as a friend,

Often I look out of the window
Often I run to the gate
I think, He will come this evening,
I think it is rather late.

I am hungry to be interrupted
For ever and ever amen
O Person from Porlock come quickly
And bring my thoughts to an end.[20]

Smith's poem envisions the person from Porlock as 'the ultimate interruption of human consciousness ... a figure of universal disruption'.[21] It is as if Chaos were incarnated in human form – 'And universal darkness buries all.' This is an extreme view, far removed from where the person from Porlock began his journey.

Porlock is associated with the exposure of malignity in Simon Gray's drama, *Otherwise Engaged* (1975), which describes a lazy afternoon on which a publisher called Hench settles down to listen to a new recording of *Parsifal*. The play describes a series of interruptions from friends, family, and colleagues – as if the person from Porlock were manifested through each. At first we perceive them through Hench's eyes – as an unwelcome distraction – but in their comings and goings they slowly reveal Hench to be a selfish, complacent monster. As one observes: 'while we may envy you your serenity, we should be revolted by the rot from which it stems. Your sanity is of the kind that causes people to go quietly mad around you.'[22]

In one of the funniest reworkings of the theme, Douglas Adams revives the visitor in the guise of Dirk Gently, a detective who must travel back in time and interrupt composition of 'Kubla Khan' if he is to save humanity from extinction. When Coleridge opens the door of his cottage and his 'slightly dazed' face peers out, Gently distracts him in the most time-wasting manner he can think of:

I was just passing by, on my way from Porlock, you understand, and I was wondering if I might trouble you to vouchsafe me an interview? It's just for a little parish broadsheet I edit. Won't take much of your time, I promise, I know you must be busy, famous poet like you, but I do so admire your work, and ...[23]

When Gently finally emerges he bids Coleridge farewell with the immortal line, 'I do hope I haven't kept you from anything important.'

Will the person from Porlock be Coleridge's most enduring imaginative creation? When the bombs have dropped, will it be he who knocks on the shelter door? He stands alongside the vampire as a mythic figure who has survived the long journey from the Romantic period to our own, continuing to preoccupy writers, film-makers, and poets. Survivor even of the much-advertised death of the printed word, he has long been a habitué of hyperspace, with his own Twitter feed and Facebook page – though who in their right mind would 'friend' such an agent of the unpredictable? Perhaps his survival might be explained by the ability to provide reassurance, reminding us of everything that is safe, suburban, and dependable – a refuge from the opium-fuelled, hypertensive world of the metaphysician. It is surely he who, in the poem's closing lines, leads the chorus:

And all should cry, Beware! Beware!
His flashing eyes, his floating hair!
Weave a circle round him thrice,
And close your eyes with holy dread:
For he on honey-dew hath fed,
And drunk the milk of Paradise.[24]

Notes

1 Samuel Taylor Coleridge, 'Of the Fragment of Kubla Khan', in *Christabel: Kubla Khan, A Vision; The Pains of Sleep* (London: John Murray, 1816), pp. 52–3.

2 The date of composition is, apparently 'Sept–Nov 1797? May 1798? Oct 1799?' See Samuel Taylor Coleridge, *Poetical Works*, ed. J. C. C. Mays (6 vols., Princeton, NJ: Princeton University Press, 2001), i. 509. See also Jack Stillinger, *Coleridge and Textual Instability: The Multiple Versions of the Major Poems* (New York: Oxford University Press, 1994), pp. 73–9.

3 Reviewing it shortly after publication, Hazlitt wrote that it 'only shews that Mr Coleridge can write better *nonsense* verses than any man in England'; see *The Selected Writings of William Hazlitt*, ed. Duncan Wu (9 vols., London: Pickering & Chatto, 1998), ix. 25.

4 See, *inter alia*, Michael Grevis, 'Notes on the Place of Composition of "Kubla Khan"', *Charles Lamb Bulletin* NS 93 (January 1991), 12–19.

5 Richard Holmes, *Coleridge: Darker Reflections* (London: HarperCollins, 1998), p. 436.

6 Quoted by David Perkins, 'The Imaginative Vision of *Kubla Khan*: On Coleridge's Introductory Note', repr. in *Bloom's Period Studies: English Romantic Poetry*, ed. Harold Bloom (New York: Infobase Publishing, 2004), p. 251.

7 Walter Jackson Bate, *Coleridge* (London: Weidenfeld & Nicolson, 1968), p. 76.

8 Norman Fruman, *Coleridge, The Damaged Archangel* (New York: George Braziller, 1971), p. 337.

9 John Worthen, *The Gang: Coleridge, the Hutchinsons and the Wordsworths in 1802* (New Haven: Yale University Press, 2001), p. 2.

10 Rosemary Ashton, *The Life of Samuel Taylor Coleridge* (Oxford: Blackwell, 1996), p. 112.

11 Hugh Haughton, 'Xanadu and Porlock: Thoughts on Composition and Interruption', in *The Book of Interruptions*, ed. David Hillman and Adam Phillips (Bern: Peter Lang, 2007), pp. 27–43, 30.

12 Ibid., p. 25.

13 Perkins, 'The Imaginative Vision of *Kubla Khan*', p. 260.

14 Sir Arthur Conan Doyle, *The Valley of Fear* (London: John Murray and Jonathan Cape, 1974), p. 17.

15 Raymond F. Jones, 'The Person from Porlock', in *The Ascent of Wonder: The Evolution of Hard SF*, ed. David G. Hartwell and Kathryn Cramer (New York: Tor, 1994), p. 644.

16 *The Nabokov-Wilson Letters*, ed. Simon Karlinsky (London: Weidenfeld & Nicolson, 1979), p. 86n4. The aptness of the title is explored by Leona Toker, *Nabokov: The Mystery of Literary Structures* (Ithaca, NY: Cornell University Press, 1989), pp. 178–9, and Brian Boyd, *Vladimir Nabokov: The American Years* (Princeton, NJ: Princeton University Press, 1991), pp. 103–4.

17 Vladimir Nabokov, *Tyrants Destroyed and Other Stories* (London: Weidenfeld & Nicolson, 1975), p. 230.

18 Vladimir Nabokov, *The Annotated Lolita*, ed. Alfred Appel, Jr (New York: Vintage, 1991), pp. 250, 426.

19 Louis MacNeice, *Persons from Porlock and Other Plays for Radio* (London: British Broadcasting Corporation, 1969), p. 144.

20 *The Collected Poems of Stevie Smith* (New York: Oxford University Press, 1976), p. 386.

21 Haughton, 'Xanadu and Porlock', p. 35.

22 Simon Gray, *Otherwise Engaged and Other Plays* (London: Methuen, 1975), p. 56.

23 Douglas Adams, *Dirk Gently's Holistic Detective Agency* (New York: Pocket Books, 1988), p. 299.

24 'Kubla Khan', ll. 49–54, in Coleridge, *Poetical Works*, ed. Mays, i. 514.

Myth 14

JANE AUSTEN HAD AN INCESTUOUS RELATIONSHIP WITH HER SISTER

> With so much true merit and true love, and no want of fortune or friends, the happiness of the married cousins must appear as secure as earthly happiness can be.
>
> Jane Austen, *Mansfield Park*[1]

'Was Jane Austen gay?' has to be one of the most provocative shouts ever to appear on the cover of a literary magazine. The *London Review of Books* ran it in 1995 when publicizing a review by Terry Castle. It worked (assuming outrage was the desired result), and letters poured in for weeks.[2]

Of Austen's letters to her niece, Castle said 'they make for rather unpleasant reading' because of their homoerotic content: 'the tone is giddy, sentimental and disturbingly schoolgirlish for a 42-year-old woman. Austen was infatuated with Fanny and slips often into embarrassing coquetries.'[3] But the relationship with her sister Cassandra was where Castle found evidence of lesbianism, in part because, as their correspondence reveals, they slept together: 'she loved and was loved by Cassandra'. Austen's interest in female clothing was evidence of 'the close terms of physical intimacy on which she and Cassandra lived and

30 Great Myths About the Romantics, First Edition. Duncan Wu.
© 2015 John Wiley & Sons, Ltd. Published 2015 by John Wiley & Sons, Ltd.

the intense psychic "mirroring" that went on between them'. Having quoted one such letter, Castle points out:

> Such passages remind us strikingly of how important a role clothes have played in the subliminal fetish life of women – how much time women spend looking at one another, dressing one another, and engaging in elaborate and mutually pleasurable 'grooming behaviour'. Austen and Cassandra were hardly exempt: the conventions of early nineteenth-century female sociability and body-intimacy may have provided the necessary screen behind which both women acted out unconscious narcissistic or homoerotic imperatives.[4]

This was what Castle recalled when, a few weeks after her article appeared, she defended herself against hostile responses: '[Austen] lived with her sister on terms of considerable physical intimacy, and ... the relationship – I believe – had its unconscious homoerotic dimensions.'[5] She argued that neither Austen nor her sister 'showed much real inclination for matrimony', finding 'greater comfort and pleasure ... in remaining with one another'.[6]

The collection in which Castle reprinted her review article on Austen bears the title *Boss Ladies, Watch Out!* – suggesting jackboot diplomacy rather than pusillanimity. Why, then, has she and so many of those who insist on Austen's lesbianism insisted it was 'unconscious'? Could it be because any such theory is impossible to test – for who is to say what passed in the unconscious mind of someone who died two hundred years ago? Which in turn inclines me to wonder: how 'unconscious' can anyone's lesbianism really be? Susan Gubar rephrases the question: 'Did [Austen] sleep in her sister Cassandra's bed only during the cold, damp English winters?' She answers with a series of hypotheticals: perhaps Austen was 'only passing as straight', or 'created texts that critique heterosexuality or express a lesbian vision evident to those readers equipped with what Barbara Johnson calls "an inner lesbometer". It all depends on how we define the term "lesbian author".'[7] The implication is that if, by our standards, the novels are judged homoerotic, it is an indication their author was attempting to communicate her 'lesbian vision' to like-minded readers – something that comes close to suggesting deliberation. But not quite.

By the turn of the century, when Gubar published her thoughts on the matter, queer readings of Austen had been in circulation for more than five decades. In June 1944, Edmund Wilson noted Emma Woodhouse's sexual ambivalence:

> Emma, who was relatively indifferent to men, was inclined to infatuations with women; and what reason is there to believe that her marriage with Knightley would prevent her from going on as she had done before: from discovering a new young lady as appealing as Harriet Smith, dominating her personality and situating her in a dream-world of Emma's own in which

Emma would be able to confer on her all kinds of imaginary benefits but which would have no connection whatever with her condition or her real possibilities? This would worry and exasperate Knightley and be hard for him to do anything about. He would be lucky if he did not presently find himself saddled, along with the other awkward features of the arrangement, with one of Emma's young protégées as an actual member of the household.[8]

In 1952 Marvin Mudrick also noted Emma's preference for women and feeling for Harriet Smith: 'Emma is in love with her: a love unphysical and inadmissible, even perhaps undefinable in such a society; and therefore safe.'[9] Claudia L. Johnson notes that, unknown to himself, Mudrick 'verges here on a theory of the closet: aware that sex and gender are not equivalent, and alert to the relation between sexuality, gender, and social power, he suggests that sexuality is a discursive practice: "inadmissible" forms of sexuality become undiscussable, "undefinable," and therefore under certain circumstances, even "safe"'.[10] Lisa L. Moore's *Sapphic History of the British Novel* (1998) returns to Emma's desire for Harriet Smith because it 'raises the possibilities of autonomous female desire and class transgression'.[11] Moore says Emma's principal shortcoming is her desire to be masculine 'lover' rather than feminine 'beloved' – that is, she is too butch to prosper in a heterosexual world. Emma's acceptance of Mr Knightley's marriage proposal is lacking in brio, Moore suggests, compared with her more enthusiastic 'first meetings with sexually available young women'.[12]

Claudia Johnson's *Equivocal Beings* (1995) concluded with an analysis of *Emma*, in which the more feminine women in the novel are said to 'give heterosexuality a rather revolting appearance, against which Emma's coolness looks sane and enviable'.[13] The argument frames Emma (and her creator) as culturally 'male' – more so than Frank Churchill, whose script is said to be 'like woman's writing'. The love of Mr Knightley for Emma is, Johnson suggests, 'fraternal rather than heterosexual'.[14] What does this mean? That the world of *Emma* is not conventionally heterosexual, but redefined by its masculine protagonist. A year later, Johnson published an article, 'The Divine Miss Jane' (1996), which took issue with the 'heteronormativity' of Austen studies by positing 'that manners are gay … and that gay manners are indeed profoundly productive'.[15] Others, such as Clara Tuite, have attacked the 'heterosexist investment' in Austen's 'national reproductive myth of heterosexual romance'.[16]

Novelists sniff truffles among the ambiguities. Emma Tennant is the author of *Emma in Love* (1996), in which the dullness of life with Mr Knightley leads its heroine to an extra-marital affair with a French noblewoman, Baroness d'Almane: 'They kissed. Emma did not leave the stool where she perched, but permitted the cool, strong hands to run from her shoulders to her neck: the pearls, still hanging loosely at her throat, tumbled to the floor.'[17] *Gay Pride and Prejudice* (2012) is the

Figure 10 Cassandra Austen (1773–1845), sister of the novelist.
Source: private collection / Bridgeman Images.

work of Kate Christie, who declares herself 'weary of the compulsive heteronormativity of the classics', and reconceives Austen's fiction as a lesbian novel, available for download on Amazon.

The most influential essay on this theme appeared in 1991, when Eve Kosofsky Sedgwick published 'Jane Austen and the Masturbating Girl', arguing (among other things) that the Dashwood sisters had a homoerotic relationship: 'the erotic axis' of *Sense and Sensibility* as a whole is 'the unwavering but difficult love of a woman, Elinor Dashwood, for a woman, Marianne Dashwood'.[18] In Marianne, Sedgwick detected 'a certain autoerotic closure, absentation, self-sufficiency' which 'signifies an excess of sexuality altogether, an excess dangerous to others but chiefly to herself'.[19] Such ideas may be what the *Historical Dictionary of Lesbian Literature* (2006) had in mind when it described Austen's novels as concerned with 'the sexual and romantic desires of young women'.[20] It is probably not what anyone would have said in 1956, but half a century later such remarks remain symptomatic of how literary criticism is shaped by contemporary preoccupations.

A tendency of the commentary surrounding Austen is the assumption that biographical insights may be inferred from the novels: the suspicion that incest had a place in Austen's life hovers behind the work of Glenda A. Hudson, who pointed out not only that Fanny and Edmund (in *Mansfield Park*) are first cousins, but that Mr Knightley, though unrelated to Emma Woodhouse, is 'symbolically oedipal: because of their ages, he is something of a father-figure to her as well as an elder brother',[21] while Elinor and Edward (*Sense and Sensibility*) 'treat one another as blood brother and blood sister', their relationship being 'very much like that of siblings'.[22] At the same time, she argued, sisterly relationships in the novels are 'in many ways analogous to a good marriage'.[23] Austen's view of incestuous unions as stabilizing and protective was due, Hudson argued, to her close relationship with Cassandra: 'Austen's death marked the end of a period of thirty-five years in which the two unmarried sisters shared the same bedroom, confided their innermost thoughts to each other, and wrote and worked together.'[24] A few years later, Misty G. Anderson postulated an unconscious 'homoerotic intimacy' between Maria Bertram and Fanny Price in *Mansfield Park* – 'an unspoken possibility, not unlike "that" of incest that cannot be named. Indeed, it is precisely the inability to name homoerotic desire, to bring it to the level of consciousness in the text, that maintains its threat to the official plot, a dangerous narrative other that moves freely in the text.'[25]

The insistence on the unconscious nature of Austen's lesbianism is a recurrent motif, and it assigns to the critic the dual role of psychiatrist and spiritualist, haruspicating the novelist's entrails. It is a frustrating situation; as more than one critic has observed, 'it is hard completely to exclude the shade of sexuality when such a relationship is described as a marriage'.[26] In other words, if critics would have Austen the partner in a lesbian 'marriage', how unaware of it can she have been? Several of those cited in this essay refer to the observation that Jane and Cassandra were 'wedded' (a comment made by their mother), as well as to Cassandra's intense grief at Jane's death: 'She was the sun of my life, the gilder of every pleasure, the soother of every sorrow, I had not a thought concealed from her, & it is as if I had lost a part of myself.'[27] None of which proves lesbianism.

The unreality is more evident when one confronts rhetoric with fact. Psychiatrists report incestuous relationships between sisters to be unusual,[28] but when they occur the consequences can be no less traumatic than in cases of brother–sister incest.[29] One reported victim in a case of sister–sister incest presented for treatment with fears of hurting her husband and children, guilt over refusing her husband sex, as well as depression and past suicide attempts. Documented after-effects include depression, guilt, anxiety, low self-esteem, self-hatred, and confusion. Victims have been known to victimize others.[30] *The Encyclopedia of Child Abuse* notes sororal incest often takes place in households where sisters have been sexually abused by father or brothers.[31] In short, it is not a lifestyle option; in the real world it has potential to cause far-reaching damage.

One searches Austen's biographical record in vain for evidence of these symptoms. Everything we know confirms her relationship with Cassandra was close and loving up to the moment of her death. There is no more hint of incest than there is of abuse or trauma, and to say so is not homophobic.

Claire Tomalin, one of Austen's more perceptive biographers, reminds us women can have loving relationships without being lesbian.

> I knew two middle-aged sisters who, in the innocent days of the 1950s, explained to my mother in so many words that they thought of themselves as being like husband and wife; the elder went out to work wearing a suit, the younger preferred flower-printed dresses and took charge of their house and garden. They were certainly sisters, and not lesbian companions, and had evolved their own way of living which both found quite satisfactory. Neither Jane nor Cassandra adopted a masculine role – they had too many brothers to compete with to allow that – but they enjoyed their complementarity. 'I know your starched notions', Jane teased Cassandra .... Their different roles were known and understood within the family.[32]

Knowing too much of our own self-befouling nature, we find the innocence Tomalin describes almost impossible to conceive. Such arguments, read in the light of recent critical discussion, appear subversive. For that reason one has to admire Mary Jane Corbett for having argued as recently as 2004 that the marriage of Edmund and Fanny in *Mansfield Park* 'offers the heroine her very best opportunity to reconcile individual desire and family interest'. Corbett's insight is that what we regard as deviant was, in Austen's day, unexceptional: 'many middle-class and elite people ... would likely have shared the view that marriages that deepen and extend family ties held decided and pronounced advantages over bonds formed with strangers'.[33] That can be proved by reference to historical data, and goes some way towards quelling unease at the union of first cousins in *Mansfield Park*.[34] It is easily argued that Austen's interest in certain kinds of relationships grew out of her own incestuous union with Cassandra, but she was merely reflecting a fact of life in the society of which she was part. Austen was, in other words, innocent of the value judgements and inferences that have been attributed to her. It is a reminder that the imposition of our ideology on historical figures is a luxury for which a price must be paid, often in the form of the truth.

Notes

1 Jane Austen, *Mansfield Park*, ed. John Wiltshire (Cambridge: Cambridge University Press, 2005), p. 547.

2 For another view of this controversy, see Claire Harman, *Jane's Fame: How Jane Austen Conquered the World* (New York: Henry Holt, 2009), p. 192.

3 Terry Castle, 'Was Jane Austen Gay?', 1st published *London Review of Books* 17 (3 August 1995), 3–6; quoted from the revised version of the essay in Castle's *Boss Ladies, Watch Out! Essays on Women, Sex and Writing* (New York: Routledge, 2002), p. 133.

4 Ibid., pp. 132–3.

5 Ibid., p. 135.

6 Ibid., p. 130.

7 Susan Gubar, *Critical Condition: Feminism at the Turn of the Century* (New York: Columbia University Press, 2000), p. 50.

8 Edmund Wilson, 'A Long Talk about Jane Austen', first published 24 June 1944; repr. in *Classics and Commercials: A Literary Chronicle of the Forties* (New York: Farrar & Strauss, 1950), p. 202.

9 Marvin Mudrick, *Jane Austen: Irony as Defense and Discovery* (Princeton, NJ: Princeton University Press, 1952), p. 203.

10 Claudia L. Johnson, *Equivocal Beings: Politics, Gender, and Sentimentality in the 1790s: Wollstonecraft, Radcliffe, Burney, Austen* (Chicago: University of Chicago Press, 1995), p. 194.

11 Lisa L. Moore, *Dangerous Intimacies: Toward a Sapphic History of the British Novel* (Durham, NC: Duke University Press, 1998), p. 121.

12 Ibid., pp. 138–9.

13 Johnson, *Equivocal Beings*, p. 202.

14 Ibid., p. 201.

15 Claudia L. Johnson, 'The Divine Miss Jane: Jane Austen, Janeites, and the Discipline of Novel Studies', *boundary 2* 23 (1996), 143–63, p. 161.

16 Clara Tuite, *Romantic Austen: Sexual Politics and the Literary Canon* (Cambridge: Cambridge University Press, 2002), p. 19.

17 Emma Tennant, *Emma in Love* (London: Fourth Estate, 1996), p. 204.

18 Eve Kosofsky Sedgwick, 'Jane Austen and the Masturbating Girl', *Critical Inquiry* 17 (Fall 1991), 818–37, pp. 822–3, 826–7.

19 Ibid., p. 829.

20 Meredith Miller, *The Historical Dictionary of Lesbian Literature* (Lanham, MD: Scarecrow Press, 2006), p. 165.

21 Glenda A. Hudson, *Sibling Love and Incest in Jane Austen's Fiction* (New York: St Martins Press, 1992), p. 53.

22 Ibid., p. 56.

23 Ibid., p. 70.

24 Ibid., p. 64.
25 Misty G. Anderson, 'The Different Sorts of Friendship: Desire in *Mansfield Park*', *Jane Austen and Discourses of Feminism*, ed. Devoney Looser (New York: St Martin's Press, 1995), pp. 167–83, 172.
26 Sarah Annes Brown, *Devoted Sisters: Representations of the Sister Relationship in Nineteenth-Century British and American Literature* (Aldershot, Hants.: Ashgate, 2003), p. 137.
27 Cassandra Austen to Fanny Knight, 20 July 1817, in *Jane Austen's Letters*, ed. Deirdre Le Faye (4th ed., Oxford: Oxford University Press, 2011), pp. 359–60.
28 See, for instance, Florence Kaslow et al., 'Homosexual Incest', *Psychiatric Quarterly* 3 (1981), 184–93, p. 190, and Robin E. Clark, Judith Freeman Clark, and Christine A. Adamec, *The Encyclopedia of Child Abuse* (3rd ed., New York: Infobase, 2007), p. 145.
29 Diana E. H. Russell, *The Secret Trauma: Incest in the Lives of Girls and Women* (New York: Basic Books, 1999), p. 304.
30 Christine A. Courtois, *Healing the Incest Wound: Adult Survivors in Therapy* (New York: Norton, 1996), p. 79.
31 Clark, Clark, and Adamec, *Encyclopedia of Child Abuse*, p. 145.
32 Claire Tomalin, *Jane Austen: A Life* (London: Viking, 1997), p. 212. A similar point is made by Jill Pitkeathley in her novel, *Cassandra and Jane* (Bath: Copperfield Books, 2004), p. 225.
33 Mary Jean Corbett, 'Cousins in Love, &c. in Jane Austen', *Tulsa Studies in Women's Literature* 23 (2004), 237–59, pp. 240, 243.
34 Scholars show that marriages which we would regard as incestuous became more common during the course of the nineteenth century; this is most obvious in the increased number of first cousins who married. See, for instance, David Warren Sabean, 'Kinship and Class Dynamics in Nineteenth-Century Europe', in *Kinship In Europe: Approaches to Long-Term Development (1300–1900)*, ed. David Warren Sabean, Simon Teuscher, and Jon Mathieu (New York: Berghahn Books, 2007), pp. 301–13, 311.

Figure 11 William Hazlitt (1778–1830), essayist and journalist, as depicted by Sir William Allan, RA, c.1821.
Source: Duncan Wu collection.

Myth 15 THE KESWICK RAPIST

On 25 July 1968 the *Times Literary Supplement* carried a letter by Sir George Mallaby that began:

> Hazlitt spent a large part of the autumn of 1803 at Keswick and at the end of his stay raped, or attempted to rape, a local girl. He narrowly escaped being ducked by the girl's friends and made a hot-foot escape from Keswick. He arrived at the door of Dove Cottage at midnight – probably on a night early in December – and was welcomed by Wordsworth and given clothes and money.[1]

The accusation of rape is a serious one and it is baffling Mallaby does not explain it. (He does not claim access to some new informant or documentary source.) It attracted two letters on Hazlitt's behalf, one from Michael Foot, the other from Stanley Jones. Years later, those letters became the fulcrum for renewed academic prosecution of Hazlitt in which his 'sexual harassment' was taken as read. In *Sexual Politics and the Romantic Author* (1998), Sonia Hofkosh argued that accounts of the Keswick incident by a host of male critics and biographers suppressed the female perspective. That most scrupulous of scholars, Stanley Jones, was accused of having described it in a manner that 'minimizes, dismisses, or appropriates the woman's side of the story'[2] – that is to say, he failed to use evidence that does not exist. It is true we know nothing about the woman's side of the Keswick incident – we do not even know her name – but that is not because she has been silenced. The incident generated no newspaper reports or legal records; it is known only from accounts in correspondence and memoirs.

Arguments concerning Hazlitt's 'sexual harassment' have continued,[3] and the repercussions are far-reaching. One textbook anthology includes

30 Great Myths About the Romantics, First Edition. Duncan Wu.
© 2015 John Wiley & Sons, Ltd. Published 2015 by John Wiley & Sons, Ltd.

only two brief extracts from the twenty-one volumes of Hazlitt's collected writings under the glum rubric, 'Historical and Cultural Context'. By way of apology, the editors refer in passing to Hazlitt's 'campaign of sexual harassment'.[4] Marginalization of a principal writer of the period as retrospective punishment is hinted at when Hofkosh remarks: 'at stake in current readings of the Keswick episode are questions about the place of a writer such as Hazlitt in a romantic tradition described primarily in terms of a Wordsworthian paradigm'.[5] The implication is that 'a writer such as Hazlitt' has no place – as if it were the privilege of a wiser and more knowing future to suppress the literary achievement of rapists. If the moral character of a writer is to determine his or her canonical standing, our judgements had better find a secure footing.

Hazlitt was in the Lake District in October 1803 making portraits of Wordsworth and Coleridge. The incident that precipitated his unplanned exodus took place one evening late that month at a Keswick tavern. Southey, Coleridge, and Wordsworth were among the first to hear what happened. Henry Crabb Robinson's diary for 15 June 1815 records Wordsworth's version:

> It appears that Hazlitt, when at Keswick, narrowly escaped being ducked by the populace, and probably sent to prison for some gross attacks on women. (He even whipped one woman, *more puerorum*, for not yielding to his wishes.) The populace were incensed against him and pursued him, but he escaped to Wordsworth, who took him into his house at midnight, gave him clothes and money (from three to five pounds).[6]

Robinson's specific claim, that Hazlitt 'whipped' someone, is cited as his ultimate crime. (In this context I take 'whip' to mean 'spank', *OED*, definition 6a.) In contemporary terms that would be assault rather than rape.

Benjamin Robert Haydon's diary records another conversation with Wordsworth, this time dating from 1824, in which

> He was relating to me with great horror Hazlitt's licentious conduct to the girls of the Lake, & that no woman could walk after dark, for 'his Satyr & *beastly* appetites.' Some girl called him a black-faced rascal, when Hazlitt enraged pushed her down, '& because, Sir', said Wordsworth, 'she refused to gratify his abominable & devilish propensities,' he lifted up her petticoats & *smote* her on *the bottom*.[7]

This is consistent with Robinson in not referring to rape. Wordsworth was not sympathetic to Hazlitt: by 1815 he was demanding he be excluded from any party to which he was invited because his former friend had taken to denouncing him in print for abandoning his early political convictions. There was every reason for him to present Hazlitt in the least flattering light, yet the worst he can say is he 'whipped' someone 'for not yielding to his wishes'. Had Wordsworth thought him a rapist, there was every reason to have said so.

Just over a month before the Keswick incident, Coleridge described Hazlitt as 'addicted to women, as objects of sexual Indulgence';[8] reprehensible such propensities may be, but they do not amount to rape. On the night of the incident, Hazlitt fled the tavern and went to Greta Hall, where he explained what had happened to Southey and Coleridge. Accounts of what then transpired date from years later, when the protagonists were no longer on friendly terms. In June 1817, Coleridge said Hazlitt was

> snatched from an infamous Punishment by Southey and myself (there were not less than 200 men on horse in search of him) – after having given him all the money, I had in the world, and the very Shoes off my feet to enable him to escape over the mountains – and since that time never, either of us, injured him in the least degree – unless the quiet withdrawing from any further connection with him (& this without any ostentation, or any mark of Shyness when we accidentally met him) – not merely or chiefly on account of his Keswick Conduct, but from the continued depravity of his Life – but why need I say more?[9]

This comes from a series of letters in response to Hazlitt's attacks on Coleridge for having betrayed his early religious and political convictions.[10] Again, in February 1818, Coleridge says:

> the sole cause of this man's hatred to me is, that for years together I had been serving him with more than brotherly zeal, till his own unmanly vices (of which I had never dreamt) forced him to run away from the Lakes, and with difficulty by Southey's and my assistance to escape the ministers of Justice, and to leave behind him a character which would have shaken even the reputation of my own, Southey's and Wordsworth's families, with whom he had by my means been almost domesticated.[11]

No one should attempt to diminish the implications – 'depravity' and 'unmanly vices' are strong terms – but Coleridge does not use the word 'rape'. He had every reason to blacken Hazlitt's name but, in letters of 1817–18, made no such accusation. None of those present in Keswick at the time of the incident are known to have done so. In December 1803, weeks afterwards, Southey referred to Hazlitt as 'a man of real genius',[12] without irony. Southey was not the kind of man to overlook a crime as heinous as rape on account of 'genius'; one recent biographer refers to his 'rigid moral views'.[13]

John Beer says Hazlitt's escapade 'does not seem to have been regarded with the utmost gravity by Wordsworth and Coleridge at the time'.[14]

That is supported by Wordsworth's letter to Hazlitt of 5 March 1804 – that is to say, roughly four months after the event, which reassured him his clothes and paintbox would be 'looked after' at Dove Cottage, and informed him Wordsworth had written '1200 Lines of the Poem on my own life' (that is, *The Prelude*), adding, 'I should have liked to shew you 200 yards or so of mountain Brook scenery which I found out yesterday above Rydale.'[15] A man as sensitive to tact and propriety as Wordsworth would not have written in this way to someone he believed a rapist. Nothing he says in his letter suggests annoyance, embarrassment, even dismay. Over the years relations between them cooled, but he felt no hostility until Hazlitt published his review of *The Excursion* in 1814.[16]

Other references to the incident deserve mention. In a letter of December 1814 to Wordsworth, Charles Lamb writes: 'The "'scapes" of the great god Pan who appeared among your mountains some dozen years since, and his narrow chance of being submerged by the swains, afforded me much pleasure. I can conceive the water nymphs pulling for him.'[17] Lamb was responding to a letter by Wordsworth which, we may infer, invoked the Keswick incident in a manner that justified levity. Wordsworth was reminded of it by Hazlitt's review of *The Excursion* which slighted the Lake District for possessing 'neither courtiers nor courtesans'.[18] That may indicate an interest in prostitutes, but not in rape.

P. G. Patmore refers to the incident in his memoirs when he mentions

> Hazlitt's alleged treatment of some pretty village jilt, who, when he was on a visit to Wordsworth, had led him (Hazlitt) to believe that she was not insensible to his attentions; and then, having induced him to 'commit' himself to her in some ridiculous manner, turned round upon him, and made him the laughing-stock of the village .... the mingled disappointment and rage of Hazlitt on this occasion led him, during the madness of the moment (for it must have been nothing less), to acts which nothing but the supposition of insanity could account for, much less excuse.[19]

The criticism is unambiguous, but while Patmore condemns Hazlitt for behaviour he regarded as insane, he does not allege rape.

The earliest occurrence of the charge occurs in a letter by J. G. Lockhart and John Wilson to John Murray, 2 October 1818: 'Wordsworth and Southey are both continually talking about the rape story'.[20] The previous month, Lockhart and Wilson had published a bitter, excoriating attack on Hazlitt's character in *Blackwood's Edinburgh Magazine*, and Murray, their London publisher, had just received notice that Hazlitt intended to sue for damages. Lockhart and Wilson's justification is that, far from giving Hazlitt what he deserved, they had concealed the full extent of his crimes. Wilson knew both Southey and Wordsworth, and may have heard them recount the events of October 1803. But that doesn't mean the accusation of 'rape' came from them: Wilson is defending his own actionable offence to an irate employer and had every reason to exaggerate. Stanley Jones characterizes Lockhart and Wilson as 'new-fledged briefless advocates with time on their hands and mischief in their minds, unhampered by respect or admiration for any man, having at their command, and capable of supplementing by invention, all the tittle-tattle of the gossiping Scottish capital'.[21] Wilson was 'by nature an overbearing bully, and when the hidden violence that stoked the nerve of his prose erupted he did not care who the victim was or what the bystanders might feel'.[22]

Blackwood was unable to send Murray documentary proof that would sustain the accusations made by his journalists, and Murray chastised him for it: 'To neglect such a thing as this when three-fourths of the talent of the Bar are in hostility to you, and when any jury will be prejudiced against you, is very reprehensible.'[23] Had it gone to court, Wordsworth would have been summoned as a witness on Hazlitt's behalf, and he 'seemed vexed that his name was connected with the thing in any way'.[24] Kurt Koenigsberger confirms Hazlitt's case was 'taken for a strong one, since both *Blackwood's* and Wordsworth appear to have been worried about the seriousness of Hazlitt's resolve'.[25] The matter was settled out of court when Blackwood agreed to make payment to Hazlitt of £100.

If the judgement upon Hazlitt is that he was a rapist, it says more about his accusers than about him. The charge is trumped-up and the evidence flimsy. No one with first-hand knowledge of the subject repeated it, and the few who did had no reason truthfully to report what they had heard. Such malicious tittle-tattle would have been forgotten had it not been rehabilitated as the excuse for casting Hazlitt out of the curriculum. Besides asking why, readers might wonder whether it is really the task of the literary critic to play judge and jury in a kangaroo court. The correct answer is 'no'; even if it were 'yes', we might expect the punishment to fit the crime, but that is one of many respects in which it fails to justify itself. Of course teachers are at liberty to deny students the chance to read one of the great prose writers of the Romantic period, but let them not demean victims of rape by framing Hazlitt's exile from the syllabus as the obvious and inevitable punishment for such crimes. I do not say Hazlitt's behaviour towards women was beyond reproach, nor do I defend the conduct of those who saved Hazlitt from a ducking, a lynching, or whatever form of legal redress might conceivably have followed the Keswick incident. I do dispute anyone's authority to convict him, post mortem, in the absence of any better testimony than the poisonous cocktail of half-recollected hearsay, axe-grinding, and outright lies that comprise the written record. And I see no ground for assuming the appropriate penalty for the retrospective conviction of rape to be removal from the curriculum. Were that so, other writers would long ago have been escorted from the premises, not least John Wilmot, Earl of Rochester, a known rapist whose favourite victims were working-class girls and whose rapsheet extended to attempted homicide. Where such arguments might be expected there is a gaping void, feminists such as Germaine Greer preferring to suggest that Rochester's rakish legend was largely myth.[26] All of which leads to the inescapable conclusion that the case against Hazlitt is underwhelming and his demotion in college textbooks illogical even by the fluctuating standards of contemporary critical discourse. It is an exceptional, unjust, arbitrary punishment, and should long ago have assumed its rightful position in the capacious trashcan of tendentiousness.

Notes

1 'Wordsworth and Hazlitt', *Times Literary Supplement* 25 July 1968, p. 788.
2 Sonia Hofkosh, *Sexual Politics and the Romantic Author* (Cambridge: Cambridge University Press, 1998), p. 110.
3 See, for example, Julie Carlson, 'Impositions of Form: Romantic Anthitheatricalism and the Case against Particular Women Author(s)', *English Literary History* 60 (1993), 149–79; Duncan Wu, 'Hazlitt's "Sexual Harassment"', *Essays in Criticism* 50 (2000), 199–214; Mark McCutcheon, 'Liber Amoris and the Lineaments of Hazlitt's Desire', *Texas Studies in Literature and Language* 46 (2004), 432–51.
4 *British Literature 1780–1830*, ed. Anne K. Mellor and Richard E. Matlak (Fort Worth, TX: Harcourt Brace, 1996), p. 149.
5 Hofkosh, *Sexual Politics*, p. 107.
6 *Henry Crabb Robinson on Books and their Writers*, ed. Edith J. Morley (3 vols., London: Dent, 1938), i. 169–70.
7 29 March 1824, in *The Diary of Benjamin Robert Haydon*, ed. Willard Bissell Pope (5 vols., Cambridge, MA: Harvard University Press, 1960–3), ii. 470.
8 S. T. Coleridge to Thomas Wedgwood, 16 September 1803, in *Collected Letters of Samuel Taylor Coleridge*, ed. Earl Leslie Griggs (6 vols., Oxford: Clarendon Press, 1956–71), ii. 990.
9 S. T. Coleridge to Francis Wrangham, 5 June 1817, ibid., iv. 735.
10 For an account of these attacks, see Duncan Wu, 'Rancour and Rabies: Hazlitt, Coleridge and Jeffrey in Dialogue', in *British Romanticism and the Edinburgh Review: Bicentenary Essays*, ed. Massimiliano Demata and Duncan Wu (Houndmills, Basingstoke: Palgrave Macmillan, 2002), pp. 168–94.
11 S. T. Coleridge to James Perry, 5 February 1818, in *Collected Letters*, ed. Griggs, iv. 831.

12 Robert Southey to Richard Duppa, 14 December 1803, in *Life and Correspondence of Robert Southey*, ed. Charles Cuthbert Southey (6 vols., London, 1849–50), ii. 238.

13 W. A. Speck, *Robert Southey: Entire Man of Letters* (New Haven: Yale University Press, 2006), p. 102.

14 John Beer, 'Coleridge, Hazlitt, and "Christabel"', *Review of English Studies* 37 (1986), 40–54, p. 43.

15 William Wordsworth to William Hazlitt, 5 March 1804, in *The Letters of William and Dorothy Wordsworth*, i, *The Early Years, 1787–1805*, ed. Ernest de Selincourt, rev. Chester L. Shaver (Oxford: Clarendon Press, 1967), pp. 446–7.

16 See Duncan Wu, *William Hazlitt: The First Modern Man* (Oxford: Oxford University Press, 2008), pp. 168–71; Stanley Jones, *Hazlitt: A Life* (Oxford: Oxford University Press, 1991), pp. 154–7; David Bromwich, *Hazlitt: The Mind of a Critic* (New York: Oxford University Press, 1983), pp. 158–85.

17 Charles Lamb to William Wordsworth, 28 December 1814, in *The Letters of Charles and Mary Anne Lamb*, ed. Edwin W. Marrs (3 vols., Ithaca, NY: Cornell University Press, 1975–8), iii. 125. References to Pan in Wordsworth's correspondence with Lamb usually have something to do with sex; see his letter of 21 November 1816 in *The Letters of Dorothy and William Wordsworth*, viii, *A Supplement of New Letters*, ed. Alan G. Hill (Oxford: Clarendon Press, 1993), p. 162.

18 *The Selected Writings of William Hazlitt*, ed. Duncan Wu (9 vols., London: Pickering & Chatto, 1998), ii. 338.

19 P. G. Patmore, *My Friends and Acquaintance* (3 vols., London: Saunders & Otley, 1854), iii. 141.

20 J. G. Lockhart and John Wilson to John Murray, 2 October 1818, as quoted in Jones, *Hazlitt: A Life*, p. 299n74.

21 Ibid., p. 288.

22 Ibid., p. 289.

23 John Murray to William Blackwood, 27 November 1818, in *Memoir and Correspondence of the Late John Murray*, ed. Samuel Smiles (2 vols., London: John Murray, 1891), i. 492.

24 Sara Coleridge to Thomas Poole, September 1818, in *Minnow among Tritons: Mrs S. T. Coleridge's Letters to Thomas Poole, 1799–1834*, ed. Stephen Potter (London: Nonesuch Press, 1934), p. 64.

25 Kurt M. Koenigsberger, 'Liberty, Libel, and *Liber Amoris*: Hazlitt on Sovereignty and Death', *Studies in Romanticism* 38 (1999), 281–309, p. 293.

26 Germaine Greer, *John Wilmot, Earl of Rochester* (Horndon, Devon: Northcote House in association with the British Council, 2000), pp. 1–8. Others take a less exculpatory view than Greer; see, for instance, Susan Kingsley Kent, *Gender and Power in Britain, 1640–1990* (London: Routledge, 1999), p. 29.

Figure 12 The Hon. Augusta Leigh, Byron's half-sister (1783–1851), portrait by James Holmes.
Source: private collection. Photo © Christie's Images / Bridgeman Images.

Myth 16

BYRON HAD AN AFFAIR WITH HIS SISTER

Rumours of marital violence, adultery with actresses and his incest with his sister began to circulate.

The Guardian, 8 November 2002

Lord Byron's tireless love of women, men, teenagers, prostitutes, his own sister, the wives of others and their 11-year-old daughters – all of them chronicled in the most famous poetry of the 19th century – helped forge a legend that has parallel only in the debauched exploits of Casanova and Sade.

The American Scholar, Summer 2009

These quotations, from reputable publications, indicate how widespread is the belief Byron had an incestuous relationship with his sister: as he didn't have a sister that can't be right. Augusta Leigh was his half-sister; they had a father in common. Did they have a physical relationship? The question is seldom asked because the answer invariably assumed is 'yes', even by scholars. Benita Eisler says, 'he had been the first man to awaken her sexually', and continues: 'Exploring the childhood intimacies they had missed earlier, they became lovers.'[1] The idea is too appalling not to be true. Michael and Melissa Bakewell structure their melodramatic account of Augusta's life round the affair with no suggestion the evidence might be fallible: 'the truth was that the two of them had not simply become lovers; they were in love – a love that neither would ever be able entirely to escape, a love that was to change their lives irrevocably and bring Augusta, at least, untold misery and suffering'.[2] That they produced a child, Medora, is so frequently the position of biographers as to have attained the status of honorary fact.[3]

30 Great Myths About the Romantics, First Edition. Duncan Wu.
© 2015 John Wiley & Sons, Ltd. Published 2015 by John Wiley & Sons, Ltd.

The evidence indicates that Byron's love of his half-sister was intense. That is probably why, in his journal for 14 November 1813, he reflected that *The Bride of Abydos* was written 'to drive my thoughts from the recollection of – "Dear sacred name, rest ever unreveal'd"' (assumed to refer to Augusta).[4] On 17 May 1819 he told her, 'I have never ceased nor can cease to feel for a moment that perfect & boundless attachment which bound & binds me to you .... It is heart-breaking to think of our long Separation – and I am sure more than punishment enough for all our sins.'[5] In October 1821 he wrote again, saying (in a heavily deleted passage) 'I was ready to have sacrificed every thing for you.'[6] These remarks may indicate the strength of his feeling, but do not prove an affair.

Nearly everyone who says Byron committed incest cites as the most explicit of his various admissions a letter of 25 April 1814 to Lady Melbourne:

> Oh! but it is 'worth while' – I can't tell you why – and it is *not* an 'Ape' and if it is – that must be my fault – however I will positively reform – you must however allow – that it is utterly impossible I can ever be half as well liked elsewhere – and I have been all my life trying to make some one love me – & never got the sort that I preferred before. –– But positively she & I will grow good – & all that – & so we are *now* and shall be these three weeks & more too.[7]

This is the principal evidence (excluding the 'minutes' of what Lady Byron was told by Lady Caroline Lamb) that Augusta Leigh's third daughter, Elizabeth Medora Leigh (1814–49), might have been Byron's. His comments stop short of an admission, both on the count of incest and on that of impregnating his sister. As Fiona MacCarthy observes, they prove little: 'This seems less a straightforward confession referring to the medieval superstition that children conceived incestuously would be born as monsters than an ambiguous joke of the kind Byron and Lady Melbourne loved to share. He could equally well be suggesting that forbidden intercourse between him and his sister might have malformed a child generated by George Leigh.'[8] MacCarthy goes on to note Byron's lack, in later years, of any interest in Medora comparable to that in Allegra, his daughter by Claire Clairmont, suggesting 'Byron was never convinced [Medora] was his child.'[9]

What, then, was he playing at, telling Lady Melbourne 'it is utterly impossible I can ever be half as well liked elsewhere' (as with Augusta)? The answer may be found in Lady Melbourne's response, which was immediate. Her letter, presumably delivered to the Albany by hand (as his to her had been), declared: 'I wish I could flatter myself I had the least influence ... for I could talk & reason with you for two Hours, so many objections have I to urge, & after all, for what … is it worth while!'[10] The exclamation mark is hers, as are the panicky cadences, which reveal she was in a flap. And not surprisingly: besides being taboo, what Byron was suggesting bordered on the criminal. 'When you return to A. I shall not dare to make use of Such a term you will deem it, irreligious.'[11]

It gave Byron a thrill to confess to crimes of which he and his sister may have been innocent. He was a poseur rather than the real thing, and those close to him knew it.[12] Augusta herself said as much: 'Byron is never so happy as when he can make you believe some atrocity against himself.'[13] Hobhouse observed he 'had the habit of marking in his books traits of singular depravity, and poor Lady Byron mistook these marks for notes of admiration'.[14] Caroline Lamb's repeated claims that Byron 'corrupted' his manservant, Rushton, are now discredited, and originated with Byron himself.[15] Thanks to Byron's own words, Goethe believed him a murderer, and Thomas Moore noted of Caroline Lamb that 'Lord Byron *did* endeavor to make her think that he murdered some one – never would give her his right hand – wore a glove on it &c. &c. This at first alarmed [Lady Caroline], but when she came to know him better, she saw through his acting.'[16] Moore was aware of Byron's tendency, in a 'self-accusing mood', to 'throw out hints of his past life with an air of gloom and mystery designed evidently to awaken curiosity and interest', and continued:

> From what I have known … of his experiments upon more impressible listeners, I have little doubt that, to produce effect at the moment, there is hardly any crime so dark or desperate of which, in the excitement of thus acting upon the imaginations of others, he would not have hinted that he had been guilty; and it has sometimes occurred to me that the occult cause of his lady's separation from him, round which herself and her legal advisor have thrown such formidable mystery, may have been nothing more, after all, than some imposture of this kind, some dimly hinted confession of undefined horrors, which, though intended by the relater but to mystify and surprise, the hearer so little understood him as to take in sober seriousness.[17]

This does not provide licence for questioning everything Byron said, but Moore advises caution where Byron volunteers himself sole witness for the prosecution. Surveying the correspondence with Lady Melbourne, G. Wilson Knight pointed out, 'Byron liked arousing people's suspicions … . This is a trait everyone recognized, and evidence of it abounds.'[18] For this reason, Alan Rawes judges the Melbourne letters 'problematic as evidence'.[19] Knight has to be right when he says Byron found the older woman 'both entertaining and shocking' and wanted to test her. It was the kind of game to which someone as narcissistic and easily bored as Byron was prone – and a Regency high-roller like Lady Melbourne presented an irresistible challenge. Her rapsheet was as colourful as his, for she employed her charms ruthlessly and systematically in the cause of social advancement. Past conquests included the Second Earl of Egremont, the Fifth Duke of Bedford, Lord Coleraine, and the Prince of Wales. Her own descendants described her as 'a spendthrift and a libertine'.[20] For Byron, the pay-off for saying he was running off to the Continent with his half-sister was the satisfaction of seeing the traumatized reaction of this experienced woman of the world filtered through the incoherent sentences, tremulous hand, and tentative wording of her written response. (That is not to say the desire to elope with Augusta was a total sham; he idealizes it in his 'Epistle to Augusta', which sees 'two things in my destiny: / A world to roam through, and a home with thee' (ll. 7–8), and actually did suggest her family accompany him to Nice ('but I should occupy a separate house').[21] In October 1822, when the invitation was extended, he must have known there was little chance of acceptance. 'Pensez', he advised her – as if daring her to say 'no', as indeed she did.)

The other principal witness is Byron's estranged wife who, according to Harriet Beecher Stowe in 1870, insisted (at length) that 'the crime which separated her from Lord Byron was incest'.[22] But that contradicts her contemporary testimony. In a letter to her mother of 24 January 1816 she wrote, 'I very much fear that she [Augusta] may be supposed the cause of the separation by many, & it would be a cruel injustice'.[23] In July that year she accepted there had been no incest, for she told Mrs Villiers: 'I have had an answer – all that it ought to be – or that I could desire. It *thoroughly* convinces me of her innocence in regard to all the period with which I was concerned.'[24] S. M. Waddams, the Canadian jurist who analysed the papers of Lady Byron's lawyer, Stephen Lushington, says there is 'no proof'[25] Byron committed incest with his sister during the course of his marriage, and that Lady Byron and her advisers accepted that as fact: 'suspicion of incest was not Lady Byron's primary reason for desiring a separation'.[26] As Doris Langley Moore has shown, Lady Byron's story changed only when she became hostile towards Augusta on other grounds, from 1824 onwards.[27] Yet that is the testimony by which many biographers justify the charge of incest without acknowledging her change of heart. As Knight suggests, they are wrong to do so.[28]

Augusta's word should be considered, if anything, more trustworthy than that of either Byron or his wife. She never admitted to an incestuous union even though, during the 'weeks leading up to the Separation, she was functioning as Lady Byron's colleague'.[29] Having examined Leigh's correspondence with Lady Byron, Knight confirmed that 'Augusta confesses to nothing', and cited Lord Lovelace as observing that at her death she left behind, 'all ready and arranged, a small selection of carefully selected documents calculated to rebut the charge [of incest]'.[30] Eisler's search through Leigh's commonplace book turned up nothing conclusive, and what it did produce suggests 'doubt rather than conviction'.[31] If Mrs Villiers' letter to Lady Byron of 26 February 1816 is correct, there were rumours in London of incest having taken place, probably circulated by Caroline Lamb.[32] But did anyone take them seriously? Less than a month later, on 16 March, Augusta became Woman of the Bedchamber to Queen Charlotte, which entitled her to an annual stipend of £300 (rising to £700 in November 1818) and a suite of apartments in St James's Palace. It is hard to believe such an appointment would have been approved were she thought to have had an affair with her half-brother.

Byron enjoyed teasing Lady Melbourne with the shocking idea he had bedded Augusta and, by saying as much to Caroline Lamb, was indirectly responsible for broadcasting the good news to London society. Augusta would suffer by this when Lady Byron turned against her, but the biggest casualty was Medora who, until the day she died, believed herself Byron's daughter.[33] True or not, it blighted her life and alienated her from her mother. Having exiled herself to France, Medora became a servant, was seduced by a soldier, had his child, and died of smallpox at the age of 35.

No one doubts that Byron had unnaturally intense feelings towards Augusta. While we cannot rule out the possibility something occurred between them (most likely in 1813 or 1814), we cannot know what it was, and there is nothing to prove Medora was theirs. All we have are rumours circulated by Byron, repeated by Caroline Lamb, and reiterated by his wife. That the trail leads back to him is suggestive: he cannot have failed to realize the incest myth bolstered that of his heterosexuality (Myth 17), which in turn concealed his interest in 15-year-old boys (for which see pp. 143–5). Incest was shocking and disreputable, but in ways that might have enriched his reputation; his interest in boys might have destroyed it. (If he had doubts on that score, he had only to consider the fate of William Beckford.[34]) In this case, as in others, the truth is more revealing than the lie: the 'crimes' to which Byron was willing to confess were not invariably those of which he was guilty. Lady Caroline might more accurately have called him 'mad, bad, and *difficult* to know' – but that would have been less memorable.

Notes

1 Benita Eisler, Byron: *Child of Passion, Fool of Fame* (London: Hamish Hamilton, 1999), p. 396.
2 Michael and Melissa Bakewell, *Augusta Leigh, Byron's Half-Sister: A Biography* (London: Chatto & Windus, 2000), p. 104.

3 It is Paul Douglass's contention, in *The Cambridge Companion to Byron* that, by the time Byron separated from his wife, he 'probably ... [had] a daughter by Augusta'; see 'Byron's Life and his Biographers', in *The Cambridge Companion to Byron*, ed. Drummond Bone (Cambridge: Cambridge University Press, 2004), p. 13.

4 Lord Byron, journal entry for 14 November 1813, in *Byron's Letters and Journals*, ed. Leslie A. Marchand (13 vols., London: John Murray, 1973–94), iii. 205.

5 Lord Byron to Augusta Leigh, 17 May 1819, ibid., vi. 129.

6 Lord Byron to Augusta Leigh, 5 October 1821, ibid., viii. 234.

7 Lord Byron to Lady Melbourne, 25 April 1814, ibid., iv. 104.

8 Fiona MacCarthy, *Byron: Life and Legend* (London: John Murray, 2002), p. 214. MacCarthy is not the only biographer to have questioned Byron's paternity of Medora; see also Doris Langley Moore, *The Late Lord Byron* (Philadelphia and New York: Lippincott, 1961), pp. 301–2.

9 MacCarthy, *Byron: Life and Legend*, p. 215.

10 Lady Melbourne to Lord Byron, 25 April 1814, in *Byron's 'Corbeau Blanc': The Life and Letters of Lady Melbourne*, ed. Jonathan David Gross (Liverpool: Liverpool University Press, 1997), p. 171.

11 Ibid., p. 172.

12 Peter Cochran writes an entire chapter on this theme in *Byron's Romantic Politics: The Problem of Metahistory* (Newcastle upon Tyne: Cambridge Scholars, 2011), pp. 191–207.

13 John Cam Hobhouse, *Contemporary Account of the Separation of Lord and Lady Byron* (London: privately printed, 1870), p. 104.

14 Ibid.

15 Roderick Beaton, *Byron's War: Romantic Rebellion, Greek Revolution* (Cambridge: Cambridge University Press, 2013), p. 21.

16 *The Diary of Thomas Moore*, ed. Wilfred Dowden, Barbara Bartholomew, and Joy L. Linsley (6 vols., Newark and London: Associated University Presses, 1983–91), iii. 1079.

17 *The Works of Lord Byron* (14 vols., London: John Murray, 1832), vi. 242.

18 G. Wilson Knight, *Lord Byron's Marriage: The Evidence of the Asterisks* (London: Kegan Paul, 1957), p. 41. On this subject see also, *inter alia*, James Soderholm, *Fantasy, Forgery, and the Byron Legend* (Lexington: University Press of Kentucky, 1996), p. 153.

19 Alan Rawes, '"That Perverse Passion" and Benita Eisler's "Byronic" Biography of Byron', in *Romantic Biography*, ed. Arthur Bradley and Alan Rawes (Aldershot, Hants.: Ashgate, 2003), pp. 74–92, 76. I am indebted throughout this essay to Rawes's thoughtful and persuasive analysis.

20 Judy Egerton, *George Stubbs, Painter. Catalogue Raisonné* (New Haven: Yale University Press, 2007), p. 319.

21 Lord Byron to Augusta Leigh, 20 October 1822, in *Byron's Letters and Journals* ed. Marchand, x. 15.

22 Harriet Beecher Stowe, *Lady Byron Vindicated: A History of the Byron Controversy* (London: Sampson Low, 1870), p. 233. In fact, Stowe first alleged

incest in September 1869: see Paul Baender, 'Mark Twain and the Byron Scandal', *American Literature* 30 (1959), 467–85, and Susan McPherson, 'Opening the Open Secret: The Stowe-Byron Controversy', *Victorian Review* 27 (2001), 86–101.

23 Lady Byron to Lady Noel, 24 January 1816, as quoted by S. M. Waddams, *Law, Politics, and the Church of England: The Career of Stephen Lushington 1782–1873* (Cambridge: Cambridge University Press, 1992), p. 128.

24 Ibid., p. 111n43.

25 Ibid., p. 129.

26 Ibid., p. 127. Waddams is dependent on Marchand's ambiguous comments on the matter for the thought that incest might have taken place prior to the marriage. G. Wilson Knight analyses Lushington's comments in *Byron and Shakespeare* (London: Routledge & Kegan Paul, 1966), pp. 359–64.

27 Moore, *The Late Lord Byron*, p. 145.

28 Knight, *Byron and Shakespeare*, p. 114. The charge that incest caused the separation is described by Knight as a 'lie'.

29 Ibid., p. 88.

30 Ibid., pp. 96, 97.

31 Rawes, '"That Perverse Passion"', p. 86.

32 For Mrs Villiers' letter, see Malcolm Elwin, *Lord Byron's Wife* (London: Macdonald, 1962), pp. 425–6.

33 Medora's sad story is recounted by, *inter alia*, Michael and Melissa Bakewell, *Augusta Leigh, Byron's Half-Sister*.

34 In 1784, something occurred at Powderham Castle, estate of Lord Courtney, father of William Courtenay, with whom Beckford was in love, that was reported as 'the detestable scene lately acted in Wiltshire, by a pair of fashionable male lovers'. The scandal ended Beckford's worldly ambitions and heralded a decline in his creativity; see William Beckford, *Vathek with the Episodes of Vathek*, ed. Kenneth W. Graham (Peterborough, Ont.: Broadview, 2001), p. 20.

Myth
17 BYRON WAS A GREAT LOVER OF WOMEN

> Woman, experience might have told me,
> That all must love thee, who behold thee;
> Surely, experience might have taught,
> Thy firmest promises are naught;
> But, plac'd in all thy charms before me,
> All I forget, but to adore thee.
>
> Byron, 'To Woman', ll. 1–6[1]

Byron's female readers had no doubt *he* adored *them* (as their fan mail proves[2]) and could not have guessed at the emptiness behind such posturing; even the editor of the *Complete Poetical Works* calls these lines 'derivative', and suggests Byron had no particular addressee in mind.[3] It didn't matter. An inveterate self-publicist, Byron forged his image through the alter ego of the misanthropic Childe Harold. By 1821 the Scottish journalist John Gibson Lockhart was heartily sick of it. 'You do not hate men, "no, nor woman neither", but you thought it would be a fine, interesting thing for a handsome young Lord to depict himself as a dark-souled, melancholy, morbid being', he moaned, before continuing:

> In spite of all your pranks, (*Beppo*, &c. *Don Juan* included), every boarding-school in the empire still contains many devout believers in the amazing misery of the black-haired, high-browed, blue-eyed, bare-throated, Lord Byron. How melancholy you look in the prints! Oh! yes, this is the true cast of face. Now, tell me, Mrs. Goddard, now tell me, Miss Price, now tell me, dear Harriet Smith, and dear, dear Mrs. Elton, do tell me, is not this just the very look, that one would have fancied for Childe Harold? Oh! what eyes and eyebrows! – Oh! what a chin![4]

30 Great Myths About the Romantics, First Edition. Duncan Wu.
© 2015 John Wiley & Sons, Ltd. Published 2015 by John Wiley & Sons, Ltd.

Lockhart waxes envious, but he has a point. The image of the Byronic nobleman rampaged through the female imagination for decades to come, perpetuated by such anti-heroes as Heathcliff and Rochester. Which may explain why a recent volume about seduction presents the noble lord as 'more than a rock-star poet who caused a tsunami of female fans – a Byronmania – he won the undying adoration of innumerable women throughout his life'.[5] Such claims buttress the argument he was a great lover, which in turn embellishes the myth he was a pre-eminent heterosexual.

As long ago as 1974, Doris Langley Moore said 'Byron was, in my belief, like many men of extreme sensibility, born with a genuinely bisexual temperament.'[6] Louis Crompton concurred: in *Byron and Greek Love* (1985) he noted Byron's 'heterosexual impulses were fully as real as his homosexual ones and, if we take his life as a whole, more persistent and significant'.[7] He was, deduces Crompton, bisexual, with periods when homosexual activity was predominant.[8] That does not mean he was uninterested in women. He seems to have loved Teresa Guiccioli, his affair with whom has been described as 'suicidal in its intensity',[9] at least until she left her husband for him, when he promptly lost interest in her. (She later claimed their relationship was Platonic, though scholars think that unlikely.[10]) And it is true he conceded that females possessed a certain *je ne sais quoi*:

> There is something to me very softening in the presence of a woman, – some strange influence, even if one is not in love with them, – which I cannot at all account for, having no very high opinion of the sex. But yet, – I always feel in better humour with myself and every thing else, if there is a woman within ken.[11]

Perhaps that was why he made the raffish Lady Melbourne his confidante, to whom he wrote more letters than anyone else with the exception of Murray, Hobhouse, and his financial advisers.[12] That friendship was echoed towards the end of his life in confessional banterings with Marguerite, Countess of Blessington. If he had 'no very high opinion of the sex', he could nonetheless empathize with women's plight. Only that would explain why, rather than seducing Lady Frances Wedderburn Webster, 'I spared her.'[13] And it explains why he elucidated the female perspective with such fidelity in *Don Juan*:

> Alas! the love of women! it is known
> To be a lovely and a fearful thing;
> For all of theirs upon that die is thrown,
> And if 'tis lost, life hath no more to bring

> To them but mockeries of the past alone,
>   And their revenge is as the tiger's spring,
> Deadly, and quick, and crushing; yet, as real
> Torture is theirs, what they inflict they feel.
>
> They are right; for man, to man so oft unjust,
>   Is always so to women; one sole bond
> Awaits them, treachery is all their trust;
>   Taught to conceal, their bursting hearts despond
> Over their idol, till some wealthier lust
>   Buys them in marriage – and what rests beyond?
> A thankless husband, next a faithless lover,
> Then dressing, nursing, praying, and all's over.[14]

Anyone reading those stanzas might be forgiven for imagining their author thought constantly about women – as was almost certainly the intention. But that phrase, 'Alas! the love of women!', is ambiguous: despite first appearances, 'the love' is not felt *towards* women, but felt *by* women for men.

His mythic power as lover continues to linger; the notion of a 'Byronic lover' implies a dark, tall stranger whose reputation makes the knees of even the most level-headed female quiver in anticipation. Byron's actual gifts may have been less noteworthy. Writing to Jane Williams in December 1826, Claire Clairmont recalled her affair with him as having 'lasted only ten minutes but these ten minutes have discomposed the rest of my life; the passion God knows for what cause, from no fault of mine however disappeared leaving no trace whatever behind it except my heart wasted and ruined as if it had been scorched by a thousand lightnings'.[15] *Ten minutes*. Byron evidently wasted no time on foreplay; he got straight down to business, as was the case with the unfortunate chambermaid upon whom, in Belgium, 'he fell like a thunderbolt'.[16] No wonder those ten minutes, which had seemed to promise so much, 'discomposed' Clairmont's life. Byron's focus was on his own gratification: when it was over, it was over. And the caravan moved on. He was typical of his day in regarding women as passive receptacles with no sexual needs or libido – and the alacrity with which he dispatched his partners indicates a disinclination to engage with them on other terms.

Only that would explain the industrial scale on which his love-making skills appear to have been deployed when in Venice, where he spent upwards of £2,500 (a king's ransom in those days) on over 200 women, 'perhaps more – for I have not lately kept the recount'.[17] Shelley attested to Byron's frenetic programme of indulgence having seen him urge 'fathers & mothers to bargain with him for their daughters, & though this is common enough in Italy, yet for an Englishman to encourage such sickening vice is a melancholy thing'.[18] Shelley felt sorry for the Venetians who were suffering poverty and starvation thanks to the Austrian occupation. Had he been asked, Byron might have said he was doing what we might now call social work: at a time of depression, the sating of his appetites generated a vigorous micro-economy in the heart of the lagoon. He told his banker, Douglas Kinnaird, that it was an appropriate use of his literary earnings: 'what I get by my brains – I will spend on my b[ollock]s – as long as I have a tester or testicle remaining'. In the same letter, dated 19 January 1819, he enumerates the hapless multitudes bedded 'since last year' – that is, *in the last two and a half weeks*:

> the Tarruscelli – the Da Mosti – the Spineda – the Lotti – the Rizzato – the Eleanora – the Carlotta – the Giulietta – the Alvisi – the Zambieri – The Eleanora da Bezzi – (who was the King of Naples' Gioaschino's mistress – at least one of them) the Theresina of Mazzurati – the Glettenheimer – & her Sister – the Luigia & her mother – the Fornaretta – the Santa – the Caligari – the Portiera [Vedova?] – the Bolognese figurante – the Tentora and her sister – cum multis aliis? – some of them are Countesses – & some of them Cobblers wives – some noble – some middling – some low – & all whores ... I have had them all & thrice as many to boot since 1817 ... .[19]

None of this suggests love; in fact, it is more consistent with someone who detested women – sexually abused in childhood by his nurse, his relationship with his mother tormented, and who referred without hesitation to 'the bitch my wife'.[20] His general attitude might be summarized by the precept, 'I always suspect a woman of being a whore'.[21] Such feelings explain why he liked Lady Caroline Lamb to cross-dress: in drag, she could be imagined 'a fair-faced delicate boy of thirteen or fourteen' – not a woman but an effeminate young man.[22] One of his favourite pastimes was sodomy practised on members of both sexes, which Thomas Moore placed under the category 'certain beastly proposals'.[23] (During his Venice debauch, his pet-name for the place was 'Sea-Sodom'.[24]) This was what Knight meant when he referred squeamishly to Byron's 'homosexuality, together with its extension into the marriage-relationship'.[25]

Those wedded to the idea of Byron as red-blooded heterosexual might wish to inspect the names in his address book. One or two significant exceptions aside, his preferred partners were adolescent males – the likes of John Edleston, the 15-year-old Cambridge chorister of whom he wrote: 'I certainly *love* him more than any human being ... . He certainly is perhaps more *attached* to *me*, than even I am in *return*.'[26] This was a romantic attachment not consummated physically,[27] and perhaps on that account Edleston remained the pre-eminent love of his life. Until the end of his days Byron treasured a lock of his blond hair upon which his wife saw him gaze with 'feeling'.[28] That liaison was echoed in others:

there was his infatuation with Efstathios Georgiou ('my dearly-beloved Eustathius'[29]), whose 'ambrosial curls' hung down over his garments while he held a parasol 'to save his complexion from the heat';[30] his affair with Niccolò Giraud, a 15-year-old Grecian of French parentage, of whom he wrote, 'I have obtained above two hundred pl & opt Cs and am almost tired of them'[31] (the phrase 'pl & opt Cs' being code for 'coitum plenum et optabilem' – 'as much full intercourse as I could wish' – from Petronius, referring to sex between an adult male and adolescent boy[32]); the young Bartolomeo di Regnier, later Professor of Italian Language and Literature;[33] and Loukas Chalandritsanos, 15 years old when Byron became infatuated with him on Cephalonia. Despite gifts of gilded firearms, a gold-bedecked jacket, an expensive saddle, and large amounts of money, Loukas fought off his benefactor's advances, for which Roderick Beaton convicts him of 'contempt, indifference, or quite possibly just uncomprehending vanity'.[34]

It was not very heterosexual of Byron, when visiting Turkey in May 1810, to beat a path to the 'Buggering shop' where he ogled the early nineteenth-century equivalent of male strippers. As Hobhouse confided to his diary: 'here I saw a boy dancing in a style indescribably beastly, scarcely moving from one place, but making a thousand lascivious motions with his thighs loins and belly'.[35] Indescribably beastly, though not beastly enough to deter them from going back two days later 'with a party' to watch 'two old and ugly boys, who wrung the sweat off their brows, dance as before, waving their long hair. Also they spread a mat and, putting on a kind of shawl, performed an Alexandrian woman's dance – much the same, except that they knelt, and, covering each other's heads, seemed as if kissing.' One of their Turkish friends told them this was foreplay: 'De Turk take and byger dem d'ye see?'[36] Unsurprisingly, these episodes failed to find a place in Hobhouse's *A Journey through Albania and Other Provinces of Turkey* (1813) based (loosely) on his journal entries.

The myth of Byron's supposed love of women is traceable either to his poems (which encourage the confusion of Don Juan with his creator) or to his publicity machine (of which Hobhouse was one of the more important cogs). Among close friends, however, he made little secret of his true inclinations. In a letter of June 1809 he describes William Beckford, lover of William 'Kitty' Courtenay, Ninth Earl of Devon (said to be the most beautiful boy in England), as 'Martyr of prejudice', 'the great Apostle of Paederasty Beckford!',[37] while he told another friend his objective in making his grand tour was to research a treatise 'to be entituled "Sodomy simplified or Paederasty proved to be praiseworthy from ancient authors and modern practice."'[38] This was only half a joke. There is no doubt Byron thought pederasty *was* praiseworthy, and that has to modify how we assess his status as a lover of women. So

Figure 13 William Beckford (1760–1844), author of one of the greatest novels of the period, *Vathek: An Arabian Tale* (1786). Byron regarded him as a 'great Apostle of Paederasty'.
Source: Paul F. Betz Collection.

far as the majority of his female conquests were concerned, Byron had no interest in them once the deed was done; they were shown the door and ushered briskly through it. Boys, on the other hand, were partners with whom he spent the long love's day. He loved more than their bodies; he loved their company and luxuriated with them, as Juan and Haidee do in their Greek idyll. That would explain why his most deeply felt poems were addressed not to women but to nubile young boys in girls' clothing.

> Ours too the glance none saw beside;
> The smile none else might understand;
> The whisper'd thought of hearts allied,
> The pressure of the thrilling hand;
> The kiss so guiltless and refin'd
> That Love each warmer wish forbore;
> Those eyes proclaim'd so pure a mind,
> Ev'n passion blush'd to plead for more.[39]

Notes

1 In Lord Byron, *The Complete Poetical Works*, ed. Jerome J. McGann (7 vols., Oxford: Clarendon Press, 1980–93), i. 45.

2 See, *inter alia*, Corin Throsby, 'Flirting with Fame: Byron's Anonymous Female Fans', *The Byron Journal* 32.2 (December 2004), 115–23.

3 Byron, *Complete Poetical Works*, ed. McGann, i. 366.

4 J. G. Lockhart, writing in 1821; even Byron enjoyed it. See *Lord Byron: The Critical Heritage*, ed. Andrew Rutherford (London: Routledge & Kegan Paul, 1970), pp. 182–3.

5 Betsy Prioleau, *Swoon: Great Seducers and Why Women Love Them* (New York: Norton, 2013), p. 21.

6 Doris Langley Moore, *Lord Byron: Accounts Rendered* (New York: Harper & Row, 1974), p. 456.

7 Louis Crompton, *Byron and Greek Love: Homophobia in 19th-Century England* (Berkeley: University of California Press, 1985), p. 8.

8 Recent critics resile from taxonomy: Andrew Elfenbein describes Byron as 'omnivorous', while Emily A. Bernhard Jackson writes: 'What precise act he performed, or with what gender, or with precisely whom he performed the acts he performed, seems not to have been important to him. The goal for Byron was sex.' See Andrew Elfenbein, *Byron and the Victorians* (Cambridge: Cambridge University Press, 1995), p. 209, and Emily A. Bernhard Jackson, 'Least Like Saints: The Vexed Issue of Byron's Sexuality', *The Byron Journal* 38 (2010), 29–37, p. 34.

9 Peter Cochran, introduction to *Don Leon*, in *Byron and Women [and Men]*, ed. Peter Cochran (Newcastle upon Tyne: Cambridge Scholars, 2010), pp. 207–21, 207. For two letters by Byron from this period, see Teresa Guiccioli, *Lord Byron's Life in Italy*, ed. Peter Cochran, tr. Michael Rees (Cranbury, NJ: Associated University Presses, 2005), p. 9.

10 See, for instance, Guiccioli, *Lord Byron's Life in Italy*, p. 19. G. Wilson Knight was inclined to belief; see *Lord Byron's Marriage: The Evidence of Asterisks* (London: Routledge & Kegan Paul, 1957), p. 254.

11 Journal entry, 27 February 1814, in *Byron's Letters and Journals*, ed. Leslie A. Marchand (13 vols., London: John Murray, 1973–94), iii. 246.

12 For this I am indebted to Mary O'Connell, who investigates its implications in *The Literary Relationship of Byron and John Murray* (Liverpool: Liverpool University Press, 2014). Paul Douglass says Lady Melbourne was Byron's last conquest; see *Lady Caroline Lamb: A Biography* (New York: Palgrave Macmillan, 2004), p. 113.

13 Lord Byron to Lady Melbourne, 17 October 1813, in *Byron's Letters and Journals*, ed. Marchand, iii. 146.

14 *Don Juan* ii, stanzas 199–200, in Byron, *Complete Poetical Works*, ed. McGann, v. 151.

15 Claire Clairmont to Jane Williams, December 1826, in *The Clairmont Correspondence*, ed. Marion Kingston Stocking (2 vols., Baltimore, MD: Johns Hopkins University Press, 1995), i. 241.

16 *The Diary of Dr John William Polidori 1816*, ed. William Michael Rossetti (London: Elkin Mathews, 1911), p. 33.

17 Lord Byron to James Wedderburn Webster, 8 September 1818, in *Byron's Letters and Journals*, ed. Marchand, vi. 66.

18 Percy Bysshe Shelley to Thomas Love Peacock, 17 or 18 December 1818, in *The Letters of Percy Bysshe Shelley*, ed. Frederick L. Jones (2 vols., Oxford: Clarendon Press, 1964), ii. 58.

19 Lord Byron to Hobhouse and Kinnaird, 19 January 1819, in *Byron's Letters and Journals*, ed. Marchand, vi. 92.

20 Lord Byron to Hobhouse, 25 January 1819, ibid., p. 95. See also, *inter alia*, Fiona MacCarthy, *Byron: Life and Legend* (London: John Murray, 2002), pp. 23, 52–3. It is intriguing to find that, according to Thomas Moore, it was widely believed 'the Monsters in Paris that stab women' were inspired by 'the study of Lord Byrons works, & the principles inculcated by him!' See *The Journal of Thomas Moore*, ed. Wilfred S. Dowden (6 vols., Newark: University of Delaware Press, 1983–91), i. 303.

21 Lord Byron to Douglas Kinnaird, 9 December 1818, in *Byron's Letters and Journals*, ed. Marchand, vi. 87.

22 Robert Charles Dallas, *Correspondence of Lord Byron with a Friend* (3 vols., Paris: Galignani, 1825), iii. 41. As Paul Douglass points out, Lamb was in the habit of cross-dressing before she met Byron; see Douglass, *Lady Caroline Lamb*, pp. 64–5.

23 Fiona MacCarthy; see *Byron: Life and Legend*, pp. 267–8.

24 Lord Byron to Richard Hoppner, 31 December 1819, in *Byron's Letters and Journals*, ed. Marchand, vi. 262. The term is used also at *Marino Faliero*, V. iii. 99.

25 Knight, *Lord Byron's Marriage*, p. 254.

26 Lord Byron to Elizabeth Pigot, 5 July 1807, in *Byron's Letters and Journals*, ed. Marchand, i. 124–5.

27 This is the view of, among others, Roderick Beaton, *Byron's War: Romantic Rebellion, Greek Revolution* (Cambridge: Cambridge University Press, 2013), p. 21.

28 Crompton, *Byron and Greek Love*, p. 218.

29 Lord Byron to John Cam Hobhouse, 29 July 1810, in *Byron's Letters and Journals*, ed. Marchand, ii. 6.

30 Ibid.

31 Lord Byron to John Cam Hobhouse, 12 October 1810, ibid., p. 23.

32 This is the translation given by Beaton, *Byron's War*, p. 22. See, *inter alia*, Crompton, *Byron and Greek Love*, p. 128.

33 See Peter Cochran, 'Byron's Boyfriends', in *Byron and Women [and Men]*, ed. Cochran, p. 32.

34 Beaton, *Byron's War*, p. 244.

35 Hobhouse, diary for 17 May 1810, transcribed by Peter Cochran, p. 219. Accessible online at <http://petercochran.files.wordpress.com/2009/12/07 -constantinople.pdf>.

36 Hobhouse, diary for 19 May 1810, transcribed by Peter Cochran, p. 221.

37 Lord Byron to Francis Hodgson, 25 June 1809, in *Byron's Letters and Journals*, ed. Marchand, i. 210. Byron comments further on Beckford in *Childe Harold*; see D. S. Neff, 'Bitches, Mollies, and Tommies: Byron, Masculinity, and the History of Sexualities', *Journal of the History of Sexuality* 11 (2002), 395–438, p. 412.

38 Lord Byron to Henry Drury, 25 June 1809, in *Byron's Letters and Journals*, ed. Marchand, i. 208.

39 'To Thyrza' ('Without a stone to mark the spot'), 29–36, ibid., p. 347.

Myth

18 BYRON WAS A CHAMPION OF DEMOCRACY

Writing in 1897, Edward Dowden described Byron as 'a democrat among aristocrats and an aristocrat among democrats'[1] – the kind of antithesis that gives rhetorical devices a bad name. More surprisingly, a recently published work of reference tells us: 'Greece enlisted the help of liberal admirers across Europe in its war for independence from the Ottoman Empire, and volunteers like the English Romantic poet Lord Byron answered the call to arms, inspired by the thought of liberating the first democracy of the ancient world.'[2] There are at least four factual slippages in that sentence: (1) Byron was not English but Scottish (contrary to what some might think, there *is* a difference); (2) he didn't answer a 'call to arms' as a 'volunteer' (a status he would have loathed), but went as representative of the London Greek Committee;[3] (3) he was an admirer of Greece only in the abstract (see p. 161); (4) he was neither liberator nor democrat but an aristocrat with a finely honed instinct for protecting his own interests.

On the sole occasion when he reflected seriously on the matter in his journal, he expressed himself in no uncertain terms:

> The Roman Consuls make a goodly show – but then they only reigned for a *year* – & and were under a sort of personal obligation to distinguish themselves. – It is still more difficult to say which form of Government is the *worst* – all are so bad. – As for democracy it is the worst of the whole – for *what is (in fact)* democracy? an Aristocracy of Blackguards. –[4]

If that sounds like snobbery, it is. And it resonates mercilessly through any analysis of Byron's politics, a symptom of the fanaticism with which he coveted his aristocratic status. (He was born in the back room of a rented apartment in a London side street and perhaps feared a revolution might

30 Great Myths About the Romantics, First Edition. Duncan Wu.
© 2015 John Wiley & Sons, Ltd. Published 2015 by John Wiley & Sons, Ltd.

send him back there.) That has not deterred supporters from arguing that he foresaw the necessity of revolution, as if he were the Che Guevara of his day: 'The king-times are fast finishing. There will be blood shed like water, and tears like mist; but the peoples will conquer in the end. I shall not live to see it, but I foresee it.'[5] In this, as in his verse, tone is everything. His words were written in horror rather than ardent anticipation. The 'Byron as revolutionary' school cites his support of Italian and Greek independence, but he never said he wanted revolution (at least not in the sense posited by Marx and Engels). He might more accurately be said to have supported anti-colonial nationalism in three occupied countries of the Mediterranean – not necessarily a good thing. After his death, the myth of Byron as 'noble warrior' killed in the cause of Greek freedom (Myth 19) granted respectability to the militant nationalism which was to be 'the most divisive and destructive element in Western civilisation'.[6]

Richard Cronin points to the glibness with which he supported the revolutionary side when discussing 'preindustrial, neo-feudal societies, [in which] he could assume his preferred political role as champion of the people without compromising his aristocratic status'.[7] In 1816–18, Byron was basically a tourist with an incomplete understanding of the political situation and of those with whom he claimed common cause. Though he struck the pose of freedom fighter in both countries, his contribution to their plights amounted to very little – and in the case of Italy it is arguable he made matters worse rather than better (see pp. 156–8). In Britain, he enjoyed being thought the saviour of labouring folk, and they read him in the belief he spoke on their behalf.[8] That would explain why, after his death, the greater part of those who mourned him publicly were from 'the commonest and the lowest orders'.[9]

Did he ever take up arms for them? No, and for that most immaculate of conceptions: self-interest. In the Appendix to *The Two Foscari* – published shortly after composition – Byron described himself as 'no revolutionist' before going on to say

> I wish to see the English constitution restored and not destroyed. Born an aristocrat, and naturally one by temper, with the greater part of my present property in the funds, what have *I* to gain by a revolution? Perhaps I have more to lose in every way than Mr. Southey, with all his places and presents for panegyrics and abuse into the bargain. But that a revolution is inevitable, I repeat. The government may exult over the repression of petty tumults; these are but the advancing waves repulsed and broken for a moment on the shore, while the great tide is still rolling on and gaining ground with every breaker.[10]

Byron insisted on the inevitability of revolution not because he wanted it, but because he had been worked into a frenzy by his banker, Douglas Kinnaird, who told him of rioting in London after Princess Caroline's funeral in July 1821. His response? Sell government bonds while profits were still to be made – orders that continued even after he reached Missolonghi.[11]

One of the problems with this myth is the failure to understand the profound hostility towards democratic forms of government in Regency Britain. It was a land in which the argument that everyone had a God-given right to political representation was alien, the only people eligible to vote being men over 21 who met certain property-related conditions. Individual boroughs determined these, and as a result only twenty constituencies in the country had more than a thousand voters. By 1830, there were no more than 250,000 voters nationwide out of a total population of around 15 million[12] – 1.7 per cent. Manchester, Birmingham, Sheffield, and Leeds (the largest industrial centres in Britain) lacked any representation at all, while the boroughs of Old Sarum (a depopulated mound of scorched earth with eleven voters, all of whom lived elsewhere) and Dunwich (which was under water) returned two MPs each. English constituencies returned two members to Parliament; those in Scotland and Wales returned only one each. In Edinburgh and Glasgow, only magistrates could vote (thirty-three in each city); in seats such as Bodmin in Cornwall, only members of the local corporation could vote; in some boroughs only freemen could vote; in the constituency of Westminster, voters had only to pay more than £10 a year in rent to qualify –11,000 were eligible.[13] Those who owned property in more than one borough had more than one vote, while graduates of the universities of Oxford and Cambridge could vote in the constituency in which they lived *as well as* in the two university seats. Votes were always available for hire; indeed, advertisements appeared in newspapers at election time announcing the sale of entire boroughs. (Thomas Coutts purchased the seat of Boroughbridge for £4,000 in 1796 and gave it to his son-in-law, Sir Francis Burdett.[14])

Crazy though it may seem, most people felt pride at the British constitution, regarded with admiration even by foreigners – and that reveals something to which we should remain acutely sensitive: the assumptions we make about the superiority of western democracy had no footing then. There were democratic agitators, the likes of Henry 'Orator' Hunt and William Cobbett (who lobbied for annual parliaments, universal male suffrage, and the secret ballot), but they were persecuted with legislation designed to marginalize them and their opinions. Cobbett fled the country in spring 1817 when the government rushed through laws designed to precipitate his imprisonment, while Hunt was incarcerated for two and a half years after the Peterloo massacre. From a modern perspective, they were martyrs. At risk to liberty and life, they helped bring about the system of political representation Britain has today.

Had Byron really been a democrat, he would have expressed soli-
darity with them; instead they were (so he said) 'low designing dirty
levellers who would pioneer their way to a democratical tyranny'[15]
and 'a pack of blackguards – who disgust one with their Cause'. Of
Hunt, he expressed the desire to 'have passed my sword-stick through
his body – like a dog's ... it would have been as public a Service as
Walworth's chastisement of Wat. Tyler. – If we must have a tyrant – let
him at least be a gentleman who has been bred to the business, and let us
fall by the axe and not by the butcher's cleaver.'[16] That was Byron: he
wanted a gentleman tyrant, not one that had crawled out of the gutter.
The irony is that Hunt *was* a gentleman who not only owned 3,000 acres
in Wiltshire but had made a fortune as a farmer – more than Byron could
claim. (As an aristocrat, Byron had nothing to brag about: he frittered
away his patrimony for short-term pleasures and bequeathed his title,
stripped of property, to a cousin, having produced no male heir.) Byron's
unsympathetic commentary postdates Peterloo, when dragoons charged
across St Peter's Field in Manchester, sabres raised, into hundreds of
unarmed men, women, and children who were peacefully agitating for
parliamentary reform. The bodies of those killed or maimed in the attack
were emblematic of everything that was wrong with Britain in 1819.

Byron's college friend, John Cam Hobhouse, had a genuine desire to
reform the system. Invited to help him campaign in the Westminster
constituency in November 1818, Byron excused himself by saying his
celebrity would distract from the serious business of politics.[17] In truth,
he hated Hobhouse's reformist views and, when in 1819 Hobhouse was
incarcerated in Newgate for having published a pamphlet in defiance
of the Whigs, he wrote a crude rhyme mocking his association with
'blackguard Hunt and Cobby O' (Cobbett).

> [But] never mind such petty things –
> My boy Hobbie O –
> God save the people – damn all Kings –
> So let us crown the Mobby O![18]

The lampoon was as unfunny as it was unfair: Hobhouse was never the
advocate of mob rule; but no matter. Its appearance in the *Morning Post*
met with widespread hilarity,[19] especially when it became known the
author was none other than its victim's old Cambridge chum. Hobhouse
protested, only to be told: 'If you *will* dine with Bristol Hunt – & such
like – what can you expect?'[20] '& such like': that is to say, those who
ventured life and liberty for reform. What had Byron done that was
comparable? Nothing. Yet he was capable of wishing Hunt had been one
of those killed on St Peter's Field:

Why our classical education alone – should teach us to trample on such unredeemed dirt as the *dis*honest bluntness – the ignorant brutality, the unblushing
baseness of these two miscreants; – and all who believe in them. – I think I
have neither been an illiberal man nor an unsteady man upon polities – but I
think also that if the Manchester Yeomanry had cut down *Hunt only* – they
would have done their duty ... [21]

Bidden by Douglas Kinnaird to contribute to a fund for the hundreds
of people injured at Peterloo, Byron might have made a donation – he
could well afford it. Instead he revealed his insecurity when faced with
a threat to his substance and responded with a series of demands: 'get
my property out of the funds' (that is, government bonds); 'get Rochdale
sold' (his estates at Rochdale, which included coal mines); and 'ask Lady
Noel not to live so very long'.[22] So far as he was concerned, the massacre
was not a cause for shame at the slaughter of the innocent but a potential
check on his champagne and caviar lifestyle.[23]

Byron's prejudices left him incapable of taking seriously those calling
themselves democrats – or, indeed, anyone other than a Foxite Whig (that
is, a conservative) like him. True, he didn't agree with making frame-
breaking a capital offence,[24] and spoke on behalf of Luddites in the
House of Lords. That has prompted admirers to perceive in *Childe
Harold's Pilgrimage* Canto III, with its celebration of Napoleon as 'the
greatest, nor the worst of men',[25] *Don Juan* Canto IX, with its barbed
apostrophe to Wellington as master of 'a brain-spattering, windpipe-
slitting art',[26] and *Don Juan* Canto XIII, stanzas 50–111, with their
restrained burlesque on a country-house weekend – more democratic
conviction than Byron actually felt. On that basis Friedrich Engels praised
'the virulence of his satire against the existing social order';[27] Chartists
such as Thomas Cooper and George Julian Harney cited him as a literary
and political hero;[28] John Morley dubbed him 'poet of the revolution'
in 1870;[29] and, over a century later, one of the great British socialists,
Michael Foot, expounded Morley's case by reference to *Don Juan*.[30]

The truth is that Byron was 'no revolutionist'. He had a seat in that
most exclusive of gentlemen's clubs, the House of Lords, which gave him
access to the powermongers among whom he might have agitated for
reform. Did he? No. He preferred to rub noses with the Holland House
set, stepped unhesitatingly into Lady Oxford's boudoir, swapped pleas-
antries with the Prince Regent, and on three occasions spoke in the Lords.
In those respects his actions reflected his thoughts, compromised as they
were by an absence of 'sustained coherent reasoning'.[31] It is little surprise
that, as Malcolm Kelsall observes, Byron's political career amounted to 'a
record of failure ending in inarticulateness'.[32] What did the noble Lord
really believe, deep down? On those rare occasions when he articulated

his inner convictions to himself, without the obligation to entertain, he dispensed remarks such as:

> I have simplified my politics into an utter detestation of all existing governments; and, as it is the shortest and most agreeable and summary feeling imaginable, the first moment of an universal republic would convert me into an advocate for single and uncontradicted despotism.[33]

Advocates of the myth should not ignore that: it is an endorsement of tyranny.

Notes

1 Edward Dowden, *The French Revolution and English Literature* (New York: Scribner's, 1897), p. 264.

2 *Advances in Democracy: From the French Revolution to the Present-Day European Union*, ed. Heather M. Campbell (New York: Britannica Educational Publishing, 2011), p. xvi.

3 His initial expectation, as Beaton points out, was that he would teach both sides to treat their prisoners better; see *Byron's War: Romantic Rebellion, Greek Revolution* (Cambridge: Cambridge University Press, 2013), p. 132.

4 *Byron's Letters and Journals*, ed. Leslie A. Marchand (13 vols., London: John Murray, 1973–94), viii. 107.

5 Ibid., p. 26. Those who use this as evidence of Byron's 'broad and deep conception of democracy' include Anthony Arblaster, *Democracy* (2nd ed., Minneapolis: University of Minnesota Press, 1994), p. 42.

6 William St Clair, *That Greece Might Still Be Free: The Philhellenes in the War of Independence* (2nd ed., Cambridge: Open Book Publishers, 2008), p. 184. As Cochran suggests, Byron's reputation gave a boost to Garibaldi, and later to Mussolini; see *Byron's Romantic Politics: The Problem of Metahistory* (Newcastle upon Tyne: Cambridge Scholars, 2011), pp. 186–9.

7 Richard Cronin, *Romantic Victorians: English Literature, 1824–1840* (Houndmills, Basingstoke: Palgrave, 2002), p. 18.

8 On this subject, see, *inter alia*, Susan J. Wolfson, 'The New Poetries', in *The Cambridge History of English Romantic Literature*, ed. James Chandler (Cambridge: Cambridge University Press, 2009), p. 416.

9 The phrase is that of John Clare; see *John Clare by Himself*, ed. Eric Robinson and David Powell (Ashington and Manchester: Carcanet, 1996), pp. 157–8.

10 Lord Byron, *Sardanapalus, The Two Foscari, Cain* (London: John Murray, 1821), p. 327.

11 This is documented by Cochran, *Byron's Romantic Politics*, pp. 30–1.

12 Judith Schneid Lewis, *Sacred to Female Patriotism: Gender, Class, and Politics in Late Georgian Britain* (London: Routledge, 2003), p. 18.

13 One reason why Hazlitt was pleased to reside in the Westminster constituency was that it enabled him to vote in the election of 1819; see Duncan Wu, *William Hazlitt: The First Modern Man* (Oxford: Oxford University Press, 2008), p. 269.

14 Frederick Bernard Singleton, *Industrial Revolution in Yorkshire* (Clapham, Yorks.: Dalesman, 1970), p. 97.

15 Lord Byron to John Cam Hobhouse, 11 May 1820, in *Byron's Letters and Journals*, ed. Leslie A. Marchand (13 vols., London: John Murray, 1973–94), vii. 99.

16 Lord Byron to John Murray, 21 February 1820, ibid., p. 44.

17 Lord Byron to Scrope Davies, 7 December 1818, ibid., xi. 168–70.

18 'A New Song', ll. 29–32, in Lord Byron, *The Complete Poetical Works*, ed. Jerome J. McGann (7 vols., Oxford: Clarendon Press, 1980–93), iv. 288.

19 A corrupt text appeared in the *Morning Post* on 15 April 1820.

20 Lord Byron to John Cam Hobhouse, 11 May 1820, in *Byron's Letters and Journals*, ed. Marchand, vii. 99.

21 Lord Byron to John Cam Hobhouse, 22 April 1820, ibid., p. 81.

22 Lord Byron to Douglas Kinnaird, 26 October 1819, ibid., vi. 232.

23 Byron may not have been unrepresentative; in the aftermath of Peterloo, the gap between Whigs and radicals opened up. See in this regard John Murray's letter to Byron of 16 November 1819, in *The Letters of John Murray to Lord Byron*, ed. Andrew Nicholson (Liverpool: Liverpool University Press, 2007), pp. 300–3, esp. p. 303n10.

24 The Luddites were textile workers whose livelihoods were threatened by the introduction of mechanical weaving and spinning machinery. Their response was to destroy the new technology, a crime punishable by sentence of death.

25 Byron, *Childe Harold's Pilgrimage*, iii. 316. Napoleon had numerous admirers in Britain, including Charles James Fox, William Godwin, Lord Melbourne, Sir John Soane, and Lord Wycombe.

26 Byron, *Don Juan*, ix, stanza 4, l. 27.

27 Friedrich Engels, *The Condition of the Working-Class in England*, tr. W. O. Henderson and W. H. Chaloner (Stanford, CA: Stanford University Press, 1958), p. 273.

28 See, for instance, Michael Foot, *The Politics of Paradise: A Vindication of Byron* (London: Collins, 1988), pp. 387–90.

29 *Lord Byron: The Critical Heritage*, ed. Andrew Rutherford (London: Routledge & Kegan Paul, 1970), pp. 384–409.

30 Foot, *The Politics of Paradise*, pp. 244, 361.

31 Andrew Rutherford, *Byron: A Critical Study* (Stanford, CA: Stanford University Press, 1961), p. 194.

32 Malcolm Kelsall, 'Byron's Politics', in *The Cambridge Companion to Byron*, ed. Drummond Bone (Cambridge: Cambridge University Press, 2004), pp. 44–55, 50.

33 Journal, 16 January 1814, in *Byron's Letters and Journals*, ed. Marchand, iii. 242.

BYRON WAS A 'NOBLE WARRIOR' WHO DIED FIGHTING FOR GREEK FREEDOM

> I believed myself on a fool's errand from the outset …
>
> Byron to Lt Col. Charles James Napier, 9 September 1823[1]

'Noble warrior!', wrote the German poet Wilhelm Müller, on hearing of Byron's death in Greece, 'thou wert worthy of the cause so nobly fought'.[2] That he knew his way round a battlefield remains one of the most enduring of Byronic myths, often invoked as part of the notion he was a freedom fighter. *The Reader's Guide to World Literature* puts it in a nutshell: 'Proud and arrogant, with a low opinion of most men, he loved mankind, abhorred injustice, and died fighting the Turks to help the Greeks secure freedom.'[3] And then again, perhaps not.

Byron's reputation as man of action depends on sympathetic readings of his time in Italy and Greece. It is true that in Ravenna (then among the Papal States, policed by Austria) he associated with, and may have joined, the Carbonari ('charcoal-burners'), a group whose declared objective was to purge Italy of drunkenness, adultery, and gambling; it is claimed he was 'capo' (head) of a branch known as the Cacciatori Americani (American Hunters). Far from being a military force, this was a secret society run by Byron's 'Carbonari cronies',[4] Counts Ruggero and Pietro Gamba (father and brother of his mistress, Teresa Guiccioli[5]), who, when it came to action, were comically inert. They have been described as 'freemasons first, and freedom-fighters not at all …. The fetishization of ritual, the

30 Great Myths About the Romantics, First Edition. Duncan Wu.
© 2015 John Wiley & Sons, Ltd. Published 2015 by John Wiley & Sons, Ltd.

secrecy, the passwords, the hierarchy, and the high-minded, impossible aims, bespeak a world of spiritual fantasy, not a political group.'[6] That was not how Byron would have preferred it, for he could hardly be said to lack pretensions as a latter-day Spartacus. He greeted the promise of an insurgent attack on the Austrians in early January 1821 with advice about guerrilla strategy, the promise of money and arms, proposals the Carbonari use his mistress's house (the Palazzo Guiccioli) as a fortress,[7] and the argument that, were the authorities to attack, the entire country 'would rise'.[8] While awaiting the revolution Byron composed his 'address' to the Neapolitan insurgents; it was entrusted to a messenger, Giuseppe Gigante, who, when arrested, ate it.[9]

In fairness to Byron, the Carbonari were a potent force in Italian politics in the south: in July 1820 they led a revolt in Naples, forcing Ferdinand I to agree to constitutional government, which convened in October.[10] To observers in the northern states it may have seemed, by early 1821, that independence was at hand. 'Only think – a free Italy!!!', Byron confided to his journal.[11] But the terms in which he conceived of the fight against the Austrians teetered on the brink of fantasy. Having been invited to dine with the Carbonari in the forest, he declared, 'I would go as a poet, or, at least, as a lover of poetry.... I will get as tipsy and patriotic as possible.'[12] He was not alone in his frivolousness, for the cell with which he was involved was less disposed to take risks than he was, and its use of him attests to its lack of commitment. Its members used the 'lower apart-ments' of his residence as an arms dump; arranged that, 'in case of a row, the Liberals were to assemble *here* (with me)';[13] then ran away 'to the chase in the forest'[14] – that is, on a hunting expedition, rendering them-selves uncontactable. Two weeks later, Byron was beginning to realize the revolution might take longer than he first thought:

> The gentlemen, who make revolutions and are gone on a shooting, are not yet returned. They don't return till Sunday – that is to say, they have been out for five days, buffooning, while the interests of a whole country are at stake, and even they themselves compromised.[15]

The problem was numbers: 'the populace are not interested, – only the higher and middle orders. I wish that the peasantry *were*; they are a fine savage race of two-legged leopards.'[16] Byron found a popular revolution in Italy desirable, but could never have felt the same way about one in England. He detested such reformers as Henry 'Orator' Hunt and William Cobbett, and in a letter to his old friend Hobhouse (who supported them) he condemned 'the *dis*honest bluntness – the ignorant brutality, the unblushing baseness of these two miscreants; – and all who believe in them'.[17] The two-legged leopards of Ravenna failed to rise up in 1821 so, instead of attempting a coup in the real world, Byron retreated into an imaginary one and composed *Marino Faliero*.[18] In due course the Gambas were exiled to Florence because the authorities hoped he would follow them; in other words, they were punished for their association with him rather than because they posed a threat in themselves. Not only did Byron fail to advance the cause of Italian independence, he made targets of his camp-followers.

As a freedom fighter in Greece he was more ineffectual still. That may not be surprising as the London Greek Committee gave him no clear mission. He did not go as a soldier (at best, he was never more than an amateur[19]), preferring to strike the pose of human rights activist, urging both sides to improve their treatment of prisoners.[20] Even so, he spoke half-heartedly of the venture: 'I do not know what I am going for. I was tired of Italy, and liked Greece, and the London Committee told me I should be of use, but of what use they do not say nor do I see.'[21]

He arrived on 4 January 1824 with funds to support a force of Suliotes (several hundred Albanian thugs, mercenaries, and banditti), who lobbied relentlessly for more pay. His luggage contained 'half a dozen military uniforms in many colours and all lavishly decorated with gold and silver braid with sashes, epaulettes, waistcoats, and cocked hats to match. He took two gilded helmets decorated with the family motto, "Crede Byron", and at least ten swords.'[22] The helmets were modelled on descriptions of Hector's armour in *Iliad* Book VI, built to Byron's design, and stored in pink cardboard boxes.[23] When not making plans for military operations that never happened, he played with Loukas Chalandritsanos, his 15-year-old pageboy, and adorned his house with swords, pistols, Turkish sabres, dirks, rifles, guns, blunderbusses, bayonets, helmets, and trumpets, 'fantastically suspended, so as to form various figures'.[24]

For a while he planned to besiege the Albanian garrison at Lepanto (Nafpaktos in Greek) whose forces were demoralized and unpaid, and whose chieftain told a spy they would surrender as soon as Byron and his Suliotes appeared, providing Byron paid 40,000 dollars for their arrears.[25] His response was to hang more cutlasses on the walls of his house. Weeks passed. Desperate not to let the opportunity pass, the chieftain at Lepanto reduced his price to 25,000 dollars.[26] It never happened: disinclined to suffer the humiliation of a fake battle, Byron's troops (also Albanian) refused to fight 'against stone walls'.[27]

The biggest obstacle to military heroism was Byron's health, which had been variable for some time. In Italy he had become grotesquely fat, and he now adopted a draconian diet of alcohol and purgatives that undermined his constitution. That, and Missolonghi itself (a mosquito-infested swamp aptly described as 'one of the most unhealthy places in Greece'[28]), were enough to make anyone ill. On 15 February, having accepted that the siege of Lepanto would have to be postponed following yet another Suliote pay demand, Byron suffered an epileptic fit from which he never properly recovered. The comely Loukas was no solace – perhaps because Byron was less interested in seducing him than in making sure he knew his place[29] – and he turned instead to Lyon, his pet Newfoundland, as William Parry recalled:

> With Lyon Lord Byron was accustomed not only to associate, but to commune very much, and very often. His most usual phrase was, 'Lyon, you are no rogue, Lyon;' or 'Lyon,' his Lordship would say, 'thou art an honest fellow, Lyon.' The dog's eyes sparkled, and his tail swept the floor, as he sat with his haunches on the ground. 'Thou art more faithful than men, Lyon; I trust thee more.' Lyon sprang up, and barked and bounded round his master, as much as to say, 'You may trust me, I will watch actively on every side.' 'Lyon, I love thee, thou art my faithful dog!' and Lyon jumped and kissed his master's hand, as an acknowledgment of his homage. In this sort of mingled talk and gambol Lord Byron passed a good deal of time, and seemed more contented, more calmly self-satisfied, on such occasions, than almost on any other. In conversation and in company he was animated and brilliant; but with Lyon and in stillness he was pleased and perfectly happy.[30]

Figure 14 'Lyon, you are no rogue, Lyon!' Byron and his beloved Newfoundland, probable source of the tic fever that led ultimately to his death. Source: Paul F. Betz Collection.

In his weakened state, Byron was more susceptible than ever to infections carried by dog tics, which probably caused the fever that struck him down on 9 April. It was not in itself fatal and he would have survived had he not surrendered himself to the quacks at his bedside, who proceeded to purge and bleed him into a premature grave.[31]

Never let the truth get in the way of a good yarn. In a florid eulogy Spyridon Trikoupis declared: 'He came ... with the determination to die in Greece, and for Greece!'[32] Almost every Greek town had a memorial service for Byron, and the Executive Body at Nauplia proclaimed that 'because Byron does not walk any more on the Greek land, which he had loved so much years ago, and because Greece is grateful to him for ever, and the Nation must give him the name of a father and benefactor ... it is ordered that the 5th of May be regarded as a day of mourning'.[33] That instigated an epidemic of Byronmania which continues to this day. Marketplaces were renamed in his honour, statues erected in town squares, and children named after him (Vyronos); as William St Clair remarks, 'Byron became by his death the hero he would never have been if he had lived.'[34] This was echoed by his canonization in the annals of European literature.[35]

The mini-myth of his death on the battlefield was quick to take root; hearing the news, Hazlitt said Byron 'died a martyr to his zeal in the cause of freedom, for the last, best hopes of man',[36] while W. G. Thompson eulogized the poet who 'on the battlefield expired, / With thy ancestral glories fired.'[37] The architect of such misconceptions was, of course, its subject:

> If thou regret'st thy youth, why *live*?
> The Land of honourable Death
> Is here – up to the Field! and give
> Away thy Breath.

> Seek out – less often sought than found,
> A Soldier's Grave – for thee the best,
> Then look around and choose thy ground
> And take thy Rest.[38]

The real Lord Byron was a flabby, effeminate man who liked wigs, jewellery, and adolescent boys; his supposed yearning for 'A Soldier's Grave' was a posture with no basis in reality. He did visit battlefields (Marathon, Troy, Cheronea, Platea), but only as a tourist. At Waterloo in 1816 he bought souvenirs and made witticisms about the battle ('How that red rain hath made the harvest glow!'[39]). His research skills enabled him to write convincingly about war zones like Cadiz ('Look o'er the ravage of the reeking plain'[40]) and Ismail ('The bayonet pierces and the sabre cleaves, / And human lives are lavished every where'[41]), and to imagine fire-breathing warriors like Sardanapalus ('Upon them – ho! there – victory is ours'[42]). It was fustian.

Although the myth depicts Byron as martyr to the Greek cause, that was not how he saw it. He told Parry, 'My situation here ... is unbearable. A town without any resources, and a government without money; imprisoned by the floods, unable to take any exercise, pestered by demands, without the means of satisfying them or doing any thing either to relieve them, or myself, I must have left this hole, had you not arrived.'[43] No wonder he was wont to rebuff 'Prince' Mavrokordatos with ruderies: 'I have already lent him one thousand dollars, and he *shall not have more*' (his emphasis).[44] Marguerite, Countess of Blessington, heard him 'calmly talk of the worthlessness of the people', and of 'the uniforms he intends to wear, entering into petty details, and always with perfect *sang froid*'; it was enough 'to chill the admiration such an enterprise ought to create'.[45] Indeed, it would be rash to assume Byron was in Missolonghi because he loved the people; the Greeks 'are returned to barbarism',[46] he once said, and elsewhere remarked:

> With all possible freedom and every desirable advantage, nothing could keep me long among the Greeks. They are the vainest and most insincere race on earth, a chemical aggregate of all the vices of their ancestors, plus many taken from the Turks, and a good dose of the Jewish – diluted and mixed in the melting pot of slavery.[47]

He also deplored their 'present burglarious and larcenous tendencies' and that 'they are such d[amne]d liars; – there never was such an incapacity for veracity shown since Eve lived in Paradise'.[48] He preferred the Turks, among whom he had friends in high places – the millionaire torturer and mass-murderer Ali Pasha, for example.[49] Greece was acceptable in the abstract; he hailed it as 'the promised land of valour, of the arts, and of liberty throughout the ages',[50] which (according to Malcolm Kelsall) proves his philhellenism 'derives from a patrician education which saw events in the Peloponnese as if they were a continuation of classical antiquity'.[51] Actual Greeks filled him with bile.[52]

Edna O'Brien says Greece was where Byron metamorphosed 'from poet to soldier';[53] perhaps, in the limited sense that it was there his fetish for military attire reached new heights of self-preening vanity. Johann Jakob Meyer, the Swiss philhellene in whose arms he expired, was more clear-sighted: in a letter to Colonel Stanhope he wrote, 'Byron is dead! Is his death harmful to Greece? No.'[54] Bishop Ignatios was similarly undeceived in a letter to Georgios Koundouriotis: 'as a poet he was frivolous and it is not unlikely that [had he lived] he would have taken umbrage, and left, and written such things against the Greeks as would have done more harm than he ever did good'.[55] Beaton says Byron wanted 'to try to create, in Greece, political conditions that could then be emulated by the rest of the continent'.[56] None of which grants him credibility as a war hero: when offered uncontested victory against an entire garrison, he stayed at home where the grim reaper did his worst – with the assistance of two incompetent physicians, a sulky catamite, and an unhygienic dog.

Notes

1 *Byron's Letters and Journals*, ed. Leslie A. Marchand (13 vols., London: John Murray, 1973–94), xi 20.
2 Wilhelm Müller, 'On the Death of Lord Byron translated from the German of W. Müller', *The Examiner* 939 (5 February 1826), 84–5.
3 *The Reader's Guide to World Literature*, ed. Lillian Herlands Hornstein, G. D. Percy, Calvin S. Brown, Sterling Allen Brown, et al. (2nd ed., New York: New American Library, 2002), p. 101.
4 Ravenna Journal, in *Byron's Letters and Journals*, ed. Marchand, viii. 47.
5 Leslie A. Marchand, *Byron: A Biography* (3 vols., New York: Alfred A. Knopf, 1957), ii. 867.
6 Peter Cochran, *Byron and Italy* (Newcastle upon Tyne: Cambridge Scholars, 2012), p. 257.
7 Peter Cochran identifies the establishment Byron refers to as 'this house' as that owned by his mistress's husband; see Teresa Guiccioli, *Lord Byron's Life in Italy*, ed. Peter Cochran, tr. Michael Rees (Cranbury, NJ: Associated University Presses, 2005), p. 6.
8 Ravenna Journal, in *Byron's Letters and Journals*, ed. Marchand, viii. 17.
9 Marchand, *Byron: A Biography*, ii. 896–7; Lord Byron to Count Giuseppe Alborghetti, 25 May 1821, in *Byron's Letters and Journals*, ed. Marchand, vii. 124n1.
10 Tim Chapman, *The Risorgimento: Italy, 1815–1871* (Penrith: Humanities-Ebooks, 2008), pp. 21–2; Martin Clark, *The Italian Risorgimento* (2nd ed., Abingdon, Oxon.: Routledge, 2013), pp. 38–9.
11 Ravenna Journal, in *Byron's Letters and Journals*, ed. Marchand, viii. 47.
12 Ibid., p. 48.
13 Ibid., p. 17.
14 Ibid.
15 Ibid., p. 36.
16 Ibid., p. 34.
17 Lord Byron to John Cam Hobhouse, 22 April 1820, ibid., vii. 81. See Roderick Beaton, *Byron's War: Romantic Rebellion, Greek Revolution* (Cambridge: Cambridge University Press, 2013), p. 61.

18 Beaton argues that the way in which Faliero is described in the play 'is transparently a projection of how Byron saw himself in 1820' (*Byron's War*, p. 62). Cochran shows how Byron twisted the historical facts to justify his protagonist; see *Byron's Romantic Politics: The Problem of Metahistory* (Newcastle upon Tyne: Cambridge Scholars, 2011), p. 202.

19 Malcolm Kelsall, *Byron's Politics* (Brighton, Sussex: Harvester Press, 1987), p. 195.

20 Beaton, *Byron's War*, p. 132.

21 Edward John Trelawny, *Records of Shelley, Byron, and the Author* (New York, 1887), p. 212.

22 William St Clair, *That Greece Might Still Be Free: The Philhellenes in the War of Independence* (2nd ed., Cambridge: Open Book Publishers, 2008), p. 154.

23 Beaton says it is not known whether Byron ever wore the helmets; Beaton, *Byron's War*, p. 133.

24 Marchand, *Byron: A Biography*, iii. 1155.

25 Ibid., p. 1177.

26 Ibid., p. 1194.

27 Lord Byron to Douglas Kinnaird, 30 March 1824, in *Byron's Letters and Journals*, ed. Marchand, xi. 145.

28 St Clair, *That Greece Might Still Be Free*, p. 170.

29 Beaton, *Byron's War*, p. 243.

30 William Parry, *The Last Days of Lord Byron* (London: Knight & Lacey, 1825), p. 75.

31 He was well aware they would kill him; see Marchand, *Byron: A Biography*, iii. 1215.

32 Beaton, *Byron's War*, p. 269. See also Cochran, *Byron's Romantic Politics*, p. 284.

33 Marchand, *Byron: A Biography*, iii. 1236.

34 St Clair, *That Greece Might Still Be Free*, p. 183.

35 See, *inter alia*, David Roessel, *In Byron's Shadow: Modern Greece in the English and American Imagination* (Oxford: Oxford University Press, 2002), pp. 79–80.

36 'Lord Byron', in *The Spirit of the Age*, in *Selected Writings of William Hazlitt*, ed. Duncan Wu (9 vols., London: Pickering & Chatto, 1998), vii. 142.

37 Samuel C. Chew, *Byron in England: His Fame and After-Fame* (London: John Murray, 1924), p. 197.

38 'January 22nd 1824. Messalonghi. On this day I complete my thirty sixth year', ll. 33–40; Lord Byron, *The Complete Poetical Works*, ed. Jerome J. McGann (7 vols., Oxford: Clarendon Press, 1980–93), vii. 81.

39 *Childe Harold's Pilgrimage*, iii, stanza 17, l. 151.

40 Ibid., i, stanza 88, l. 901.

41 *Don Juan*, viii, stanza 88, lines 697–8.

42 *Sardanapalus*, III. i. 283.

43 Parry, *The Last Days of Lord Byron*, p. 193.

44 James Kennedy, *Conversations on Religion with Lord Byron and Others* (Philadelphia, 1833), p. 164. Beaton indicates that Mavrokordatos's treachery may have been a factor in Byron's decline and death; see Beaton, *Byron's War*, pp. 257–60.

45 Marguerite, Countess of Blessington, *Conversations of Lord Byron with the Countess of Blessington* (London: Henry Colburn, 1834), p. 138.

46 Trelawny, *Records of Shelley, Byron, and the Author*, p. 212.

47 Marchand, *Byron: A Biography*, iii. 1123.

48 *Byron's Letters and Journals*, ed. Marchand, xi. 32–3.

49 Cochran, *Byron's Romantic Politics*, pp. 342–3.

50 Lord Byron to Andreas Londos, January 1824, in *Byron's Letters and Journals*, ed. Marchand, xi. 103.

51 Kelsall, *Byron's Politics*, p. 195.

52 Cochran thinks Byron was in two minds about the Greeks; see *Byron's Romantic Politics*, p. 236.

53 Edna O'Brien, *Byron in Love* (London: Weidenfeld & Nicolson, 2009), p. 190.

54 Beaton, *Byron's War*, p. 269.

55 Ibid.

56 Ibid., p. 266.

Figure 15 An illustration from Trelawny's *Recollections*, apparently based on a sketch by Daniel Roberts, which shows the Casa Magni in San Terenzo, where Shelley lived, with what scholars believe to be the *Don Juan* in the foreground.
Source: Bayerische Staatsbibliothek, Munich, Biogr. c. 313 g.

Myth 20

SHELLEY COMMITTED SUICIDE BY SAILBOAT

On Monday 8 July 1822 Shelley set sail for San Terenzo from Leghorn (Livorno), a northbound course up the western coast of Italy of about 50 miles. He didn't make it. Within about two or three hours his boat, the *Don Juan*, encountered a squall; swamped, it took Shelley down with two crew members, Edward Williams and the boy sailor Charles Vivian. There were no survivors.

When recounted by biographers, the recklessness of Shelley in even contemplating the journey receives emphasis. Daniel Roberts and Edward Trelawny, both of whom had more seafaring experience than Shelley, are credited with concern – Trelawny to the point of wanting to accompany the *Don Juan* into the offing in his boat, the *Bolivar*, Roberts to that of advising Shelley against the journey, then running to the end of the mole and watching Shelley's boat through a spy-glass as it receded to the horizon. After the *Don Juan* is said to have disappeared from sight, biographers report an encounter in the midst of bad weather:

> Two Livornese boats, however, appear to have seen Shelley's craft shortly after Captain Roberts retired from his watch-tower. The captain of the first of these, doubting the ability of the *Don Juan* to weather the squall, offered to take the crew aboard, but was refused. Then, as a large wave broke over the little boat, he shouted: ' … For God's sake reef your sails or you are lost.' One of the gentlemen (supposed to be Williams) started to lower the sails, but the other (supposedly Shelley) seized his arm and restrained him. The crew of the second vessel … kept their own counsel, but when the boat was finally salvaged it was only too clear that she had sunk as the result of a collision.[1]

This account of Shelley's demise, from Newman Ivey White's biography, gives the impression he tried to commit suicide by shipwreck just before

---

30 Great Myths About the Romantics, First Edition. Duncan Wu.
© 2015 John Wiley & Sons, Ltd. Published 2015 by John Wiley & Sons, Ltd.

his boat was rammed, and most subsequent biographers have repeated the story.[2] It depends on the testimony of three men – Trelawny, Roberts, and Count John Taaffe.

Trelawny produced at least ten, possibly more, versions of the narrative leading up to and following Shelley's death.[3] None is consistent with the other, and many of their claims are invented. That does not mean everything he says is untrue, but his testimony must be treated with extreme caution. Most biographers rely on the version in his *Recollections of the Last Days of Shelley and Byron* (1858), one of the least accurate.[4] In my quotations below I have drawn principally on his earliest account, dated September 1822, which contains fewer untruths than later versions.[5]

Trelawny claims he intended to sail Byron's schooner, the *Bolivar*, alongside the *Don Juan* for part of the journey. The implication was that Shelley would have been safe had Trelawny been able to do this; however, Trelawny was detained 'from not having my bill of health on board and obliged to reanchor'.[6] As a result 'I staid on deck with a telescope anxiously looking out in the direction of my friends, every instant expecting and hoping to see them returning'. He describes the storm that sank the *Don Juan* as follows: 'The whole face of heaven, the waters became agitated *and foaming* and we saw the effects of the wind rushing along the surface of the sea *gathering* lifting it up into *swirling* waves *which – with the force & rapidity of the Typhoon* – it was now a gale – the thundering over our heads *became tremendous*' (his italics).[7]

Captain Roberts's account was mailed to Mary Shelley and is known from her letter to Maria Gisborne of 15 August 1822; it thus pre-dates Trelawny's. He says he urged Shelley not to travel on the fatal day because of uncertainties about the weather. 'Stay until tomorrow to see if the weather is settled', he insisted. Shelley might have done so, but Williams 'was in so great an anxiety to reach home – saying they would get there in seven hours with that wind – that they sailed!'[8] In this early account, the least likely to be contaminated by self-serving fantasy, it was Williams who insisted they sail – not Shelley. Roberts claimed to be so concerned that he climbed the lighthouse at the end of the mole and watched the *Don Juan* until it was 'about ten miles out at sea, off Via Reggio, they were taking in their topsails'.[9]

And then there is Taaffe, whose claims come to us from the journal of Clarissa Trant, who met him four years after Shelley's death. He said Shelley and his companions were urged not to leave Leghorn by several people, including the waiter at their hotel. Even Byron warned them not to go, but was allegedly told by Shelley: 'Well, to satisfy you, I will not embark if the Storm increases, but I confess that if the Gale freshens when we are at Sea I shall not be sorry; you know how I enjoy a storm – the sea is my element; from a boy I loved it.' Taaffe said the crew of a vessel bound for Leghorn passed close to the *Don Juan* soon after they set out,

> and foreseeing that they could not long contend with such tremendous waves, bore down upon them and offered to take them on board. A shrill voice, which is supposed to have been Shelley's, was distinctly heard to say 'NO.' The Captain, amazed at their infatuation, continued to watch them with his telescope. The waves were running mountains high – a tremendous surf dashed over the boat which to his astonishment was still crowded with sail. 'If you will not come on board for God's sake reef your sails or you are lost,' cried a sailor thro' the speaking trumpet. One of the gentlemen (Williams it is believed) was seen to make an effort to lower the sails – his companion seized him by the arm as if in anger.[10]

Richard Holmes says Mary Shelley's letter of 15 August to Maria Gisborne 'underwrites'[11] these claims:

> I have left out a material circumstance – A Fishing boat saw them go down – It was about 4 in the afternoon – they saw the boy at mast head, when baffling winds struck the sails, they had looked away a moment & looking again the boat was gone ... [12]

For biographers, Shelley's suicide by boat is the culminating act of a tragedy that includes his skirmish with a Tuscan Dragoon (late March); news of Allegra Byron's death (25 April); Shelley's 'shattered health and spirits' (May); hallucinations, probably of Allegra; Mary Shelley's near-fatal miscarriage (16 June); requests for a lethal dose of prussic acid (18 June); infatuation with Jane Williams; alienation from Byron; more hallucinations ('Edward & Jane came into him, they were in the most horrible condition, their bodies lacerated – their bones starting through their skin, the faces pale yet stained with blood, they could hardly walk'[13]); visions of floods, and Shelley's 'Zoroastrian double'.[14] One biographer presents the disaster as the culmination of 'visions' including that of 'Shelley's astral self'.[15]

All of which might sound like an open and shut case until one interrogates the witnesses, who prove strangely unreliable. In one version, Trelawny claims the *Don Juan* went down 13 miles from land, while in another it sank 'four or five miles at sea'; in one he says Shelley weighed anchor at noon, in another at 'half past twelve', and in yet another 'past two o'clock'. Roberts claimed Shelley sailed 'at one' and that he could see the *Don Juan* from the lighthouse when it was 10 miles off.[16] Joseph A. Dane finds that 'nothing whatsoever would be visible at ten miles and fifteen is completely out of the question'.[17] Roberts altered his account completely in 1828, claiming he set out with Shelley in the *Don Juan* and returned in a dinghy before it encountered stormy waters.[18] That, like much else he said on the subject, was a lie. In that respect, he was not the sole culprit. Trelawny's claim that 'we saw the effects of the wind rushing along the surface of the sea *gathering* lifting it up into *swirling* waves', along with Taaffe's description of the waves 'running mountains high', are entirely bogus. As Dane notes, weather conditions in which the wind comes off the land, which is what all accounts describe, can result in 'nasty chop' but not in waves 'mountains high'.[19]

Trelawny and Roberts later claimed the *Don Juan* sank after being rammed by a felucca, and embroidered their story to involve pirates. Pieces of the vessel, later recovered, were invoked as evidence, with Trelawny's wholly invented additions to Roberts's written account of the disaster.[20] As Mary Shelley wrote to Jane Williams: 'Trelawny tells me that it is his, Roberts & every other sailor's opinion that [the *Don Juan*] was run down; of course by that Fishing boat – which confessed to have seen them.'[21] This is one of the lies most frequently repeated, perhaps because it saves us from thinking Shelley the self-destructive maniac his erstwhile friends would have us suppose. White correctly realized that the so-called 'confession' of a crew member from the felucca was false,[22] yet still credited the story. As recently as 2002, one biographer said it was possible 'that the boat was rammed and sunk by a marauding vessel'.[23] Even Miranda Seymour, who admits Trelawny and Roberts had impure motives, suggests the crew of a felucca 'could have deliberately rammed the boat'.[24] None of this is necessary, let alone true. As long ago as 1977 William St Clair exposed the pirate story as invention, proving Trelawny doctored the evidence.[25] Which indicates in turn that the account of the fishing boat provided by Roberts to Mary Shelley (see p. 168, above) was also false.

There are widely varying descriptions and accounts of the *Don Juan*; White says it was a 'little boat', but Dane's reconstruction indicates a seven-sailed boat with an 8 foot beam, around 25 feet in length vastly overladen with sail, such that it required '29 Piggs of Iron Ballast' to make her seaworthy. She was unstable in a breeze, despite her wide beam.[26] The day she sank, the *Don Juan* was weighed down by provisions, wine-casks, and two trunks, and towed an 8 foot-long dinghy 86 pounds in weight. The topsails alone would have predisposed her to become overpowered by wind, which would have resulted in immediate swamping. St Clair describes her as 'one of the most unseaworthy vessels ever constructed',[27] James Bieri as 'an accident waiting to happen in the hazardous Mediterranean'.[28]

Who was to blame? Who else but Trelawny and Roberts? Trelawny played a major part in its design;[29] Roberts supervised its construction and the refit of June 1822 in which the rigging was replaced and higher topmasts fitted.[30] As Diana Pugh says, 'the design of the boat [Roberts] had built made it certain that inexperienced yachtsmen in a heavy sea and strong winds would meet with disaster'; in the words of B. C. Barker-Benfield, 'Captain Roberts could possibly be considered the person most directly responsible for Shelley's death'; or, as James Rieger put it: 'if the *Don Juan* did capsize with all sail set, [Roberts] was morally guilty of manslaughter'. [31] That explains why Trelawny and Roberts reacted as they did, contriving stories that deflected responsibility onto Williams, Shelley, and a crew of sailors who were (as Dane puts it) 'largely fictional'.[32] Anyone but themselves.

Taaffe's testimony is the basis on which biographers suggest Shelley prevented Williams furling the topsail during the storm – and thus (in effect) committed suicide.[33] It is baseless. Taaffe was not even in Leghorn and could not have been 'sole witness' to what he claimed.[34] Which explains why his remarks make no sense: his account of weather conditions is inconsistent with those of other witnesses; there would have been no need of a telescope where voices were clearly audible; and, in the conditions he describes, a telescope could not have been held steadily enough to be of use. It beggars belief that anyone shouting (in broken English, presumably) in the midst of a violent storm would be heard above the elements, let alone that they could safely get from one vessel to the other. Taaffe's story was designed to elevate its teller by association with Shelley and Byron. His testimony has no authority despite being invoked, time and again, as proof of Shelley's suicidal conduct.

In most accounts, Shelley takes the blame for the sinking of the *Don Juan*, but that does not square with what we know of his relationship with Williams. Dane notes Williams was accident-prone. He caused an earlier swamping of 16 April 1821 when he 'stood up in the frail boat to do something, and unfortunately laid hold of the mast to steady himself, and over we went'.[35] In a description by Trelawny of an outing in the *Don Juan* in mid-June 1822, Williams captained the vessel, shouting commands incomprehensible to Shelley, who ended up stalling the boat, inviting his reproaches.[36] These anecdotes show Williams tended to assume command over Shelley, blaming him when things went wrong, and Williams's insistence they sail on the fatal day might be one of the few details in any of the early accounts that chimes with what we know of those involved.

What is known of the last voyage of the *Don Juan*? Almost nothing, despite the profusion of testimony. As Bieri says: 'The actions of Shelley, Williams, and Vivian during the fatal storm will never be known.'[37] We do not know at what time the *Don Juan* weighed anchor, far less what occurred when it encountered bad weather. We do not even know where

Figure 16 Edward John Trelawny (1792–1881), the least reliable of Romantic memoirists who, with Daniel Roberts, was responsible for designing the boat in which Shelley drowned.
Source: Paul F. Betz Collection.

it sank or in what depth of water. What little we do know is stated in the first paragraph to this essay.

Shelley had a complex personality susceptible to depressive episodes which have been invoked to explain his suicide by shipwreck. Yet the concatenation of circumstances was enough to sink the *Don Juan* without that: a sudden squall; the absence of an experienced seaman; and, most of all, the boat's design. Though less dramatic than conventional depictions of Shelley's death, it would be closer to the truth to say that, in foul weather, on a vessel so ill made, Shelley, Williams, and Vivian (none of whom could swim) had little chance of survival. Knowing it was a matter of time before someone would draw that most obvious of conclusions, Roberts and Trelawny rewrote history to portray themselves as concerned onlookers whose warnings were disregarded, and those who perished as reckless, self-endangering daredevils. Taaffe then jumped on the bandwagon, claiming access to eyewitness testimony. It was lies. The story of Shelley's refusal to furl the sails of the *Don Juan*, like those of the felucca and, later, marauding pirates, were self-serving fictions designed either to protect or promote their tellers. None is true, and all do Shelley an injustice.

Notes

1 Newman Ivey White, *Shelley* (2 vols., London: Secker & Warburg, 1947), ii. 377.

2 See, for instance: 'The captain of an Italian vessel which had made it back to the safety of the harbor reported sighting the *Don Juan* in mountainous seas. He had offered to take its crew aboard, but a voice had cried back "No"': David Crane, *Lord Byron's Jackal: The Life of Edward John Trelawny* (London: HarperCollins, 1998), p. 47.

3 They are enumerated by Leslie A. Marchand, 'Trelawny on the Death of Shelley', *Keats-Shelley Memorial Bulletin* 4 (1952), 9–34, pp. 10–11. Marchand is among the more judicious of the various biographers of Shelley and his circle in his use of Trelawny's various narratives; see *Byron: A Biography* (3 vols., New York: Alfred A. Knopf, 1957), iii. 1015.

4 Dowden quotes it wholesale; see *The Life of Percy Bysshe Shelley* (2 vols., London: Kegan Paul, 1886), ii. 523.

5 I am grateful to Luca Caddia of the Keats-Shelley Memorial House in Rome for sending me a copy of the manuscript of Trelawny's account, which I have collated with the published text edited by Marchand.

6 Marchand, 'Trelawny on the Death of Shelley', pp. 29–30.

7 Ibid., p. 30.

8 Mary Shelley to Maria Gisborne, 15 August 1822, in *The Letters of Mary Wollstonecraft Shelley*, ed. Betty T. Bennett (3 vols., Baltimore, MD: Johns Hopkins University Press, 1980–8), i. 248.

9 Ibid.

10 *The Journal of Clarissa Trant, 1800–1832*, ed. C. G. Luard (London: John Lane, The Bodley Head, 1925), pp. 198–9.

11 Richard Holmes, *Shelley: The Pursuit* (London: Quartet Books, 1974), p. 789n56.

12 Mary Shelley to Maria Gisborne, 15 August 1822, in *The Letters of Mary Wollstonecraft Shelley*, ed. Bennett, i. 250.

13 Ibid., p. 245.

14 Holmes, *Shelley: The Pursuit*, p. 727.

15 Walter Edwin Peck, *Shelley: His Life and Work* (2 vols., Boston: Houghton Mifflin, 1927), ii. 287n32.

16 Throughout this essay I am indebted to Joseph A. Dane, 'On the Instability of Vessels and Narratives: A Nautical Perspective on the Sinking of the *Don Juan*', *Keats-Shelley Journal* 47 (1998), 63–86; for these and other discrepancies, I follow Dane, pp. 65–6.

17 Ibid., p. 67.

18 James Bieri, *Percy Bysshe Shelley: A Biography* (2 vols., Newark: University of Delaware Press, 2004–5), ii. 326; B. C. Barker-Benfield, 'The Honeymoon of Joseph and Henrietta Chichester, with Daniel Roberts' Memories of Byron and Shelley', *Bodleian Library Record* 12 (1986), 119–41, p. 122.

19 Dane, 'On the Instability of Vessels and Narratives', p. 67.

20 William St Clair, *Trelawny: The Incurable Romancer* (London: John Murray, 1977), pp. 184–5.

21 Mary Shelley to Jane Williams, 15 October 1822, in *The Letters of Mary Wollstonecraft Shelley*, ed. Bennett, i. 282.

22 White, *Shelley*, ii. 377.

23 Fiona MacCarthy, *Byron: Life and Legend* (London: John Murray, 2002), p. 428

24 Miranda Seymour, *Mary Shelley* (London: John Murray, 2000), p. 302n.

25 St Clair, *Trelawny*, pp. 183–5.

26 Ibid., p. 226; Dane, 'On the Instability of Vessels and Narratives', p. 78. Crane cites the letter in which Trelawny told Roberts to reduce the length of the boat from 30 feet to 17. or 18 feet; Crane, *Lord Byron's Jackal*, p. 46.

27 St Clair, *Trelawny*, p. 69.

28 Bieri, *Percy Bysshe Shelley: A Biography*, ii. 312.

29 St Clair, *Trelawny*, p. 67. See also Donald B. Prell, 'Discovering Byron's Boat (the *Bolivar*)', *The Byron Journal* 35.1 (2007), 53–9, p. 56.

30 *Maria Gisborne and Edward E. Williams, Shelley's Friends: Their Journals and Letters*, ed. Frederick L. Jones (Norman: University of Oklahoma Press, 1951), pp. 154–5.

31 Diana Pugh, 'Captain Roberts and the Sinking of the *Don Juan*', *Keats-Shelley Memorial Bulletin* 16 (1975), 18–22, p. 22; Barker-Benfield, 'The Honeymoon of Joseph and Henrietta Chichester', p. 123; James Rieger, *The Mutiny Within: The Heresies of Percy Bysshe Shelley* (New York: George Braziller, 1967), p. 223.

32 Dane, 'On the Instability of Vessels and Narratives', p. 68.

33 It is cited by, among many others, Holmes, *Shelley: The Pursuit*, p. 729, as if it were beyond reproach.

34 Dane, 'On the Instability of Vessels and Narratives', p. 83.

35 *Maria Gisborne and Edward E. Williams*, ed. Jones, p. 70.

36 This episode is cited by White as proof of Shelley's lack of seamanship (see White, *Shelley*, ii. 367), but is persuasively glossed by Dane as evidence of Williams's tendency to blame the crew for the boat's failures (Dane, 'On the Instability of Vessels and Narratives', p. 85).

37 Bieri, *Percy Bysshe Shelley: A Biography*, ii. 327.

Myth 21

SHELLEY'S HEART

In primitive societies relics had power: the blood of slaughtered animals was thought to confer strength on those who drank it. Such beliefs, far-fetched though they may be, are echoed throughout the early nineteenth century and before, when the preservation of hair was a popular means of memorializing the living and the dead. Leigh Hunt owned a hair collection and composed three sonnets on a lock of Milton's, to which he attributed extraordinary powers, having it utter the words:

> Patience and Gentleness is Power. In me
> Behold affectionate eternity.[1]

If such was the potency attributed a mere lock of hair, how much greater was that invested in a heart? Shelley's orphaned body-part was not merely a prized souvenir, gloated over and caressed by proprietors of the shrines through which it passed; it would acquire the status of mythic object by being widely discussed – in letters, memoirs, even poems. Curiously, Richard Holmes's widely read biography, *Shelley: The Pursuit*, says nothing of it;[2] its story demands to be told, even if only to dispel some of the mystique its elusiveness continues to foster.[3]

Shelley went down with the *Don Juan*, in the middle of a storm, on 8 July 1822 (see Myth 20). It was ten days before what was left of him washed up about $4\frac{1}{2}$ miles north of Viareggio. Trelawny identified him by his white nankeen sailing trousers, silk socks, double-breasted reefer jacket, and the copy of Keats's final volume of poems in his pocket, lent him by Leigh Hunt, doubled back on itself 'as if it had been thrust in, in the hurry of a surprise'.[4] Besides that, the corpse was unrecognizable because 'the face, hands, head had been so mauled by small fish so as not to leave a trace of what they had been'.[5] Genoan quarantine laws

30 Great Myths About the Romantics, First Edition. Duncan Wu.
© 2015 John Wiley & Sons, Ltd. Published 2015 by John Wiley & Sons, Ltd.

demanded bodies of those drowned at sea be quicklimed until cremated, so it became necessary to inter the corpse in a temporary grave while a furnace was constructed which could be transported to the burial site.[6] Nearly a month later, on 16 August, Trelawny returned with Byron and Leigh Hunt to find the body 'plundered of his clothes; it was naked and dreadfully mutilated, loathsome'.[7] As a means of confirming it as that of his friend, Byron asked to see the teeth but 'they were terribly mangled'. 'What, are we to resemble that?' asked Byron. 'It may be the carcass of a sheep for all I can distinguish.' Pointing to Shelley's handkerchief, he added, 'See, an old rag retains its form longer. What a degrading reflection!'[8] Trelawny noted Shelley's remains were 'in the worst state of putridity and very offensive.... Both the legs were separated at the knees, the thigh bones bared and the flesh hung about in shreds; the hands were off and the arm bones protruded, the skull black & neither features nor face remaining.'[9] Those involved in the hapless task of transferring the fragments to the furnace had to fortify themselves with slugs of brandy.

As the fire was set, Trelawny and Byron threw handfuls of frankincense, honey, wine, and sugar on the flames, which gave a 'singular appearance' to the fire.[10] After three hours, Trelawny observed the corpse's chest open up, revealing the heart, which 'remained unaltered; a quantity of thin fluid still flowing and occasioning a bright blue flame ... I took the heart out to examine it, and the oily fluid flowed freely from it; the only visible effect the fire appeared to have had was to change its colour to a dingy blue.'[11] Various reasons have been given for its ability to withstand fire, the most persuasive being that 'Shelley suffered from a progressively calcifying heart, which might well have caused diffuse symptoms with its increasing weight of calcium and which would have resisted cremation as readily as a skull, jaw, or fragments of bone. Shelley's heart, epitome of Romanticism, may well have been a heart of stone.'[12] Whatever the cause, its refusal to incinerate helps explain its elevation to the status of sacred relic – as if that most emblematic of organs aspired to a transcendence denied the rest of Shelley's corpse.

Trelawny wanted to hang on to it,[13] but Hunt 'begged'[14] him for it as the pyre burned down. Trelawny cannot have given it up easily. Hunt probably harped on his lengthy friendship with the deceased, having known him since late 1816; Trelawny's acquaintance was of less than eight months' vintage. 'Good God! How shall I say it? My beloved friend Shelley, – my dear, my divine friend, the best of friends and men – he is no more', Hunt was capable of declaring in self-dramatizing moods.[15] He may also have mentioned the copy of Keats's poems found in Shelley's pocket, which was his: 'Dear Shelley had retained a book in his pocket, which he told me he

Figure 17   Shelley's jawbone, today preserved at the Keats-Shelley House, Rome.
Source: Photograph by Flavio Ianniello, courtesy of the Keats-Shelley House, Rome.

would not part with till he saw me again, – Keats's last publication.'[16] To a former jailbird like Hunt, whose assets amounted to nothing, Shelley's heart provided incontrovertible evidence of his standing in the world. (By 'some unknown manner'[17] Hunt managed also to procure Shelley's jaw-bone, now at the Keats-Shelley Memorial House in Rome.[18])

So began Hunt's 'cult of Shelley's heart'.[19] He could not resist flaunting the thing in front of Mary Shelley on return to Casa Lanfranchi in Pisa – an insensitive gesture, given that no one had thought to bring her any of her former husband's body-parts. She asked Byron to intercede on her behalf. 'Of course you should have it!', Byron exclaimed (or something of the kind), and he lobbied Hunt to hand it over. Whatever he said, he succeeded only in extracting from Hunt a reproachful letter protesting his prior claim because of 'my love for my friend; and for this to make way for the claims of any other love, man's or woman's, I must have great reasons indeed brought me ... they must be great, unequivocal, and undeniable'.[20] An astonishingly pompous remark given that he was addressing Shelley's widow. She was so appalled she preferred not to discuss him with her friend Maria Gisborne, saying she would speak of him 'when I see you'.[21]

For the next ten days, Shelley's heart remained *chez* Hunt – a locus of ribaldry or grief, depending on one's point of view. Byron noted its presence when, on 27 August, he told Thomas Moore it was 'now preserved in spirits of wine'.[22] But not for long. Mary Shelley was, understandably, in a state of agitation, Hunt's obduracy serving only to aggrieve her. She confided to Jane Williams, whose lover also drowned in the *Don Juan*; she in turn wrote to Hunt, saying 'how grievous and melancholy it was that Shelley's remains should become a source of dissension between his dearest friends. Could he be conscious of such bitterness between Mary and Hunt, how would his gentle spirit be moved and agitated!'[23]

That did the trick. Hunt saved face by admitting this was 'the only argument that could have induced him to yield'[24] and conveyed the heart to Mary Shelley. All the same, 'he never gave up his instinct that Shelley was his'.[25] (Leigh Hunt's biographer, Edmund Blunden, notes that 'in Hunt there was an element not merely of the unconventional but of the abnormal'.[26]) The rapprochement was in everyone's interest; insecure finances compelled Mary and her son Percy Florence to cohabit with the Hunts when in September they followed Byron to Genoa. Mary wrapped the heart in a silken pouch and secreted it inside a copy of Shelley's *Adonais* in her travelling desk, where it remained for the next three decades.[27]

In the meantime, Shelley's ashes enjoyed the rare distinction of receiving two burials. For months they sat in the cellar of a wine merchant in Via Condotti in Rome until, on 21 January 1823, Joseph Severn (who nursed Keats through his final illness) and two British clergymen walked them to the non-Catholic cemetery in Testaccio and placed them 'in a heap with five or six common vagabonds'.[28] One of the clergymen, Richard Burgess, read the burial service over the remains of the renowned 'atheist' (see Myth 27, especially pp. 233–4). A few months later Trelawny arrived and promptly set about offending everyone concerned, as Severn told Charles Brown:

> There is a Mad Chap come here – whose name is Trelawny I do not know what to make of him further than his queer and I was near saying shabby behavior to me – He comes as the friend of Shelly – great – glowing and rich in romance – of course I show'd all my paint-pot politeness to him – to the very brim – assisted him to remove the Ashes of Shelly to a spot where he himself (when this world has done with his body) will lie – He wished me to think, myself, and consult my Friends about a Monument to Shelly ... [29]

Under Trelawny's supervision, the ashes were exhumed and reinterred in part of the cemetery which he planted with six cypresses and four laurels.[30] The grave was marked by a stone inscribed 'Cor Cordium' (heart of hearts) – Hunt's idea, proving his knack for irony. Misled by the inscription, tour guides and writers continue to repeat the mini-myth that Shelley's heart was interred there.[31]

It travelled with Mary Shelley across the Continent in July 1823 back to England, arriving at the end of August, and was in her possession when she died at 24 Chester Square, London, on 1 February 1851. During her last days, Mary Shelley was comatose, though her doting daughter-in-law, Lady Jane Shelley, thought she knew better: according to her, the dying novelist was surprisingly vigorous given her condition: she 'turned her beautiful great grey eyes on us and towards her desk so often with a longing and beseeching look in them as if she wanted to speak and tell us something. I did not know what she wanted to say; we could not understand, though we longed to do so, and she passed away.'[32]

Sir Percy Florence Shelley (who inherited the baronetcy from his grandfather in 1844) was so 'unstrung' by his mother's death he 'could not bear to have any of her precious things touched'.[33] The contents of the silken pouch remained undefiled by human hand even after the desk had been transported, with the rest of her possessions, to their new residence, Boscombe Lodge in Bournemouth. In 1852, the desk was finally unlocked to reveal the copy of *Adonais* 'with a page torn loose and folded over in four. We opened it reverently and found ashes – dust – and we then knew what Mary had so longed to tell us: all that was left of Shelley's heart lay there.'[34] This gave Lady Shelley the inspiration for the 'sanctum' – a hallowed recess in her drawing-room enclosed by crimson curtains, illuminated by a red lamp, its ceiling painted with gold stars. It housed 'Etruscan and Greek figures and tear-bottles',[35] manuscripts, portraits of Shelley and his circle, hair-bracelets, Shelley's gloves, his watch, his guitar, a copy of Sophocles alleged to have been in his pocket when he drowned,[36] and – in an urn – what was left of the heart.[37] At some point Lady Shelley transferred it to a silver casket lined with silk, perhaps for use in séances.[38] (At the same period Teresa Guiccioli was diligently transcribing Byron's communiqués from the spirit world.[39])

In the meantime, Trelawny got down to the important task of mythologizing the heart and his role in its preservation. Readers might have thought they knew about it from Byron's letters, published in 1830, but they had so far been spared the minutiae refracted through the distorting lens of Trelawny's self-aggrandizing memory. In chapter 12 of his *Recollections of the Last Days of Shelley and Byron* (1858), published at his own expense, he recounted the tale of Shelley's incineration in much-embroidered detail, featuring himself as the protagonist who 'severely burnt' his hand while snatching the heart from the flames, while the poet's brains 'literally seethed, bubbled and boiled'.[40] Feeling himself insufficiently acknowledged, Trelawny rewrote the book as *Records of*

Shelley, Byron and the Author (1878), casting himself as peer to the writers alongside whom he had been little more than a hanger-on. In this final testament he condemned Mary Shelley for being so disgusted by the heart as to have given it to Leigh Hunt, an obvious falsehood. Yet this version of his narrative is widely cited.[41]

In 1885, an article appeared in *The Athenæum* suggesting the 'heart' was actually Shelley's liver.[42] Perhaps, but it hardly mattered. It was nothing more than dust and ashes, and was not long for this world – nor was Sir Percy Florence Shelley, who died on 5 December 1889. His wife apparently placed the remaining fragments of the 'heart' in his coffin before it made its way to the family mausoleum at St Peter's Church in Bournemouth. She feared it might continue on its travels when she was gone, perhaps as one of the trophies fought over by those glorified rag-and-bone men, Harry Buxton Forman and Thomas James Wise.[43]

That might have been the end of this tale were it not for a piece of evidence come recently to light. In a handwritten note in his copy of Trelawny's *Recollections*, E. Gambier Parry claimed the heart was long ago buried at Christchurch Abbey by Canon Ferdinand St John of Gloucester Cathedral.[44] Where is it now? No one knows, but the heart lives on in mythologized form. Who could forget that cadence from Byron's letter of August 1822, 'All of Shelley was consumed, except his heart, *which would not take the flame*'?[45] Those words went into print in 1830, and have bewitched us ever after. Such phrases have the power to transform water into wine, to transmogrify tin-can into holy grail. Shelley's heart continues to enjoy an independent life – as fetish, source of power, symbol of the manner in which the culture cannibalizes itself. It has resonated through literature, making guest appearances in Malcolm Lowry's 'Strange Comfort (Afforded by the Profession)' (published 1961), Charles McCarry's bestselling spy thriller *Shelley's Heart* (1995),[46] and William Michael Rossetti's sonnet, which boasts the most intractable final line in literary history:

Shelley's Heart

To Edward John Trelawny

'What surprised us all was that the heart remained entire. In snatching this relic from the fiery furnace, my hand was severely burnt.' – Trelawny's 'Recollections of Shelley'

> Trelawny's hand, which held'st the sacred heart,
> The heart of Shelley, and hast felt the fire
> Wherein the drossier framework of that lyre
> Of heaven and earth was molten – but its part

Immortal echoes always, and shall dart
    Pangs of keen love to human souls, and dire
    Ecstatic sorrow of joy, as higher and higher
They mount to know thee, Shelley, what thou art –
Trelawny's hand, did then the outward burn
    As once the inward? O cor cordium,
        Which *wast* a spirit of love, and now a clot,
    What other other flame was wont to come
Lambent from thee to fainter hearts, and turn –
    Red like thy death-pyre's heat – their lukewarmth hot![47]

Notes

1 Leigh Hunt, 'To the Same, on the Same Subject', ll. 13–14, in *Foliage* (London: C. & J. Ollier, 1818), p. cxxxii. Jane Stabler discusses Hunt's sonnet on Milton's hair, and Hunt's hair collection more generally, in 'Leigh Hunt's Aesthetics of Intimacy', in *Leigh Hunt: Life, Poetics, Politics*, ed. Nicholas Roe (London: Routledge, 2003), pp. 95–117.

2 The place for this would be chapter 30 (page 730) of Richard Holmes, *Shelley: The Pursuit* (London: Quartet Books, 1976).

3 It has been spoken of by others, as the following notes attest. See, *inter alia*, Hermione Lee, *Virginia Woolf's Nose: Essays on Biography* (Princeton, NJ: Princeton University Press, 2007), ch. 1, which recounts the story using the least reliable versions of Trelawny's narrative, and without consulting the full range of scholarly sources. Intriguingly, Howard E. Hugo's *Portable Romantic Reader* (New York: Viking, 1960) concludes with Trelawny's account of Shelley's *al fresco* cremation.

4 Leigh Hunt to Horace Smith, 25 July 1822, in *The Correspondence of Leigh Hunt*, ed. Thornton Leigh Hunt (2 vols., London: Smith, Elder, 1862), i. 194.

5 From the manuscript of Trelawny's essay quoted by Timothy Webb, 'Correcting the Irritability of His Temper: The Evolution of Leigh Hunt's *Autobiography*', in *Romantic Revisions*, ed. Robert A. Brinkley and Keith Hanley (Cambridge: Cambridge University Press, 1992), pp. 268–90, 283. It is worth pointing out Trelawny wrote at least ten accounts of the cremation, with varying levels of accuracy, most enumerated by Leslie A. Marchand, 'Trelawny on the Death of Shelley', *Keats-Shelley Memorial Bulletin* 4 (1952), 9–34, pp. 10–11. My quotations are taken from early versions more likely to be accurate.

6 Trelawny knew what to do because he had cremated his Arab wife some years before; see Leslie A. Marchand, 'A Note on the Burning of Shelley's Body', *Keats-Shelley Memorial Bulletin* 6 (1955), 1–3, p. 1.

7 From Trelawny's initial account of what happened, as quoted by Marchand, 'Trelawny on the Death of Shelley', p. 28.

8 Ibid. I have punctuated the wording of Trelawny's 1822 manuscript for ease of reading.

9 Webb, 'Correcting the Irritability of His Temper', p. 284.

10 Marchand, 'Trelawny on the Death of Shelley', p. 28. Byron to Thomas Moore, 27 August 1822, in *Byron's Letters and Journals*, ed. Leslie A. Marchand (13 vols., London: John Murray, 1973–94), ix. 197.

11 Webb, 'Correcting the Irritability of His Temper', p. 284. For other versions of Trelawny's commentary on the heart, see Marchand, 'Trelawny on the Death of Shelley', pp. 22–3.

12 Quoted in *The Letters of Mary Wollstonecraft Shelley*, ed. Betty T. Bennett (3 vols., Baltimore, MD: Johns Hopkins University Press, 1980–8), i. 256n2.

13 Trelawny clearly took other items, including three pieces of Shelley's skull and two of the jawbone.

14 Hunt's term; see his letter to Mary Shelley of 17 August 1822, quoted in *The Letters of Mary Wollstonecraft Shelley*, ed. Bennett, i. 255n2. The term is used also by Newman Ivey White, *Shelley* (2 vols., London: Secker & Warburg, 1947), ii. 382.

15 Leigh Hunt to Elizabeth Kent, 20 July 1822, in *The Correspondence of Leigh Hunt*, ed. Hunt, i. 190.

16 Ibid.

17 The phrase is that of White, *Shelley*, ii. 382.

18 Marchand suggests the jawbone may have belonged to Williams; see 'Trelawny on the Death of Shelley', pp. 20–1.

19 See Timothy Webb, 'Religion of the Heart: Leigh Hunt's Unpublished Tribute to Shelley', *The Keats-Shelley Review* 7 (1992), 1–61, p. 27, and 'Correcting the Irritability of His Temper', p. 285. The phrase is echoed by Roe, *Fiery Heart: The First Life of Leigh Hunt* (London: Pimlico, 2005), p. 348.

20 Leigh Hunt to Mary Shelley, 17 August 1822, in *The Letters of Mary W. Shelley*, ed. Frederick L. Jones (2 vols., Norman: University of Oklahoma Press, 1944), i. 187n2. See also *The Letters of Mary Wollstonecraft Shelley*, ed. Bennett, i. 255n2.

21 Mary Shelley to Maria Gisborne, c. 27 August 1822, in *The Letters of Mary Wollstonecraft Shelley*, ed. Bennett, i. 253.

22 Lord Byron to Thomas Moore, 27 August 1822, in *Byron's Letters and Journals*, ed. Marchand, ix. 197.

23 *Maria Gisborne and Edward E. Williams, Shelley's Friends: Their Journals and Letters*, ed. Frederick L. Jones (Norman: University of Oklahoma Press, 1951), pp. 88–9.

24 Ibid., p. 89.

25 Edmund Blunden, *Leigh Hunt: A Biography* (London: Cobden-Sanderson, 1930), p. 176.

26 Ibid.

27 A likely moment for this would have been after 7 October 1822, when it arrived at Genoa; see *The Letters of Mary Wollstonecraft Shelley*, ed. Bennett, i. 283. The copy of *Adonais* in which the heart was preserved is now at the Bodleian Library; B. C. Barker-Benfield reports 'The first four leaves are now missing': *Shelley's Guitar* (Oxford: Bodleian Library, 1992), p. 161.

28 The phrase is Trelawny's; see William St Clair, *Trelawny: The Incurable Romancer* (London: John Murray, 1977), p. 82. Severn's account of Shelley's

first funeral can be found in his letters to Charles Brown and Leigh Hunt, both of 21 January 1823, in *Joseph Severn: Letters and Memoirs*, ed. Grant F. Scott (Aldershot, Hants.: Ashgate, 2005), pp. 227–31.

29 Joseph Severn to Charles Brown, 9 April 1823, in *Joseph Severn: Letters and Memoirs*, ed. Scott, p. 237.

30 Mary Shelley to Maria Gisborne, 3 May 1823, in *The Letters of Mary Wollstonecraft Shelley*, ed. Bennett, i. 334.

31 Frederick L. Jones in 1944: 'Much controversy has raged about Shelley's heart, and even at the present time Roman tourist guides, pointing to "Cor Cordium" on the tombstone, tell travelers that the heart lies under the stone.' See *The Letters of Mary W. Shelley*, ed. Jones, i. 187n2. See also Kim Wheatley's helpful article, 'Attracted by the Body: Accounts of Shelley's Cremation', *Keats-Shelley Journal* 49 (2000), 162–82, pp. 178–9, and Frank J. Korn, *Hidden Rome* (Mahwah, NJ: Paulist Press, 2002), p. 174.

32 Maud Rolleston, *Talks with Lady Shelley* (London: George G. Harrap, 1897), p. 30.

33 Ibid., pp. 30–1.

34 Ibid., p. 31.

35 Stephen Hebron and Elizabeth C. Denlinger, *Shelley's Ghost: Reshaping the Image of a Literary Family* (Oxford: Bodleian Library, 2010), p. 142.

36 This is now at the Bodleian Library. Trelawny did not mention the Sophocles until 1858, and it seems highly implausible, given how long it would have been underwater and afterwards in quicklime, that it would have fared any better than the copy of Keats's poems. The Bodleian's website, however, insists that it may have been on board the *Don Juan* when it sank. For more on this topic see Marchand, 'Trelawny on the Death of Shelley', pp. 17–18.

37 For other items in the sanctum, see Miranda Seymour, *Mary Shelley* (London: John Murray, 2000), p. 543.

38 For more on Lady Jane's spiritualism, see ibid., p. 546. The part played in the creation of the Shelley legend by the Shelley sanctum has been discussed by Julie A. Carlson, *England's First Family of Writers: Mary Wollstonecraft, William Godwin, Mary Shelley* (Baltimore, MD: Johns Hopkins University Press, 2007), p. 259ff.

39 James Soderholm, *Fantasy, Forgery, and the Byron Legend* (Lexington: University Press of Kentucky, 1996), pp. 126–8.

40 Edward James Trelawny, *Recollections of the Last Days of Shelley and Byron* (London, 1858), pp. 134–5.

41 I refer those who write on this matter to William St Clair: 'It is difficult to establish for certain exactly what happened on and after the fatal day of 8 July 1822 despite the wealth of relevant material. Many of the participants were concerned within a short time of the disaster to vindicate their own conduct, to blame others, or to lay claim to credit, and all but the most contemporaneous documents have to be treated with caution': *Trelawny: The Incurable Romancer*, p. 216.

42 A. S. Bicknell, 'The "Cor Cordium"', *The Athenæum* 3009 (27 June 1885), 823.

43 Those unfamiliar with these Dickensian delinquents will find an introduction to them, including Forman's mugshot, in Hebron and Denlinger, *Shelley's Ghost*, pp. 164–7.

44 See Seymour, *Mary Shelley*, p. 562.

45 Lord Byron to Thomas Moore, 27 August 1822, in *Byron's Letters and Journals*, ed. Marchand, ix. 197.

46 Christopher Hitchens assesses McCarry's attitude to Shelley in his essay, 'Ode to the West Wing', in *Unacknowledged Legislation: Writers in the Public Sphere* (London: Verso, 2000), pp. 303–14.

47 This is the text which appeared in *The Dark Blue* 1 (1 March 1871), p. 35. Rossetti was aware the final line was problematic and, when reprinted in Laura Valentine's *Gems of National Poetry* (London: Frederick Warne, 1880), p. 314, he revised it to read: 'Their frost to fire of the sun's chariot!' Rossetti's difficulties in finding a publisher for the sonnet are recounted by Michelle Hawley, 'Recollections of P. B. Shelley: William Michael Rossetti, Political Commitment and Literary Capital', in *Outsiders Looking In: The Rossettis Then and Now*, ed. David Clifford and Laurence Roussillon (London: Anthem Press, 2004), pp. 77–96, 81–3.

Myth
22
KEATS'S 'HUMBLE ORIGINS'

> I see a schoolboy when I think of him,
> With face and nose pressed to a sweet-shop window,
> For certainly he sank into his grave
> His senses and his heart unsatisfied,
> And made – being poor, ailing and ignorant,
> Shut out from all the luxury of the world,
> The coarse-bred son of a livery-stable keeper –
> Luxuriant song.
>
> W. B. Yeats, 'Ego Dominus Tuus'

It wasn't Yeats's fault his portrait of Keats was a wayward caricature; he was correct by scholarly standards of the time. A decade before he composed these lines,[1] Ernest de Selincourt introduced his 1905 edition of Keats's poems by saying, 'John Keats was born a member of that section of the community in which, perhaps, we are least accustomed to suspect the presence of poetic thought and feeling.'[2] If the idea that poetic thought is alien to those of working-class origins seems shocking now, it was not so to de Selincourt's Victorian readers. He went on to describe Keats's education as 'scanty': 'Of Greek he had learned nothing; and though he had some knowledge of Latin, for he had already begun, as a pastime, a translation of Vergil's *Aeneid*, he could hardly have reached that stage of scholarship in which the influence of classical literature begins to make itself felt.'[3] This is one of the most misleading passages in his introduction: by suggesting Keats merely *began* to translate as a 'pastime', he reinforces the image of an air-headed amateur. He should have known better. Since 1838, when Charles Brown published his pamphlet on Shakespeare, it had been known that Keats made a literal translation of the entire *Aeneid*

30 Great Myths About the Romantics, First Edition. Duncan Wu.
© 2015 John Wiley & Sons, Ltd. Published 2015 by John Wiley & Sons, Ltd.

in order to remedy the effects of his 'early removal from school'. And, as Brown went on to recall, 'I have seen him deeply absorbed in the study of the Greek and Italian, both which languages he then commenced, and to which he allotted a portion of each day.'[4] Brown was one of the first to demonstrate, if only by implication, Keats's affinity with Shakespeare.[5]

De Selincourt's edition remained in print until 1961, but is not the myth's ultimate source; the allegation that Keats was a lower-class ignoramus is traceable to his literary and political foes – Tory critics such as John Gibson Lockhart, who combined critical rigour with social snobbery in a series of venomous cocktails entitled 'The Cockney School of Poetry'. Lockhart began by aligning Keats with the servant class: 'our very footmen compose tragedies, and there is scarcely a superannuated governess in the island that does not leave a roll of lyrics behind her in her band-box'.[6] He concluded by invoking Keats's medical training as evidence of his lowly status:

> It is a better and a wiser thing to be a starved apothecary than a starved poet; so back to the shop Mr John, back to 'plasters, pills, and ointment boxes,' &c. But, for Heaven's sake, young Sangrado, be a little more sparing of extenuatives and soporifics in your practice than you have been in your poetry.[7]

Sangrado was the useless quack from Le Sage's once popular novel *Gil Blas* (1715–35), who knew no treatment besides bleeding and the drinking of hot water; Lockhart invokes him as representative of apothecaries – semi-literate tradesmen ignorant of Latin,[8] on a par with grocers and barbers.[9] Lockhart's readers probably found this amusing, without realizing his jokes were themselves superannuated. As recently as 1815 the Worshipful Society of Apothecaries had been granted the right to examine and license general medical practitioners throughout England and Wales. Candidates had to be proficient in Latin; to produce certificates of attendance at lectures and of at least six months' attendance at a public hospital, infirmary, or dispensary; and to have completed a five-year apprenticeship. The new regulations stemmed the tidal wave of Sangrados by creating a new class of 'qualified general practitioners' regarded as 'well-educated gentlemen'.[10]

In short, the medical profession was no longer the resort of snake-oil salesmen; at the upper end, surgeons were members of the gentry.[11] Keats studied with one – Astley Cooper, pioneer in the surgery of blood vessels, experimental surgery, and surgery of the ear, who was awarded a baronetcy after removing a cyst from the scalp of George IV.[12] Thanks in part to Cooper's good offices, Keats passed the relevant examination at Apothecaries' Hall and was listed as 'certificated apothecary' in the

London Medical Repository for October 1816.[13] All of which Lockhart disregards for the sake of a lampoon.

His slurs might have decayed quietly in the archives had they not been lent currency by Leigh Hunt, who in 1828 declared,

> Mr Keats's origin was of the humblest description: he was born 29 October 1796, at a livery stables in Moorfields, of which his grandfather was the proprietor .... He never spoke of it, perhaps out of a personal soreness which the world had exasperated.[14]

This is the most damaging of the myth's various reiterations, being that to which scholars most often refer, and almost every part of it is incorrect, yet it comes from someone Keats regarded as a friend – whose association with him was the principal reason for the 'Cockney School' attacks. In 1964 Robert Gittings observed, 'Leigh Hunt could hardly have been more mistaken in his remarks on "Mr Keats's origin"',[15] yet it continues to shape scholarly and popular preconceptions. As recently as 2008, none other than *The New Yorker* could be found misinforming readers about Keats's 'working-class origins': 'Keats was the son of a stable-keeper, and he had trained as an apothecary' (as if the one followed from the other).[16]

Yeats, de Selincourt, Lockhart, Leigh Hunt, and *The New Yorker* all seem to think that, as tavern proprietor, Keats's grandfather was straight out of *The Beggar's Opera*, the cohort of highwaymen, prostitutes, and petty criminals. They couldn't be more wrong. The Swan and Hoop was at 24 The Pavement, immediately outside old Moorgate. It was a grand establishment occupying a large, three-storey building, with a passage leading to two coach houses, a large stable yard, stabling for fifty horses, and room for a number of carriages. A large and profitable concern owned by John Jennings (1730–1805), Keats's grandfather on his mother's side, it was upgraded in 1774 at a cost of £670 – in those days a considerable sum. It was neither gambling den nor brothel; despite the anachronism, modern readers would be closer to the mark were they to consider it the eighteenth-century equivalent of a leisure complex and hotel with car hire facilities.

Jennings exemplified the upwardly mobile middle-class businessmen who joined the London guilds. On 1 January 1774, he purchased his freedom of the City of London, and of the Innholders' Company three days later. In 1785, he took a lease on the next-door property, 22 The Pavement, which he let for £46 a year; the combined frontage measured 117 feet.[17] Jennings's portfolio was varied: he took up mortgages on other properties, lent money on property security, and invested in government funds and East India stock. 1798 may have been a tricky year financially,[18] but its effect was not to render Jennings any less middle-class than he had been previously. When he died on 8 March 1805, his estate was valued at more than £13,600.[19]

Keats's father is a shadowy figure about whom little is known before he turned up as an employee at the Swan and Hoop. He married Jennings's daughter Frances on 9 October 1794, elevating himself 'above his sphere in life',[20] and over the years gained his father-in-law's trust, for in 1802 Jennings would sublease the Swan and Hoop to him at £44 a year. Like his father-in-law before him, Thomas Keats was admitted to the Innkeepers' Company in 1803 and became Freeman of the City.[21] None of this supports the contention he was working-class; the evidence suggests he was middle-class. It was a matter of his demeanour – which struck no one as 'humble' – as well as his conduct. John Taylor, Keats's publisher, recalled he 'kept a remarkably fine Horse for his own Riding, & on Sundays would go out with others who prided themselves in the like Distinction, to Highgate, Highbury, or some other place of public Entertainment for Man & Horse'.[22] George Keats heard his father 'praised as a man of good sense and very much liked',[23] probably recalling Charles Cowden Clarke. Clarke remembered him for 'his excellent natural sense, and total freedom from vulgarity, and assumption, on account of his prosperous alliance with the family of his employer'.[24] Clarke elsewhere characterizes him as 'a man of so remarkably fine a commonsense and native respectability, that I perfectly remember the warm terms in which his demeanour used to be canvassed by my parents after he had been to visit his boys'.[25]

At his death in 1804, Thomas Keats left an estate worth £2,000,[26] which 'need not have been, as has sometimes been assumed, solely the result of his fortunate marriage'.[27] By the standards of the time, he died a wealthy man with an income considerably larger than that of artisans and skilled workers. Some confusion about his standing may be caused by the description of him as an ostler, often glossed as 'servant'. It is not evident he ever occupied precisely that position but, if he began in it, Frederick Salmon took care to describe him as '*Head* Ostler at the Swan & Hoop' (his italics),[28] which means his role was managerial and his income commensurate with that status. Either way, the mere fact his father occupied that post does not prove John Keats was born 'at a livery stables', as Hunt implied; in fact, Keats's baptism at the church of St Botolph-without-Bishopsgate indicates he was born in the neighbouring parish.[29]

If the level of education to which parents aspire on their children's behalf is any indication, the Keatses should be regarded as members of the cultural elite. Frances Keats (who herself enjoyed an upbringing 'of comfortable affluence and good education'[30]) told her sons she would have wanted to send them to Harrow, one of the finest public schools in the land, 'if she could have afforded'.[31] In fact, Keats went to John Clarke's Enfield Academy, which Nicholas Roe has described as 'the most extraordinary school in the country'.[32] It was a dissenting institution at the forefront of educational theory and practice. Instead of the floggings suffered by pupils elsewhere, boys kept records of their behaviour, and made 'voluntary' translations from Latin and French texts. The science of astronomy was taught by means of the living orrery, a schoolyard game.[33] It gave Keats an excellent (if unconventional) education and the mentorship of Charles Cowden Clarke, eight years his senior and an assistant teacher at the school, who nurtured his literary talent up to the moment at which he began to write his greatest work.[34] None of which is characteristic of working-class people at this period, who were lucky if they were taught to read. Education, for most outside the monied classes, was 'characteristically episodic, fractured, and contingent';[35] that could not be said of Keats's, which was 'crucial to the formation of [his] genius'.[36] An oft-repeated myth concerning his schooling is that he had no classical education; as I have already pointed out, he made up for that in later life. Though at school he did not venture far with ancient Greek, he won prizes for translations from Latin and French.[37]

One way of assessing Keats's working-class credentials is to compare him with those who really were from a humble background. Stephen Duck (1705–56) left school at 14 to become an agricultural labourer; Ann Yearsley (baptized 1753, died 1806) was daughter of a milkwoman, her only schooling received at home from her mother; John Clare (1793–1864), son of a thresher and local wrestler, attended dame- and vestry-school before becoming a ploughboy at 14. By contrast, Keats received an education that equipped him for a profession, had he wished to pursue one: after Clarke's academy, he was apprenticed to Thomas Hammond, an apothecary and surgeon, before entering Guy's Hospital as a student. There he attended lectures by the finest surgeon of the day, became dresser to William Lucas, and qualified as Licentiate of the Society of Apothecaries in July 1816. This was a path of academic distinction beyond the reach of those who left school at 14.

Yeats's Keats was 'poor, ailing and ignorant, / Shut out from all the luxury of the world' – a mini-myth of poverty corroborating proletarian ignorance. In fact, the Keatses were well-to-do. The siblings inherited two separate funds, one amounting to £20,000,[38] on which they could have drawn in later years. Their difficulty was not knowing their situation or how to claim their due. In the autumn of 1816, at a time when he supposed himself without resources, Keats actually had £800 in Chancery. When he discussed money with Fanny Brawne, he was prone to affect an aristocratic disdain which may reflect his true feelings: 'by heaven, I am as entirely above all matters of interest as the Sun is above the Earth – And though of my own money I should be careless; of my Friends I must be spare'.[39]

Either way, Keats was never the deprived yokel he is reputed to have been. His family was prosperous by the standards of the day, and his mother had ambitions for him that his schooling helped him achieve. If we must label him, we should use the terms endorsed by Charles and Mary Cowden Clarke: 'John Keats was born on the 29th of October, 1795, in the upper rank of the middle class'.[40] Keats's social standing, like that of anyone else in English society, was echoed in that of his friends: Leigh Hunt (son of a lawyer); Charles Brown (son of a stockbroker); Charles Dilke (son of the chief clerk in the paymaster branch at the Admiralty); Benjamin Robert Haydon (son of a printer, publisher, and bookseller); and William Haslam (son of a solicitor). 'The coarse-bred son of a livery-stable keeper' would never have kept such company.

Notes

1 Yeats's poem was written in December 1915, according to Warwick Gould, 'The Mask before *The Mask*', in *Yeats's Mask: Yeats Annual 19*, ed. Margaret Mills Harper and Warwick Gould (Cambridge: Open Book Publishers, 2013), p. 36.
2 *The Poems of John Keats*, ed. Ernest de Selincourt (London: Methuen, 1905), p. xx.
3 Ibid., p. xxi.
4 Charles Brown, *Shakespeare's Autobiographical Poems* (London: James Bohn, 1838), pp. 133–4.
5 E. H. McCormick, *The Friend of Keats: A Life of Charles Armitage Brown* (Wellington, NZ: Victoria University Press, 1989), p. 154.
6 *John Keats: The Critical Heritage*, ed. G. M. Matthews (London: Routledge & Kegan Paul, 1971), pp. 97–8.
7 Ibid., pp. 109–10. Roe cites the evidence revealing that Benjamin Bailey was Lockhart's chief informant; see Nicholas Roe, *John Keats and the Culture of Dissent* (Oxford: Clarendon Press, 1997), p. 24.
8 *Health, Disease and Society in Europe, 1500–1800: A Sourcebook*, ed. Peter Elmer and Ole Peter Grell (Manchester: Manchester University Press, 2004), p. 20.
9 In Smollett's translation, Sangrado is described as having 'acquired great reputation with the public, by a pomp of words, a solemn air, and some lucky cures': Le Sage, *The Adventures of Gil Blas of Santillane*, tr. Tobias Smollett (3 vols., London, 1819), i. 131.
10 Richard W. Schoch, *Not Shakespeare: Bardolatry and Burlesque in the Nineteenth Century* (Cambridge: Cambridge University Press, 2002), p. 122.

For more on the 1815 Act and its consequences, see Christopher Lawrence, *Medicine in the Making of Modern Britain, 1700–1920* (Abingdon, Oxon.: Routledge, 1994).

11 *Health, Disease and Society in Europe, 1500–1800*, ed. Elmer and Grell, p. 192.

12 See, for an excellent account of Cooper's career, William John Bishop, *The Early History of Surgery* (London: Robert Hale, 1960), pp. 135–40.

13 Nicholas Roe, *John Keats: A New Life* (New Haven: Yale University Press, 2012), p. 92.

14 Leigh Hunt, *Lord Byron and Some of His Contemporaries* (2nd ed., 2 vols., London, 1828), i. 409.

15 Robert Gittings, 'Mr Keats's Origin', *Times Literary Supplement*, 5 March 1964, p. 200.

16 Adam Kirsch, 'Cloudy Trophies; John Keats's Obsession with Fame and Death', *The New Yorker* 84 (7 July 2008), 92. The article surveys Stanley Plumly's excellent *Posthumous Keats* (2008), which stays clear of this solecism.

17 Lawrence M. Crutcher, *George Keats of Kentucky* (Lexington: University Press of Kentucky, 2012), p. 12.

18 Roe, *Keats: A New Life*, pp. 13–14.

19 This figure varies depending on who is reporting it; I refer to Crutcher, *George Keats of Kentucky*, p. 6. Crutcher describes the various lawsuits that followed Jennings's death.

20 'Richard Woodhouse: Notes on Keats's Life', in *The Keats Circle: Letters and Papers 1816–1878*, ed. Hyder Edward Rollins (2 vols., Cambridge, MA: Harvard University Press, 1948), i. 274. It is hard to be sure who was Woodhouse's source for this point, as he seems to be taking notes from a conversation with both Frederick Salmon and Charles Cowden Clarke.

21 Crutcher, *George Keats of Kentucky*, p. 12.

22 John Taylor to Richard Woodhouse, 20, 23 April 1827, in *The Keats Circle*, ed. Rollins, i. 304.

23 George Keats to Charles Dilke, 20 April 1825, ibid., p. 288.

24 Ibid., ii. 288.

25 *Keats: The Critical Heritage*, ed. Matthews, p. 385.

26 I follow Gittings, 'Mr Keats's Origin', who examined the original Chancery documents.

27 Robert Gittings, *John Keats* (Harmondsworth: Penguin, 1968), p. 11. Andrew Motion follows Gittings: Andrew Motion, *Keats* (London: Faber & Faber, 1997), p. 9.

28 Frederick Salmon to Richard Woodhouse, 15 February 1822, in *The Keats Circle*, ed. Rollins, i. 270.

29 Gittings, *John Keats*, p. 32.

30 Ibid., p. 31. This contention is underwritten by other findings concerning her family; see, *inter alia*, Phyllis G. Mann, 'New Light on Keats and His Family', *Keats-Shelley Memorial Bulletin* 11 (1960), 33–8.

31 George Keats to Charles Dilke, 20 April 1825, in *The Keats Circle*, ed. Rollins, i. 288.

32 Roe, *A New Life*, p. 20.

33 See Roe, *Keats and the Culture of Dissent*, pp. 36–7, and Roe's essay, 'A Cockney Schoolroom: John Keats at Enfield', in *Keats: Bicentenary Readings*, ed. Michael O'Neill (Edinburgh: Edinburgh University Press, 1997), pp. 11–26.

34 Clarke remembered Keats reading Burnet's *History of His Own Time* at school, and it was at that period Keats first came across Leigh Hunt's newspaper, *The Examiner*; see Roe, *Keats and the Culture of Dissent*, p. 25.

35 Philip Gardner, 'Literacy, Learning, and Education', in *A Companion to 19th-Century Britain*, ed. Chris Williams (Oxford: Blackwell, 2004), pp. 353–68, 354.

36 *Keats and the Culture of Dissent*, p. 23.

37 Roe, *Keats: A New Life*, pp. 38–9, 42–3, 92. See also Martin Aske, *Keats and Hellenism: An Essay* (Cambridge: Cambridge University Press, 1985), pp. 34–5.

38 Roe, *Keats: A New Life*, p. 42.

39 John Keats to Fanny Brawne, 16 August 1819, in *The Letters of John Keats 1814–1821*, ed. Hyder Edward Rollins (2 vols., Cambridge, MA: Harvard University Press, 1958), ii. 141.

40 Charles and Mary Cowden Clarke, *Recollections of Writers* (Fontwell, Sussex: Centaur Press, 1969), p. 121.

Myth
23 KEATS WAS GAY

The myth is an anachronism. In Keats's day there was no such thing as 'gay', and to be exposed as homosexual was to make oneself vulnerable to prosecution. (If proven, sodomy was punishable with a capital penalty, two men a year being executed for it on average.[1]) All the same, Keats did go in for cross-dressing, after a fashion: when planning to publish 'The Jealousies', he said he would do so under the pseudonym Lucy Vaughan Lloyd, in the hope that, as a woman, he would sell more books than as a man.[2] But since when did transvestism say anything about one's orientation?

We have no evidence Keats was homosexual; in fact, what we know points in the other direction. This was a man who could be haunted for two days by the 'voice and shape of a woman', and declare, 'I forget myself entirely because I live in her'.[3] He has been described as 'one of the boys',[4] a keen cigar-smoker, snuff-taker, and claret-drinker who played billiards, attended boxing matches, cockfights, and bearbaitings. Biographers suggest he was treated for syphilis caught from a female prostitute.[5]

Yet it would be fantasy to pretend there was not something in Keats that resonates with the modern gay sensibility, and critics such as James Najarian and Sarah Wootton, on whose work I have drawn in this essay, have noted inferences drawn by some readers, particularly during the Victorian period.[6] Visiting Keats's grave at the non-Catholic cemetery in 1877, Oscar Wilde prostrated himself, calling it 'the holiest place in Rome',[7] and was moved to write a sonnet.[8] Shortly after, he recalled his visit in 'The Tomb of Keats':

> As I stood beside the mean grave of this divine boy, I thought of him as a Priest of Beauty slain before his time; and the vision of Guido's St. Sebastian came before my eyes as I saw him at Genoa, a lovely brown boy, with crisp, clustering hair and red lips, bound by his evil enemies to a tree, and though pierced by arrows, raising his eyes with divine, impassioned gaze towards the Eternal Beauty of the opening heavens.[9]

30 Great Myths About the Romantics, First Edition. Duncan Wu.
© 2015 John Wiley & Sons, Ltd. Published 2015 by John Wiley & Sons, Ltd.

Figure 18 Guido Reni's depiction of St Sebastian: 'a lovely brown boy, with crisp, clustering hair and red lips'.
Source: Palazzo Bianco, Genoa, Italy / Mondadori Portfolio / Electa / Antonio Quattrone / Bridgeman Images.

Five years later he described the poet as 'that god-like boy, the real Adonis of our age',[10] and in a lecture delivered to American audiences said he exemplified 'the sensuous life of verse': 'for our delight his despair will gild its own thorns, and his pain, like Adonis, be beautiful in its agony; and when the poet's heart breaks it will break in music'.[11] Wilde fetishized the manuscript of Keats's 'Sonnet in Blue' which he kept on his drawing-room wall, declaring: 'I am half enamoured of the paper that touched his hand and the ink that did his bidding. I have grown fond of the sweet comeliness of his charactery'[12] – a rare occasion on which a poet was worshipped for the sweep of his cursives. ('Charactery', meaning handwriting, was a term Keats had used in one of his greatest sonnets about mortality, 'When I have fears that I may cease to be'.)

Almost from the start, critics thought Keats's poetry lady-like.[13] In 1817, a reviewer described his style as 'namby-pamby',[14] which may have prompted John Gibson Lockhart, the following year, to dragoon him into 'The Cockney School of Poetry', ridiculing him for having 'adopted the loose, nerveless versification and Cockney rhymes of the poet of *Rimini*' – that is, Leigh Hunt.[15] Besides referring to someone born within the sound of Bow Bells, 'Cockney' could be taken to mean 'effeminate', and with that in mind fellow-traveller Benjamin Robert Haydon once mused: 'How could Byron sympathise with the mawkish, unmanly namby pamby effeminacy of Leigh Hunt'.[16] It may have been that Hunt (who became a mentor to Keats) affected what we would call a 'camp' manner, as Haydon seems to imply; even at their first meeting, 'I listened with something of curiosity to his republican independence, though hating his effeminacy and cockney peculiarities.'[17]

For all his 'peculiarities' (whatever they were), there is no shortage of witnesses to Hunt's orientation; besides being passionately in love with his wife, he cultivated what Haydon described as a 'smuggering fondness' for his sister-in-law, Bess, over whose overflowing bosoms he liked to 'dawdle'.[18] Keats's problem was that, for every witness to his heterosexuality, another testified to his being 'namby-pamby'; in some cases they were one and the same person. No one could have been more assured of Keats's love of women than that seasoned habitué of the West End stews, William Hazlitt – yet it was he who, within a year of Keats's death, wrote,

> I cannot help thinking that the fault of Mr Keats's poems was a deficiency in masculine energy of style. He had beauty, tenderness, delicacy, in an uncommon degree, but there was a want of strength and substance .... All is soft and fleshy, without bone or muscle. We see in him the youth, without the manhood of poetry.[19]

Hazlitt is describing the qualities of the verse, but it was inevitable someone would turn his comments into a test of Keats's preferences – and that someone turned out to be none other than Leigh Hunt: 'Mr Keats's natural tendency to pleasure, as a poet, sometimes degenerated, by reason of his ill health, into a poetical effeminacy.'[20] In one sentence, Hunt equated Keats's poetic manner with physical debility, hedonism, and girlishness – giving renewed currency to the Cockney School attacks of a decade before. The irony is that, were it not for Hunt, Keats would probably not have been branded Cockney in the first place – something Hunt was unlikely to admit. And so the name-calling continued, from allies and former friends, in ever more exotic forms: in 1842 George Darley described Keats as 'one of those beauties who fed upon rose-leaves instead of wholesome flesh, fish and fowl'.[21]

Byron was unusually agitated by Keats's verse, one of the peculiarities of his animus being the impulse to compare it with deviant sexual practices. In the most spectacular of his numerous outbursts against the 'miserable mountebanks of the day', Byron expressed horror at Jeffrey's favourable review of Keats in the Edinburgh Review:[22]

> The Edinburgh praises Jack Keats or Ketch or whatever his names are; – why his is the Onanism of Poetry – something like the pleasure an Italian fiddler extracted out of being suspended daily by a Street Walker in Drury Lane – this went on for some weeks – at last the Girl went to get a pint of Gin – met another, chatted too long – and Cornelli was hanged outright before she returned. Such like is the trash they praise – and such will be the end of the outstretched poesy of this miserable Self-polluter of the human Mind.[23]

Byron is saying he disapproved of such works as 'The Eve of St Agnes' because its pleasures were akin to those derived from auto-erotic asphyxiation – except that, in his story, the Italian 'fiddler' is supervised by a prostitute whose comic inattentiveness precipitates his demise (which may explain his reference to Jack Ketch, a public hangman of the 1670s). This came hot on the heels of his initial snarl at Keats's final lifetime publication, containing Lamia, The Eve of St Agnes, and the odes, or 'Johnny Keats's p-ss a bed poetry'[24] as he called it, which elicited the proposal that his publisher John Murray (who had been kind enough to send him Keats's book) 'flay him alive – if some of you don't I must skin him myself[;] there is no bearing the drivelling idiotism of the Mankin'[25] (a 'mankin' is a diminutive or puny man). As traumatized scholars have observed, Byron's implication is that excessive self-abuse has rotted the brains of 'that dirty little blackguard KEATES'[26] – a theory explored in yet another paroxysm: 'such writing is a sort of mental masturbation – he is always fr-gg-g his Imagination. – I don't mean that he is indecent but viciously soliciting his own ideas into a state which is neither poetry nor any thing else but a Bedlam vision produced by raw pork and opium.'[27]

Byron accuses Keats of arousing sexual desire in the reader, something he thought unhealthy. But why has the jaded roué of the Romantic period adopted the matronly guise of mother superior? This was someone whose bedtime reading was De Sade's *Justine* and who by this date had done things with adolescent boys Keats never contemplated. What's more, Byron's image (not Keats's) was the emblem on Benbow's House of Regency Porn in Leicester Square, while pirated copies of *Don Juan* retailed alongside Harriette Wilson's *Memoirs* and lurid French novels at William Dugdale's bookshop in Holywell Street, the unintended result of reviewers having labelled it 'vulgar and obscene', 'thoroughly depraved', and 'spawned in filth and darkness'.[28] But therein, of course, lies the answer.

It is no accident that most of Byron's written denunciations of Keats were addressed to John Murray, who he knew read them aloud to the courtiers of Albemarle Street;[29] to that audience he declared his disapproval of someone whose poetry was 'continually in for – and filling some other Body'.[30] The negatively capable Keats invested himself shamelessly in the sensuous experience of others, leading the *Quarterly Review* (Murray's house organ) to admonish him for having used 'the most uncouth language'.[31] No wonder Byron, brought up a Calvinist,[32] bruised by recent attacks on *Don Juan* Cantos I and II (and denounced by the *British Critic* for 'shameless indecency'[33]), took the opportunity to expose what he thought the more egregious sins of Keats's verse, soiled by its ripe awareness of the physicality of things, drenched in unreleased passion and a kind of innocence that manifested itself as earnestness. And that innocence, that unaffected lack of sophistication, was what Byron most despised: he could not bear Keats's refusal to undermine his poems with the cynical language games and high-tea manners with which his own writing was encrusted. How understandable, then, that one of the most dissipated readers of the period should denounce as obscene the one contemporary whose offences were restricted to the realm of literary style. It was a form of self-exoneration performed in a semi-public forum. Perhaps a similar anxiety inspired Whitman's criticism of Keats as 'sweet – oh! very sweet – all sweetness: almost lush: lush, polish, ornateness, elegancy'.[34]

You didn't have to be Calvinist to disown Keatsian excess; you had only to be human enough to enjoy the sensation as it tickled the soles of your feet – and that kind of pleasure, most Victorians were obliged to say, was depraved. Sidney Colvin observed that Keats's youthful heroes were characterized by 'effeminacy and physical softness',[35] while William Michael Rossetti described Keats as 'almost an alien in the region of morals', noting 'two or three of Keats's minor poems have a certain unmistakable twang of erotic laxity'.[36] Gerard Manley Hopkins sensed something similar. He was aware of 'how his work is at every turn abandoning itself to an unmanly and enervating luxury'[37] – something that offended what modern critics have described as his homoerotic asceticism.[38]

These comments develop a quality first analysed by Hazlitt into something else – immorality, with the suggestion Keats was dissolute or 'deviant'. Suspicions deepened with publication of Keats's love letters in 1878: they prompted Matthew Arnold to deplore the 'complete enervation' of a 'sensuous man of a badly bred and badly trained sort'.[39] Swinburne described him as 'a vapid and effeminate rhymester in the sickly stage of whelphood', adding the letters 'ought never to have been written…a manful kind of man or even a manly sort of boy, in his love-making or in his suffering, will not howl and snivel after such a lamentable fashion'.[40] (One can but marvel at such hypocrisy – though it must be admitted that, as one of the most enthusiastic sado-masochists of the century, Swinburne knew about howling and snivelling.) In 1887 Coventry Patmore divided poetry into two different classes: in one, intellect predominated (masculine); in the other, beauty and sweetness (feminine), and in that 'Keats stands as high as any other, if not higher'.[41] If there is a theme, it is that of presumed sexual ambiguity, invoked by friend and foe alike: 'In poetry', Mrs Oliphant wrote, 'his was the woman's part.'[42] Critical approaches of recent times have continued to explore this aspect of his reputation; Barbara Charlesworth Gelpi and Adrienne Rich cast him 'an honorary woman'.[43]

The Romantic period may be the first in history in which literary style provided the basis for speculation concerning sexual orientation. It matters not that Keats's actual sex life was uneventful, even dull, at least by comparison with those of such witnesses for the prosecution as Byron and Swinburne; it was enough he align himself with Leigh Hunt, whose poetry displayed what its critics described as 'extreme moral depravity' and 'a noxious and disgusting mixture of libertinism and jacobinism'.[44] Keats was aware of the danger: in October 1817 he told Benjamin Bailey of his fear that 'I shall have the Reputation of Hunt's elevé' (or pupil).[45] It made him aspire to a more 'manly' style, but the forging of a poetic manner is the work of decades, and he had no more than months.

His appropriation as gay icon may be inspired in part by his protracted disintegration over many months in the arms of Joseph Severn, which resonates in a period devastated by AIDS. Najarian notes that, in an AIDS anthology, four poems mention Keats by name, each written 'for or about a person who has died from the disease'.[46] And teachers report that 'students seem better able to grasp Keats's attitudes toward death through comparisons with views in AIDS poetry'.[47] Catherine Payling, Curator of the Keats-Shelley Memorial House in Rome from 1997 to

2011, tells me visitors to the room in which the poet died sometimes asked whether Keats and Severn were lovers. No, she would say, to be greeted with pitying looks. Which prompts the thought that this is one of those rare occasions on which the myth points to an ultimate truth. The queering of Keats echoes a recognition that readers of the poetry, beginning with Hazlitt, have always had: it was written by a man unabashed by his own femininity. When he discussed imaginative power, Keats conceived it as 'chameleon' in its ability to embody whatever it chose to describe, regardless of sex – or, for that matter, sexual orientation. Why, then, should he *not* be claimed by contemporary gay and lesbian culture? It is to be welcomed that Keats House in Hampstead is one of a handful of attractions to which the *Time Out* guide to *Gay and Lesbian London* directs readers,[48] and that Keats is mentioned in Timothy F. Murphy's comprehensive *Reader's Guide to Gay and Lesbian Studies*.[49] If poetry is to continue being read it must renew itself, whether written by a medical school drop-out called John Keats or a cross-dressing Cockney called Lucy Vaughan Lloyd.

Notes

1 I refer to Louis Crompton's excellent history of homosexuality in the opening chapter of *Byron and Greek Love: Homophobia in 19th-Century England* (Berkeley: University of California Press, 1985), esp. pp. 14–15. See also A. D. Harvey, *Sex in Georgian England: Attitudes and Prejudices from the 1720s to the 1820s* (London: Duckworth, 1994), pp. 122–53.

2 John Keats to Charles Brown, 21 June 1820, in *The Letters of John Keats 1814–1821*, ed. Hyder Edward Rollins (2 vols., Cambridge, MA: Harvard University Press, 1958), ii. 299; *John Keats: Complete Poems*, ed. Jack Stillinger (Cambridge, MA: Harvard University Press, 1982), p. 482.

3 In both cases he was referring to Jane Cox; see his letters of 22 September 1818 to John Hamilton Reynolds and 14 October 1818 to the George Keatses, in *The Letters of John Keats 1814–1821*, ed. Rollins, i. 370, 395.

4 Joseph Epstein, 'The Medical Keats', *Hudson Review* 52.1 (Spring 1999), 44–64, p. 55.

5 For a useful summary of the various arguments, see Susan L. Davis, 'John Keats and "The Poison": Venereal or Mercurial?', *Keats-Shelley Journal* 53 (2004), 86–96.

6 James Najarian, *Victorian Keats: Manliness, Sexuality, and Desire* (Houndmills, Basingstoke, 2002); Sarah Wootton, *Consuming Keats: Nineteenth-Century Representations in Art and Literature* (Houndmills, Basingstoke: Palgrave Macmillan, 2006).

7 Wilde's letter to the Revd J. Page Hopps, 14 January 1885, in *The Letters of Oscar Wilde*, ed. Rupert Hart-Davis (London: Hart-Davis, 1962), p. 169.

8 Alex R. Falzon reprints the two versions of Wilde's poem inspired by his visit to Keats's grave in 'Wilde and Keats: *La Donnée*', in *The Challenge of Keats: Bicentenary Essays 1795–1995*, ed. Allan C. Christensen, Lilla Maria Crisafulli Jones, Giuseppe Galigani, and Anthony L. Johnson (Amsterdam: Rodopi, 2000), pp. 249–55.

9 Oscar Wilde, *Miscellanies* (London: Methuen, 1908), pp. 3–4.

10 *The Letters of Oscar Wilde*, ed. Hart-Davis, p. 108.

11 *The Essays of Oscar Wilde* (New York: Cosmopolitan Books, 1916), p. 464.

12 *The Letters of Oscar Wilde*, ed. Hart-Davis, p. 38.

13 Susan J. Wolfson surveys the various sources in *Borderlines: The Shiftings of Gender in British Romanticism* (Stanford, CA: Stanford University Press, 2006), ch. 8.

14 *John Keats: The Critical Heritage*, ed. G. M. Matthews (London: Routledge & Kegan Paul, 1971), p. 74.

15 *Romanticism: An Anthology*, ed. Duncan Wu (4th ed., Oxford: Wiley-Blackwell, 2012), p. 1382.

16 Written on the verso of the front flyleaf of Haydon's copy of Medwin's *Journal of the Conversations of Byron* (London, 1824), now retained at Newstead Abbey. See, *inter alia*, David Blayney Brown, Robert Woof, and Stephen Hebron, *Benjamin Robert Haydon 1786–1824: Painter and Writer, Friend of Wordsworth and Keats* (Grasmere: Wordsworth Trust, 1996), p. 128, and Ronan Kelly, *Bard of Erin: The Life of Thomas Moore* (Dublin: Penguin Ireland, 2005), p. 448.

17 *The Autobiography of Benjamin Robert Haydon*, ed. Tom Taylor (3 vols., London: Longman, 1853), i. 158.

18 Nicholas Roe, *Fiery Heart: The First Life of Leigh Hunt* (London: Pimlico, 2005), pp. 193–5.

19 'On Effeminacy of Character', *Table Talk*, vol. ii, in *The Selected Writings of William Hazlitt*, ed. Duncan Wu (9 vols., London: Pickering & Chatto, 1998), vi. 228.

20 Leigh Hunt, *Lord Byron and Some of His Contemporaries* (2nd ed., 2 vols., London, 1828), i. 418–19.

21 *Keats: The Critical Heritage*, ed. Matthews, p. 34.

22 The review appeared in the *Edinburgh* for August 1820.

23 Lord Byron to John Murray, 4 November 1820, in *Byron's Letters and Journals*, ed. Leslie A. Marchand (13 vols., London: John Murray, 1973–94), vii. 217.

24 Lord Byron to John Murray, 12 October 1820, ibid., p. 200.

25 Ibid., p. 202.

26 Lord Byron to John Murray, 18 November 1820, ibid., p. 229.

27 Lord Byron to John Murray, 9 November 1820, ibid., p. 225.

28 See Iain McCalman, *Radical Underworld: Prophets, Revolutionaries and Pornographers in London, 1795–1840* (Cambridge: Cambridge University Press, 1988), ch. 10; William St Clair, *The Reading Nation in the Romantic Period* (Cambridge: Cambridge University Press, 2004), p. 678; Tom Mole,

'Ways of Seeing Byron', in *Byron: The Image of the Poet*, ed. Christine Kenyon-Jones (Cranbury, NJ: Associated University Presses, 2008), p. 72; and *Lord Byron: The Critical Heritage*, ed. Andrew Rutherford (London: Routledge & Kegan Paul, 1970), pp. 259–60.

29 Peter Cochran tells me that all Byron's letters to Murray from April 1816 onwards were designed for publication.

30 John Keats to Richard Woodhouse, 27 October 1818, in *The Letters of John Keats 1814–1821*, ed. Rollins, i. 387.

31 John Wilson Croker in the *Quarterly Review* for April 1818, published in September 1818; see John O. Hayden, *Romantic Bards and British Reviewers* (London: Routledge & Kegan Paul, 1971), p. 324.

32 On this subject, see, *inter alia*, G. Wilson Knight, *Lord Byron: Christian Virtues* (London: Routledge & Kegan Paul, 1952), p. 247ff.

33 Hayden, *Romantic Bards*, p. 271.

34 *The Routledge Encyclopedia of Walt Whitman*, ed. J. R. LeMaster and Donald D. Kummings (New York: Routledge, 1998), p. 76.

35 Sidney Colvin, *Keats* (London, 1887), p. 100.

36 William Michael Rossetti, *Life of John Keats* (London, 1887), p. 195.

37 Gerard Manley Hopkins to Coventry Patmore, 6 May 1888, in *Further Letters of Gerard Manley Hopkins*, ed. Claude Colleer Abbot (2nd ed., London: Oxford University Press, 1956), p. 387.

38 See Julia F. Saville, *A Queer Chivalry: The Homoerotic Asceticism of Gerard Manley Hopkins* (Charlottesville: University Press of Virginia, 2000).

39 Matthew Arnold, *Essays in Criticism: Second Series* (London: Macmillan, 1888), pp. 103–4.

40 Matthew Arnold, 'John Keats', in *The English Poets: Selections*, ed. Thomas Humphry Ward (London, 1880), p. 429; *Encyclopedia Britannica* (1882).

41 As quoted by Susan J. Wolfson, 'Feminizing Keats', in *Critical Essays on John Keats*, ed. Hermione de Almeida (Boston: G. K. Hall, 1990), pp. 317–56, 331.

42 Ibid., p. 325.

43 Margaret Homans, 'Keats Reading Women, Women Reading Keats', *Studies in Romanticism* 29 (1990), 341–70, p. 343. Other critics have been surveyed by Susan J. Wolfson in 'Feminizing Keats', pp. 346–9. See also, *inter alia*, Marlon Ross, *The Contours of Masculine Desire: Romanticism and the Rise of Women's Poetry* (New York: Oxford University Press, 1989), pp. 167–72; Philip Cox, *Gender, Genre and the Romantic Poets* (Manchester: Manchester University Press, 1996), ch. 4; Nicholas Roe, *John Keats and the Culture of Dissent* (Oxford: Clarendon Press, 1997), pp. 226–9; Richard Marggraf Turley, *Keats's Boyish Imagination* (London: Routledge, 2004); and Wolfson, *Borderlines*, ch. 8.

44 For more such criticisms, see Jeffrey N. Cox, *Poetry and Politics in the Cockney School: Keats, Shelley, Hunt and Their Circle* (Cambridge: Cambridge University Press, 1998), p. 26.

45 John Keats to Benjamin Bailey, 8 October 1817, in *The Letters of John Keats 1814–1821*, ed. Rollins, i. 170.

46 Najarian, *Victorian Keats*, p. 12. Najarian's is an exemplary study of the manner in which Keats helped Victorian writers approach the subject of male relationships.
47 Sheryl Stevenson, 'Learning through AIDS Poetry', *Feminist Teacher* 5 (Spring 1991), 30–3, p. 33.
48 *Time Out Gay and Lesbian London*, ed. Hugh Graham and John Shandy Watson (London: Time Out Guides, 2010), p. 209.
49 *Reader's Guide to Gay and Lesbian Studies*, ed. Timothy F. Murphy (Chicago: Fitzroy Dearborn, 2000), p. 517.

Myth 24

KEATS WAS KILLED BY A REVIEW

This myth is really a fairy tale – that of a poet condemned by an unreceptive public only to receive in death the acclaim denied him in life.

The implication that Keats's reviews were uniformly hostile is enforced by critical fixation with the attacks by John Wilson Croker in the *Quarterly* and by John Gibson Lockhart, author of the 'Cockney School' essays, in *Blackwood's*. But they are not the whole story. Even for his uneven first volume, Keats 'received a majority of favourable reviews'; *Endymion* 'also met with a generally favourable reception';[1] and reviews of Keats's last lifetime volume were 'almost wholly positive',[2] including one by Francis Jeffrey. Throughout his life, in contemporary newspapers, Keats 'was given an extraordinarily good reception'.[3] The trouble was that when the bad boys arrived, they spoke in very loud voices and made everyone else feel stupid. Even so, it is one thing to say Keats was the recipient of two decidedly unsympathetic reviews, another to suggest they finished him off.

'I am very sorry to hear what you say of Keats', Byron told Shelley when he received the news of Keats's death, 'is it *actually* true? I did not think criticism had been so killing.'[4] That was *slightly* disingenuous coming from the man who wanted to shoot the reviewer who declared he would have been whipped at Harrow but that 'they have there … an undue respect for lords' bottoms'[5] – enough to challenge him to a duel.[6] However, that was at the start of his career and by the time he published *Cain* (which he admitted was 'inconceivably ridiculous & dull') he hardly batted an eyelid when told he was a 'cool, unconcerned fiend', 'the professed and systematic poet of seduction, adultery and incest'.[7] Reviews of later cantos of *Don Juan* were sufficiently brutal to make Keats's worst look like cheap imitations – the *Edinburgh Magazine* called Byron's poem 'a piece of unredeemed and unrelieved sensuality and indecency' and pleaded, 'Why is this ridiculous and disgusting farce to go on, unnoticed by the

30 Great Myths About the Romantics, First Edition. Duncan Wu.
© 2015 John Wiley & Sons, Ltd. Published 2015 by John Wiley & Sons, Ltd.

more powerful critical journals of the day?'[8] Knowing how it felt to be the literary world's Aunt Sally, Byron was well placed to enquire whether the experience was really fatal.

The correct answer was 'No, it's an outrageous fantasy' – but that was not what Byron's informant, Percy Bysshe Shelley, was likely to say. It was, after all, a myth in which he was heavily invested: 'Young Keats', he had informed Byron, 'died lately at Rome from the consequences of breaking a blood-vessel, in paroxysms of despair at the contemptuous attack on his book in the *Quarterly Review*.'[9] He later embroidered it enough to establish a connection with the disease that actually did the job: 'in the first paroxysms of his disappointment [Keats] burst a blood-vessel; and thus laid the foundation of a rapid consumption'.[10] Like Byron, he had been the target of notices that made Croker's savaging of *Endymion* look like gentlemanly back-scratching. The *Quarterly* declared him 'in the downward course of infidelity and immorality' while the *Literary Gazette*

Figure 19 John Wilson Croker (1780–1857), lawyer, politician, secretary to the Admiralty, and putative murderer of Keats. His review of *Endymion* condemned Keats's poetry as 'unintelligible'.
Source: Paul F. Betz Collection.

declared of *Prometheus Unbound*, 'were we not assured to the contrary, we should take it for granted that the author was lunatic – as his principles are ludicrously wicked, and his poetry a melange of nonsense, cockney-ism, poverty, and pedantry'.[11] Shelley knew reviews could kill: they kill creativity. And by turning metaphor into myth, he furnished himself with the means to return fire on the philistines who denounced his poems as 'drivelling prose run mad'.[12]

'I weep for Adonais – he is dead!' runs the first line of Shelley's great elegy – fifty-five stanzas lamenting Keats, prefaced by an essay that explained their context:

> The savage criticism on his *Endymion*, which appeared in the *Quarterly Review*, produced the most violent effect on his susceptible mind; the agitation thus originated ended in the rupture of a blood-vessel in the lungs; a rapid consumption ensued, and the succeeding acknowledgments from more candid critics of the true greatness of his powers, were ineffectual to heal the wound thus wantonly inflicted.[13]

This might mean something if it could be proved Keats cared about his reviews, but there is little evidence he did. In December 1818 he declared that 'Reviews have had their day – that the public have been surfeited – there will soon be some new folly to keep the Parlours in talk'; less than two months later he sneered, 'the Reviews have enervated and made indolent mens minds – few think for themselves'; and in October 1819 he comforted Haydon with the thought 'the Reviewers will no more be able to stumble-block me than the Academy could you .... What the Reviewers can put a hindrance to must be – a nothing – or mediocre which is worse.'[14] Perhaps Keats was more disturbed by attacks on *Endymion* than he let on,[15] but why, in that case, was he capable, in the face of Croker's attack, of declaring, 'I shall be among the English Poets after my death', and saying in his final year to Fanny Brawne: 'I will not die without being remember'd'?[16]

Today those remarks are accessible to anyone with access to Hyder Rollins's edition of Keats's correspondence, something unavailable to Shelley. But had a copy been at his bedside, I doubt it would have made any difference, for he was expounding a truth distinct from any related to Keats's physiology, as James A. W. Heffernan has written: 'Shelley's celebration of Keats required a poet weak enough to have been killed by the words of a reviewer so that he might be resurrected by the words of Shelley, whose elegy would be a sublime *reviewing*, a visionary transformation of the pastoral dreamer into a Miltonic genius, and hence a demonstration of Shelley's own power.'[17] That was the myth: it enacts

Shelley's martyrdom at the hands of unfeeling critics, of whose culpability he is certain:

> the curse of Cain
> Light on his head who pierced thy innocent breast,
> And scared the angel soul that was its earthly guest!
>
> (*Adonais*, ll. 151–3)

The story that Keats was 'killed' by the *Quarterly* preceded Shelley, though he was the most determined of its promoters: in July 1820, a year before publication of *Adonais*, Mary Russell Mitford lamented this 'young, delicate, imaginative boy – that withering article fell upon him like an east wind. I am afraid he has no chance of recovery'.[18] As that suggests, the misconception that Keats was dispatched by a reviewer was accompanied by the equally misguided notion that he was a fragile blossom, easily bruised. 'Poor Keats...' began J. W. Dalby in the *Pocket Magazine* of 4 April 1821, who attributed Keats's death to 'the attacks of grovelling and merciless critics', and the fact he 'was not bold or brave enough to encounter the struggles of life'.[19] Charles Cowden Clarke informed readers of the *Morning Chronicle* on 27 July 1821 that Keats had 'lain awake through the whole night talking with sensative-bitterness of the unfair treatment he had experienced'.[20] 'What was sport to the town was death to him', wrote William Hazlitt, who said the reviews 'stuck like a barbed arrow in his heart... and unable to endure the miscreant cry and idiot laugh, [Keats] withdrew to sigh his last breath in foreign climes'.[21] Even Fanny Brawne (it was claimed) had seen him 'with that review in his hand, reading as if he would devour it – completely absorbed – absent, and drinking it in like mortal poison'.[22]

Several of these witnesses had known Keats, and there is no reason to assume they agreed with Shelley's version of his decline; indeed, Clarke questioned it.[23] But Keats's humiliation at the punishment meted out by the *Quarterly* and *Blackwood's* was easily conceived – and perhaps that lent the myth currency. By the time Cyrus Redding wrote the introduction to the Galignani edition of the poetry in 1829, few doubted its critics were assassins in all but name. 'The unmerited abuse poured upon Keats', wrote Redding, 'is supposed to have hastened his end':[24] the myth was 'an accepted reading of history'.[25]

It was hammered into Keats's gravestone. He had asked for the simplest of inscriptions, 'Here lies one whose name was writ in water',[26] without name or date, and trusted Joseph Severn, who accompanied him to Rome, to honour the request. And Severn might have done so were it not for Charles Brown, who composed a more elaborate inscription referring to Keats's supposed 'bitterness' at the 'malicious power of his enemies'.[27] Brown justified this by saying 'an epitaph must necessarily be considered as the act of the deceased's friends and not of the deceased himself'.[28] Severn hesitated, then agreed. He added an incorrect date of death (24 rather than 23 February) to a lightly revised version of what Brown had written and erected the stone during the course of May 1823.[29]

> This grave contains all that was mortal of a young English poet who, on his death-bed, in the bitterness of his heart at the malicious power of his enemies, desired these words to be engraven on his tombstone – HERE LIES ONE WHOSE NAME WAS WRIT IN WATER.[30]

Because Keats's poetry was not reprinted in England, American readers were compelled to obtain copies of the Galignani edition (which declared itself 'infinitely more perfect than any of those published in London'[31]) – explaining why, as early as 1833, one American writer claimed Keats had been 'killed by criticism',[32] while in 1845 another said he was killed by a review 'because he was weak'.[33] The Galignani edition helpfully reproduced the gravestone's inscription and gave directions to the cemetery, where admirers appeared, weeping openly as they bore witness to what in their minds was nothing less than murder. As one wrote, 'I have read of broken hearts, but nothing ever indicated to me half so lonely and desolate a heart, as the dying language of Keats.'[34]

Severn knew better than anyone how this distorted the truth, and quickly came to regret his part in it. By July 1836 he described 'the present grave stone with its inscription [as] an eye sore to me and more', hoping to replace it with something 'in the Greek style'.[35] In 1859 (more than three and a half decades after Keats's death) it was still causing him anxiety, and in a letter to Charles Dilke he complained he wanted 'to do away with poor Keats's gravestone, so disrespe[c]tfull & unjust to his memory as it is & distressing to my feelings – No doubt you are aware that it was written by Charles Brown & is one of his saddest mistakes'. It was, he continued, an 'unseemly stone', 'a downright anomaly' which he wanted to replace with 'a true inscription beyond ridicule'.[36] Too late: Brown's sentiments, engraved in stone and circulated by Galignani, had acquired the authority of fact.

Brown's certainty about the cause of Keats's untimely demise was restated in his manuscript biography, which he never published; its penultimate paragraph declares Keats was 'destroyed by hirelings, under the imposing name of Reviewers.... Month after month, an accumulation of ridicule and scoffs against his character and person, did worse than tear food from the mouth of a starving wretch, for it tore honour from the poet's brow.'[37] When he sent it to R. M. Milnes, Brown insisted on 'the propriety, the truth of what I have written against the Quarterly and the Edinburg, and against Blackwood's Magazine'.[38] Brown had reason to place his faith in a story that deflected attention from himself. He failed to respond when Keats asked him to go to Rome with him, and his flirtation with Fanny Brawne elicited from Keats the harshest words he ever wrote to her:

> When you were in the habit of flirting with Brown you would have left off, could your own heart have felt one half of one pang mine did. Brown is a good sort of Man – he did not know he was doing me to death by inches. I feel the effect of every one of those hours in my side now; and for that cause, though he has done me many services, though I know his love and friendship for me, though at this moment I should be without pence were it not for his assistance, I will never see or speak to him until we are both old men, if we are to be. I *will* resent my heart having been made a football.[39]

This suggests Keats had spoken frankly of his resentment to Brown and discontinued the friendship, at least for a while. It gave Brown cause to invest himself in a fiction that would suppress the more credible story of a poet betrayed by his friend.[40]

Byron forced himself to mouth the expected pieties to Shelley but, when addressing John Murray (who, as owner of the *Quarterly*, placed the stiletto in Croker's grasp) was at liberty to speak as he wished. Could reviews *really* be fatal? After all, he was taking his share of punishment. Having caught up with 'the homicide review of *J. Keats*' in August 1821 Byron thought it 'harsh certainly and contemptuous but not more so than what I recollect of the Edinburgh R[eview] of "the Hours of Idleness" in 1808 …. though very provoking it was hardly so bitter as to kill – unless there was a morbid feeling previously in his system'.[41] Shelley's explanation may have been true to what he thought had taken place and consistent with medical opinion at the time.[42] And perhaps Keats's reading of the reviews brought about palpitations or other cardiovascular symptoms that reduced his ability to combat the dread bacillus. But Byron's point remains valid. Keats's death was not the result of his critical reception (which was good overall) but of a disease for which no cure then existed, and which contemporary therapies such as leeching and dieting can only have aggravated. Never one to waste such insights, Byron channelled his thoughts on Shelley's poetic martyrology into one of the most memorable stanzas of *Don Juan*, combining them with doubts as to Keats's education.

One of the most famous things ever written on the subject, it manages to query the myth while perpetuating it.

> John Keats, who was killed off by one critique,
>   Just as he really promised something great,
> If not intelligible, – without Greek
>   Contrived to talk about the Gods of late,
> Much as they might have been supposed to speak.
>   Poor fellow! His was an untoward fate: –
> 'Tis strange the mind, that very fiery particle,
> Should let itself be snuffed out by an Article.[43]

Notes

1 John O. Haydon, *The Romantic Reviewers 1802–1824* (London: Routledge & Kegan Paul, 1969), pp. 188, 190.

2 Nicholas Roe, *John Keats: A New Life* (New Haven: Yale University Press, 2012), p. 374.

3 Lewis M. Schwartz, 'Keats's Critical Reception in Newspapers of His Day', *Keats-Shelley Journal* 21/22 (1972/73), 170–87, p. 186.

4 Byron to Percy Bysshe Shelley, 26 April 1821, in *Byron's Letters and Journals*, ed. Leslie A. Marchand (13 vols., London: John Murray, 1973–94), viii. 103.

5 Unsigned review of Byron, *Hours of Idleness* (1807), in *The Monthly Mirror* 3 (1808), 28–30, p. 30.

6 The reviewer appears to have been Mr Twiddie; see Byron's letter to Edward Noel Long, 28 January 1808, in *Byron's Letters and Journals*, ed. Marchand, i. 150.

7 Fiona MacCarthy, *Byron: Life and Legend* (London: John Murray, 2002), pp. 414–15.

8 *Lord Byron: The Critical Heritage*, ed. Andrew Rutherford (London: Routledge & Kegan Paul, 1970), p. 260.

9 Percy Bysshe Shelley to Lord Byron, 17 April 1821, in *The Letters of Percy Bysshe Shelley*, ed. Frederick L. Jones (2 vols., Oxford: Clarendon Press, 1964), ii. 284.

10 Percy Bysshe Shelley to Lord Byron, 4 May 1821, ibid., p. 289.

11 *Shelley: The Critical Heritage*, ed. James E. Barcus (London: Routledge & Kegan Paul, 1975), pp. 134, 226.

12 Ibid., p. 266.

13 Quoted from the text in *Romanticism: An Anthology*, ed. Duncan Wu (4th ed., Oxford: Wiley-Blackwell, 2012), p. 1249.

14 John Keats to George and Georgiana Keats, December 1818 and 19 February 1819; John Keats to Benjamin Robert Haydon, 3 October 1819, in *The Letters*

of John Keats, ed. Hyder Edward Rollins (2 vols., Cambridge, MA: Harvard University Press, 1958), ii. 15–16, 65, 220.

15 John Barnard, 'Keats's Sleepless Night: Charles Cowden Clarke's Letter of 1821', *Romanticism* 16.3 (2010), 267–78, pp. 271–2.

16 John Keats to George and Georgiana Keats, 14 October 1818; John Keats to Fanny Brawne, March 1820, in *The Letters of John Keats*, ed. Rollins, i. 394, ii. 277.

17 '*Adonais*: Shelley's Consumption of Keats', in *Romanticism: A Critical Reader*, ed. Duncan Wu (Oxford: Blackwell, 1995), p. 179.

18 Mary Russell Mitford to Sir William Elford, 5 July 1820, in *The Life of Mary Russell Mitford*, ed. A. G. L'Estrange (3 vols., London: Richard Bentley, 1870), ii. 105.

19 Lewis M. Schwartz, *Keats Reviewed by His Contemporaries: A Collection of Notices for the Years 1816–1821* (Metuchen, NJ: Scarecrow Press, 1973), p. 318.

20 My quotation from the text presented by Barnard, 'Keats's Sleepless Night', p. 269.

21 *The Selected Writings of William Hazlitt*, ed. Duncan Wu (9 vols., London: Pickering & Chatto, 1998), vi. 86.

22 *John Keats: The Critical Heritage*, ed. G. M. Matthews (London: Routledge & Kegan Paul, 1971), p. 17.

23 Barnard, 'Keats's Sleepless Night', pp. 270–1.

24 *Keats: The Critical Heritage*, ed. Matthews, p. 262.

25 Susan J. Wolfson, 'Keats Enters History: Autopsy, *Adonais*, and the Fame of Keats', in *Keats and History*, ed. Nicholas Roe (Cambridge: Cambridge University Press, 1995), pp. 17–45, 27.

26 The request can be dated to 14 February 1821; see Severn's letter to Brown of February 1821 in *The Keats Circle: Letters and Papers 1816–1878*, ed. Hyder Edward Rollins (2 vols., Cambridge, MA: Harvard University Press, 1948), ii. 91.

27 For the full story behind the stone, and Severn's misgivings about the inscription, see Sue Brown, *Joseph Severn, A Life: The Rewards of Friendship* (Oxford: Oxford University Press, 2009), pp. 150–1.

28 Charles Brown to Joseph Severn, 28 August 1822, in *The Letters of Charles Armitage Brown*, ed. Jack Stillinger (Cambridge, MA: Harvard University Press, 1966), p. 91.

29 In this I follow Sue Brown, *Joseph Severn, A Life*, pp. 149–50.

30 Quoted from the Galignani text: *The Poetical Works of Coleridge, Shelley, and Keats* (Paris: A. and W. Galignani, 1829), p. vi.

31 Hyder Edward Rollins, *Keats' Reputation in America to 1848* (Cambridge, MA: Harvard University Press, 1946), p. 27.

32 Ibid., p. 49.

33 Ibid., p. 74.

34 Ibid., pp. 51–2.

35 Joseph Severn to Charles Brown, 13 July 1836, in *Joseph Severn: Letters and Memoirs*, ed. Grant F. Scott (Aldershot, Hants.: Ashgate, 2005), p. 338.

36 Joseph Severn to Charles Dilke, 3 February 1859, ibid., pp. 468–9.

37 *The Keats Circle*, ed. Rollins, ii. 95–6.

38 Charles Brown to R. M. Milnes, 19 March 1841, in *The Letters of Charles Armitage Brown*, ed. Stillinger, p. 409.

39 John Keats to Fanny Brawne, 5 July 1820, in *The Letters of John Keats*, ed. Rollins, ii. 303.

40 Henry Crabb Robinson, who knew Charles Brown in later years, testified that Brown 'was mysterious towards me And seemed afraid of my betraying his secret – He was not an agreeable man' (MS Reminiscences, vol. 4 (1834–43), f. 278, Dr Williams's Library, London).

41 Lord Byron to John Murray, 7 August 1821, in *Byron's Letters and Journals*, ed. Marchand, viii. 173.

42 Anthony D. Knerr points out it was consistent with what Shelley had heard from the Gisbornes, Hunts, and others who had seen Keats in England; see *Shelley's Adonais: A Critical Edition* (New York: Columbia University Press, 1984), p. 6.

43 *Don Juan*, xi, stanza 60, in Byron, *The Complete Poetical Works*, ed. Jerome J. McGann (7 vols., Oxford: Clarendon Press, 1980–93), v. 483.

Myth
25
PERCY BYSSHE SHELLEY WROTE *FRANKENSTEIN*

When it appeared anonymously on 1 January 1818, some readers mistakenly assumed *Frankenstein* was not by Mary Shelley but by her husband, Percy Bysshe Shelley. Charlotte Grove, Percy's cousin, recorded in her diary for 4 May 1818, 'Bysshe's novel of Prometheus came',[1] and some early reviewers believed him to be its author, including Sir Walter Scott, who wrote: 'it is said to be written by Mr Percy Bysshe Shelley, who, if we are rightly informed, is son-in-law to Mr Godwin'.[2]

One might expect the appearance of the novel under Mary Shelley's name in 1831 to have settled the matter – but that would be to underestimate the ingenuity of the critic. In 1974, James Rieger examined the manuscript of the novel and argued that the effect of Percy Bysshe Shelley's contributions was more far-reaching than had been recognized, such that 'one hardly knows whether to regard him as editor or minor collaborator':

> Not only did he correct her frequent grammatical solecisms, her spelling, and her awkward phrasing; the surviving manuscript fragments show marginal suggestions (all adopted by Mary) for the improvement of the narrative, interpolations that run for several sentences, and final revisions of the last pages …. Finally, in 1817, he corrected the proofs, with his wife's 'carte blanche to make what alterations you please'.[3]

Rieger overstated his case, but he was on to something. He found in the manuscript layers of revision that were not Mary Shelley's work alone, that would preoccupy critics for years. The manuscript is long and difficult, and its pitfalls are illustrated by the work of E. B. Murray, who underestimated by a considerable margin the number of words contributed by Percy Shelley, putting the total at a 'thousand or so'.[4] This was in

30 Great Myths About the Romantics, First Edition. Duncan Wu.
© 2015 John Wiley & Sons, Ltd. Published 2015 by John Wiley & Sons, Ltd.

part because, as Charles E. Robinson has noted, he failed to distinguish between the two authors' handwriting – an understandable error.[5]

Anne K. Mellor's reservation about Rieger was that he was 'so biased in Percy Shelley's favor' that his work amounted to 'a tissue of facts, half-truths, and pure speculation'.[6] Her *Mary Shelley: Her Life, Her Fiction, Her Monsters* (1988) was designed to redress the balance. In her view, Percy's revisions fell into two categories, 'those that improve the novel and those that do not',[7] and by far the majority fell into the latter. In her view, Percy was responsible for 'much of the most inflated rhetoric in the text';[8] he 'distorted the meaning of the text'[9] and 'imposed his own favorite philosophical, political, and poetic theories on a text which either contradicted them or to which they were irrelevant'.[10] In short, by means of condescension and egotism, he suppressed his wife's distinctive vision. Worse still, Mary Shelley 'shared Percy's opinion of her inferior literary abilities' and 'substituted Percy's style for her own'.[11] It proved their marriage was one 'in which the husband played the dominant role'.[12]

This provided the footings for what was to come. In 1992 Johanna M. Smith, editor of a *Frankenstein* textbook, marshalled Mellor's arguments in an essay based on her own 'examination of the rough-draft and fair-copy manuscripts'.[13] She condemned Percy Shelley's 'heavy editorial hand [which] marks the novel throughout', and went on to point out that 'a man's influence on a woman writer remains complicated':

> Mary Shelley felt unable 'to put [her]self forward unless led, cherished & supported,' and she perceived this need for support as feminine, 'the woman's love of looking up and being guided' (*Journal* 555). It might be, then, that this ideology of dependent femininity rendered her unable to write her own text without her husband's help. Moreover, collaboration forced by a more dominant writer on a less powerful and perhaps unwilling 'partner' is a kind of rape; if *Frankenstein* is the product of such a union, then it evinces a debilitating femininity.[14]

Marie-Hélène Huet's *Monstrous Imagination* (1993) purported to base its arguments on manuscript evidence though without first-hand examination of the notebooks. Yet Huet wrote with confidence: 'We know that Percy Shelley was responsible for the contrast between Victor's character and that of Elizabeth. He also suggested that Victor should travel to England to create a female companion for the monster.'[15] Both arguments were flawed: Mary Shelley established the contrast and conceived the idea that Victor would create a female. By way of proving her larger theory that *Frankenstein* was turned by Percy Shelley into a 'repudiation of the idea of human procreation', Huet said he wrote 'the monster's final words', which 'offer the strongest image of the Romantic poet as sterile monster'.[16]

Up to this point, the problem for those venturing to comment on the *Frankenstein* manuscripts was the difficulty of getting to grips with their contents. However serious their intent, they did not yet have access to a properly edited transcription which revealed precisely who wrote what. The notebooks contain two different hands not always easy to decipher or, indeed, distinguish. It would take an expert conversant with the manuscripts of both to produce an authoritative account of the *Frankenstein* drafts. The academic world waited until 1996 for the first full survey, edited by Charles E. Robinson of Delaware University. This edition, which stands as one of the most accomplished of modern scholarship, comprised photofacsimiles of each page alongside Robinson's transcriptions, the authorship of each word clearly indicated. Only now was it possible to see that Shelley contributed between 4,000 and 5,000 words to the novel and only now could those contributions be accurately assessed. (Today, anyone can check his findings by logging on to the Shelley-Godwin Archive website, where the manuscript can be viewed alongside his transcriptions.) Robinson's view of the Shelleys' collaborative relationship supersedes those of his predecessors and continues to stand as the definitive account:

> If, as this edition will make evident, MWS is the creative genius by which this novel was conceived and developed, we can call PBS an able midwife who helped his wife bring her monster to life …. A reading of the evidence in these *Frankenstein* Notebooks should make clear that PBS's contributions to *Frankenstein* were no more than what most publishers' editors have provided new (or old) authors or, in fact, what colleagues have provided to each other after reading each other's works in progress. What MWS actually thought of PBS's involvement in her text we will never know, no matter what methodology or facts we bring to the issue. I personally prefer to give both of them the benefit of the doubt and conjecture that (1) PBS suggested and made alterations to the text of *Frankenstein* for the purpose of improving an already excellent narrative (in [?February 1818] he wrote a review that judged the published novel 'one of the most original and complete productions of the day') and that (2) MWS accepted the suggestions and alterations that she agreed with.[17]

Robinson supplemented his transcriptions, which distinguished Percy's contributions to the text, with the first detailed chronology of composition, publication, and afterlife of the novel.[18]

Another twelve years would pass until the appearance of *The Original Frankenstein*, in which Robinson presented a text of the novel drawn exclusively from manuscript. For the first time it became possible to read the novel exactly as Mary Shelley had written it, distinct from her husband's interventions. In his introduction, Robinson again described the relationship between author and husband as collaborative:

we may conclude that [Percy] contributed at least 4,000 to 5,000 words to this 72,000 word novel. Despite the number of Percy's words, the novel was conceived and mainly written by Mary Shelley, as attested not only by others in their circle (e.g. Byron, Godwin, Claire and Charles Clairmont, Leigh Hunt) but by the nature of the manuscript evidence in the surviving pages of the Draft.[19]

On dust-jacket and title page, Robinson's *Frankenstein* was credited to 'Mary Shelley (with Percy Shelley)'.

As the years have passed, the idea that husband and wife worked alongside each other in ways that did not entail bullying, harassment, or physical violence has begun to find acceptance, and in the second edition of her 'Authoritative Text', published in 2000, Johanna M. Smith deleted any such implication from the revised version of her essay.[20] To some extent, critics were misled by Mary Shelley's own account of the collaboration, which 'exaggerated her meekness and dependency', as Zachary Leader points out. Those who knew Shelley testify to 'quite different qualities: directness, precision, irony, command, qualities frequently found in the early journal entries'.[21] Indeed, in Mary's own self-assessments, Leader finds evidence of her 'belief in herself as an author'. It is more likely that, when writing *Frankenstein*, she 'consciously, willingly welcomed Percy Shelley's contributions', an act that 'calls into question the supposedly inevitable conflict'.[22] Nora Crook adds that Percy's attitude towards his wife's writing was positive. He encouraged her to translate Alfieri's *Mirra*, 'supplied lyrics for her mythological dramas *Proserpine* and *Midas* (1820)', and welcomed her contributions to his translation of Spinoza's *Tractatus Theologico-Politicus*.[23]

It might be expected, after spillage of so much critical ink, that the debate might have died a natural death. Not at all. In 2007, 'independent scholar' John Lauritsen published a weird cocktail of emails, essays, items of correspondence, and web postings under the title *The Man who Wrote Frankenstein*. Incensed by feminists, irritated by Robinson, annoyed with academics of all kinds for never admitting they were wrong ('Do academics *ever* admit it?', he wrote in desperation[24]), Lauritsen reverted to the idea put about by Sir Walter Scott: *Frankenstein* was written entirely by Percy Shelley. He argues, with lapel-grabbing insistence, that the novel's true theme (which the world had been too stupid to perceive) was 'male love', and that it was intended 'for a select audience, gay men'.[25] Scott Douglas de Hart, author of *Shelley Unbound*, hails Lauritsen's book as 'a groundbreaking new approach', and argues Shelley was *Frankenstein*'s only begetter. For him, '*Frankenstein* is an autobiographical novel inspired by the thoughts and experiences of its author, Percy Bysshe Shelley .... a subtle, albeit powerful, manifesto for atheism'. The nuttiness of the thesis aside, that sounds almost rational until de Hart starts claiming the novel to be 'a story combining the mystery of alchemy with the advances in science, joined to an Illuminati agenda'.[26] Wishful and credulous at once, de Hart devotes a chunk of his book to the theory that the attribution to Mary Shelley is the work of an elaborate conspiracy,[27] at which point he drifts into X-Files territory.

To Lauritsen and de Hart, Robinson's scholarly labours are irrelevant, for they say Mary Shelley was acting as her husband's copyist when she wrote the *Frankenstein* manuscript. Lauritsen may be a failed scholar and de Hart no scholar at all, but a qualification in bibliography isn't necessary to prompt the question: if the novel was written by Percy Shelley, why do none of his notebooks contain a single paragraph in rough draft in his hand from *Frankenstein*?[28] And why does he nowhere in any of his voluminous correspondence refer to it as his? The obvious answer is the one Lauritsen and de Hart turn cartwheels to avoid: he was not its author.

Were they to examine Robinson's work rather than dismiss it, Lauritsen and de Hart might see that the interrelation between the hands of Mary Shelley and her husband in the manuscript is more complex than if she were acting merely as copyist. As Robinson says, Percy 'at times improved the diction and syntax of individual sentences; he replaced some of her more colloquial phrasings with more formal or more Latinate constructions; he occasionally introduced his more skeptical judgments about God and the afterlife; and he added a half dozen passages that developed some of the domestic and scientific and political issues in the novel'.[29] He also made a number of editorial adjustments he would never have made had he been the author, including corrections to orthography, punctuation, capitalization, errors of fact, and grammatical solecisms – interventions that declare the collaborative interaction of two people.

If the critical history of *Frankenstein* teaches us anything, it is that the most important piece of evidence in any discussion about its authorship is the manuscript. Lauritsen and de Hart pursue their respective cases only by misinterpreting it or, where it fails to serve their purposes, ignoring it. Which makes their inability to find anything in Shelley or Mary Shelley's correspondence and journals to support their claims an irrelevance. They are embarrassingly silent about the wealth of evidence by which they are contradicted, for instance Mary's journal entry for 21 August 1816 which records 'Shelley & I talk about my story' – not 'his' story but '*my* story'.[30]

One does not have to read very far into either Lauritsen or de Hart before hearing, amidst their flighty logic and bludgeoning certitudes, the voice of obsession. It would take a woman writer, Germaine Greer, to offer the common-sense response that might have given them pause: '*Frankenstein* really was written by Mary Shelley. It's obvious – because the book is so bad.'[31]

Greer's comment is provocative, and deliberately so. Most of us regard the novel as a masterwork. Why else would its sullen tale of creative intensity reverberate so insistently into the present day? (See, in that regard, the 'Coda' to this book, especially pages 271–2.) Which helps explain why these debates have taken place. Those who have expounded the various arguments want to claim as theirs one of the greatest novels in literature. The diversity of those interests makes the myth exemplary of a larger truth about critics, for it demonstrates their readiness to impose upon the evidence interpretive grids designed to illustrate pre-existing agendas, eccentric though they may be (something indicated by other myths in this volume, including numbers 8, 11, 14, and 18). Only that explains why we are bidden to think of Percy Shelley as both wife-beater and gay advocate, roles of which he was innocent. As for the scholarship, it points in only one direction: *Frankenstein* 'was conceived and mainly written by Mary Shelley'.

Notes

1 *The Grove Diaries: The Rise and Fall of an English Family 1809–1925*, ed. Desmond Hawkins (Wimborne, Dorset: Dovecote Press, 1995), p. 137.

2 [Sir Walter Scott], 'Remarks on Frankenstein', *Blackwood's Edinburgh Magazine* 2 (March 1818), 613–20, p. 614.

3 Mary Shelley, *Frankenstein or The Modern Prometheus: The 1818 Text*, ed. James Rieger (Chicago: University of Chicago Press, 1974), p. xviii.

4 E. B. Murray, 'Shelley's Contribution to Mary's *Frankenstein*', *Keats-Shelley Memorial Bulletin* 29 (1978), 50–68, p. 51.

5 Mary Wollstonecraft Shelley, *The Frankenstein Notebooks: A Facsimile Edition of Mary Shelley's Manuscript Novel, 1816–17*, ed. Charles E. Robinson (2 vols., New York: Garland: 1996), i. lxviii.

6 Anne K. Mellor, *Mary Shelley: Her Life, Her Fiction, Her Monsters* (New York: Methuen, 1988), p. 58.

7 Ibid., p. 59.

8 Ibid., p. 61.

9 Ibid., p. 62.

10 Ibid., p. 64.

11 Ibid., p. 69.

12 Ibid.

13 *Mary Shelley, Frankenstein: Complete, Authoritative Text with Biographical and Historical Contexts, Critical History, and Essays from Five Contemporary Critical Perspectives*, ed. Johanna M. Smith (Boston: Bedford Books of St Martin's Press, 1992), p. 273.

14 Ibid., p. 274.

15 Marie-Hélène Huet, *Monstrous Imagination* (Cambridge, MA: Harvard University Press, 1993), p. 154.

16 Ibid., p. 155.

17 *The Frankenstein Notebooks*, ed. Robinson, i. lxvii.

18 Ibid., i. lxxvi–cx.

19 *The Original Frankenstein*, ed. Charles E. Robinson (Oxford: Bodleian Library, 2008), p. 25.

20 See Johanna M. Smith, 'Cooped Up with Sad Trash: Domesticity and the Sciences in Frankenstein', in *Mary Shelley, Frankenstein: Complete, Authoritative Text with Biographical, Historical, and Cultural Contexts, Critical History, and Essays from Contemporary Critical Perspectives*, ed. Johanna M. Smith (2nd ed., Boston: Bedford/St Martin's Press, 2000), pp. 313–33.

21 Zachary Leader, *Revision and Romantic Authorship* (Oxford: Clarendon Press, 1996), p. 169.

22 Ibid., p. 171.

23 Nora Crook, 'Shelley and Women', in *The Oxford Handbook to Percy Bysshe Shelley*, ed. Michael O'Neill and Anthony Howe with the assistance of Madeleine Callaghan (Oxford: Oxford University Press, 2013), p. 80.

24 John Lauritsen, *The Man who Wrote Frankenstein* (Dorchester, MA: Pagan Press, 2007), p. 55.

25 Ibid., p. 80.

26 Scott Douglas de Hart, *Shelley Unbound: Discovering Frankenstein's True Creator* (Port Townsend, WA: Feral House, 2013), pp. 23, 61, 79, 123.

27 Ibid., pp. 47–54.

28 Robinson confirms there is no draft for *Frankenstein* in Shelley's hand other than the last eleven pages of the fair copy that he copied from Mary's working manuscript. In doing so, Shelley considerably embellished it, again in a way that indicates he was emending a draft that had not originated with him.

29 Charles E. Robinson, 'Collaboration and Ventriloquism in Mary Shelley's *Frankenstein*', *La Questione Romantica* (Mary Shelley special issue in memory of Betty T. Bennett) 1.1 (2009), 29–39; see also 'Percy Shelley's Text(s) in Mary Shelley's *Frankenstein*', in *The Unfamiliar Shelley*, ed. Alan M. Weinberg and Timothy Webb (Aldershot, Hants.: Ashgate, forthcoming).

30 *The Journals of Mary Shelley*, ed. Diana Scott-Kilvert and Paula Feldman (2 vols., Oxford: Clarendon Press, 1987), i. 130.

31 *The Observer*, Sunday, 8 April 2007.

Figure 20 Hannah More (1745–1833), one of the most successful authors of the Romantic period.
Source: Paul F. Betz Collection.

Myth

26

WOMEN WRITERS WERE AN EXPLOITED UNDERCLASS – UNKNOWN, UNLOVED, AND UNPAID

One of the most financially successful writers of the period was female. Hannah More made £30,000 during the course of her career,[1] a larger sum than the £20,000 Byron made over the nine years he published with Murray.[2] Two million copies of her *Cheap Repository* tracts had been distributed by March 1796.[3] Her conduct book in the form of a novel, *Coelebs in Search of a Wife* (1808), sold 14,500 copies up to 1826, more than Jane Austen's six novels combined during the same period.[4] Averaged across the sixty or so years of her career, More would have had a weekly income of between £9 and £10; by comparison, the cook who worked for Austen's family was content to receive £8 a year.[5]

Success on that scale was not entirely genteel; when More was a young woman, literature was regarded as an accomplishment rather than as the means of earning a living. She was lucky to be introduced to the Bluestockings by David Garrick, and through them came to know Edmund Burke, Dr Johnson, Sir Joshua Reynolds, and Elizabeth Montagu, queen of the Blues. Other members included Anna Laetitia Barbauld, the Duchess of Beaufort, the Duchess of Portland, Horace Walpole, and Lord Lyttelton. Under their protection, she composed two of her most famous early poems, 'Sensibility' and 'The Bas-Bleu'.[6] Another Blue, Elizabeth Carter, made £1,000 by subscription publication

30 Great Myths About the Romantics, First Edition. Duncan Wu.
© 2015 John Wiley & Sons, Ltd. Published 2015 by John Wiley & Sons, Ltd.

of her translation of Epictetus. The Blues fostered an interest in women's writing by promoting it: 'several ladies of the bluestocking club, while [Mary] Robinson remained unknown, even ventured to admire – nay, more, to recite her productions in their learned and critical coterie'.[7] Though not established on feminist principles, the Blues made literature a more acceptable activity for women than it had been previously. Marguerite, Countess of Blessington, continued the tradition of the literary salon in the 1830s and 1840s, to which she invited Letitia Landon, Jane Porter, Caroline Norton, Edward Bulwer-Lytton, John Forster, Benjamin Disraeli, and Charles Dickens.[8]

This was a good time to be a woman writer, but there is no denying the existence of anti-feminist diatribes. 'We heartily abjure Blue Stockings', wrote one critic,[9] while the Reverend Richard Polwhele condemned *The Unsex'd Females* (1798) who 'were tinged with Rousseauistic revolutionaryism and therefore veered mindlessly in the direction of lust'.[10] Polwhele was a Tory whose motivation was to discredit political

Figure 21 Anna Laetitia Barbauld (1743–1825), former Bluestocking, whose literary career came to a sudden halt when her *Eighteen Hundred and Eleven* (1812) received a hostile review from John Wilson Croker.
Source: Paul F. Betz Collection.

opponents; consequently he approved of conservative Bluestockings (Montagu and Carter) but criticized revolutionary sympathizers like Mary Wollstonecraft, Helen Maria Williams, Charlotte Smith, and Anna Laetitia Barbauld.[11] In fact, political differences explain most attacks on women over the course of the period. When Barbauld deplored the state of the nation in her political poem, *Eighteen Hundred and Eleven* (1812), she was caricatured by a Tory, John Wilson Croker, as having cast 'down her shagreen spectacles and her knitting needles' in order to 'sally forth ... in the magnanimous resolution of saving a sinking state'.[12] Other reviewers condemned her for being unpatriotic and having 'a peculiarly frigid temperament'.[13] The onslaught silenced her: she published no more poetry during her lifetime.[14] In the mid-1820s Letitia Landon received more than her share of bad reviews and, being a single woman, had also to face allegations about her private life. (The debate continues: Germaine Greer points out that 'there is no proof L.E.L. ever had a lover by day or night, let alone several',[15] while others say she was the mistress of her editor, William Jerdan.[16]) Nonetheless, Landon was not afraid to bite back, and published one article condemning 'personal attacks; virulent sneers; the coarse and false statements; the foolish opinions of a set whose incognito is indeed their existence' and another specifically targeting 'the two pseudo-called great Reviews, the Edinburgh and the Quarterly'. As Glennis Stephenson observes, Landon 'cannot be seen only as a victim'.[17]

It is hard to imagine Hannah More behaving in that way in the 1780s. Things changed in part because women wrote for an increasingly female readership. When More was in her twenties, private circulating libraries and book clubs were already catering for a female clientele, the principal borrowers of novels and romances.[18] By 1800, most copies of any given edition of a novel were sold not to individuals but to libraries of which, by that time, there numbered over a thousand in England alone. Throughout the period, books were expensive enough to be regarded as luxury items (see pp. xxvii–xxviii) and library membership became a popular way of pursuing a love of literature. Fanny Price in Austen's *Mansfield Park* was typical: 'She became a subscriber – amazed at being any thing *in propria persona*, amazed at her own doings in any way; to be a renter, a chuser of books!'[19]

The other thing that changed was that, whereas at the end of the eighteenth century women worked in an environment in which earning power was perceived as disreputable, in the new century more women began to take charge of their financial negotiations with publishers, and to profit by them. Publishers appear not to have discriminated against women: male and female writers were offered similar terms for similar work. If anything, women were given privileges not allowed to men, such as the ability to remain in debt, often over years.[20]

As many as a third of all novels were 'by a Lady',[21] including leisured gentlewomen, high-profile aristocrats, destitute merchants' wives, reformed (and some unreformed) prostitutes, and pious autodidacts.[22] Although some of the more successful were credited on title pages (Charlotte Smith, Amelia Opie, Lady Morgan, and Maria Edgeworth), anonymity was the norm, over 80 per cent of all novels published in the 1770s and 1780s, and nearly half those published during the first three decades of the nineteenth century, appearing unsigned.[23] The likely reasons? Fear of ridicule, modesty, and desire for a 'disguised' entrance into the literary arena[24] (though women seldom published books of poetry anonymously[25]).

The sums earned by authors rose sharply during the Romantic period, and women writers benefited as much as male counterparts, especially when publishing multi-volume works such as novels. The going rate for a triple-decker ranged from £150 to £200, though established authors could haggle for more: Charlotte Smith made £330 from the first edition of *The Romance of Real Life* (1787);[26] Fanny Burney made £250 for *Cecilia* (1795) and £1,500 for the first edition of *The Wanderer* (1814);[27] Ann Radcliffe earned £500 for *The Mysteries of Udolpho* (1794) and £800 for *The Italian* (1797) (a sum which, up to that time, was unprecedented);[28] Lady Caroline Lamb accepted £500 for *Glenarvon* in 1816;[29] and in 1824 Susan Ferrier was paid £1,000 for *The Inheritance*[30] – though that pales by comparison with the £2,000 earned by More's *Coelebs in Search of a Wife* (1808) in its first year of publication[31] or the £2,100 Maria Edgeworth earned for *Patronage* (1814).[32] Successful novelists could make a respectable living: Edgeworth put her lifetime earnings at £11,062. 8s. 10d.[33]

By comparison, Jane Austen's lifetime earnings, amounting to £600, seem unspectacular. But she had little reputation during her lifetime, and her publishing career was short (seven years, compared with Ferrier's thirty-four, Edgeworth's thirty-eight, and Burney's fifty-five years). Her best-selling work was *Pride and Prejudice* (1814), 3,000 copies of which were in circulation up to 1835, though Burney's *Camilla* (1796) outsold it (4,000). These figures hardly compare with those of Scott, whose *Waverley* (1814) sold 40,000 copies in the years up to 1836.[34] Which explains why offers made to Austen were unappetizing; Murray was willing to pay £450 for *Emma*, but also wanted the copyright to *Mansfield Park* and *Sense and Sensibility*. Austen preferred to publish 'on commission' – that is, to take the risk herself, paying the publisher a 10 per cent royalty on sales. By that means, she earned £140 for *Sense and Sensibility* and

£221. 6s. 4d for *Emma*.[35] Had she lived another twenty years, her reputation would have grown with her earnings.

Increased earnings were in line with the growing price of books throughout the wartime period and beyond. The Romantic period saw a boom in
poetry that ended with the publishing crash of 1826.[36] One authority cal-
culates that, between the 1780s and 1830s, there were 5,000 new books
of verse written by about 2,000 living poets, as well as a vast amount
of poetry reprinted from earlier times.[37] J. R. de J. Jackson documents
around 900 female poets between 1770 and 1835, responsible for 2,584
new titles.[38] All were beneficiaries of the boom but (then as now) poetry
was no way to make a living unless you were a best-seller. At the upper end
of the market, returns were impressive: Murray was confident he would
see a return on the £2,000 he gave Byron for Canto III of *Childe Harold's
Pilgrimage*, while Longman was prepared to offer Thomas Moore £3,000
for a poem he had not even read.[39] But those authors sold books in tens
of thousands (or, in the case of *Don Juan*, hundreds of thousands[40]),
which was not the norm. Amelia Opie's *Poems* (1804) did well to make
£61. 16s. 7d. in its first year,[41] while Charlotte Smith's *Beachy Head* made
£300.[42] Male writers were not always so fortunate: *Lyrical Ballads* (1798)
made £20. 18s. 6d.[43]

Women writers were sometimes at a disadvantage when dealing with
publishers, some of whom were not above fleecing them. Richard Dodsley
reacted to the suggestion he publish Charlotte Smith's sonnets by saying
'he should not object to print the poems – when, should any profit arise, he
might take it for his pains',[44] an idea Smith wisely rejected. Mary Robinson was an industrious writer, but in her four-and-a-half-year association
with Hookham netted less than £10. She attributed that to his sharp practice, but scholars now know she misjudged the market. She did better with
Longman, who paid her an average of £150 per annum for the last three
years of her life.[45]

Some treated women writers better than others. Two publishers,
Thomas Cadell and Sampson Low, were willing to make loans to
Charlotte Smith. There was a price to be paid, of course: Cadell charged
interest.[46] All the same, he paid more than agreed for the first edition
of *Emmeline, the Orphan of the Castle* (1788), so that she received
£200, and £40 each from two further editions.[47] Smith was a canny
businesswoman who did her best to wangle a good deal, earning £180
on the fifth edition of *Elegiac Sonnets* (1789),[48] which was published on
subscription – a goodly sum for a volume that appeared five years before.

All of which shows female authors could prosper in the literary marketplace if they had a modicum of business sense. Those whose principal
talent was for poetry were constantly struggling with its failure to pay as

well as fiction. Among the more successful, Letitia Landon made £2,585 from her writings in the course of a very productive career, £900 of which came from *The Improvisatrice* (1824) and *The Troubadour* (1825).[49] Averaged across her seventeen-year career, that gave her an income of £2. 18s. 6d. a week. Felicia Dorothea Hemans, probably the best-known female poet of her time, earned £62 from *The Siege of Valencia* (1823), and £75 from *Records of Woman* (1828), both issued on a profit-sharing basis,[50] and her lifetime earnings are estimated as in excess of £2,988. Across the twenty-seven years of her publishing career, that would have yielded an average of at least £2. 2s. 6d. per week. Poets who could write novels did better: over the course of a thirty-year career, Amelia Opie earned £4,181. 10s. 4d;[51] over two decades, Charlotte Smith made about £4,190.[52] They were among the exceptions. It was normal for poets to earn nothing at all, such as Keats and Shelley,[53] or end up in debt to their publishers: by 1827 John Clare owed Taylor and Hessey £150.[54]

Women poets gained from the growing popularity of newspapers, periodicals, and albums, which paid well.[55] Careers were launched in them. Mary Robinson began publishing her poetry in *The World* as Anna Matilda, and at the end of her life was taking an income from *The Morning Post*.[56] Isabella Lickbarrow started publishing poetry in the *Westmorland Advertiser* in 1811. A local woman whose life was one of financial hardship, she wrote verse to support herself and her two sisters. Had it not been for the *Advertiser*, her work would probably not have appeared in print at all, nor would her first volume of poems, published in 1814 on a subscription basis by the *Advertiser*'s proprietor at a cost of 5 shillings.[57]

As readers demanded more (and better) poetry, rewards increased. In 1827, after hard-fought negotiations, Felicia Hemans was given 24 guineas a sheet for contributions to *Blackwood's Magazine* (£1. 11s. 6d. per page[58]), making her its highest-paid writer, her rates exceeding those of Thomas Hood, William Godwin, Thomas De Quincey, and Walter Scott. (By comparison, William Hazlitt began work as a journalist in 1812 for the princely sum of 4 guineas a week and was content, a decade later, to receive 15 guineas a sheet for contributions to the *London Magazine*.) Letitia Landon provided most of the poems and prose for *Fisher's Drawing Room Scrap Book* (1832–8), earning £2. 2s. each for her poems, and £100 for the entire text.[59] The work was congenial and lucrative, and inclined her to edit other annuals, including *The Easter Gift*, *Heath's Book of Beauty*, *A Birthday Tribute*, and *Flowers of Loveliness*.[60] Between 1826 and 1832, Hemans published ninety-four poems in thirteen annuals, from which she made more than £930.[61]

Such sums testify to the popularity of annuals at this period: in 1827 *The Keepsake* sold an estimated 15,000 copies.[62]

By the time Harriet Martineau began to sell stories for £5 each in 1826, the female writer was an unremarkable feature on the literary landscape; by 1844 she calculated she had made 'between £5000 & £6000'[63] by her pen – more than either Hemans or Landon. For the opportunities that came her way, Martineau could thank the generation that preceded hers, as the Romantic period was the first in which women could take their place in a profession that was once male-dominated. That is not to say that they were always able to write in the way they wanted or on the subjects they chose, that they received kinder reviews than male authors, or that they escaped the exploitation of unscrupulous publishers. In fact they were constrained by numerous cultural and commercial pressures.[64] However, those with the stamina to keep producing over decades, capable of dealing in a businesslike manner with publishers, could enjoy rewards equivalent to, and sometimes greater than, those earned by men.[65] Some, such as Charlotte Smith and Fanny Burney, even enjoyed their share of celebrity.

Notes

1 This was More's own estimate; see M. G. Jones, *Hannah More* (Cambridge: Cambridge University Press, 1952), p. 186. See also *The Annual Biography and Obituary, 1834* (London: Longman, 1834), p. 405, and Henry Thompson, *The Life of Hannah More* (London: Cadell, 1838), p. 324.

2 William St Clair, *The Reading Nation in the Romantic Period* (Cambridge: Cambridge University Press, 2004), p. 162.

3 Sales figures from *Selected Writings of Hannah More*, ed. Robert Hole (London: Pickering & Chatto, 1996), p. vii.

4 St Clair, *The Reading Nation in the Romantic Period*, pp. 221, 621. For a detailed analysis of Austen's dealings with one of her publishers, see Kathryn Sutherland, 'Jane Austen's Dealings with John Murray and His Firm', *The Review of English Studies* 64 (2013), 105–26.

5 Claire Tomalin, *Jane Austen: A Life* (London: Viking, 1997), p. 212.

6 See *Romantic Women Poets: An Anthology*, ed. Duncan Wu (Oxford: Blackwell, 1996), pp. 24–43.

7 *Romanticism: An Anthology*, ed. Duncan Wu (4th ed., Oxford: Wiley-Blackwell, 2012), p. 251. For more on the Bluestockings, see Sylvia Harcstark Myers, *The Bluestocking Circle: Women, Friendship, and the Life of the Mind in Eighteenth-Century England* (Oxford: Clarendon Press, 1990), and *Bluestockings Displayed: Portraiture, Performance, and Patronage,*

1730–1830, ed. Elizabeth Eger (Cambridge: Cambridge University Press, 2013).

8 See, *inter alia*, Susanne Schmid, *British Literary Salons of the Late Eighteenth and Early Nineteenth Centuries* (New York: Palgrave Macmillan, 2013), ch. 6.

9 Susan J. Wolfson quotes the entire thing in 'The New Poetries', in *The Cambridge History of English Romantic Literature*, ed. James Chandler (Cambridge: Cambridge University Press, 2009), p. 423.

10 G. J. Barker-Benfield, *The Culture of Sensibility: Sex and Society in Eighteenth-Century Britain* (Chicago: University of Chicago Press, 1992), p. 377. For another view of Polwhele's poem, see Katherine Binhammer, 'Thinking Gender with Sexuality in 1790s' Feminist Thought', *Feminist Studies* 28 (2002), 667–90.

11 William Stafford comments: 'in a sense the conservative Polwhele's list of "unsex'd" female writers, with the exceptions of Yearsley and Robinson, was made up within the ranks of radicalism' (*English Feminists and Their Opponents in the 1790s: Unsex'd and Proper Females* (Manchester: Manchester University Press, 2002), p. 3). Eleanor Ty observes Polwhele was opposing 'their support of the French people's desire for a republican government, and hence their meddling in politics' (*Unsex'd Revolutionaries: Five Women Novelists of the 1790s* (Toronto: University of Toronto Press, 1993), p. 13).

12 *Romanticism: An Anthology*, ed. Wu, p. 36.

13 Ibid., p. 37.

14 William Keach has observed that Barbauld's poem was not liked by her political allies either; see 'A Regency Prophecy and the End of Anna Barbauld's Career', *Studies in Romanticism* 33 (1994), 569–77.

15 Germaine Greer, *Slip-Shod Sibyls: Recognition, Rejection and the Woman Poet* (London: Viking, 1995), p. 311.

16 See, *inter alia*, Cynthia Lawford, '"Thou shalt bid thy fair hands rove": L.E.L.'s Wooing of Sex, Pain, Death and the Editor', *Romanticism on the Net* 29–30 (February–May 2003).

17 Glennis Stephenson, *Letitia Landon: The Woman Behind L.E.L.* (Manchester: Manchester University Press, 1995), pp. 41–2.

18 St Clair, *The Reading Nation in the Romantic Period*, pp. 242–3, 665–75.

19 Jane Austen, *Mansfield Park*, ed. John Wiltshire (Cambridge: Cambridge University Press, 2005), p. 461.

20 The information in this paragraph comes from Jan Fergus and Janice Farrar Thaddeus, 'Women, Publishers, and Money, 1790–1820', *Studies in Eighteenth-Century Culture* 17 (1987), 191–207, pp. 200–1.

21 Ibid., p. 204.

22 *The English Novel 1770–1829: A Bibliographical Survey of Prose Fiction Published in the British Isles*, ed. James Raven, Peter Garside, and Rainer Schöwerling (2 vols., Oxford: Oxford University Press, 2000), i. 17.

23 Ibid., i. 41, ii. 66.

24 Mary Poovey analyses why women became more likely to publish during the Romantic period in the opening chapter of *The Proper Lady and the Woman*

Writer: Ideology as Style in the Works of Mary Wollstonecraft, Mary Shelley, and Jane Austen (Chicago: University of Chicago Press, 1984), esp. pp. 36–7.

25 For further discussion, see Paula R. Feldman, 'Women Poets and Anonymity in the Romantic Era', *New Literary History* 33 (2002), 279–89.

26 Judith Phillips Stanton, 'Charlotte Smith's "Literary Business": Income, Patronage, and Indigence', *The Age of Johnson* 1 (1987), 375–401, p. 391; Loraine Fletcher, *Charlotte Smith: A Critical Biography* (Houndmills, Basingstoke: Macmillan, 1998), p. 86.

27 St Clair, *The Reading Nation in the Romantic Period*, p. 584.

28 Ibid., p. 631.

29 *The Whole Disgraceful Truth: Selected Letters of Lady Caroline Lamb*, ed. Paul Douglass (New York: Palgrave Macmillan, 2006), p. 151.

30 St Clair, *The Reading Nation in the Romantic Period*, p. 173.

31 Ann Stott, *Hannah More: The First Victorian* (Oxford: Oxford University Press, 2004), p. 281.

32 *The Letters of Sarah Harriet Burney*, ed. Lorna J. Clark (Athens: University of Georgia Press, 1997), p. 180n2; *The English Novel 1770–1829*, ed. Raven, Garside, and Schöwerling, ii. 45.

33 This figure is cited by Fergus and Thaddeus, 'Women, Publishers, and Money, 1790–1820', p. 205n27.

34 St Clair, *The Reading Nation in the Romantic Period*, p. 222.

35 Joan Aiken Hodge, 'Jane Austen and Her Publishers', in *Jane Austen: Bicentenary Essays*, ed. John Halperin (Cambridge: Cambridge University Press, 1975), pp. 75–88, 82–4; St Clair, *The Reading Nation in the Romantic Period*, p. 580.

36 Tim Chilcott, *A Publisher and His Circle: The Life and Work of John Taylor, Keats's Publisher* (London: Routledge & Kegan Paul, 1972), p. 184.

37 St Clair, *The Reading Nation in the Romantic Period*, p. 172.

38 J. R. de J. Jackson, *Romantic Poetry by Women: A Bibliography 1770–1835* (Oxford: Clarendon Press, 1993), p. xxii.

39 *Lalla Rookh*, the rights to which Longman purchased in December 1814; see Stephen Gwynn, *Thomas Moore* (London: Macmillan, 1905), p. 73.

40 St Clair estimates 200,000 copies were in circulation prior to 1840, with a readership of as many as a million and a half; it 'was read by more people in its first twenty years than any previous work of English literature' (*The Reading Nation in the Romantic Period*, p. 333).

41 I am grateful to John B. King for this figure, drawn from Longman's account book for the relevant period.

42 Stanton, 'Charlotte Smith's "Literary Business"', p. 392; Fletcher puts the figure at £235 (p. 337).

43 *Lyrical Ballads, and Other Poems, 1797–1800*, ed. James A. Butler and Karen Green (Ithaca, NY: Cornell University Press, 1992), p. 21.

44 Fletcher, *Charlotte Smith*, p. 65.

45 Fergus and Thaddeus, 'Women, Publishers, and Money, 1790–1820', pp. 196–7.

46 Stanton, 'Charlotte Smith's "Literary Business"', p. 390.
47 Ibid., p. 391; Fletcher, *Charlotte Smith*, p. 101.
48 Stanton, 'Charlotte Smith's "Literary Business"', p. 391.
49 St Clair, *The Reading Nation in the Romantic Period*, p. 615; Letitia Elizabeth Landon, *Selected Writings*, ed. Jerome J. McGann and Daniel Riess (Peterborough, Ont.: Broadview, 1997), p. 12.
50 Felicia Hemans, *The Siege of Valencia: A Parallel Text Edition*, ed. Susan J. Wolfson and Elizabeth Fay (Peterborough, Ont.: Broadview, 2002), p. 17; *Felicia Hemans: Selected Poems, Letters, Reception Materials*, ed. Susan J. Wolfson (Princeton, NJ: Princeton University Press, 2000), p. 500. For a lucid explanation of profit-sharing, see St Clair, *The Reading Nation in the Romantic Period*, p. 164.
51 Paula R. Feldman, 'The Poet and the Profits: Felicia Hemans and the Literary Marketplace', *Keats-Shelley Journal* 46 (1997), 148–76, p. 175n67; Fergus and Thaddeus, 'Women, Publishers, and Money, 1790–1820', p. 198. Shelley King and John B. Pierce counsel caution with regard to this figure, as a full set of financial records relating to Opie's works is not available.
52 Stanton, 'Charlotte Smith's "Literary Business"', p. 390.
53 In September 1820, Taylor and Hessey calculated their loss from *Endymion* and the 1820 poems at £250; see Chilcott, *A Publisher and His Circle*, p. 53. Shelley estimated he sold five or six copies of *Prometheus Unbound* (1820). His poor sales are ironic in view of his extensive knowledge of the print technology; see Andrew Bennett, *Romantic Poets and the Culture of Posterity* (Cambridge: Cambridge University Press, 1999), p. 163. For an illuminating discussion of Shelley's dealings with his main London publisher, Charles Ollier, see Charles E. Robinson, 'Percy Bysshe Shelley, Charles Ollier, and William Blackwood: The Contexts of Early Nineteenth-Century Publishing', in *Shelley Revalued: Essays from the Gregynog Conference* (Leicester: Leicester University Press, 1983), pp. 183–226.
54 Chilcott, *A Publisher and His Circle*, p. 123.
55 Desperate for money, Keats told his friend Dilke on 22 September 1819: 'I am determined to spin – home spun any thing for sale. Yea I will trafic. Any thing but Mortgage my Brain to Blackwood': *The Letters of John Keats 1814–1821*, ed. Hyder Edward Rollins (2 vols., Cambridge, MA: Harvard University Press, 1958), ii. 178–9.
56 Daniel Robinson points out that, contrary to what is often claimed, Robinson was not the poetry editor of *The Morning Post*, at least not in anything approaching the modern understanding of that term; see *The Poetry of Mary Robinson: Form and Fame* (New York: Palgrave Macmillan, 2011), pp. 32–9, 183–8.
57 Isabella Lickbarrow, *Collected Poems*, ed. Constance Parrish (Grasmere: Wordsworth Trust, 2004), pp. 7–8. One of Lickbarrow's poems concerns 'The Fate of Newspapers' (see ibid., p. 160).
58 Feldman, 'The Poet and the Profits', pp. 161–2.
59 St Clair, *The Reading Nation in the Romantic Period*, p. 230.

60 Julie Watt, *Poisoned Lives: The Regency Poet Letitia Elizabeth Landon (L.E.L.) and British Gold Coast Administrator George Maclean* (Eastbourne: Sussex Academic Press, 2010), p. 134.

61 Feldman, 'The Poet and the Profits', p. 160. At the same time, both Landon and Hemans expressed dissatisfaction at the compromises they made in order to provide poetry for the market; see Stephen C. Behrendt, *British Women Poets and the Romantic Writing Community* (Baltimore, MD: Johns Hopkins University Press, 2009), p. 293.

62 Chilcott, *A Publisher and His Circle*, p. 185.

63 For these figures I am grateful to Linda H. Peterson, 'From French Revolution to English Reform: Hannah More, Harriet Martineau, and the "Little Book"', *Nineteenth-Century Literature* 60 (2006), 409–50, pp. 413, 415.

64 Susan J. Wolfson demonstrates how Hemans's literary repute was shaped by notions of 'femininity'; see her introduction to *Felicia Hemans: Selected Poems, Letters, Reception Materials*, pp. xvii–xxi.

65 They also built up a solid literary reputation, so that even in mid-century they were memorialized in an anthology, *The Female Poets of Great Britain, Chronologically Arranged*, ed. Frederic Rowton (Philadelphia: Henry Baird, 1856).

Myth

27

THE ROMANTICS WERE ATHEISTS

Atheists are not our preachers; madmen are not our lawgivers.

Burke, *Reflections on the Revolution in France*, 1790[1]

The Enlightenment was a period of deepening scepticism. On the Continent, H. S. Reimarus denied the existence of the supernatural, condemned the Bible as unreliable and fraudulent, and argued religion was dependent on reason for its existence; he was consistent with the thought of Leibniz and Wolff, who dominated German universities. In France, d'Holbach and his coterie of *philosophes* flirted with a form of dogmatic atheism that shocked David Hume (an avowed sceptic) when he dined with them in 1764.[2] When Burke crossed the Channel in January and February 1773 he was appalled by the 'infidels and atheists' he encountered.[3] Little wonder that, when it came, the revolution was brutally anticlerical, designed to dechristianize: some estimate that as many as three bishops and 220 priests were killed in the September massacres.[4] During the Terror, the actress Marie Maillard was enthroned as Goddess of Reason in Notre Dame Cathedral, afterwards designated the Temple of Reason. But if British Romantics tended to support the aims of the French Revolution, they did not necessarily share its more extreme impulses.

David Jasper points out that during the Romantic period 'the traditional frameworks of belief and understanding' disintegrated, giving rise to dissent.[5] This was partly the result of disillusionment with the Established Church, which (as it had political power) was implicated in what many regarded as the oppressive tactics of a government that represented

30 Great Myths About the Romantics, First Edition. Duncan Wu.
© 2015 John Wiley & Sons, Ltd. Published 2015 by John Wiley & Sons, Ltd.

a small number of wealthy landowners and was responsible for the sufferings of millions through war and industrialization. It was hardly surprising that dissent flourished, including Arianism, Arminianism, and Socinianism, all of which gave rise to Unitarianism. Adherents included Anna Laetitia Barbauld, Joseph Priestley, Josiah Wedgwood, Charles Lamb, Mary Wollstonecraft, and the publisher Joseph Johnson, to name a few. Those who might be described as deists or pagans included Samuel Horsley (Bishop of Rochester),[6] Sir Humphry Davy,[7] Erasmus Darwin,[8] Sir William Jones, Thomas Paine, William Bartram, Daniel Isaac Eaton, Daniel O'Connell, and the artist John Martin. Coleridge's poetry has been identified with a pagan Neoplatonism, though he regarded himself as a devout Unitarian in the second half of the 1790s.[9]

Atheism was a stance more extreme than most were willing to contemplate, and it came with a stigma. Though its Jacobinical resonances were fashionable in 1789, it was to become associated with unpatriotic feeling and Continental immorality – a cause for shame. All the same, there were noteworthy atheists, including William Godwin; Richard Porson;[10] Robert Owen, the socialist and philanthropist; mathematician John Leslie; Sir James Hall, the chemist and geologist; John Oswald, journalist and poet (a vegetarian); John 'Walking' Stewart (also a vegetarian);[11] radical agitator Francis Place; phrenologist George Combe; radical publisher Richard Carlile (the self-styled 'Christian atheist'); writer and publisher William Hone;[12] John Thelwall;[13] physician and mesmerist John Elliotson; and historian and politician George Grote. Yet it would be wrong to say atheism was widespread. It was not.

Of the poets, Shelley is claimed as the most eminent atheist. When in late 1810 Harriet Grove spurned him for his deistic beliefs, he became violently anti-Christian: 'Oh! I burn with impatience for the moment of Xtianity's dissolution, it has injured me', he told his best friend, Jefferson Hogg.[14] 'I am convinced too that it is of great disservice to society that it encourages prejudice which strikes at the root of the dearest the tenderest of its ties. Oh how I wish I *were* the Antichrist, that it were *mine* to crush the Demon, to hurl him to his native Hell never to rise again.... Oh! Christianity when I pardon this last this severest of thy persecutions may God (if there be a God), blast me!'[15]

Compared with that, *The Necessity of Atheism* (1811) was a sober affair that concluded: 'Every reflecting mind must allow that there is no proof of the existence of a Deity. Q.E.D.'[16] It was impolitic to send it to Oxford heads of house and bishops, though Shelley was in shock when University College decided to expel him. A few years later he wrote *A Refutation of Deism* (1814), aiming to prove 'there is no alternative between Atheism and Christianity'.[17] 'The Atheist is a monster among men', he wrote:

> He dreads no judge but his own conscience, he fears no hell but the loss of his self esteem. He is not to be restrained by punishments, for death is divested of its terror, and whatever enters into his heart to conceive, that will he not scruple to execute.[18]

But Shelley's views are less clear-cut than they appear: his insistence that 'There is no God!' in the notes to *Queen Mab* continues, 'This negation must be understood solely to affect a creative Deity. The hypothesis of a pervading Spirit coeternal with the universe, remains unshaken.'[19] None of this sounds like atheism, as it presumes the existence of a divine being. Perhaps he took pleasure in confusing his readers with comments that contradicted his bolder, atheistic declarations. Accordingly, he signed himself in hotel registers αθεος,[20] and at the same time wrote, in 'Hymn to Intellectual Beauty', 'The awful shadow of some unseen Power / Floats though unseen amongst us'; and, in 'Mont Blanc', 'the Power is there, / The still and solemn Power of many sights / And many sounds'.[21] What exactly is this 'Power'?

> This power is God. And those who have seen God, have, in the periods of their purer and more perfect nature, been harmonized by their own will, to so exquisite a consentaneity of powers, as to give forth divinest melody when the breath of universal being sweeps over their frame.[22]

If 'On Christianity' (1817) is credited, Shelley never rejected the idea of God – or, apparently, immortal life;[23] to that extent, far from being a sceptic, he was among the more devout of the Romantics. After the outburst of 1810, he reconceived Christ as a major figure in his mythology: 'Jesus Christ represents God as the fountain of all goodness, the eternal enemy of pain and evil: the uniform and unchanging motive of the salutary operations of the material world.'[24] Christ was the rebel who 'opposed with earnest eloquence the panic fears and hateful superstitions which have enslaved mankind for ages'.[25] None of this is atheistic; by the time Shelley composed his 'Defence of Poetry', suggests Robert M. Ryan, he believed poets were responsible for helping make religion 'a more beneficent force in society. Of all the Romantics, Shelley had the clearest vision of the relationship connecting literature and religious reform.'[26]

Shelley drew encouragement from the author of 'Tintern Abbey' (1798) (a man once described as 'a Republican & at least a *Semi*-atheist'[27]), who in 1791 took his place among the dissenters at the Old Jewry underneath the pulpit of Unitarian preacher Joseph Fawcett. Coleridge was so

admiring of Wordsworth's poetic talent he did not hesitate to recognize
the achievement of a poem which praised

> A presence that disturbs me with the joy
> Of elevated thoughts; a sense sublime
> Of something far more deeply interfused,
> Whose dwelling is the light of setting suns,
> And the round ocean, and the living air,
> And the blue sky, and in the mind of man,
> A motion and a spirit, that impels
> All thinking things, all objects of all thought,
> And rolls through all things.
>
> ('Tintern Abbey', ll. 95–103)

The 'presence' is a 'motion and a spirit' in the natural world and 'the
mind of man' – not God as Trinitarians knew him but something closer
to pagan conceptions. That was because Wordsworth followed Coleridge
who, in 'Religious Musings', declared,

> 'Tis the sublime of man,
> Our noontide majesty, to know ourselves
> Parts and proportions of one wondrous whole;
> This fraternizes man, this constitutes
> Our charities and bearings – but 'tis God
> Diffused through all that doth make all one whole.
>
> (ll. 140–5)

Coleridge's belief in a unitary God 'Diffused' through the cosmos offered
Wordsworth a way of conceiving 'something far more deeply interfused'
in the natural world. Both write in unconventional terms – Coleridge as
Unitarian, Wordsworth as pantheist – and their reluctance to conform
exercised a powerful attraction for both Shelley and Keats, the latter of
whom, in *Endymion* (1818), would praise Pan: 'Thou, to whom every
faun and satyr flies / For willing service' (ll. 263–4). By the time those lines
were read to Wordsworth, he had returned to the Church of England[28]
and regarded them as 'a Very pretty piece of Paganism'.[29] But they were
not, in that respect, very different from 'Tintern Abbey'.

Keats's scepticism was fuelled by his association with Leigh Hunt, who
teased Benjamin Robert Haydon for his religious faith.[30] Keats's correspondence shows him thinking intensely about the subject. On 19 March
1819, he admitted the 'splendour' of Christ, while regretting his story
had been 'written and revised by Men interested in the pious frauds of
Religion',[31] a remark in which scholars perceive the anticlericalism of
Voltaire.[32] A month later, Keats formulated a critique of Christianity in

which he said the idea of being 'taken to Heaven' was a 'little circum-scribe[d] straightened notion!', rejecting it in favour of his 'System of Soul-making'.[33] Yet throughout his discussion he takes for granted the existence of the soul, its immortality, and the afterlife. This was not athe-ism. Ryan suggests Keats finally rejected organized religion despite con-tinued attachment to a providential and benevolent Deity.[34]

Byron found 'infidel' 'a cold and chilling word'[35] even though, in *Manfred, Cain, Heaven and Earth*, and *Don Juan*, he flirted with various forms of scepticism; as Francis Jeffrey saw it, *Cain* was 'directed against the goodness or the power of the Deity, and against the reasonableness of religion in general'.[36] That was not how Byron saw himself; aspects of his biography suggest an urge to embrace religion. His study of Armenian with Father Aucher at the monastery of San Lazzaro in late 1816 cultivated his spiritual leanings so that by the end of December he described Aucher as 'My spiritual preceptor'.[37] In later years he admitted the attraction of Catholicism, saying it was 'by far the most elegant worship, hardly excepting the Greek mythology. What with incense, pictures, statues, altars, shrines, relics, and the real presence, confession, absolution, – there is something sensible to grasp at.'[38] In 1823 Byron attended a meeting at which Dr Kennedy, physician to the British garrison at Cephalonia, attempted to prove the truth of Christian doctrines, and on that occasion displayed a familiarity with the Bible that surprised his interlocutors.[39] During his final illness he kept the Bible on his breakfast table.[40] As he began the final canto of *Don Juan* he shed the poker-faced playfulness with which he sometimes wrote about religion, to speak directly to the reader:

> I do not speak profanely, to recall
> > Those holier mysteries, which the wise and just
> Receive as gospel, and which grow more rooted,
> As all truths must, the more they are disputed.[41]

It is not religion Byron frog-marches off the premises, but doubt. The 'holier mysteries' that constitute true faith are robust enough to gain strength from interrogation. By a sleight of hand, he becomes one of the disputants as well as one of the 'wise and just'. This was as close as he would ever get in verse to a confession of faith.[42]

Of the Romantics, Blake was more influenced by the Bible than any, yet he was a dissenter who arrived, via the works of philosophical alchemists such as Jacob Boehme, at the door of Emanuel Swedenborg's New Jerusalem Church in Great Eastcheap, in April 1789.[43] Swedenborg said the Last Judgement occurred in 1757 and that angels had disclosed to him the spiritual nature of creation. Blake read and annotated a number of his prophecies and attended meetings of the New Church[44] but became disillusioned, in part because Swedenborg 'was wrong in endeavouring to explain to the rational faculty what the reason cannot comprehend', and 'His sexual religion is dangerous'.[45] For the rest of his life Blake attended no church, detesting 'Lies & Priestcraft',[46] though he was 'in every real sense the Christian poet and visionary he claimed to be'.[47] His aim, as Ryan has pointed out, was to 'purify and restore the Christian faith, which he saw as offering a revolutionary alternative... to the existing social and economic order'.[48] That said, he was unconventional to a fault; one biographer suggests Blake followed his teacher Richard Cosway into ritual magic,[49] while E. P. Thompson suggested the source for many of his ideas was a radical Protestant sect, the Muggletonians.[50]

William Hazlitt trained as a Unitarian minister but, having lost his faith, left Hackney New College 'an avowed infidel'.[51] Until recently, this was an aspect of his life biographers preferred not to discuss. But it is important: Hazlitt had been a disciple of Priestley and his atheism links the English Enlightenment with Romantic scepticism. Visiting the Lake District in 1803, Hazlitt found an ally in Wordsworth; together they spoke 'so irreverently so malignantly of the Divine Wisdom' that Coleridge responded (by his own account) 'too contemptuously'.[52] Hazlitt's early beliefs, though abandoned, enabled him to write affectionately of those who 'had been brought up and lived from youth to age in the one constant belief of God and of his Christ, and who thought all other things but dross compared with the glory hereafter to be revealed'.[53] He would never, like Wordsworth and Coleridge, have conceived a poem that anticipated the millennium, but his early religious enthusiasm made him appreciative of 'The Recluse'.

The myth regards the Romantics as atheist because of the presumed influence of the French Revolution. But atheism was for the few who could engage with the idea of nothing as opposed to the something to which most contemporaries remained attached. In truth, most were prone to belief rather than doubt, and would have agreed with Charles Lamb when he described atheists as 'Short-lived, short-sighted, impotent to save.'[54] Of those who experimented with various forms of dissent, there were some who, like Coleridge, returned to the Church of England in later years. (He would advocate Trinitarian Christianity and envisage a society based on its doctrines.[55]) Nonetheless, the liberty to speculate defined much literature of the time, including (in addition to works already mentioned) Robinson's *Sappho and Phaon* (1796), Southey's *The Curse of Kehama* (1810),[56] Tighe's *Psyche* (1805),[57] Shelley's *Frankenstein* (1818), and Hogg's *Private Memoirs and Confessions of a Justified Sinner* (1824).[58] If none propound atheism, they do reflect

Figure 22 Charles Lamb (1775–1834), essayist, poet, and Unitarian. Source: Paul F. Betz Collection.

a climate in which the failure of the Established Church adequately to answer contemporary needs led many to consider alternatives. When, in 1796, Coleridge told John Thelwall he loved and reverenced deists, Calvinists, and Moravians, and would 'realize my *principles* by *feeling* love & honor for an Atheist',[59] he wrote with an optimism released by that sense of enquiry which, far from suggesting atheism, indicates belief. In that, as in much else, he was typical of the moment.

Notes

1 *Romanticism: An Anthology*, ed. Duncan Wu (4th ed., Oxford: Wiley-Blackwell, 2012), p. 14.
2 Although it is worth noting that, according to Alan Kors, only d'Holbach and Naigeon can be called proselytizing atheists; see *D'Holbach's Coterie: An Enlightenment in Paris* (Princeton, NJ: Princeton University Press, 1976), p. 49. The best available account of the larger debate concerning atheism during the years prior to the French Revolution may be found in

Martin Priestman, *Romantic Atheism: Poetry and Freethought, 1780–1830* (Cambridge: Cambridge University Press, 1999), chs. 1 and 2.

3 D. O. Thomas, *The Honest Mind: The Thought and Work of Richard Price* (Oxford: Clarendon Press, 1977), p. 311. When Joseph Priestley visited the Continent in 1774, he found that 'all the eminent Frenchmen whom he met there, were entirely destitute of any religious belief – sheer atheists': *Reminiscences and Table-Talk of Samuel Rogers*, ed. G. H. Powell (London: R. Brimley Johnson, 1903), pp. 84–5.

4 John McManners, *The French Revolution and the Church* (London: SPCK for the Church Historical Society, 1969), p. 67.

5 David Jasper, *The Sacred and Secular Canon in Romanticism: Preserving the Sacred Truths* (Houndmills, Basingstoke: Macmillan, 1999), p. 105.

6 Coleridge said Horsley was regarded as a deist in September 1794; see *Collected Letters of Samuel Taylor Coleridge*, ed. Earl Leslie Griggs (6 vols., Oxford: Clarendon Press, 1956–71), i. 102.

7 Davy believed in the immortality of the soul; see David Knight, *Humphry Davy: Science and Power* (Oxford: Blackwell, 1992), p. 71.

8 For a discussion of his deist views in relation to evolutionary theory, see Desmond King-Hele, *Doctor of Revolution: The Life and Genius of Erasmus Darwin* (London: Faber & Faber, 1977), pp. 244–5.

9 Priestman, *Romantic Atheism*, pp. 146–7.

10 'He absolutely infests you with *Atheism*': *Collected Letters of Samuel Taylor Coleridge*, ed. Griggs, i. 139.

11 Oswald and Stewart were old friends who had served in India together; see David V. Erdman, *Commerce des Lumières: John Oswald and the British in Paris, 1790–1793* (Columbia: University of Missouri Press, 1986), p. 119.

12 Hone inherited from his father a violent aversion to priestcraft; he converted to Christianity, though not the Established Church, in the early 1830s. See, *inter alia*, *Regency Radical: Selected Writings of William Hone*, ed. David A. Kent and D. R. Ewen (Detroit: Wayne State University Press, 2003), p. 26.

13 Though the possibility of a softening in his staunch atheism has been observed after 1817; see Patty O'Boyle, '"A Son of John Thelwall": Weymouth Birkbeck Thelwall's Romantic Inheritance', *Romantic Circles*: 'John Thelwall: Critical Reassessments', ed. Yasmin Solomonescu (September 2011), online periodical, para. 3.

14 Percy Bysshe Shelley to Thomas Jefferson Hogg, 20 December 1810, in *The Letters of Percy Bysshe Shelley*, ed. Frederick L. Jones (2 vols., Oxford: Clarendon Press, 1964), i. 27.

15 Percy Bysshe Shelley to Thomas Jefferson Hogg, 3 January 1811, ibid., p. 35.

16 *The Prose Works of Percy Bysshe Shelley*, vol. i, ed. E. B. Murray (Oxford: Clarendon Press, 1993), p. 5.

17 Ibid., p. 94.

18 Ibid., p. 110.

19 *The Complete Poetry of Percy Bysshe Shelley*, ed. Donald H. Reiman, Neil Fraistat, et al. (3 vols. so far, Baltimore: Johns Hopkins University Press, 2000–), ii. 263.

20 See Peter Cochran, 'Robert Southey, the "Atheist" Inscription, and the "League of Incest"', *Notes and Queries* 37 (1990), 415–18, p. 416. See also Byron's letter to the editor of *The Courier*, 5 February 1822, in *Byron's Letters and Journals*, ed. Leslie A. Marchand (13 vols., London: John Murray, 1973–94), ix. 97.

21 Shelley, 'Hymn to Intellectual Beauty', ll. 1–2; 'Mont Blanc', ll. 127–9.

22 *The Prose Works of Percy Bysshe Shelley*, vol. i, ed. Murray, pp. 251–2.

23 See Lord Byron's letter to Thomas Moore, 6 March 1822, in *Byron's Letters and Journals*, ed. Marchand, ix. 121.

24 *The Prose Works of Percy Bysshe Shelley*, vol. i, ed. Murray, p. 255.

25 Ibid., p. 256.

26 Robert M. Ryan, *The Romantic Reformation* (Cambridge: Cambridge University Press, 1997), p. 41.

27 S. T. Coleridge to John Thelwall, 13 May 1796, in *Collected Letters of Samuel Taylor Coleridge*, ed. Griggs, i. 216.

28 For a persuasive reading of this process, see Ryan, *The Romantic Reformation*, pp. 94–6.

29 *The Keats Circle: Letters and Papers 1816–1878*, ed. Hyder Edward Rollins (2 vols., Cambridge, MA: Harvard University Press, 1948), ii. 144. Ryan observes that the Hymn to Pan reflects 'some serious metaphysical thinking', and is designed to 'express a modern conception of what religion ought to be (and thus to demonstrate the defects and inadequacies of Christianity)' (Ryan, *The Romantic Reformation*, pp. 159–60).

30 See, for instance, Haydon's diary entry for 20 January 1817, in *The Diary of Benjamin Robert Haydon*, ed. Willard Bissell Pope (5 vols., Cambridge, MA: Harvard University Press, 1960–3), ii. 80–4.

31 John Keats to George and Georgiana Keats, 19 March 1819, in *The Letters of John Keats 1814–1821*, ed. Hyder Edward Rollins (2 vols., Cambridge, MA: Harvard University Press, 1958), ii. 80.

32 Stuart M. Sperry Jr., 'Keats's Skepticism and Voltaire', *Keats-Shelley Journal* 12 (1963), 75–93, pp. 85–6.

33 John Keats to George and Georgiana Keats, 21 April 1819, in *The Letters of John Keats 1814–1821*, ed. Rollins, ii. 102–3.

34 Robert M. Ryan, *Keats: The Religious Sense* (Princeton, NJ: Princeton University Press, 1976), pp. 188–211.

35 Leslie A. Marchand, *Byron: A Biography* (3 vols., New York: Alfred A. Knopf, 1957), iii. 1105.

36 *Lord Byron: The Critical Heritage*, ed. Andrew Rutherford (London: Routledge & Kegan Paul, 1970), pp. 233–4.

37 Lord Byron to John Murray, 27 December 1816, in *Byron's Letters and Journals*, ed. Marchand, v. 152.

38 Lord Byron to Thomas Moore, 8 March 1822, ibid., ix. 123. For more on this subject, see, *inter alia*, James Soderholm, *Fantasy, Forgery, and the Byron Legend* (Lexington: University Press of Kentucky, 1996), p. 123.

39 Marchand, *Byron: A Biography*, iii. 1105.

40 Ibid., p. 1244.

41 Byron, *Don Juan*, xvi, stanza 6, ll. 45–8.

42 These lines are discussed by Ryan, *The Romantic Reformation*, p. 151.

43 Bentley reports Blake and his wife subscribed to a statement of belief in Swedenborg's doctrines on 13 April 1789; see G. E. Bentley, Jr, *The Stranger from Paradise: A Biography of William Blake* (New Haven: Yale University Press, 2001), p. 127.

44 For further details of Blake's interest in Swedenborg see the excellent introduction to *The Marriage of Heaven and Hell* in William Blake, *The Early Illuminated Books*, ed. Morris Eaves, Robert N. Essick, and Joseph Viscomi (London: William Blake Trust/Tate Gallery, 1993), pp. 118–19.

45 G. E. Bentley, Jr, *Blake Records* (Oxford: Clarendon Press, 1969), pp. 312–13.

46 *The Complete Poetry and Prose of William Blake*, ed. David V. Erdman (New York: Doubleday, 1988), p. 609.

47 James D. Boulger, *The Calvinist Temper in English Poetry* (The Hague: Mouton, 1980), p. 356.

48 Ryan, *The Romantic Reformation*, p. 46.

49 Peter Ackroyd, *Blake* (London: Sinclair-Stevenson, 1995), pp. 210–11.

50 E. P. Thompson, *Witness against the Beast: William Blake and the Moral Law* (Cambridge: Cambridge University Press, 1993), pt. I. Kevin Gilmartin writes on sectarianism of the period more generally in 'Romanticism and Religious Modernity', in *The Cambridge History of English Romantic Literature*, ed. James Chandler (Cambridge: Cambridge University Press, 2009), pp. 644–7.

51 *Henry Crabb Robinson on Books and Their Writers*, ed. Edith J. Morley (3 vols., London: Dent, 1938), i. 6.

52 Duncan Wu, 'The Road to Nether Stowey', in *Metaphysical Hazlitt: Bicentenary Essays*, ed. Duncan Wu, Tom Paulin, and Uttara Natarajan (Abingdon, Oxon.: Routledge, 2005), pp. 93–4.

53 'On Court-Influence', in *The Selected Writings of William Hazlitt*, ed. Duncan Wu (9 vols., London: Pickering & Chatto, 1998), iv. 224.

54 Charles Lamb, 'Living Without God in the World', l. 46.

55 See, *inter alia*, Stephen Prickett, *Romanticism and Religion: The Tradition of Coleridge and Wordsworth in the Victorian Church* (Cambridge: Cambridge University Press, 1976), and Luke Savin Herrick Wright, *Samuel Taylor Coleridge and the Anglican Church* (Notre Dame, IN: University of Notre Dame Press, 2010), pp. 145, 181.

56 Priestman, *Romantic Atheism*, pp. 131–2.

57 Ibid., pp. 225–8.

58 Peter Garside points out that Hogg's target is the 'misuse of religion generally'; see *The Private Memoirs and Confessions of a Justified Sinner*, ed. P. D. Garside (Edinburgh: Edinburgh University Press, 2001), pp. xxviii–xxix.

59 S. T. Coleridge to John Thelwall, 22 June 1796, in *Collected Letters of Samuel Taylor Coleridge*, ed. Griggs, i. 221–2.

Figure 23   Lord Byron smoking a cigar in an illustration that hints at stronger substances with its inclusion, on the borders, of hookahs.
Source: Paul F. Betz Collection.

Myth
28
THE ROMANTICS WERE COUNTER-CULTURAL DRUG USERS

Any vaguely detailed study of Romanticism exposes the huge level of drug use amongst Romantic era writers.

KwikMed website

Drug use is a very common practice in the romantic artist.

Cognitive Circle website

The idea that opium opens the floodgates of inspiration is as old as the Romantic period, perhaps older. Reviewing 'Kubla Khan' in 1816, Hazlitt and Jeffrey said the poem 'smells strongly, it must be owned, of the anodyne' (Coleridge's word for the drug), implying it could have been written only under the influence,[1] while the *Monthly Review* quoted Kenelm Digby: 'he is more beholding to Morpheus for learned and rational as well as pleasing dreams, than to Mercury for smart and facetious conceptions'.[2] This has sometimes been coupled with another myth – that of genius gripped by inspiration, composing great poetry spontaneously (see Myth 6). It is some distance from the truth.

The therapeutic properties of opium have been known for more than 6,000 years. From the time of the Greek philosopher Galen, it was a cure-all – the answer to depression, earache, toothache, diarrhoea, gout, coughs, colds, and rheumatism. A well-known antidote to sleeplessness, it 'undoubtedly found its way into every home'.[3] More serious ailments

30 Great Myths About the Romantics, First Edition. Duncan Wu.
© 2015 John Wiley & Sons, Ltd. Published 2015 by John Wiley & Sons, Ltd.

such as syphilis, tuberculosis, cholera, and dysentery were treated with it, as well as insanity, the menopause, and 'women's ailments' in general. In his *Elements of Medicine* (1795), Dr John Brown made opium central to his regimen, to the dismay of those alert to the dangers of prolonged use. That made little difference: a huge industry was predicated on it. Even the poorest could obtain opium from street hawkers and country peddlers, from grocers, general stores, clothing stores, and at markets. Many purchased it from apothecaries or druggists such as the Quaker William Allen, a close friend of Humphry Davy, who included among the sixteen preparations sold in 1810 at his Plough Court shop off Lombard Street a syrup, an extract, and numerous forms of laudanum, the most popular of the over-the-counter preparations (cheaper than either beer or gin).[4] Others stocked it in the form of vinegar, wine, lozenge, powder, confection, or liniment, as well as local preparations such as Kendal Black Drop (said to be four times stronger than laudanum), favoured by Coleridge and De Quincey.[5] Another rendering, Lancaster Black Drop, was said to contain crushed pearls, nutmeg, saffron, crab apple, and yeast.[6] The combination of widespread availability and readiness to self-medicate meant that, 'at all levels of society, opium and laudanum were commonly and unselfconsciously bought and used'.[7]

This was encouraged by the government, which kept import duty on opium low at 9 shillings per pound up to 1826 (the bulk of it shipped from Turkey); that decreased, until by 1860 taxation was eliminated entirely. In 1830, Britain imported 22,000 pounds of it; three decades later that amount had quadrupled. It has rightly been described as 'the largest commerce of the time in any single commodity' and was highly lucrative.[8] An army of people was involved, including Jane Austen's brother Francis, who made £1,500 from a voyage to China in 1809, largely by importing opium.[9] John Wordsworth, younger brother of the poet, made a profit of £100 on a chest of opium brought back from China in 1797, and at the time of his death in 1805 was embarked on another journey in the hope of making even more.[10]

Coleridge and De Quincey are cited as exemplary of the Romantic artist, liberal in their use of narcotics in pursuit of unfettered creativity. But that would be to ignore the fact that they lived in a society in which opium was the most effective analgesic available, legally available to anyone who could afford it, and in which it was self-administered as a panacea for almost everything. That is to say, they would have been exceptional had they not used it.

Coleridge was given laudanum when seriously ill with jaundice and rheumatic fever as a schoolboy of 18 at Christ's Hospital; to that early encounter Dr James Gillman attributed 'all his bodily sufferings in future life'.[11] Coleridge would continue to dose himself, sometimes when afflicted with rheumatism or other physical problems, sometimes to correct feelings of depression: 'Dejection meant an opium jag; opium meant further neglect of work and more domestic fighting; these brought anxiety and guilt; anxiety and guilt in turn meant more opium; more opium spelled illness and so the tragic carousel revolved.'[12] But Coleridge had good reason for taking it: for the best part of his life he suffered from rheumatic disease, which would ultimately cause the heart failure that would kill him. Opium provided the only available symptomatic relief.[13]

Coleridge's surrender to chronic addiction took place in Malta, where he went to seek a cure. By the time he was back in London, in the autumn of 1806, his body chemistry was wholly dependent on the drug: 'His world was now the junkie's exclusive world of irrational, irrelevant delusion.'[14] That was why he believed he saw Wordsworth having sex with his own sister-in-law, Sara Hutchinson,[15] and why his lectures at the British Institution in early 1808 faltered: opium left him incapable of rising from his bed, unable to concentrate.[16] It made him no easier to live with. His addiction was punctuated by screaming fits, hysteria, and inebriation.

Coleridge's 1816 Preface to 'Kubla Khan' is one reason for the misconception that the Romantics found inspiration in drugs. Those who make that claim do not always attend to what he actually says: 'In consequence of a slight disposition, an anodyne had been prescribed.' And in the manuscript of the poem, probably dating from a time before publication was envisaged, he noted: 'This fragment with a good deal more, not recoverable, composed in a sort of reverie brought on by two grains of opium taken to check a dysentery.'[17] It was taken for medicinal purposes, not to inspire poetry. In any case, Molly Lefebure suggests, most of the poetry Coleridge wrote under its influence was 'doggerel', while Alethea Hayter thinks 'Kubla Khan' cannot have 'emerged complete, word for word as it now stands, from his reverie. Its pattern of images and sounds is too polished for that to be possible. He must have worked on it afterwards.'[18] If either is right, the myth of the Romantic poet inspired by opium becomes harder to argue.

De Quincey said he was 18 when he self-medicated for a toothache that tormented him for nearly three weeks but, as Robert Morrison has shown, this is probably a fiction. He had almost certainly taken opium before that. In any case, he recounted his first fix in typical style:

> Heavens! what a revulsion! what an upheaving, from its lowest depths, of the inner spirit! what an apocalypse of the world within me! That my pains had vanished, was now a trifle in my eyes: – this negative effect was swallowed up in the immensity of those positive effects which had opened before me – in the abyss of divine enjoyment thus suddenly revealed. Here was a panacea ... for all human woes: here was the secret happiness, about which philosophers had disputed for so many ages, at once discovered: happiness might now be bought for a penny, and carried in the waistcoat pocket ....[19]

He continued to take opium not for its curative properties but because he enjoyed the relief it gave from anxiety, increased intellectual activity, and the occasional sense of euphoria. He also believed it protected him from tuberculosis, from which his father died at the age of 39. As Morrison observes, 'More than half a century later, De Quincey remained convinced laudanum staved off tuberculosis, and had saved him from an early grave.'[20] He boosted his intake when sitting examinations at Oxford, believing it the key to 'imaginative insight and vast intellectual exertion',[21] after which opium became a daily necessity. At its peak, his addiction led him to consume 480 grains, or 12,000 drops of laudanum, a day.[22] Sara Hutchinson reported he was 'often tipsey .... He doses himself with Opium & drinks like a fish'.[23]

De Quincey's *Confessions of an English Opium Eater* (1821) 'invents recreational drug-taking'.[24] No one before him had written about it as if it were a supernatural power: 'Oh! just, subtle, and mighty opium! that to the hearts of poor and rich alike, for the wounds that will never heal, and for "the pangs that tempt the spirit to rebel," bringest an assuaging balm.'[25] The musicality of his cadences suggests he may have been on opium as he wrote; if so, it was for medical reasons – to combat 'my infernal persecution, the Rheumatism' and 'a sore throat which ... increased into a return of fever'.[26] Perhaps he hoped it would increase his productivity; if so, he was disappointed: 'his Copy comes in so very slow that I cannot complete anything more for want of it', complained John Taylor, his publisher.[27] It can be no coincidence that the two most opium-addicted writers among the Romantics, Coleridge and De Quincey, were in the habit of projecting ambitious literary projects they failed to write; in 1821, his publishers gave De Quincey an advance of £157. 10s. on a novel he never produced.[28]

Although the *Confessions* enjoyed 'a generally favourable reception',[29] some reviewers condemned its author for consorting with prostitutes and indulging in the 'moral turpitude' of opium consumption,[30] though the *Medical Intelligencer* (of all papers) concluded its account of this 'beautiful narrative' by saying it should be more widely used.[31] Far from prompting demands for legal sanctions, De Quincey's memoir renewed interest in the drug, and encouraged readers to try it.[32] It enjoyed considerable popularity on the Continent: Alfred de Musset's translation influenced the opium dream section of Berlioz's *Symphonie Fantastique* (1830), while Baudelaire produced his own translation which contained additions to the original.[33] As people became more aware of the dangers of drug addiction, De Quincey's advocacy of opium drew criticism; having taken the drug to treat his insomnia, Thomas Carlyle exclaimed, 'Better, a thousand times better, *die* than have anything to do with such a Devil's own drug!'[34] It was true De Quincey had presented opium as 'the true hero of the tale',[35] but he resisted the idea that he had misled readers: 'Teach opium-eating! – Did I teach wine-drinking? Did I reveal the mystery of sleeping? ... My faith is – that no man is likely to adopt opium or to lay it aside in consequence of anything he may read in a book.'[36]

One did not have to be a qualified apothecary to dose oneself with laudanum – but that's what John Keats was when in 1818 he administered it to his dying brother Tom and himself, plagued as he was by a sore throat and raging tooth.[37] It was the standard treatment for such ailments, and Keats's recent biographer, Nicholas Roe, suggests he continued with it while consumption took hold throughout the spring of 1819; according to Roe, opium may have inspired Keats's 'Ode on Indolence'.[38] When he set out for Italy the following year, he took sufficient to end his life if the suffering became too much, though he was denied that mercy when his friend Joseph Severn confiscated it.[39]

Keats, Coleridge, and De Quincey were not alone. Byron and Shelley occasionally took opium: Lady Byron found Black Drop in her husband's trunk with a copy of De Sade's *Justine*; Shelley started taking opium at Eton and at times was 'a compulsive and immoderate user'.[40] When Dorothy Wordsworth descended into dementia in the 1830s, she was given opium as a sedative and soon became addicted. When her brother tried to wean her off it, she flew into violent rages. 'We can give *her no* neighbours but ourselves', wrote Mary Wordsworth, 'or she would terrify strangers to death.'[41] Contemporaries who shared her dependency included the poets Mary Robinson and George Crabbe, the actor John Philip Kemble, politician William Wilberforce, Clive of India, the banker and economist Philip Thornton, Charles Lloyd, George Burnett, landscape gardener John Loudon, photographer Tom Wedgwood, James Mackintosh, and Baptist preacher Robert Hall. Their status indicates opium use was not confined to those of a single social class; it was widespread.

Even George IV consumed it, though to say so would be an understatement. He had been addicted since 1811 when he twisted his ankle while attempting the highland fling, the treatment being 100 drops of laudanum every three hours. Accession to the throne unleashed a series of binges; by 1827 he needed 100 drops before he could face Lord Aberdeen, the Foreign Secretary. In 1828 bladder pains led him to increase his intake, and he would spend entire days in a stupor. By his final year, he was on 250 drops a day. 'What do you think of His breakfast yesterday for an Invalid?' Wellington enquired in April 1830. 'A Pidgeon and Beef Steak Pye of which he ate two Pigeons and three Beef-Steaks, Three parts of a bottle of Mozelle, a Glass of Dry Champagne, two Glasses of Port & a

Glass of Brandy! He had taken Laudanum the night before, again before this breakfast, again last night and again this Morning!' Two months later, the 'spoiled, selfish, odious beast' (as he was described by Charles Greville, clerk to the Privy Council) was dead.[42]

The myth is that by using drugs the Romantics were being transgressive. Nothing could be further from the truth: it was conventional behaviour. Nor were they seeking to stimulate creativity. None of De Quincey's longer works was written when his addiction was at its peak, though 'partial withdrawal, total abstinence, a low but steady addiction, or inter-mittent boosts, seem all to have been propitious to his creative powers at one time or another. De Quincey's case reinforces the conclusion that opium neither promotes nor inhibits literary output; it only influences the kind and quality that is put out.'[43] De Quincey's *Suspiria de Profundis*, for instance, was not written while its author was consuming vast quan-tities of opium, even though one of its leading subjects is addiction. Not that this precludes the possibility De Quincey experimented with it, just as William S. Burroughs was to do in the 1950s, in 'a spirit of scientific curiosity'.[44] Neither would have claimed he was in search of inspiration, and there is little evidence that opium is much use for that purpose.

Notes

1 *New Writings of William Hazlitt*, ed. Duncan Wu (2 vols., Oxford: Oxford University Press, 2007), i. 215. The attribution to Hazlitt and Jeffrey is mine.

2 *Coleridge: The Critical Heritage*, ed. J. R. de J. Jackson (London: Routledge & Kegan Paul, 1970), pp. 246–7.

3 Virginia Berridge and Griffith Edwards, *Opium and the People: Opium Use in Nineteenth-Century England* (London: Allen Lane, 1981), p. xxv.

4 A. E. Musson and Eric Robinson, *Science and Technology in the Industrial Revolution* (Reading, Berks.: Gordon & Breach, 1989), pp. 137–8; Alethea Hayter, *Opium and the Romantic Imagination* (London: Faber & Faber, 1968), p. 33.

5 See Molly Lefebure, *The Bondage of Love: A Life of Mrs Samuel Taylor Coleridge* (London: Gollancz, 1988), p. 134.

6 Thomas Dormandy, *The Worst of Evils: The Fight Against Pain* (New Haven: Yale University Press, 2006), p. 133.

7 Berridge and Edwards, *Opium and the People*, pp. 34–5, 49.

8 Richard E. Matlak, *Deep Distresses: William Wordsworth, John Wordsworth, Sir George Beaumont 1800–1808* (Cranbury, NJ: Associated University Presses, 2003), p. 36.

9 Paul Byrne, *The Real Jane Austen: A Life in Small Things* (New York: Harper-Collins, 2013), p. 251.

10 *The Letters of John Wordsworth*, ed. Carl E. Ketcham (Ithaca, NY: Cornell University Press, 1969), pp. 41, 143; Matlak, *Deep Distresses*, p. 47. These exploits have been the subject of enquiry by Peter J. Kitson, 'The Wordsworths, Opium, and China', *The Wordsworth Circle* 43 (Winter 2012), 2–12.

11 As quoted in Molly Lefebure, *Samuel Taylor Coleridge: A Bondage of Opium* (London: Quartet, 1977), p. 83.

12 Ibid., p. 328.

13 Ibid., pp. 46–9.

14 Ibid., p. 447.

15 Ibid., pp. 452–3; Duncan Wu, *Wordsworth: An Inner Life* (Oxford: Blackwell, 2002), p. 275.

16 The sad details are given in Samuel Taylor Coleridge, *Lectures 1808–1819: On Literature*, ed. R. A. Foakes (2 vols., Princeton, NJ: Princeton University Press, 1987), i. 11–21.

17 *Romanticism: An Anthology*, ed. Duncan Wu (4th ed., Oxford: Wiley-Blackwell, 2012), pp. 639, 642.

18 Lefebure, *Coleridge: A Bondage of Opium*, p. 254; Hayter, *Opium and the Romantic Imagination*, p. 223.

19 Thomas De Quincey, *Confessions of an English Opium-Eater and Other Writings*, ed. Robert Morrison (Oxford: Oxford University Press, 2013), p. 39.

20 Robert Morrison, *The English Opium Eater: A Biography of Thomas De Quincey* (London: Weidenfeld & Nicolson, 2009), p. 107.

21 Ibid., p. 133.

22 Ibid., p. 163.

23 Quoted ibid., p. 174.

24 Ibid., p. 207.

25 De Quincey, *Confessions of an English Opium-Eater*, p. 49.

26 Morrison, *The English Opium Eater*, p. 205.

27 Tim Chilcott, *A Publisher and His Circle: The Life and Work of John Taylor, Keats's Publisher* (London: Routledge & Kegan Paul, 1972), p. 137.

28 Ibid., p. 140.

29 John O. Hayden, 'De Quincey's *Confessions* and the Reviewers', *The Wordsworth Circle* 6 (1975), 273–9, p. 273.

30 Ibid., p. 277.

31 Ibid.

32 See Morrison, *The English Opium Eater*, pp. 211–12.

33 E. S. Burt, *Regard for the Other: Autothanatography in Rousseau, De Quincey, Baudelaire, and Wilde* (Bronx, NY: Fordham University Press, 2009), pp. 176–9.

34 Morrison, *The English Opium Eater*, p. 211.

35 De Quincey, *Confessions of an English Opium-Eater*, p. 77.

36 Ibid., pp. 250–1.

37 See Nicholas Roe, *John Keats: A New Life* (New Haven: Yale University Press, 2012), p. 264.

38 Ibid., pp. 307, 309.

39 Ibid., p. 394.
40 Nora Crook and Derek Guiton, *Shelley's Venomed Melody* (Cambridge: Cambridge University Press, 1986), p. 30. See also Newman Ivey White, *Shelley* (2 vols., London: Secker & Warburg, 1947), ii. 108; Malcolm Elwin, *Lord Byron's Wife* (London: Macdonald, 1962), p. 413; Leslie A. Marchand, *Byron: A Biography* (3 vols., New York: Alfred A. Knopf, 1957), ii. 559.
41 Mary Wordsworth to Mary Hutchinson, 8 October 1838, in *The Letters of Mary Wordsworth*, ed. Mary E. Burton (Oxford: Clarendon Press, 1958), p. 218. See also Lucy Newlyn, *William and Dorothy Wordsworth: 'All in Each Other'* (Oxford: Oxford University Press, 2013), p. 292.
42 Richard Davenport-Hines, *The Pursuit of Oblivion: A Global History of Narcotics* (New York: W. W. Norton, 2004), pp. 63–5; E. A. Smith, *George IV* (New Haven: Yale University Press, 1999), p. 269.
43 Hayter, *Opium and the Romantic Imagination*, p. 233.
44 Ted Morgan, *Literary Outlaw: The Life and Times of William S. Burroughs* (New York: Avon Books, 1988), p. 121. The necessary distinctions to be made between the Romantics and the Beats are indicated by Al Alvarez, 'Drugs and Inspiration', *Social Research* 68 (2001), 779–93.

Myth 29

THE ROMANTICS PRACTISED FREE LOVE ON PRINCIPLE

I cry, Love! Love! Love! happy happy Love! free as the mountain wind!

Blake, *Visions of the Daughters of Albion*, plate 10[1]

It is often claimed the Romantics engaged in free love, in the sense that they swapped sexual partners regardless of marital status. At this period such behaviour was highly unconventional, and of those who preached it few were practitioners. For progressives, hypocrisy was the norm, even in the case of William Godwin, whose proto-anarchistic *Political Justice* (1793) envisaged a rationalistic world in which all property would be shared, including sexual partners. 'The abolition of marriage will be attended with no evils', he declared,

> We are apt to represent it to ourselves as the harbinger of brutal lust and depravity. But it really happens (in this as in other cases) that the positive laws which are made to restrain our vices, irritate and multiply them – not to say that the same sentiments of justice and happiness which in a state of equal property would destroy the relish for luxury, would decrease our inordinate appetites of every kind, and lead us universally to prefer the pleasures of intellect to the pleasures of sense.[2]

Godwin saw himself not as the advocate of promiscuity but as the herald of a new society governed by 'pleasures of intellect'. He foresaw a world in which the species would be propagated by 'reasonable men … regulated by the dictates of reason and duty',[3] disinclined to

30 Great Myths About the Romantics, First Edition. Duncan Wu.
© 2015 John Wiley & Sons, Ltd. Published 2015 by John Wiley & Sons, Ltd.

Figure 24 William Godwin (1756–1836) described marriage as 'the most odious of all monopolies', but it was a careless reading of his work that led acolytes to regard him as the advocate of free love.
Source: Paul F. Betz Collection.

pursue sexual gratification for its own sake. If that was 'free love' as the Romantics understood it, it was a misnomer, for Godwin nowhere used the word 'love' in *Political Justice*. His Utopia was governed by reason, the dominance of which would render marriage (along with other institutions) useless. In time, he predicted, sexual activity would diminish, to be used only for 'rational' acts of procreation. It was a cerebral, ascetic vision that would be misinterpreted as providing licence for excess.

Mary Wollstonecraft was a more austere thinker than Godwin. Her wish was that 'chastity must more universally prevail',[4] and that when people married, they 'ought not to continue to love each other with passion'[5] – an anti-sensualist vision in which sex was purely functional. Wollstonecraft described monogamous marriage as 'the best refuge from care',[6] and that may be the most important reason why critics of the institution continued nonetheless to wed, as when Godwin took his vows with Wollstonecraft in March 1797. It was a paradoxical step for the man who condemned marriage as 'an affair of property, and the worst of all properties',[7] but Wollstonecraft was insistent: she was pregnant, and wanted her child to have a father.[8]

The propensity of Godwin's acolytes to misconceive him is illustrated by three of the most famous – Samuel Taylor Coleridge, Robert Southey, and Robert Lovell – who, in 1794, planned a 'pantisocratic' commune in America on rationalist principles. It was as well they got no further than the planning stage because they were never more than lukewarm about Godwin's views on marriage: why else begin by marrying the women they intended to take with them (Coleridge tied the knot with Sara Fricker, Southey with her sister Edith, and Robert Lovell her sister Mary)? Free love as a concept sits uneasily with Southey's account of the scheme by which 'every motive for vice should be annihilated and every motive for virtue strengthened',[9] and with Coleridge's letter to John Thelwall of 13 May 1796, in which he asked

> Why should you not have intercourse with *the Wife* of your friend? ... Because it would be *criminal*? What more do we mean by *Marriage* than that state in which it would be criminal to tempt to, or permit, an act of inconstancy? But if criminal *at one moment*, criminal always: in other words, *Marriage is indissoluble*.[10]

The evidence suggests Southey and Coleridge soon came to regret the adoption of what they assumed to be the Godwinian view of marriage.[11]

Nonetheless they were, at least for a brief time, Godwinians, along with William Wordsworth, Basil Montagu, Francis Place, and James Webbe Tobin. Wordsworth's later recollection was that Godwin's philosophy 'promised to abstract the hopes of man / Out of his feelings',[12] yet its denial of emotion caused him to reject it. It was fast receding from the public consciousness by the time Godwin published his *Memoir of Wollstonecraft* (1798), which precipitated a hailstorm of abuse, Robert Bisset in the *Anti-Jacobin Review* using Wollstonecraft's unhappy affair with Gilbert Imlay as basis for a lampoon: 'We must observe, that Mary's theory, that it is the right of women to indulge their inclinations with every man they like, is so far from being new, that it is as old as prostitution.'[13] Wollstonecraft was never the advocate of promiscuity, but that was not the point: the Tory practice of smearing radicals by association with immorality was well under way.[14]

One weapon was the novel, several of which targeted Godwin's philosophy, including Charles Lloyd's *Edmund Oliver* (1798), Sophia King's *Waldorf* (1798), and Edward Dubois's *St Godwin* (1800).[15] That with most impact was the work of a former friend. Amelia Alderson met Godwin in the summer of 1794 when she perceptively observed that 'his theory had not yet gotten entire ascendancy over his practice'.[16] Their dalliance reached the point at which she could tell Wollstonecraft that 'every day pass'd with him, has indeared him to me more strongly – and made me cease to regret he was not what I expected to find him'.[17] In August 1796, having spoken with her, Wollstonecraft teased Godwin that 'you, I'm told, were ready to devour her – in your little parlour. Elle est tres jolie – n'est pas?'[18] Two days later Alderson asked Wollstonecraft whether Godwin '*ever* kissed a maiden fair'.[19]

After Wollstonecraft and Godwin began their own affair they lost touch with her – not surprisingly. Alderson took her revenge with a fiction, *Adeline Mowbray* (1805), published after she married portrait painter John Opie. Its heroine falls for a philosophical anarchist, Frederic Glenmurray, 'who drew so delightful a picture of the superior purity, as well as happiness, of an union cemented by no ties but those of love and honour'.[20] On his deathbed Glenmurray urges Adeline to marry his kinsman, Charles Berrendale. Adeline does so, but Berrendale runs off with another woman, precipitating Adeline's deathbed recantation:

> I am convinced, that if the ties of marriage were dissolved, or it were no longer judged infamous to act in contempt of them, unbridled licentiousness would soon be in general practice …. marriage is a wise and ought to be a sacred institution; and I bitterly regret the hour when, with the hasty and immature judgement of eighteen, and with a degree of presumption scarcely pardonable at any time of life, I dared to think and act contrary to this opinion and the reverend experience of ages, and became in the eyes of the world an example of vice, when I believed myself the champion of virtue.[21]

The renunciation misrepresents Mowbray's real-life model, Mary Wollstonecraft. Neither she nor Godwin was an advocate of 'unbridled licentiousness', but by employing such terms Opie bolstered the popular view of them as libertines.[22]

Harriet Westbrook gave a copy of *Adeline Mowbray* to Percy Bysshe Shelley shortly before they eloped to Scotland in August 1811.[23] It was a weirdly prophetic gesture (how many times in after-years must she have rued her association with him?), as well as pointed: she wanted him to marry her, and thought the novel might tip the balance. She was right to be anxious. Shelley was a militant Godwinian who, months before, told his friend Thomas Jefferson Hogg, '*marriage* is hateful detestable, – a kind of ineffable sickening disgust seizes my mind when I think of this most despotic most unrequired fetter which prejudice has forged to confine it's energies'.[24] That was what he believed but, confronted with

Harriet's urgings, he agreed to matrimony; in that respect, he followed in his mentor's footsteps, as St Clair points out: 'Shelley, like Godwin, reluctantly chose hypocrisy.'[25] That did not prevent him proposing that another female friend, Elizabeth Hitchener, join their *ménage*, or encouraging Thomas Jefferson Hogg in his infatuation, first, with Harriet and then with Godwin's daughter Mary.[26] These were failed attempts to realize what he mistakenly believed the doctrines of *Political Justice* to be.

Shelley's attachment to rationalism found its articulation in *Queen Mab*, the notes to which provide a preposterously elaborate scaffolding of anarchist, socialist, republican, atheist, and vegetarian propaganda: 'Love is free: to promise for ever to love the same woman, is not less absurd than to promise to believe the same creed: such a vow, in both cases, excludes us from all enquiry.'[27] Marriage, he wrote, was 'a despotism'[28] and should be abolished. Were that to happen, he said, 'I by no means assert that the intercourse would be promiscuous'.[29] Lawyers prosecuting the poem in 1821 pleaded these views be prohibited from general circulation, but in vain:[30] *Queen Mab* was pirated many times and became 'Shelley's most easily available, most frequently printed, cheapest, and most widely read book'.[31] It was also one of the most energetically condemned: appalled by its 'pages of raving atheism', the *Literary Gazette* imagined that

> A disciple following his tenets, would not hesitate to debauch, or, after debauching, to abandon any woman: to such, it would be a matter of perfect indifference to rob a confiding father of his daughters, and incestuously to live with all the branches of a family whose morals were ruined by the damned sophistry of the seducer; to such it would be a sport to tell a deserted wife to obtain with her pretty face support by prostitution; and, when the unhappy maniac sought refuge in self-destruction, to laugh at the fool while in the arms of associate strumpets.[32]

Like most of literary London, whoever wrote this was aware of the human wreckage that littered the poet's trail. Shelley had known Godwin's 16-year-old daughter Mary for a mere two months when in early July 1814 he proposed they run off to Switzerland. He probably thought Godwin would not object, the philosopher having written in *Political Justice*: 'So long as two human beings are forbidden by positive institution to follow the dictates of their own mind, prejudice is alive and vigorous.'[33] But an unbridgeable chasm divided theory and practice. Incensed, Godwin refused permission for the escapade, only for Shelley, Mary, and Jane Clairmont to elope as a threesome. Shelley wanted also to take his wife Harriet, who would have been, like Jane, a non-sexual participant, but she refused, thinking her husband 'profligate and sensual, owing entirely to Godwin's *Political Justice*'.[34] Fanny Wollstonecraft (the orphaned child of Mary Wollstonecraft and Gilbert Imlay) attempted to mediate between Shelley and Godwin, the stress of which led her to suicide in October 1816.[35] A few weeks later Harriet was fished out of the Serpentine, in which she had committed suicide; she was pregnant, having cohabited with several men as the sole means of maintaining herself.

By this time, Shelley, Mary, and Jane (who had now changed her name to Claire) had visited the Continent a second time, where they were said to be embroiled (with Byron) in a 'league of incest'. Byron attributed the rumour to Robert Southey (who had seen the hotel register in which Shelley described himself as an atheist[36]); it was untrue, as he told John Murray:

> I understand the scoundrel said, on his return from Switzerland two years ago, that 'Shelley and I were in a league of Incest, etc., etc.' He is a burning liar! for the women to whom he alludes are not sisters – one being Godwin's daughter, by Mary Wollstonecraft, and the other daughter of the *present* (second) Mrs. G, by a *former* husband; and in the next place, if they had even been so, there was no *promiscuous intercourse* whatever.[37]

Byron never forgave Southey, attacking him in the Dedication to *Don Juan* (1819) and other works, including *The Vision of Judgement* (1822).[38] But his ire was misdirected: the true culprit was lawyer and politician Henry Brougham. Thanks to him, Lady Frances Shelley believed in summer 1816 that 'Lord Byron is living near here with Percy Shelley, or rather, with his wife's sister, as the *chronique scandaleuse* says',[39] and Lady Anne Romilly reported that Byron 'and his equally delectable party ... lived together in a way to shock common decency'.[40] Had that been true, it would have owed nothing to Godwin and Wollstonecraft. Nor did their theories have any bearing on the marriage of Percy Shelley and Mary Godwin on 30 December 1816, in accordance with English law and the rites of the Anglican Church.[41]

William Blake was absent from the wedding but had known Shelley's mother-in-law, Mary Wollstonecraft, and perhaps had her futile pursuit of Henry Fuseli (a married bisexual) in mind when composing *Visions of the Daughters of Albion* (1793). Its editors suggest 'Oothoon's rejection of jealousy and her willingness to find "girls" for Theotormon's pleasure may be idealized projections of what Blake hoped, but did not receive, from Catherine' (his wife).[42] That is not editorial whimsy: Blake once shocked his straitlaced friend Henry Crabb Robinson by telling him 'wives should be in common',[43] while G. E. Bentley, Jr, reminds me that Part I of George Cumberland's novel, *The Captive of the Castle of Sennaar* (1796), describes an alternative society the inhabitants of which, besides being vegetarians, were exponents of free love and naturism. Blake read it eagerly and was friendly with its author.[44] But that proves nothing about his practice and, so far as we know, he never strayed from his wife.

One of the few known practitioners of the day was radical writer and publisher Richard Carlile, whose Zetetic movement in the mid- to late 1820s advocated women's rights, contraception, and free-love liaisons; he led by example, engaging in such a relationship with Eliza Sharples, citing as inspiration the work of Shelley, Godwin, and Wollstonecraft who (misunderstood or not) would encourage subsequent free-love advocates on both sides of the Atlantic.[45] But in practising what he preached Carlile remained in a minority. Those who promoted free love tended to be conventional in practice because women had the ultimate say: for them, marriage promised a modicum of security, something not otherwise in plentiful supply.

Notes

1 William Blake, *The Early Illuminated Books*, ed. Morris Eaves, Robert N. Essick, and Joseph Viscomi (London: William Blake Trust/Tate Gallery, 1993), p. 260.
2 *Romanticism: An Anthology*, ed. Duncan Wu (4th ed., Oxford: Wiley-Blackwell, 2012), p. 159.
3 Ibid., p. 160.
4 Mary Wollstonecraft, *A Vindication of the Rights of Woman* (3rd ed., London: J. Johnson, 1796), pp. vii–viii.
5 Ibid., p. 58.
6 Ibid., p. 269.
7 *Romanticism: An Anthology*, ed. Wu, p. 159.
8 St Clair calls Godwin's marriage to Wollstonecraft 'a shameful and squalid compromise': William St Clair, *The Godwins and the Shelleys: The Biography of a Family* (London: Faber & Faber, 1989), p. 170.
9 Robert Southey to Horace Walpole Bedford, 22 August 1794, in *New Letters of Robert Southey*, ed. Kenneth Curry (2 vols., New York: Columbia University Press, 1965), i. 70.
10 S. T. Coleridge to John Thelwall, 13 May 1796, in *Collected Letters of Samuel Taylor Coleridge*, ed. Earl Leslie Griggs (6 vols., Oxford: Clarendon Press, 1956–71), i. 213.
11 I am grateful to Seamus Perry for assistance in this matter. See also St Clair, *The Godwins and the Shelleys*, p. 97; Michael Wiley, *Romantic Migrations: Local, National and Transnational Dispositions* (New York: Palgrave Macmillan, 2008), p. 67; and Anya Taylor, *Erotic Coleridge: Women, Love, and the Law against Divorce* (New York: Palgrave Macmillan, 2005), pp. 22–3.
12 Wordsworth, *The Thirteen-Book Prelude*, x. 807–8.

13 *The Anti-Jacobin Review and Magazine* 1 (July 1798), 94–102, p. 97. The attribution to Bisset is given by Emily Lorraine de Montluzin, *The Anti-Jacobins 1798–1800: The Early Contributors to the 'Anti-Jacobin Review'* (Houndmills, Basingstoke: Macmillan, 1988), p. 165.

14 A helpful summary of the critical reception is given by Pamela Clemit and Gina Luria Walker in their edition of Godwin's *Memoirs* (Peterborough, Ont.: Broadview, 2001), pp. 32–6.

15 For details on these and other anti-Godwinian novels, see Peter Marshall, *William Godwin* (New Haven: Yale University Press, 1984), pp. 217–18.

16 St Clair, *The Godwins and the Shelleys*, p. 148.

17 Ibid., p. 165.

18 Mary Wollstonecraft to William Godwin, 4 August 1796, in *Godwin and Mary: Letters of William Godwin and Mary Wollstonecraft*, ed. Ralph M. Wardle (London: Constable, 1967), p. 12.

19 Mary Wollstonecraft to William Godwin, 6 August 1796, ibid.

20 Amelia Opie, *Adeline Mowbray; or The Mother and Daughter* (3 vols., London: Longman, 1805), i. 37.

21 Ibid., iii. 208–10.

22 That may be why, having read it in 1812, Dorothy Wordsworth wrote: 'Adeline Mowbray made us quite sick before we got to the end of it': letter to William Wordsworth, 23 April 1812, in *The Letters of William and Dorothy Wordsworth*, iii, *The Middle Years, Part 2: 1812–1820*, ed. Ernest de Selincourt, rev. Mary Moorman and Alan G. Hill (2nd ed., Oxford: Clarendon Press, 1970), p. 7. Critics continue to disagree over their interpretations of this novel; for various views, see, *inter alia*, Roxanne Eberle, 'Amelia Opie's *Adeline Mowbray*: Diverting the Libertine Gaze; or, the Vindication of a Fallen Woman', *Studies in the Novel* 26 (1994), 121–52; Carol Howard, 'The Story of the Pineapple: Sentimental Abolitionism and Moral Motherhood in Amelia Opie's *Adeline Mowbray*', *Studies in the Novel* 30 (1998), 355–76; Joanne Tong, 'The Return of the Prodigal Daughter: Finding the Family in Amelia Opie's Novels', *Studies in the Novel* 36 (2004), 465–83; and Claire Tomalin, *The Life and Death of Mary Wollstonecraft* (London: Weidenfeld & Nicolson, 1974), pp. 238–9.

23 F. S. Schwarzbach, 'Harriet 1812: Harriet Shelley's Commonplace Book', *Huntington Library Quarterly* 56 (1993), 40–66, p. 45.

24 Percy Bysshe Shelley to Thomas Jefferson Hogg, 8 May 1811, in *The Letters of Percy Bysshe Shelley*, ed. Frederick L. Jones (2 vols., Oxford: Clarendon Press, 1964), i. 80.

25 St Clair, *The Godwins and the Shelleys*, p. 322.

26 James Bieri deals with Hogg's attempt to seduce Harriet in *Percy Bysshe Shelley: A Biography* (2 vols., Newark: University of Delaware Press, 2004–5), i. 213–14. For the love letters between Mary and Hogg, see Muriel Spark, *Mary Shelley* (London: Cardinal, 1989), pp. 42–5.

27 *The Complete Poetry of Percy Bysshe Shelley*, ed. Donald H. Reiman, Neil Fraistat, et al. (3 vols. so far, Baltimore: Johns Hopkins University Press, 2000–), ii. 253.

28 Ibid.
29 Ibid., p. 255. The editors of the Johns Hopkins text point to Godwin, Wollstonecraft, and James Henry Lawrence as Shelley's sources.
30 Iain McCalman, 'Unrespectable Radicalism: Infidels and Pornography in Early Nineteenth-Century London', *Past and Present* 104 (1984), 74–110, p. 100.
31 William St Clair, *The Reading Nation in the Romantic Period* (Cambridge: Cambridge University Press, 2004), p. 320.
32 *Shelley: The Critical Heritage*, ed. James E. Barcus (London: Routledge & Kegan Paul, 1975), p. 79.
33 *Romanticism: An Anthology*, ed. Wu, p. 159.
34 St Clair, *The Godwins and the Shelleys*, p. 376.
35 Few writers have better explained the motivation than Janet Todd, *Death and the Maidens: Fanny Wollstonecraft and the Shelley Circle* (London: Profile, 2007).
36 Peter Cochran, 'Robert Southey, the "Atheist" Inscription, and the "League of Incest"', *Notes and Queries* 37 (1990), 415–18.
37 Lord Byron to John Murray, 24 November 1818, in *Byron's Letters and Journals*, ed. Leslie A. Marchand (13 vols., London: John Murray, 1973–94), vi. 82; his italics.
38 See, *inter alia*, Peter Cochran, *Byron and Bob: Lord Byron's Relationship with Robert Southey* (Newcastle-upon-Tyne: Cambridge Scholars, 2010).
39 *The Diary of Lady Frances Shelley 1787–1817*, ed. Richard Edgcumbe (2 vols., New York: Scribner's, 1912–13), i. 231.
40 *The Romilly–Edgeworth Letters 1813–1818*, ed. Samuel Henry Romilly (London: John Murray, 1936), p. 165.
41 It was, as William St Clair points out, something for which Shelley can only have been 'ashamed of his own retreat from principle' (*The Godwins and the Shelleys*, p. 417).
42 Blake, *The Early Illuminated Books*, ed. Eaves, Essick, and Viscomi, p. 231.
43 G. E. Bentley, Jr., *Blake Records* (Oxford: Clarendon Press, 1969), p. 332.
44 This fascinating novel should be read in Bentley's edition, which contains in its introduction a discussion of Blake's friendship with its author; George Cumberland, *The Captive of the Castle of Sennaar: An African Tale*, ed. G. E. Bentley, Jr (Montreal: McGill-Queen's University Press, 1991). There were other Utopian novels which criticized marriage, such as Lawrence's *The Empire of the Nairs* (1811); for its influence on Mary Shelley's *Frankenstein* see, *inter alia*, Bieri, *Percy Bysshe Shelley: A Biography*, i. 257–8, and D. S. Neff, 'The "Paradise of the Mothersons": *Frankenstein* and *The Empire of the Nairs*', *Journal of English and Germanic Philology* 95 (1996), 204–22. Thomas Love Peacock was also interested in Lawrence's novel; see Nicholas A. Joukovsky, '"A Dialogue on Idealities": An Unpublished Manuscript of Thomas Love Peacock', *Yearbook of English Studies* 7 (1977), 128–40, p. 131.
45 See in this regard, *inter alia*, Iain McCalman, 'Females, Feminism and Free Love in an Early Nineteenth Century Radical Movement', *Labour History* 38 (1980), 1–25; Sandra Stanley Holton, 'Free Love and Victorian Feminism:

The Divers Matrimonials of Elizabeth Wolstenholme and Ben Elmy', *Victorian Studies* 37 (1994), 199–222, pp. 204–5; Michael Mason, *The Making of Victorian Sexual Attitudes* (Oxford: Oxford University Press, 1994), esp. pp. 219–21; and Eugenia DeLamotte, 'Refashioning the Mind: The Revolutionary Rhetoric of Voltairine de Cleyre', *Legacy* 20 (2003), 153–74.

Myth

30

THE ROMANTICS WERE THE ROCK STARS OF THEIR DAY

The Satanic/Byronic hero is the prototypical rock star, the timeless representation of hero as outsider.

Chris Mathews, *Modern Satanism*, p. 26

1816–1819   Romantic poets Lord Byron and Percy Bysshe Shelley cavort like rock stars

Jim DeRogatis, *Turn on Your Mind: Four Decades of Great Psychedelic Rock*, entry in chronology, p. 23

The Romantic poets were the badly behaved rock stars of their time, involved with drug use and indiscriminate sex.

Carlisle K. Webber, *Gay, Lesbian, Bisexual, Transgender and Questioning Teen Literature: A Guide to Reading Interests*, p. 91

Of course they were! Look at the lives of Wollstonecraft, Coleridge, Shelley, Keats, Byron, and Lady Caroline Lamb: heedless of conventional morality; prone to wallow in recreational sex, drugs, and drink; determined to die young – what else would one call them? One recent biographer says Byron's celebrity was 'recharged by the rock culture's canonization of self-destructive artists hallowed by early death: Elvis and James Dean, while "His Satanic Majesty" Mick Jagger still pays tribute to the sneering, demonic Byron of Victorian nightmare.'[1] This may owe something to Camille Paglia's nomination of Byron as one of her

30 Great Myths About the Romantics, First Edition. Duncan Wu.
© 2015 John Wiley & Sons, Ltd. Published 2015 by John Wiley & Sons, Ltd.

'revolutionary men of beauty': 'Energy and beauty together are burning, godlike, destructive. Byron created the youth-cult that would sweep Elvis Presley to uncomfortable fame.'[2] Too erudite to be unaware how easily such comparisons can bog themselves down in nonsense, Paglia navigates the pitfalls with aplomb, but her conceit has been recycled by less knowing writers in ever more confused form.

The idea the Romantics were rock stars is sometimes espoused by those who want to sex up a subject that to a readership weaned on a predominantly visual culture might be thought to have limited appeal. These are desperate measures, but we live in desperate times when almost anything seems justified in the fight to reclaim readers from the video shack. The plight is one with which I have sympathy, and it is worth saying that, though the focus of this short essay is on ways in which the Romantics were not rock stars, there is one apparent similarity deserving of notice: Byron was the first poet to be famous in something resembling the modern sense.

Fascination with Byron as a personality culminated in a form of hysteria fuelled more by morbid fascination with his private life than by knowledge of his poetry. In 1816, on his visit to Geneva, he recalled, 'I was watched by glasses on the opposite side of the Lake, and by glasses too that must have had very distorted optics. I was waylaid in my evening drives – I was accused of corrupting all the *grisettes* in the Rue Basse.'[3] Made monstrous by the fug of scandal that followed him across the Continent, he caused Elizabeth Hervey to faint when he entered the salon at Coppet.[4] These experiences induced in him a reticence that made him 'turn my horse's head the other way'; at the sight of an Englishman.[5] But he did not stand in the same relation to fainting women as Elvis and the Beatles: it was his soiled reputation that made him a spectacle. Nonetheless, that may be sufficient to distinguish him from his peers.

When the case is argued for the Romantics at large, it is on the basis of what we call lifestyle choices, drug abuse and sexual proclivities being high on the list. But comparisons with modern crack, cocaine, and heroin addicts are misleading: as I show in Myth 28, 'hard drugs' were legally obtainable by anyone with the means to buy them – a crucial distinction because it meant the opium trade was open to view, while consumption (which did not occur intravenously, the hypodermic needle not being invented until c.1857) did not turn users into criminals. Huge numbers of all social classes, including (at the upper end) George IV (see pp. 247–8), consumed opium on a routine basis. There may have been some recreational drug use, but the drug was known to prove fatal when taken in excess, and that must have deterred many from using it for other than therapeutic reasons. Which may explain why, in an un-hip moment,

Byron confided to his diary that he had drunk grog because 'I don't like laudanum now as I used to do'.[6] And in October 1821 he told Thomas Moore he could consume laudanum 'without any effect at all' and so preferred 'a dose of *salts*' (his emphasis)[7] – which sound more like the words of someone in a convalescent home than those of a hellraiser.

Their sex lives are no easier to interpret, the last two hundred years having seen drastic changes in sexual attitudes. Advocates of the rock star myth might argue the Romantics are 'the same' as us because of the rampant sexual abandon characteristic of the latter part of the eighteenth century. The evidence is seen in increasing birth rates and the widespread availability of prostitutes in London – perhaps as many as 50,000 in 1797 (9 per cent of its female population).[8] In 1817 there were 360 brothels in just three parishes in the City employing over 2,000 prostitutes – and their trade was not concealed from view. As one historian says, prostitution was 'a fact of life',[9] most of its practitioners being based in taverns, pubs, theatres, circuses, and the pleasure-gardens of Vauxhall and Ranelagh.[10] Not only was it carried on in plain sight, it was paraded thrice daily, as streetwalkers trooped in phalanx across the city at regular hours.[11] This was a culture in which, far from being the cause of shame, a visit to the whorehouse was routine. Few poets escape suspicion: scholars speculate Wordsworth went as an undergraduate;[12] Coleridge admitted to it in his letters and notebooks;[13] Keats may have caught syphilis by that means, and was haunted for years by the memory of a prostitute he saw at Vauxhall;[14] Shelley possibly had sex with one at Eton;[15] Lamb and Hazlitt may have visited brothels *à deux*;[16] De Quincey's friendship with 'Ann' is recounted in his *Confessions* (1821), and biographers affirm (contrary to later protestations) he was on 'familiar and friendly terms' with her colleagues.[17] All of which was lawful. Prostitutes in the Romantic period engaged in a trade not prohibited by law.[18]

The most elite class comprised women whose attentions were confined to select clients, sometimes only one, whom it was proper to accompany socially and, under certain circumstances, to marry – as Emma Lyon (aka Emma Hart, Amy Lyon) became mistress to Sir William Hamilton, ambassador to the court at Naples, having been cast off by Hamilton's nephew, Charles Greville. Sir William stage-managed his future wife's 'attitudes' – a choreographed series of scantily clad poses designed to evoke heroines of classical myth, performed in front of an invited (and, one imagines, startled) audience.[19] Hamilton married his performing statue in 1791; the union seems always to have been casual, and in autumn 1798 turned into a *ménage à trois* with Admiral Horatio Nelson. Lyon's antics were unlikely to meet with distaste in a society inured to the behaviour of the royal princes who made it fashionable to live openly

Figure 25 Lady Emma Hamilton (baptized 1765, died 1815) was the focus of rumour-mongers, not least the claim that she had engaged in a lesbian relationship with the queen. Thomas Rowlandson depicts her 'Attitudes' – postures in which she impersonated classical heroines – with her much older husband holding the curtain.
Source: Bridgeman Images.

with women to whom they were not married. Maria Fitzherbert actually did marry the Prince of Wales in 1785 in a ceremony later deemed unlawful, and was rewarded with a pension of £5,000 for the remainder of her life.[20]

This might appear to support the idea that the Romantics were precursors of the modern rock star, but that would be to ignore contemporary attitudes: as one historian notes, the widespread availability of sex coincided with 'the closing down of traditional female occupations, such as midwifery, and the increasing denigration of traditional forms of female knowledge, such as those associated with magic and healing, [which] all contributed to a set of circumstances which undermined the negotiated nature of women's power and position'.[21] In Georgian England women were marginal, not permitted to have careers in the modern sense. In the bedroom, they were regarded as imperfect men and treated as receptacles, devoid of libido or any other kind of sexual need.[22] By contrast, rock stars entered the culture at the same time as a sexual revolution by which women were empowered. From the 1950s onwards, for the first time in centuries, female sexuality was made the subject of study and discussed in print. Thanks in part to their contribution to the war effort, the value of women as work colleagues was acknowledged, and they regained a footing in the workplace. And for the first time in history birth control became widely available (something that existed only in rudimentary form in the Romantic period[23]).

This is where the rock star comparison breaks down. Proponents would have us place Courtney Love, Yoko Ono, and Jerry Hall in the same relation to their celebrated partners as Mary Shelley, Jane Williams, Lady Caroline Lamb, and Claire Clairmont. But that is anachronistically to project modern attitudes onto the past. Women in Regency times were acutely vulnerable to social disapproval: Mary Godwin was ostracized after running off to the Continent with Shelley in July 1814, and as his widow continued to suffer the consequences, while Jane Williams endured a similar fate after her return in 1822. Claire Clairmont preferred to suppress her riotous past and became a governess and female companion in such places as Pisa, Vienna, London, Carlsbad, Moscow, and Dresden. Lady Caroline Lamb's *Glenarvon* (1816), a *roman-à-clef* concerning her affair with Byron, led to exile from Whig high society, as Hobhouse gloatingly remarked: '*Glenarvon* has done nothing but render the little vicious author more odious if possible than ever.'[24] Women continued to be judged harshly for decades: Fanny Brawne was unknown to the reading public until publication of Keats's love letters in 1878, thirteen years after her death, which prompted critics to call her 'shallow-hearted, with sympathies and brain as shallow as her heart',[25] and 'unworthy, commonplace, unresponsive, and negative'.[26] This was typical of a culture that valued femininity less highly than we do today.

The argument seems always to gravitate towards Byron. It is true he had numerous encounters with women, but his most intense relationships were not (despite one or two notable exceptions) heterosexual. He preferred 15-year-old boys, with several of whom he seems to have fallen in love. Even in that respect, his experience was unlike that of our time. During the Romantic period, sodomy was a capital offence and would remain so until 1861; moreover, the repugnance felt by the public towards 'deviance' gave the authorities cause to step up prosecutions in the early part of the nineteenth century.[27] Mob violence against homosexuals took place in London, culminating in 'semi-lynchings'.[28] In short, Byron's England was brutally intolerant of sexual activity between men, as distinct from the easing of attitudes after the decriminalization of homosexuality in 1967. As time has passed the English have become more accepting still: from 2000 it became possible for gays and lesbians to serve openly in Her Majesty's Armed Forces, and in 2005 they gained the right to enter into civil partnerships and adopt children. At the time of writing, LGBT citizens in England and Wales have most of the same rights as anyone else. It is misleading to imply Byron enjoyed the same liberties as today's rock stars; he didn't. Georgian attitudes drove him into exile and made him reluctant to return.[29]

The Romantics' early deaths are sometimes invoked by way of comparison with such figures as James Dean, Sid Vicious, Amy Winehouse, Michael Hutchence, and Kurt Cobain. There is no getting round the fact that Mary Wollstonecraft, Percy Bysshe Shelley, Byron, and Keats died before their time, but comparisons on this basis are misleading. Dean died in a car accident; the deaths of Vicious and Cobain were drug-related; Winehouse died of alcohol poisoning; Hutchence committed suicide using alcohol and drugs. These deaths were either self-induced or the result of high-risk behaviour, their correlation with those of Romantic writers questionable at best. Wollstonecraft died in childbirth. Her death, the result of unhygienic medical practices, was a tragedy. It had nothing to do with a hedonistic lifestyle. From the time Keats contracted consumption, an illness that ran in his family, his days were numbered. He did not want to die, knowing better than anyone his artistic potential. Despite what some biographers say, there is no evidence Shelley wanted to die, and claims he raised the sails of the Don Juan in the middle of a storm are false (see Myth 20). Byron would have survived the fever he contracted in Missolonghi had it not been for his doctors, whose determination to leech him was the cause of his premature death (see p. 160).

I have suggested Byron's fame might bear comparison on a superficial level with that of modern celebrities, but there are important distinctions not to be overlooked. Unlike those with whom he is compared, he was not a performer but a writer, an originator of ideas. It is easy to gloss over that even if, in the context in which these comparisons are made, the distinction between poets and songwriters is easily blurred. Nor did Byron know the pressures of appearing in front of a mass public of a kind that would not come into being for the best part of a century after his death. The celebrities with whom he is compared were products of a wholly different world. It is true Byron cared about posterity, the opinion of a future he could not live to see,[30] but that is not the same as caring about personal renown during one's lifetime – that is, about fame, its vulgar, showy, down-at-heel neighbour which Byron dismissed with a clear-sightedness that stands as the rebuke to the suggestion he possessed rock star status *avant la lettre*.

> What is the end of fame? 'tis but to fill
>   A certain portion of uncertain paper:
> Some liken it to climbing up a hill,
>   Whose summit, like all hills', is lost in vapour;
> For this men write, speak, preach, and heroes kill,
>   And bards burn what they call their 'midnight taper,'
> To have, when the original is dust,
> A name, a wretched picture, and worse bust.[31]

Notes

1 Benita Eisler, *Byron: Child of Passion, Fool of Fame* (London: Hamish Hamilton, 1999), p. 752.
2 Camille Paglia, *Sexual Personae: Art and Decadence from Nefertiti to Emily Dickinson* (London: Penguin Books, 1992), p. 364. Paglia's work is cited by Greil Marcus in *Dead Elvis: A Chronicle of a Cultural Obsession* (London: Penguin Books, 1991), pp. 193–4.
3 Leslie A. Marchand, *Byron: A Biography* (3 vols., New York: Alfred A. Knopf, 1957), ii. 627.
4 Fiona MacCarthy, *Byron: Life and Legend* (London: John Murray, 2002), p. 301.
5 Jane Stabler, *The Artistry of Exile: Romantic and Victorian Writers in Italy* (Oxford: Oxford University Press, 2013), pp. 50–1.
6 Ravenna Journal, 14 January 1821, in *Byron's Letters and Journals*, ed. Leslie A. Marchand (13 vols., London: John Murray, 1973–94), viii. 27.
7 Lord Byron to Thomas Moore, 6 October 1821, ibid., p. 236.

8 This figure appears in William St Clair, *The Godwins and the Shelleys: The Biography of a Family* (London: Faber & Faber, 1989), p. 88. Patrick Colquhoun, stipendiary magistrate in Westminster, also produced a figure of 50,000 in 1800; see A. J. Harvey, *Sex in Georgian England: Attitudes and Prejudices from the 1720s to the 1820s* (London: Duckworth, 1994), pp. 92–3.

9 Antony E. Simpson, 'The Ordeal of St Sepulchre's: A Campaign against Organized Prostitution in Early Nineteenth-Century London and the Emergence of Lower Middle-Class Consciousness', *Social and Legal Studies* 15 (2006), 363–87, p. 367.

10 Marius Kwint reports that in 1817 the Commons Police Committee heard complaints about the hundreds of brothels supported by the Royal Circus and Astley's Amphitheatre; see 'The Legitimization of the Circus in Late Georgian England', *Past and Present* 174 (2002), 72–115, p. 104.

11 See Nora Crook and Derek Guiton, *Shelley's Venomed Melody* (Cambridge: Cambridge University Press, 1986), p. 11.

12 Kenneth R. Johnston, *The Hidden Wordsworth: Poet Lover Rebel Spy* (New York: W. W. Norton, 1998), pp. 128–30.

13 See, *inter alia*, *The Notebooks of Samuel Taylor Coleridge*, vol. i, ed. Kathleen Coburn (New York: Pantheon Books, 1957), entry 1726, which dates from December 1803. It is discussed by Jennifer Ford, *Coleridge on Dreaming: Romanticism, Dreams and the Medical Imagination* (Cambridge: Cambridge University Press, 1998), pp. 78–9. Molly Lefebure says Coleridge was 'scared of intimacy with women', which made him 'an incurable philanderer'; see *Samuel Taylor Coleridge: A Bondage of Opium* (London: Gollancz, 1977), p. 107.

14 Andrew Motion, *Keats* (London: Faber & Faber, 1997), pp. 196–7; Nicholas Roe, *John Keats: A New Life* (New Haven: Yale University Press, 2012), pp. 60–1, 191. See also Robert Gittings's appendix on 'Keats and Venereal Disease', in *John Keats* (Harmondsworth: Penguin, 1968), pp. 446–50.

15 Crook and Guiton, *Shelley's Venomed Melody*, ch. 2. See also James Bieri, *Percy Bysshe Shelley: A Biography* (2 vols., Newark: University of Delaware Press, 2004–5), ii. 225–6.

16 There is no record of this, but both men liked prostitutes and spent much time together in the streets of London; see Duncan Wu, *William Hazlitt: The First Modern Man* (Oxford: Oxford University Press, 2008), pp. 59–60; A. C. Grayling, *The Quarrel of the Age: The Life and Times of William Hazlitt* (London: Weidenfeld & Nicolson, 2000), pp. 86–8.

17 Robert Morrison, *The English Opium Eater: A Biography of Thomas De Quincey* (London: Weidenfeld & Nicolson, 2009), pp. 76–7.

18 Although that did not discourage the authorities from attempting to clamp down on the trade using vagrancy laws; see Harvey, *Sex in Georgian England*, pp. 100–1.

19 Samuel Rogers was among one such audience, and reported that 'her performance was very beautiful indeed': *Reminiscences and Table-Talk of Samuel Rogers*, ed. G. H. Powell (London: R. Brimley Johnson, 1903), p. 109.

20 For more information on mistresses, see Venetia Murray, *An Elegant Madness: High Society in Regency England* (London: Penguin Books, 1998), ch. 7.

21 Tim Hitchcock, 'Redefining Sex in Eighteenth-Century England', *History Workshop Journal* 41 (1996), 72–90, p. 77.

22 The obvious source for the 'one-sex' model by which women were judged in eighteenth-century England is Thomas Lacqueur's *Making Sex: Body and Gender from the Greeks to Freud* (Cambridge, MA: Harvard University Press, 1992). See also Harvey, *Sex in Georgian England*, pp. 42–4, and Karen Harvey, 'The Century of Sex? Gender, Bodies, and Sexuality in the Long Eighteenth Century', *The Historical Journal* 45 (2002), 899–916, p. 903.

23 The vaginal sponge and the sheath appear to have been the principal instruments; Iain McCalman deals briefly with them in 'Females, Feminism and Free Love in an Early Nineteenth Century Radical Movement', *Labour History* 38 (1980), 1–25, pp. 16–17.

24 Paul Douglass, *Lady Caroline Lamb: A Biography* (New York: Palgrave Macmillan, 2004), p. 191.

25 Abby Sage Richardson, *Old Love Letters* (10th ed., Boston, MA: Houghton Mifflin, 1893), p. 156.

26 Walter Littlefield, *Love Letters of Famous Poets and Novelists* (New York: John McBride, 1909), p. 274.

27 Harvey, *Sex in Georgian England*, p. 144.

28 Louis Crompton, *Byron and Greek Love: Homophobia in 19th-Century England* (Berkeley: University of California Press, 1985), pp. 163–7.

29 Ibid., pp. 228–35.

30 Andrew Bennett, *Romantic Poets and the Culture of Posterity* (Cambridge: Cambridge University Press, 1999), ch. 8.

31 *Don Juan*, i, stanza 218, in Byron, *The Complete Poetical Works*, ed. Jerome J. McGann (7 vols., Oxford: Clarendon Press, 1980–93), v. 79.

CODA

The biggest myth of all might be that the Romantics invented Romanticism in 1798, practised it till 1830, then died. Its negation is closer to the mark: no one invented Romanticism; there were no Romantics, and no *terminus ad quem* or *a quo*. There were just writers who lived at roughly the same period, leaving their writings behind them. They did not call themselves Romantics, nor attach labels to themselves. Yet the ivory-tower mythographers might say that was irrelevant. And I suppose that is what this book is about: the way later generations have interpreted the Romantic period, and the manner in which the accumulated mythology has shaped our understanding of it.

British Romanticism is definable by its resistance to definition: successive generations have understood it in ways that made sense to them, only for their prescriptions to become outmoded. As if in response, the shelf life of fresh definitions decreases in duration. Take the work of Ernest Bernbaum, whose *Anthology of Romanticism* (1930) was among the first such texts to appear.[1] Though he was working with resources that now seem primitive, his volume is knowledgeable, meticulous, and readable. He was among the first to determine Blake's place among the Romantic poets and to argue Scott's innovations as a historical novelist. Bernbaum's insights, both in his *Anthology* and its accompanying *Guide*, are persuasive: Byron 'liked to attract general attention by parading his woes or posing as satanically wicked',[2] while Hazlitt was 'certain that his principles were the only just ones'.[3] Yet Bernbaum's Romanticism was the product of its moment. To read him is to gaze into a vanished world – not that of Regency England but that of post-war America. In the third edition of his anthology (1948)

30 Great Myths About the Romantics, First Edition. Duncan Wu.
© 2015 John Wiley & Sons, Ltd. Published 2015 by John Wiley & Sons, Ltd.

he speaks of the Romantics as enshrining an optimism needed by those whose task it was to reconstruct.

> Much of the literature produced after World War I was rooted in worldliness, and bore the bitter fruits of cynicism and pessimism. Now that World War II has ended, and a new generation is trying to rebuild civilization, there are signs of a revival of the spirit of resolute idealism. If we wish to 'move forward with an active faith,' to quote the last words of a great modern idealist, we can gain encouragement from the Romantics. In them there is neither fear nor defeatism. Their inspiration and imagination, guiding our own good will, can help save our world from the abyss of falsehood, evil, and ugliness.[4]

Bernbaum's words, and those of FDR (which he cites), are moving because they testify to faith in the power of literature to create a better society, and to the hopes of those who lived through two world wars and bore witness to our ability to turn everything we touch to ash. We know what has followed – the endless wrong turns, acts of bad faith, and moral failures, which continue to accumulate. Few scholars today would claim Romanticism can change the world, and I wonder how many would attribute such power to any writer? Yet the lives and work of the Romantics remain more widely studied than ever, as reflected in the explosion of scholarly editions of their writings and critical approaches to the subject.

Since Bernbaum's death in 1958, everything has changed: his was a conception of Romanticism that, for all its thoughtfulness, excluded many writers and works studied today. Thanks to a combination of scholarly brilliance and technological wizardry, almost everything published during the period is now retrievable by almost anyone, anywhere in the world. Bibliographers and scholars have catalogued the full range of novels, poetry, and non-fiction prose of the age, and texts may be obtained, if not in scholarly editions then in libraries without walls, suspended in cyberspace. Except for those works placed permanently out of reach by censorious onlookers or by chance (for example, Wordsworth's 'A Somersetshire Tragedy', Byron's Memoirs, Shelley's Hubert Cauvin), much that once slipped from view has resurfaced, even works unpublished at the time. The fortuitous discovery of Scrope Davies's trunk in the bowels of the Pall Mall branch of Barclays Bank in 1976, containing Byron's manuscripts and Shelley's drafts of 'Mont Blanc' and 'Hymn to Intellectual Beauty', is the best-known example.[5]

It is not just a matter of the past remaining with us, even when it appears forgotten; the Romantics themselves are resurrected alongside us. You can see it in the way certain motifs are perpetuated in modern culture – such as Frankenstein and his monster, reincarnated in the novels of Thomas Harris. Harris's protagonist, Hannibal Lecter, is both scientist and monster. He is highly trained, with a medical degree from Johns Hopkins and qualifications to practise as an 'experienced clinical psychiatrist'. His research papers appear in academic journals.[6] Yet there is no escaping his dark side. 'I know he's a monster', says FBI agent Clarice Starling before first meeting him,[7] and he proves it when, upon escape from prison, he tears the face off a guard and 'wears' it in an ambulance.[8] Or when, towards the end of *Hannibal*, he feeds Deputy Assistant Inspector Paul Krendler his own brains fried in Charente butter, lemon juice, and fresh truffles: 'In dealing with the item absolutely fresh, the challenge is to prevent the material from simply disintegrating into a handful of lumpy gelatin.'[9]

Such baroque tendencies prompt us to imagine Lecter as *übermonster* – which in turn suggests that, since the moment Mary Shelley's creature advanced towards its maker 'with superhuman speed',[10] he has been on the verge of becoming a superhero. Lecter is such a beast, for he will save Clarice's life in the required manner, nurse her 'with infinite care',[11] psychoanalyse her,[12] and dress her as his consort. He has impeccable taste, giving her 'a long dinner gown in cream silk, narrowly but deeply décolleté beneath an exquisite beaded jacket'.[13] The couple run away to Buenos Aires and live happily ever after in a Beaux Arts building near the French embassy.[14]

The Lecter story is foreshadowed in Shelley's novel when Frankenstein agrees to make the monster a mate, but Harris has customized it for modern tastes. Bernbaum described post-First World War literature as 'rooted in worldliness'; that of our time is more deeply mired in materialism, alienation, and pessimism than he could ever have imagined. And those qualities are reflected in the emollient consumerism of Harris's narrative and Clarice's escape to the Shangri-La of urban Argentina having taken as her lover one of the most repulsive serial killers in literary history. She finally becomes, as the tabloids predict, 'Bride of Frankenstein',[15] while Lecter emerges as the ultimate antihero in a world peopled by scientists and monsters. He is a psychopath whose story is laden with a late twentieth-century knowledge of cynicism and injustice.

Successive ages recapitulate Romantic ideas in ways that reflect anxieties of their own; in turn, they shape the manner by which we reflect our own image back into the culture. You can see it as much in the way 'Jerusalem' has been harnessed to causes unimaginable to Blake as in the relentless embellishment of the vampire myth (which first entered literature with Polidori's novella of 1819), most notably in the *Twilight* novels and the HBO series *True Blood*. Polidori's *The Vampyre* is an especially good example of the way mythic concepts, released into the ether, assume lives independent of their makers. Henry Colburn, publisher of the novella, was aware of Polidori's authorship, but in order to stimulate sales marketed it as 'The Vampyre; A Tale by Lord Byron'. Its appearance on April Fool's Day 1819 was a clue to the deception, but readers were content to believe it Byron's, which explains why it went through five editions in the next eight months.[16] The Vampyre is an extraordinary book in its own right, though without the attribution to Byron it would probably not have been translated into French, German, Italian, Spanish, and Swedish by 1830. In France and Germany it appeared as part of Byron's collected works. Such was the vampire's popularity, other writers 'borrowed' his services: Cyprien Bérard's Lord Ruthwen ou les Vampires (Paris, 1820) told the story of 'ce Don Juan vampirique' and his European escapades. In summer 1820 Charles Nodier adapted it for the stage in Paris at the Théâtre de la Porte Saint-Martin, where it was hugely successful; six other adaptations sprang up across the city during the year. When J. R. Planché's 'free translation' of the French play opened at the English Opera House on 9 August 1820, it was a sellout. And it was no less successful as opera, first performed in Leipzig in 1828.

This was one of those rare occasions in history when a runaway success was denounced both by the man who wrote it and by the one to whom it was attributed. From the moment John Murray forwarded to Byron 'a Copy of a thing called the Vampire which Mr Colburn has had the temerity to publish with your Lordships name as its author',[17] Byron distanced himself from it. He wrote to the papers declaring 'a personal dislike to Vampires'[18] and in private was even more dismissive: 'Damn "the Vampire," – what do I know of Vampires? it must be some bookselling imposture'.[19] But the myth of the lordly Ruthven was caviar to a public fixated by tales of Byron's serial ravishments. The Vampyre continued to appear under his name until the 1890s and was read as his self-portrait.[20] It is one of the ironies of the period that a man with no interest in vampires was assumed to be author and model of the original nosferatu.

Polidori had serious literary ambitions. He tried his hand at drama, poetry, and fiction, but everything he published sank without trace. The Vampyre enjoyed more success than the rest put together, yet no one believed he had anything to do with it. Having sold it for a fee, he gained nothing by its growing popularity, and was doomed to stand mutely by while endless reprintings served only to burnish the reputation of a man he despised, making others rich from the proceeds.[21] He must have felt like one of the damned. In August 1821 he disappeared to Brighton on a gambling spree and 'incurred a debt of honour which he had no present means of clearing off'.[22] He returned to his father's house in London, drank a glass of prussic acid and died, though the coroner's jury decreed his life ended 'by the visitation of God'.[23] He was buried in St Pancras' churchyard, London, on 29 August 1821. Though no one now reads his verse tragedy *Ximenes*, or two-canto Miltonic poem *The Fall of the Angels*, his infamous vampire, the aristocratic Ruthven, resonated through subsequent decades in such characters as Sheridan Le Fanu's Carmilla and Bram Stoker's Count Dracula, without whom our current craving for vampires would not exist.

The point is that, more than almost any other writings, those of the British Romantics possess the ability to renew themselves in the human consciousness. Without that power, only the most determined scholars would continue to burrow into the corpus like so many maggots. Instead, almost everything from the period continues to compel a mass readership, including Frankenstein and Dracula – cruel tales sprung from Romanticism's dark side, designed to lend substance to the childhood nightmare of the shadow at the door. There are other respects in which the literature continues to display its enduring vitality. Over the last five decades an army of editors has produced new scholarly editions of the work of the canonical Romantic poets[24] – as well as that of hitherto neglected writers of both verse and prose. As editors know, there is no such thing as a 'definitive' edition. The work has always to be approached provisionally, and texts are produced for each occasion. None of which can discourage others from doing the same job of work in a different way, for a different time and a different readership.

In the end it hardly matters how we define the Romantic. (Such rococo gestures as definitions, however well argued, soon come to appear like a Louis Quatorze sconce, all gilt and curlicues, hopelessly enmeshed in their own time and place.) It is not just that different generations will always see the concept in a new light but that a life-long wrestling match with critical abstraction could never enable anyone to account for the strangeness and unpredictability of the literature. The idea of the Romantic functions best when not hemmed in by prescriptive boundaries. It is more important that the works of that unusually creative time in literary history – whether we call it the late Georgian, Regency, or Revolutionary and Napoleonic periods – continue to speak, providing us with the light by which to understand the obsessions, desires, and petty madnesses we share with their authors. That can happen only when we are able to see their lives and works clear-sightedly. If myth is a form of blindness, I hope this book has the power to help readers shake free of it and to appreciate the Romantics for what they were.

Notes

1 *Anthology of Romanticism*, ed. Ernest Bernbaum (1930; 3rd ed., New York: Ronald Press, 1948).

2 Ernest Bernbaum, *Guide through the Romantic Movement* (2nd ed., New York: Ronald Press, 1949), p. 197. I am intrigued by the fact that the copy of this book currently held by Georgetown University was formerly in the possession of W. K. Wimsatt, a Georgetown graduate.

3 Ibid., p. 128.

4 *Anthology of Romanticism*, ed. Bernbaum (3rd ed.), p. xxviii.

5 See, *inter alia*, Judith Chernaik and David Burnett, 'The Byron and Shelley Manuscripts in the Scrope Davies Find', *Review of English Studies* 29 (1978), 36–49; *Fair-Copy Manuscripts of Shelley's Poems in European and American Libraries: Including Percy Bysshe Shelley's holographs and copies in the hand of Mary W. Shelley, located in the United States, England, Scotland, Ireland, and Switzerland, as well as the holograph draft of Keats's Robin Hood*, ed. Donald Reiman and Michael O'Neill (New York: Garland, 1997), p. 125. Werner Glinga writes engagingly about Davies's playboy lifestyle in *Legacy of Empire: A Journey through British Society* (Manchester: Manchester University Press, 1986), pp. 12–13.

6 Thomas Harris, *The Silence of the Lambs* (New York: St Martin's Press, 1988), pp. 17, 5.

7 Ibid., p. 6.

8 Ibid., pp. 222–3, 229–30.

9 Thomas Harris, *Hannibal* (New York: Delacorte, 1999), p. 473.

10 Mary Wollstonecraft Shelley, *The Frankenstein Notebooks: A Facsimile Edition of Mary Shelley's Manuscript Novel, 1816–17*, ed. Charles E. Robinson (2 vols., New York: Garland, 1996), i. 252–3.

11 Harris, *Hannibal*, p. 435.

12 Ibid., p. 453.

13 Ibid., p. 464.

14 Ibid., p. 482.

15 Harris, *The Silence of the Lambs*, p. 59.

16 These are listed by Henry R. Viets, 'The London Editions of Polidori's *The Vampyre*', *Papers of the Bibliographical Society of America* 63 (1969), 83–103, pp. 101–3.

17 John Murray to Byron, 27 April 1819, in *The Letters of John Murray to Lord Byron*, ed. Andrew Nicholson (Liverpool: Liverpool University Press, 2007), p. 269.

18 Byron to the editor of *Galignani's Messenger*, 27 April 1819, in *Byron's Letters and Journals*, ed. Leslie A. Marchand (13 vols., London: John Murray, 1973–94), xiii. 50.

19 Byron to Douglas Kinnaird, 24 April 1819, ibid., vi. 114.

20 See William St Clair, *The Reading Nation in the Romantic Period* (Cambridge: Cambridge University Press, 2004), p. 721.

21 Within days of the first appearance of the story in the *New Monthly Magazine*, Polidori realized his foolishness in having sold it for 'a small sum'. Having tried unsuccessfully to extract further payment, he wrote a letter to the *Morning Chronicle* denouncing the whole thing as a hoax. Colburn visited him, persuaded him to withdraw the letter, and made one more payment. For further details see D. L. Macdonald, *Poor Polidori: A Critical Biography of the Author of The Vampyre* (Toronto: University of Toronto Press, 1991), pp. 180–1.

22 *The Diary of Dr John William Polidori 1816*, ed. William Michael Rossetti (London: Elkin Mathews, 1911), p. 4.

23 See Henry R. Viets, '"By the Visitation of God": The Death of John William Polidori, M.D., in 1821', *British Medical Journal* 2 (30 December 1961), 1773–5, p. 1774.

24 More new poetry by Wordsworth was published in the last three decades of the twentieth century than in the first three of his own life (including 'poems' he was not aware of having written); reasonably priced facsimiles of Blake's hand-produced illuminated books are now within reach of any interested reader; Coleridge is no longer the genius who under-produced (the standard edition of his poetry stretches to six packed volumes, and we have access to his extensive correspondence, notebooks, and a massive *Collected Works* completed in the first years of the new century); an exhaustive survey of Shelley's manuscripts continues to transform our reading of his poetry and prose; and Byron and Keats are now read in editions more reliably edited, and better informed, than any previously available.

FURTHER READING

The guidelines for this series require a brief, partial account of those works and editions I would recommend to readers. What follows is an avowedly personal selection designed for the student and general reader rather than the specialist.

Editions

Those wishing to dive straight into the literature have at their disposal some excellent new paperback editions from Penguin and Oxford University Press containing introductions and notes by the finest scholars in the field: Robert Morrison's Oxford World's Classics edition of De Quincey's *Confessions* (2013); Fiona Stafford's *Lyrical Ballads 1798 and 1802* (2013); Richard Holmes's thematically organized *Coleridge: Selected Poems* (2013); Susan Wolfson and Peter Manning's *Lord Byron: Selected Poems* (2005); G. E. Bentley, Jr's *William Blake: Selected Poems* (2005); John Barnard's *John Keats: Selected Poems* (2007); and Stephen Gill's *William Wordsworth* in the 21st-Century Oxford Authors series (2010). The new Broadview editions are useful when seeking paperback texts of works otherwise hard to obtain; among others, I recommend William McCarthy and Elizabeth Kraft's edition of Anna Laetitia Barbauld's *Selected Poetry and Prose* (2002); Susan Wolfson and Elizabeth Fay's edition of Felicia Hemans's *The Siege of Valencia* (2002); and Anne McWhir's edition of Amelia Opie's *Adeline Mowbray* (2009). Charles E. Robinson's Vintage Classics edition of *The Original Frankenstein* (2009) makes it possible for the first time to read a text for which Mary Shelley was solely responsible. More lavish, but worth the price, Robert Morrison's edition of *Persuasion: An Annotated Edition* (2011) is an enjoyable and learned rendering of Austen's last complete fiction. The other volumes in the Harvard Annotated Austen are highly recommended. There are several poetry

30 Great Myths About the Romantics, First Edition. Duncan Wu.
© 2015 John Wiley & Sons, Ltd. Published 2015 by John Wiley & Sons, Ltd.

anthologies of the period: a useful one for the engaged reader is *Romantic Poetry: An Annotated Anthology*, ed. Michael O'Neill and Charles Mahoney (2007).

Biographies

Full immersion in the period may be attained by reading the excellent available biographies of Romantic writers – Thomas De Quincey, for instance, whose ramshackle career is recounted by Robert Morrison in *The English Opium-Eater* (2009). De Quincey was not the most likeable of men: racist, self-confessed hedonist, probable paedophile, and back-stabber. One of his most clear-sighted readers, Morrison gives us scant cause to doubt Wordsworth's judgement: 'He is quite mad with pride.' How De Quincey came to live to such a great age, given that he seemed to consume little but booze and drugs, I have no idea – but Morrison makes him an object of fascination.

Other volumes approach the challenge of biography in original ways. Lucy Newlyn reveals the joint lives of William and Dorothy Wordsworth in '*All in Each Other*' (2013). 'Their nesting instinct was connected with the trauma of loss', she tells us, explaining the desire to set up house in Grasmere. Such intuitions make sense of a compulsion inadequately acknowledged by others; here, it becomes a telling detail in the portrait of siblings whose intense love was the product of grief. Stanley Plumly's *Posthumous Keats: A Personal Biography* (2009) has similar virtues. Plumly describes his study as one of 'reflection, contemplation, mediation'. By an act of empathy he uses the scholarly record to recreate Keats's world as it appeared to the poet and his contemporaries. His is a nuanced evocation of the relationships between Keats and his friends, demonstrating how profoundly Keats was shaped by anxiety and loss. Ann Wroe's *Being Shelley: The Poet's Search for Himself* (2007) invokes the poet as principal witness to his personality through the notebooks and manuscripts at the Bodleian Library, drawing not just on drafts of poems but on hesitations, second thoughts, doodles, corrections, and false starts. Wroe is one of the first to let us eavesdrop on Shelley's innermost utterances, with their self-doubt, self-argument, and self-reflection. In that sense, this must be the most comprehensive biography currently in print.

Reference Works

Countless reference works address Romanticism, and more roll off the presses by the month. I have space to nominate only a handful. Jane Moore and John Strachan's *Key Concepts in Romantic Literature* (2010) is by me as I write; I can think of no more effective (or complete) introduction to the subject in a mere 300 pages. *The Cambridge Companion to English Literature, 1740–1830*, ed. Jon Mee and Tom Keymer (2004), is not principally designed as a book about the Romantics, and is all the better for it. All the same, it makes the case that the period it surveys was remarkably coherent.

William St Clair's *The Reading Nation in the Romantic Period* (2004) gathers together publication data for authors and publishers, and is a primary source for discursive analysis on such topics as publishing, intellectual property, and readerships. The chapter on *Frankenstein* is one of the most useful, as well as compulsively readable, pieces of writing on the subject currently in print. Of the many reference volumes tagged to individual writers, I have found *The Oxford Handbook of Percy Bysshe Shelley*, ed. Michael O'Neill and Anthony Howe, with the assistance of Madeleine Callaghan (2013), excellent. *Jane Austen in Context*, ed. Janet Todd (2005), is designed principally for student readers, but contains a number of essays, especially those on the historical and cultural context, which everyone will find informative. I particularly like that on 'Food'.

More Advanced Reading

Here is a brief selection of books that address the way we think about the period and its authors; they are less for those approaching the subject for the first time than for the enthusiast, but all are written in an accessible manner. Isaiah Berlin's *The Roots of Romanticism* (1999) originated as a series of lectures delivered in Washington, DC, in 1965. Though focused on Continental writers and thinkers, his account casts invaluable sidelights on British Romanticism, and goes some way towards defining it.

I have been impressed by Ian Haywood's *Bloody Romanticism: Spectacular Violence and the Politics of Representation, 1776–1832* (2006), a reminder of its terrible history, including the abuses of the slave trade, suppression of the United Irishmen, and conflict in America. As well as describing the atrocities by which the period was punctuated, Haywood expands the literary canon, discussing popular visual prints, newspapers, and pamphlets. His 'bloody vignettes' emphasize brutality rather than the more optimistic qualities associated with Romanticism. John Gardner's *Poetry and Popular Protest: Peterloo, Cato Street and the Queen Caroline Controversy* (2011) could be seen as extending Haywood's investigation, examining a moment (August 1819 to August 1821) when it seemed England was on the verge of revolution. Gardner looks at the full range of works that helped foment change, from printed caricatures to William Hone's political booklets. Few write so persuasively about that still neglected poet, Samuel Bamford.

I admire Paul Fry's *Wordsworth and the Poetry of What We Are* (2008) for the way it challenges commonly held assumptions about its subject. At one point, he tells us the spots of time 'mean absolutely nothing at all', a judgement that may go against what we have been taught but which seems to me unimpeachable. If the function of criticism is to challenge us, to anatomize our beliefs and provoke us into fresh interrogation, this has to be one of the most powerful books on Wordsworth to have appeared in the last fifty years.

In '*Romanticism*' – *and Byron* (2009) Peter Cochran profiles the life and work of Byron through his relations with such figures as Blake, Keats, and Coleridge. His book is full of perceptive commentary on such matters as Byron's 'obsession' with Wordsworth, his hankering for approval from Tory man of letters William Gifford, flirtation with Lord Holland, dislike of the numerous Leigh Hunt offspring, and reluctance to praise Shelley's poetry. When Cochran reads the final section of 'Ode to the West Wind' as 'the desperate cry of a failure', he is being provocative but is surely correct.

Joseph Viscomi's *Blake and the Idea of the Book* (1993) must be one of the most important studies of Blake to have appeared in recent decades. It describes Blake's printing technique in greater detail than we have ever seen before, demonstrating by example – there are photographs of Viscomi repeating Blake's procedures. He shows also how Blake exploited the immediacy of the medium, composing his poetry directly onto copper plates.

There are numerous books about the culture of the period; Robert M. Ryan's *The Romantic Reformation: Religious Politics in English Literature, 1789–1824* (1997) takes us to one of the most important issues of the time. Ryan argues Romantic writers were engaged in a reformation – an attempt to purify and redefine the national faith – and that no reading of Romanticism should fail to take that into account.

The Enlightenment

As a topic, the Enlightenment is as sprawling as Romanticism. While preparing my thoughts on Myth 2, I was guided initially by Dorinda Outram's *The Enlightenment* (3rd ed., 2013), her lavishly illustrated *Panorama of the Enlightenment* (2006), and Dan Edelstein's *The Enlightenment: A Genealogy* (2010). Roger Scruton's *An Intelligent Person's Guide to Modern Culture* (2000) offers a brilliantly incisive account of what the Enlightenment was and how it gave rise to Romanticism. He then shows how the two movements shaped the world in which we live. I have also enjoyed Anthony Pagden's *The Enlightenment and Why It Still Matters* (2013). Pagden is a declared advocate of the Enlightenment and its numerous achievements, and has much to say about why the Enlightenment turned out as it did, and how the Romantics reacted to it.

More focused analysis of the Enlightenment may be found in Isaiah Berlin's *Three Critics of the Enlightenment: Vico, Hamann, Herder*, ed. Henry Hardy (2nd ed., 2013). Berlin's focus is Continental thought, which means his analysis is only peripherally relevant to students of British Romanticism; however, he is well worth reading for the clarity with which he outlines the failings of Enlightenment thinkers and the kind of response it provoked among those with whom he is concerned. 'The Magus of the North', about Hamann, must be one of the most readable studies of any philosopher ever written. Hugh Trevor-Roper's bracing *History and the Enlightenment* (2010) is valuable for collecting his finest essays and lectures on Enlightenment thinkers, including three on Gibbon. Trevor-Roper approaches Romanticism through Scott and the Germans, arguing its principal innovation was to encourage historians 'to make the past live'. He identifies Coleridge (quite rightly) as the source of the view that Gibbon was a dry, passionless writer, and suggests he lacked appreciation of Gibbon's life and work. Besides being one of the most erudite authors on this subject, Trevor-Roper writes some of its most elegant and considered prose.

Electronic Resources

Here are some of the e-resources to which I turn regularly. Blake is well served by *The William Blake Archive*, established by three of the most eminent scholars in the Blake world: Joseph Viscomi, Morris Eaves, and Robert N. Essick. It carries reproductions of many of Blake's illuminated books, as well as David V. Erdman's printed edition of the *Works*. Those who yearn for hard copy should turn to the Tate Gallery/Blake Trust editions, but *The William Blake Archive* is the best online resource. *Romantic Circles* is host to a number of textual editions by some of the finest scholars in their fields, including the complete correspondence of Robert Southey and a text of *Frankenstein* edited by Stuart Curran. The site as a whole is edited to an exemplary standard. *Frankenstein* is a feature of *The Shelley-Godwin Archive*, which makes available its various manuscript pages online, with Charles E. Robinson's erudite commentary. Two academic journals have made either all or part of their archive freely available online. *The British Association of Romantic Studies Bulletin and Review* can be accessed through the BARS website, and *The Charles Lamb Bulletin* through that of the Charles Lamb Society.

One of the best electronic resources is *Google Books*, which makes available pdf files of complete literary works, taken from first editions. However, these are unmediated by editors and are accompanied by none of the auxiliary materials available in the paperback editions listed above, such as an introduction, list of further reading, and scholarly annotations. They are, in other words, raw, and should be approached with caution. For those with no alternative, they remain a possible starting-point and have the virtue of being free of charge.

Electronic Resources

INDEX

Page references to illustrations are in bold.

---

30 Great Myths About the Romantics, First Edition. Duncan Wu.
© 2015 John Wiley & Sons, Ltd. Published 2015 by John Wiley & Sons, Ltd.